RENEWALS 458-4574.

Security and Development in the Pacific Islands

A project of the International Peace Academy
and the
Australian Centre for
Peace and Conflict Studies

WITHDRAWN
UTSA LIBRARIES

Security and Development in the Pacific Islands

Social Resilience in Emerging States

edited by
M. Anne Brown

LYNNE
RIENNER
PUBLISHERS

BOULDER
LONDON

Library
University of Texas
at San Antonio

Published in the United States of America in 2007 by
Lynne Rienner Publishers, Inc.
1800 30th Street, Boulder, Colorado 80301
www.rienner.com

and in the United Kingdom by
Lynne Rienner Publishers, Inc.
3 Henrietta Street, Covent Garden, London WC2E 8LU

© 2007 by the International Peace Academy, Inc.
All rights reserved by the publisher

Library of Congress Cataloging-in-Publication Data
Security and development in the Pacific Islands : social resilience in emerging states /
edited by M. Anne Brown.
     p. cm.
Includes bibliographical references and index.
ISBN-13: 978-1-58826-505-0 (hardcover : alk. paper)
ISBN-13: 978-1-58826-530-2 (pbk. : alk. paper)
1. Political stability—Oceania. 2. Conflict management—Oceania.
3. Oceania—Economic conditions. I. Brown, M. Anne.
JQ5995.S43 2007
995—dc22

2006035990

British Cataloguing in Publication Data
A Cataloguing in Publication record for this book
is available from the British Library.

Printed and bound in the United States of America

∞   The paper used in this publication meets the requirements
of the American National Standard for Permanence of
Paper for Printed Library Materials Z39.48-1992.

5   4   3   2   1

**Library
University of Texas
at San Antonio**

Contents

Foreword

Terje Rød-Larsen,
President, International Peace Academy

IT IS A PLEASURE for the International Peace Academy (IPA) to present this volume, *Security and Development in the Pacific Islands: Social Resilience in Emerging States,* at a critical moment for the South Pacific. This thoughtful and provocative work offers insights both for the communities in the South Pacific and for the broader international community as they reflect on many decades engaged in state building and embark on new cooperative enterprises to build peace in and among emerging states. Of the many conclusions that emerge from the rich contributions to this collection, none is more important than the common refrain of the importance of partnerships— between the international community and regional actors, between states and societies—if we are to achieve both security and development.

It is therefore appropriate that the book is itself a product of a partnership between the IPA and the Australian Centre for Peace and Conflict Studies (ACPACS) at the University of Queensland. Led by Kevin Clements, director of ACPACS, and Neclâ Tschirgi, then vice president of the IPA, the two institutions joined together in 2004 in the Pacific Peacebuilding Partnership. This research initiative aimed to improve our understanding of security and development strategies from a South Pacific perspective and to generate lessons learned with implications beyond the region. To that effect, the program organized a number of workshops and conferences in the region and conducted field research and outreach. In particular, the Pacific Peacebuilding Partnership worked to bring together research and policy expertise from the Pacific Islands region and New York, so that each might benefit from the other.

Within the IPA, this project contributed to our broader Security-Development Nexus Program. This research program—envisioned and realized by Neclâ Tschirgi and her capable staff, in this case particularly Gordon Peake and Kaysie Studdard Brown—has contributed to a better understanding of the linkages among the various dimensions of violent conflicts in the contemporary era and the need for multidimensional strategies in conflict management. At ACPACS, the partnership was furthered by Professor Clements and M. Anne Brown, who brought her considerable diplomatic experience and interdisciplinary research expertise to bear in shaping this volume. We are particularly grateful to Dr. Brown for her perseverance in bringing this project to a successful completion.

The Security-Development Nexus Program was generously supported by the governments of Belgium, Canada, Germany, Luxembourg, Norway, and the United Kingdom (the latter through its Department for International Development), as well as the Rockefeller Foundation. The program also benefited from core support to the IPA from the governments of Denmark, Sweden, and Switzerland, as well as the Ford Foundation and the William and Flora Hewlett Foundation.

Our deep gratitude also goes to the Australian Agency for International Development (AusAID), whose support for the partnership extended well beyond its considerable financial contribution. AusAID knows well the relevance of the lessons of security and development in the South Pacific for similar enterprises elsewhere in the world, and, through the Australian government's contribution to this partnership, it has enabled us to bring some of those lessons to a broader audience in the United Nations community and beyond. I would particularly like to thank John Dauth, an old friend of the IPA, who played an integral role throughout.

The social portraits offered in the pages that follow hold rich insights for all those interested in the emergence of functioning and responsible states, whether in the South Pacific or elsewhere. The diverse group of authors whom Dr. Brown has assembled, ranging from voices from the states concerned to regional commentators, offer perspectives from a wide variety of disciplines. What results is a vivid portrayal of resilient Pacific Islands societies actively engaged with the external political, social, economic, and military forces that they have confronted during colonization and since, striving to build states that serve their wants and needs.

My own involvement with Middle Eastern politics began with a study of living conditions in the Occupied Palestinian Territories and led me to a search for regional solutions; it will perhaps come as no surprise, therefore, that I see a particular importance for international policymakers and theorists alike in the emphasis that this volume places on engaging with communities, both local and regional, in building states. Only through such partnerships will we find the common security and generate the sustainable development that states ultimately protect.

Acknowledgments

THIS PROJECT would not have been possible without the inspiration, determination, and drive of Kevin Clements (director of the Australian Centre for Peace and Conflict Studies [ACPACS]), Neclâ Tschirgi (then vice president of the IPA), and Beris Gwynne (then director of the Foundation for Development Cooperation). It would not have come to fruition without the support and hard work of Wendy Foley, Anna Nolan, Bindi Borg, and Nadia Mizner at ACPACS in Brisbane, and Gordon Peake, Kaysie Studdard Brown, James Cockayne, and Adam Lupel at the IPA. My particular thanks to Wendy Foley for her time and energy. I would also like to thank the contributors to the volume for their participation and support. Clive Moore and Max Quanchi went well beyond the requirements of duty.

I would also like to thank many others who have offered conversation, critique, and support. This is a long list, but includes Neva Wendt (Australian Council for International Development), Steve Darvill (AusAID), John Henderson (University of Canterbury), Peter Wallensteen (Uppsala University), Jenny Corrin-Care (University of Queensland), and Volke Boege (the Bonn International Center for Conversion and ACPACS). Finally, I am grateful to AusAID for their generous support and patience in the production of this volume.

—*M. Anne Brown*

The Pacific Islands Region

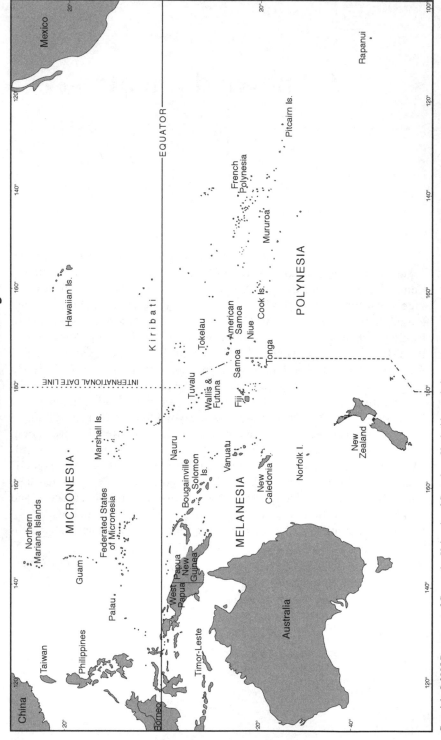

Copyright © 2005 Department of Geography, University of Canterbury. Used with permission.

1

Security and Development: Conflict and Resilience in the Pacific Islands Region

M. Anne Brown

THIS BOOK EXPLORES the interactions of development and security in the Pacific Islands region—the great stretch of largely tropical and subtropical islands and ocean that, in approximate terms, approaches Australia in the west and New Zealand in the south, and includes the Federated States of Micronesia in the north and French Polynesia in the west.[1] While this book focuses on the Pacific Islands, the significance of the questions it explores is global. Questions of development and security lie close to the heart of political community. There is a growing awareness of the complex interactions of these fundamental but often elusive public goods at all the levels at which they are sought: human, national, regional, and international. The Pacific Islands region not only provides an important arena in which to investigate some of these interactions, but also offers insights relevant to other regions grappling with the joint challenges of development and security.

Development and security cannot exist without each other. Good development can untie the entrenched patterns of need, want, or fundamental inequity that often generate the conditions for violent conflict, but development can also produce or intensify patterns of inequity or marginalization. Development involves significant and sometimes rapid change; it creates new winners and losers, recasts the contexts in which communities give substance to their beliefs, and plays into dynamics of conflict already present, perhaps triggering latent violence. "Development" can be forced on people, fragmenting communities, creating conflict with their values and priorities, or alienating them from the values and relationships that animate or give meaning to their collective and ethical life. Different views of what development means for a community can themselves generate deep conflict, as Anthony Regan's discussion of Bougainville (Chapter 5) makes clear. The safety and relationships of trust that security implies are fundamental to good development, as they are to all forms of community well-being. Violent conflict undoes the work of development, and can lay the ground for intergenerational suffering, but security approaches that are dominated by inappropriate or narrow frames of reference (an essentially military approach in a non-war situation, for example) can also compete with or distort broad-based efforts to deal with underlying structural sources of violence.

Despite this interplay, for many decades "development" and "security" operated as sharply different policy worlds and distinct scholarly orientations, the disjunction embedded both in institutional structures and in the political and ideological contests of the Cold War. International work against violent conflict since the end of the Cold War, however, has further underscored the complex interdependence of questions of security and development in causing as well as addressing conflict. This has led to renewed efforts to bring policy, practice, and scholarly agendas in these areas together—to shape development orientations in ways that are sensitive to the vulnerability of communities and their potential for destructive violence, and to find security approaches that are responsive to structural sources of violence and to their own impact on development. Awareness of these intersections changes the way we might look at development approaches, by consistently bringing to the fore questions of their impact on the generation of division and violence. And similarly, it changes the way we look at security, by including questions of what constitutes fundamental well-being and how to support that well-being more clearly within its scope.

What can an exploration of the Pacific Islands region tell us about these intersections? The following chapters explore different dimensions of the security and development nexus in various countries in the region (including the impact of socially inappropriate patterns of development; conflict over land, self-determination, and resource extraction; the challenges of external intervention, development, and gender; and reconciliation) with a view to drawing out insights into common problems and approaches. Four fundamental points can be drawn from this wide-ranging exploration.

The first point is that the region is characterized by high levels of social resilience. The social resilience of the region is grounded largely in its community life. Resilience and the sources of that resilience are the too often unremarked backdrop to analyses of the crises and problems the region faces. Yet acknowledging the strengths of the region changes subtly but profoundly the ways the region is approached. While the problems are real and pressing, if the focus is only on problems, there is a danger that they will be seen out of context and as disconnected from either potential sources of creative response or capacities for endurance.

The second point from this exploration of the Pacific is the emerging nature of states in the region. As will be discussed later, parts of the region are now almost routinely described as failed or failing states—such a view can carry significant implications for development and security approaches to the region. But while the peoples of the region have long, deeply rooted traditions, states as such are young. Across the region a slow, difficult, but also potentially creative process is under way as governments and communities grapple with profound social, economic, and political change and with the challenge of forging states that are grounded in Pacific Islands societies. Many of the problems of the region reflect the turbulent nature of these processes. This is an essential context for understanding security and development in the region, and one that has considerable ramifications for policy.

The third point evident from many chapters in this volume is that there is often a significant disconnection between the institutions of the state and the life and values of Pacific Island communities. It is part of being an emerging state that central government institutions often lack roots in the patterns of legitimacy that have weight on the ground in Pacific Islands communities. As a number of the following chapters make clear, introduced or formal political, justice, policing, and administrative systems often do not fit easily with customary or local governance mechanisms and cultural norms. At times they interact destructively, becoming the context, the source, or a significant contributing factor to many of the problems that beset regional states. At the same time, there is tension between subsistence food production and the communal land tenure that largely underpins it, and the dynamics of international markets and commercial life. As with the lack of fit between introduced and indigenous political and social governance, so tension between indigenous and international economic life can be an underlying factor encouraging insecurity and conflict. These tensions are part of being an emerging state; they need to be recognized and consciously engaged as such.

The centrality of community life to the region is the final point that emerges from this exploration of security and development in the Pacific Islands. Community life is the basis for much of the social cohesion and resilience in the region, and for the food production that sustains most of the population. For those outside the region, but seeking to understand or work with it, engaging with communities is at least as important as focusing on governments and central institutions. For Pacific states to work well, they must be concerned with the health of their evolving communities, including customary sociopolitical and economic life.

This chapter briefly introduces the region and this volume; it reviews some of the challenges faced by efforts to strengthen security and support development in the region. The concluding chapter continues these themes and draws out broad implications for approaches to the region.

■ The Place

The Pacific Islands region (also known as Oceania) is an area of extraordinary cultural, social, and political diversity. (Table 1.1, which summarizes

Table 1.1 Characteristics of States and Territories Represented in This Volume, 2006

	Land Area (km²)[a]	Population[a]	Population Density (people per km²)[a]	Languages[b]	Population Age 14 and Under (%)[c]	Population Urban (%)[b]	Adult Literacy Rate[b]		Life Expectancy at Birth[b]	Infant Mortality Rate (deaths per 1,000 live births, before age 1)[b]	GDP per Capita (US$)[d]
							Male	Female			
Fiji	18,333	890,000	48	10	32	46	95	91	67	20	3,229
Nauru	21	10,100	481	2	40	100	89	75[e]	58	13	4,322
New Caledonia	18,576	237,000	13	40	28[f]	71	92	90	73	7	17,538
Papua New Guinea	462,243	5,695,000	12	826	41	15	50	40	54	77	824
Solomon Islands	28,370	460,000	16	71	41	13	27	14	61	38	585
Tonga	649	101,700	157	4	36	32	96	96	71	19	1,930
Vanuatu	12,190	216,000	17	110	41	21	33	33	63	45	1,405
West Papua[g]	410,660	2,200,000	5	257	n/a	6	58	44[h]	58	80	450[i]

Sources: a. 2004, http://www.spc.int/demog/en/stats/2004/pacific%20island%20populations%202004%20by%20sex%20and%205yr%20age%20grps.xls (accessed 18 April 2006); http://www.spc.int/demog/en/stats/2003/posterupdate03.xls (accessed 18 April 2006).
b. http://www.abc.net.au/ra/pacific/places/stat_table.htm (accessed 26 June 2006).
c. 2004 UNESCO data, http://www.uis.unesco.org/profiles/en/edu/countryprofile (accessed 26 June 2006).
d. 2004 GDP US$, http://www.unescap.org/stat/data/statind/pdf/t16_dec05.pdf (accessed 26 June 2006).
e. http://www.uis.unesco.org/profiles/en/edu/countryprofile_en.aspx?code=5200 (accessed 26 June 2006).
f. http://www.cia.gov/cia/publications/factbook/print/nc.html(accessed 20 April 2006).
g. http://www.abc.net.au/ra/pacific/places/country/papua.htm (accessed 19 April 2006).
h. http://www.ciir.org/templates/internal.asp?nodeid=91181 (accessed 26 June 2006).
i. 2002 GDP US$, http://www.newint.org/issue344/facts.htm (accessed 26 June 2006).
Note: Estimates and measurements of these characteristics vary considerably across sources.

characteristics of the places represented in this volume, gives some illustration of this.) The region's twenty-eight island states and territories, comprising thousands of individual islands, reach over 30 million square kilometers (12 million square miles), of which 98 percent is ocean. National populations range from over 5 million (for Papua New Guinea) to around 1,000 (for Niue), with an approximate total of 8 million for the region, or 10 million if West Papua (a province of Indonesia, also called Irian Jaya) is included.[2]

A number of states have considerable reserves of strategic metals, including copper, gold, nickel, and cobalt, as well as timber resources. Oceania's extensive sea territories (exclusive economic zones) are believed to contain oil and gas reserves as well as polymetallic nodules. Fishing is also a substantial resource, although it is pillaged by rogue operations from outside the region. Tourism is growing in some states, as is commercial agriculture.

The region's geography varies, from tiny coral atolls to mountainous land masses. Because of the ocean, and the extremely rugged terrain of many islands, many indigenous communities have developed within distinct ecological pockets, in isolation from each other or in far-flung networks of exchange. As a result, more than one-quarter of the world's total number of languages are spoken in the region. The majority of the region's population are sustained by subsistence agriculture; many live in small communities and lineage groups. Melanesia, a cultural and ethnic subregion that includes Papua New Guinea (PNG), the Solomon Islands, Fiji and Vanuatu, New Caledonia, West Papua (a province of Indonesia), and the Torres Strait Islands (part of Australia), makes up approximately 85 percent of the region's population and also holds most of the region's land-based mineral and timber resources.

The region's diversity also extends to the variety of political structures. Although the political system of most independent states in the region is some form of liberal democracy, Tonga is a slowly liberalizing monarchy, Samoa is a state where only chiefs can stand for election, while Fiji has "communal" parliamentary seats (voting within one's ethnic identification) as well as "common" parliamentary seats. New Caledonia and French Polynesia hold shared sovereignty with France, in a sometimes turbulent relationship; Niue and the Cook Islands are independent, but in free association with New Zealand; Palau, the Federated States of Micronesia, and the Marshall Islands are in association with the United States; Tokelau is a largely self-governing territory under the administration of New Zealand; West Papua is part of Indonesia; and the small islands scattered across the Torres Strait between PNG and Australia are part of Australia.

Despite this diversity, the Pacific Islands do form a region, although the exact borders may shift, depending on the perspective and purpose of discussion. Patterns of ethnic and cultural family resemblance weave across the region, alongside important historical, political, and geographical commonalities. Elements of a voyaging culture are widely held, and values of reciprocity, tolerance, restraint, family, spirituality, performance, and storytelling remain deeply embedded. Small communities have meant that in much of the region, societies are relatively participative and oriented toward consultation and conflict resolution.

Ocean and distance dominate much of the region, making communication, transport, trade, and the provision of services challenging. This has meant that, to those outside the region, the Pacific Islands can be seen as isolated and vulnerable, far from major lines of international trade. Countering this, commentators such as Tongan author Epeli Hau'ofa speak of "our sea of islands,"[3] where the ocean is understood as a unifying and binding force rather than an isolating one, and a shared source of environmental, material, cultural, and spiritual resources. The region is also linked through an active network of intergovernmental agencies, nongovernmental organizations, civil society associations, and faith-based linkages. Efforts at greater regionalization are discussed in the concluding chapter.

■ A Security Overview

From the international strategic point of view, the security environment of the Pacific Islands region is generally agreed to be benign—the region's security problems are essentially intrastate.[4] Nevertheless, this should not suggest that the region's crises are simply endogenous; they flow to a significant extent from histories and patterns of exchange in which other parts of the world at least equally share. The Pacific Islands states and economies are small developing entities grappling with the demands and structural inequities of globalization, and working with the very mixed effects of their colonial inheritances, which are still current in the region.

The region, or parts of it, confronts many of the patterns of vulnerability and risk that are evident in other parts of the developing world: low economic growth coupled with high population growth, resulting in a very significant youth bulge; growing unemployment and underemployment, and poverty and the social problems that accompany it; growing inequality; very low human development indicators (particularly in parts of PNG and the Solomon Islands); poor leadership, corruption, and political instability; economic mismanagement on a grand scale (Nauru, Fiji, Tonga, and the Solomon Islands); protracted intercommunal confrontation or violence (Fiji, the Solomon Islands, PNG, Bougainville, and West Papua), including serious law and order problems (PNG); conflict around development and the use of resources and land; serious environmental degradation; and social violence, particularly violence against women.

HIV/AIDS is a rapidly growing disaster in PNG, with about 80,000 people infected (2 percent of the population),[5] and there is deepening concern regarding its spread in other parts of the region. Environmental degradation is a pressing problem that often accompanies poverty and resource extraction. Questions of self-determination are still alive in the region, now most notably (though not only) in West Papua, an ethnically Melanesian province of Indonesia, where conflict with the Indonesian army has led to significant levels of violence.

As a recent analysis of security and peacebuilding in the Asia Pacific noted,[6] violent conflict is not the norm for Pacific Island states. Nevertheless, there have been a number of serious crises in the region over the past twenty-five years. The 1980s saw conflict in Vanuatu, where a francophone movement sought a path independent of the newly formed government, dominated by Anglophones; in New Caledonia, over independence from France; and in Fiji, where elements within the army (dominated by indigenous Fijians) mounted successful coups in 1987, overthrowing the first government in Fiji to be led by a party dominated by Indo-Fijians. All three conflicts were significantly shaped by the colonial legacy of the states and territories involved.

The Bougainville conflict also broke into violence in the late 1980s. Lasting almost ten years, and fought across the island group at the eastern boundary of PNG, this was the region's most bloody post–World War II struggle. Several thousand people died in fighting that erupted over a complex mix of factors—the intense social and environmental impact on subsistence communities of what was then the largest open-pit mine in the world, intercommunal conflict, and demands for greater self-determination from PNG. Intercommunal conflict around the capital of the Solomon Islands, again rooted in patterns of uneven development intensified by grievances over land tenure, "the predatory practices of logging companies from South-East Asia,"[7] government corruption, and the availability of small weapons from Bougainville, lasted from 1998 until the arrival of an Australian-led regional assistance mission in 2003. Hundreds of people died, and up to 20,000 were internally displaced. In 2000, another coup in Fiji, and an associated mutiny by an elite unit of armed forces, followed the second election of the predominantly Indo-Fijian Labour Party to government (with eight deaths). To varying degrees the legacies or unresolved elements of these three conflicts (in Bougainville, the Solomon Islands, and Fiji) continue to challenge social and political life. In the Solomon Islands in early 2006, rioters, disgruntled with the newly elected parliament's choice of prime minister, burned down many businesses owned by Chinese settlers, who were popularly seen as being associated with vote buying and corruption in business and politics. In Fiji in December 2006, the commander of Fiji's military forces took executive power in a bloodless coup, motivated in part by deep disagreement with the government of the day over how to handle those responsible for the coup and mutiny in 2000.

In Tonga in November 2006, the slow and peaceful process of democratization faltered when, despite the democratizing agenda of the government, elements of the prodemocracy movement, calling for a faster pace of reform, sparked a riot and looting spree in which seven people were killed and more than 80 percent of the capital's business district was burned down. The government, however, appears to remain committed to steady democratization, while those pushing for a faster pace of reform seem likely to be discredited by the tragedy. Further from international sight, a simmering conflict in West Papua stems from demands by Papuan groups for increased control over their own affairs in confronting the violent suppression of the Indonesian military, but also involves large-scale resource extraction. While already violent, this conflict has the potential to develop into a protracted and particularly serious conflict with regional implications.

Many of these crises have roots in historical patterns of uneven development, disruption of land tenure, or conflict around highly destructive resource extraction. Particularly in the context of fundamental tension between the demands and promises of the international market economy and scarcely monetized subsistence or exchange economies, large-scale resource-based projects can generate extreme confusion, social discontent, and envy. Bougainville is a leading example of this, but conflicts represented as "ethnic," such as in the Solomon Islands and Fiji, also have roots in histories of uneven economic development. Moreover, national or provincial governments in young states often do not have the capacities, or the popular authority and legitimacy, needed to manage these deep-rooted social and economic dilemmas. The rapid pace of social, political, and economic change has severely disrupted traditional structures, values, and societies, while new structures are still taking shape. The underlying political and economic tensions—between international and subsistence economies, and between structures of authority in state institutions and local communities—reflect the fundamental nature of the political, economic, and social changes under way, the profoundly long-term nature of state building, and the states' colonial legacies.

▨ Emerging States or Failing States?

The significantly heightened international security concerns that followed the terrorist attacks in New York in 2001 and in Bali in 2002 changed the framework for security assessments in many parts of the world, including in Australia—the local major power for the Pacific Islands region. The genuine challenges presented by security in the Pacific Islands—which at the opening of the twenty-first century were dominated by the worsening crisis in the

Solomon Islands, law and order problems and political instability in PNG, the still recent coup in Fiji, the legacy of hostilities in Bougainville, and weak economies across the region—were seen through the charged lenses of this concern. Parts of the Pacific Islands region drew some sharp epithets, identified as "an arc of instability" and "a collective basket case," and cast as zones of failing governance, insecurity, and economic disintegration. These sentiments were vividly captured by one leading Australian media commentator: "Melanesia is on fire and one day the flames will engulf Australia."[8] Comparisons were drawn with Africa and the Balkans. There was concern that the "ability to resist penetration by outsiders . . . is almost nil" in such states, leading to them being potential "havens for terrorists."[9]

Pacific Islands countries struggle with serious problems of state capacity and with the intense pace of social, political, and economic change. Left unchecked, these problems are likely to deteriorate further, undermining social cohesion with grave consequences for local populations. Nevertheless, violent conflicts and crises, while significant, have been limited in comparison to many other developing regions. It is important to appreciate both patterns of resilience and patterns of vulnerability. Whatever the relevance of the category of state failure to Africa and the Balkans, the studies in this volume do not find that regional states are failing; nor does the concept of state failure help us to understand the challenges of state building with which the region is grappling. Rather, Pacific Islands states are *emerging*—and this realization entails a somewhat different perspective on supporting state capacity and security.

The idea of "failing states" is misleading in its application to the region in some fundamental ways. It overlooks sources of social cohesion, including customary life, and so misrepresents both the nature of the states themselves and the extent of the region's crises; it implies greater vulnerability to transnational conflict than is present; it suggests a failure of established state institutions rather than the long process of developing sustainable state institutions grounded in their own societies and citizenry.

Sources of Resilience

Talk of "failed or failing states" can encourage us to view all states in the region through alarmist lenses. But while some states face very serious difficulties, violent conflict has not been widespread, and social collapse is both rare and geographically confined. Allegations of state failure discount the considerable strengths of Pacific Islands states, demonstrated by the resilience of Pacific Islands societies but also by robust aspects of the state across the region. Justice systems remain vigorous, for example. While parliamentary and electoral systems have not translated easily into Pacific societies, in ways that are discussed briefly below, with the exception of Fiji

(1987 and 2000) and the Solomon Islands (2000), governments are not changed or held in place by violence or the threat of violence. With the partial exception of Tonga (a monarchy), there has been no pattern of postindependence authoritarian rule in the region. As commentator Graeme Dobell has pointed out, democracy has been relatively successful in the Pacific.[10]

If we understand the "state" as comprising not solely mechanisms of government but also orderly communities, then it is far from disintegrating in the region, although in places it is undergoing intense strains. Writing of the crisis in the Solomon Islands in Chapter 9, Clive Moore notes that "what had failed was the introduced modern centralized processes of government . . . not the lives of the 84 percent of Solomon Islanders who still live in villages and remain dependent on subsistence agriculture and fishing." Most of Oceania, even in those countries that have been marked by periods of serious violence, is orderly and peaceful—this is almost entirely the work of local norms and justice practices.

Community and custom, including customary governance, are still relatively strong and evolving in the Pacific Islands. Paralleling this, subsistence food production remains the central form of livelihood and sustenance. By and large, people can sustain their lives, well so in many areas, and food is distributed through networks of kinship relations. Most people have access to local produce, with poor urban dwellers being the most vulnerable. While nutrition levels can be a problem, there is none of the widespread starvation associated with sub-Saharan Africa, for example. Most people still have access to communal land, in contrast to the situation in many developing countries, where there are significant numbers of landless poor. Growth in the formal economy, while weaker than East Asia or the Caribbean, is substantially better than in sub-Saharan Africa. Fundamental security in the Pacific Islands, in terms of both food and social order, is substantially provided by kin and village. Formal policing, by contrast, has little profile.

Factors containing violence and promoting order in the region have often been local, whether customary or state-based—community work to restrain combatants, customary authority initiating reconciliation processes, the vigorous operation of the legal system, and the active role of civil society in the search for consensus. In some cases the assistance of other regional parties has been critical in restoring order (in Vanuatu, the Solomon Islands, and Bougainville). The long-term viability of the current intervention in the Solomon Islands is likely to depend on how well it collaborates with those indigenous factors supporting order and reconciliation. As Nic Maclellan notes in Chapter 7, there are long traditions of local conflict management and resolution approaches that, while not always adequate to recent forms of conflict, have played a central role in restraining violence and opening the way for resolution and reconciliation. These capacities need to be utilized by interventions from beyond the immediate region.

"Melanesia Is on Fire"

In the Pacific Islands, in a further distinction from Africa and the Balkans, transnational conflict formations are not a feature, reflecting the island nature of the geography and perhaps the continuing strength of social characteristics. With the important exceptions of the Solomon Islands and Bougainville (which are close neighbors) and West Papua and Papua New Guinea (which share a land border), there are natural geographic barriers that inhibit violent conflicts from directly crossing borders. (In a small but worrying development, Fijian mercenaries have been working in Bougainville for a local con-man.) The illegal movement of small arms into Papua New Guinea poses serious security problems, while the availability of small arms has had a profoundly destructive impact on community and customary processes in the Solomon Islands and parts of PNG, including Bougainville, which is now working on reconstructing these processes. According to recent studies the illicit trade in small weapons in the region is relatively limited,[11] though it is nevertheless a problem that needs a regional response.

Military and security forces in the region have played a leading or complicit role in crises in Fiji, the Solomon Islands, Vanuatu, and (more contentiously) Papua New Guinea, as well as being a key factor sparking conflict in Bougainville. The role of the Fijian military in political life (discussed by Steve Ratuva in Chapter 10) is complex and problematic. Military officers have three times led coups, the first two in 1987 and the third in 2006. There was considerable difference between the 1987 and the 2006 coups, with the 1987 coups motivated by ethnic Fijian nationalism and the 2006 coup motivated in part by the pursuit of legal punishment for those behind the 2000 attempted coup and mutiny. While the 2006 coup was ostensibly mounted to uphold the rule of law, the tendency of the military to intervene directly in political life seriously threatens the scope of the rule of law in Fiji. There are concerns about "the blurring of roles and responsibilities between military and unarmed constabulary" in the region, and a militarization of conflict.[12] Donor focus on strengthening security capacities through training, weapons supply, and joint exercises needs to be careful not to contribute negatively to this process. The region is not, however, characterized by systematic abuse of military power, with military forces themselves being small.

Emerging States

The concept of "state failure" implies a disintegration of already-established state institutions and a breakdown of social order that is assumed to rely directly or indirectly on these institutions. But as various commentators have pointed out, the state is still in the process of being created in the Pacific Islands region.[13] Social order is not dependent on central institutions to the extent that it is in developed or mature states. Rather than illuminating the circumstances of the Pacific Island region, the label "state failure" indicates the prevalence of the unrealistic expectation that working, modern nation-states are essentially a set of institutions that can be delivered like a product, rather than complex political processes and institutions embedded in society, within which they must construct their legitimacy. This has significant implications for efforts to strengthen states in Oceania.

Across much of the region there is a fractured relationship, and at times a deep disconnection, between the institutions of the state and society. While efforts to transfer liberal state institutions have met varying levels of success across the region, the institutions and processes of the state often lack roots in, or clear articulation with, the patterns of legitimacy and authority that have weight in grassroots communities. As in some other postcolonial regions, in the Pacific Islands many small, localized, and highly diverse communities, with their own traditionally oriented governance mechanisms organized around clan or language-based patterns of loyalty, now sit within the structures and institutions of the contemporary state and the dynamics of globalized markets. The institutions of the state, however, from parliaments to police systems, do not mesh automatically with customary or local community governance mechanisms and cultural norms. State institutions can also face the challenges of working effectively with complex patterns of political and cultural difference within the one state. This "thin" connection between society and the institutions of the state weakens the legitimacy of institutions, citizenship, and democratic participation. It can work to distort the proper functioning of both state institutions and community processes, and so has profound effects on the potential for violent conflict and crime, and for development across the region.

The disjunction between state and society creates the conditions from which other critical problems emerge or intensify. At worst, it generates governments characterized by intense self-interest, localism, structural instability, and opportunities for corruption. This seriously weakens the capacity of parliaments to represent either the electorate to government, or government to the electorate, and enables opportunistic criminality from within or without the region. Conflicts over resources are exacerbated by the disjunction between state and society, as the processes that deal with fundamental questions of the management, use, and distribution of resources are often fractured or dysfunctional.

However, rather than grasping this situation as state failure, it is more accurate to see Pacific Islands nations as states not yet born, as former Solomon Island prime minister Solomon Mamaloni commented in regard to the Solomons,[14] or more simply, as states not yet mature. But even "not mature" may not capture what is happening. People and governments across the region are struggling with processes of reshaping and reimagining the way political community is lived, understood, and institutionalized. The region could be better understood as undergoing a generative process, rather than being in a state of collapse, as people search for more constructive relationships between their own collective social values and the processes of the state of which they are now part. Such a process inevitably involves significant confusion and conflict, between values and cosmologies as much as between changing interest groups. The challenge is to support these processes in ways that avoid violent conflict and minimize the potential for patterns of criminality and corruption to become established.

Case Studies

Addressing development and security means that "conflict" is a term used frequently in this book, usually with negative significance. Conflict, particularly when violent and embedded, can destroy lives, well-being, and community trust, undermining the potential for participative politics and prosperity. However, conflict is often not violent and certainly is not always or only negative. Pacific Islands states and societies are undergoing demanding processes of change that are inevitably full of uncertainty and wrong turns, both creative and conflictual.

The case studies in this book cross a spectrum of political status, including independent states (Papua New Guinea, the Solomon Islands, Fiji, Vanuatu, Tonga, and Nauru), a territory (New Caledonia, which shares sovereignty with France), an autonomous region (Bougainville, which is part of PNG), and a province (West Papua, which is part of Indonesia). While the legal standing of most is settled, the search for appropriate forms of governance is ongoing in them all. In some cases, however, the legal status of the territory is still taking shape. In response to earlier periods of violent conflict, New Caledonia and Bougainville have both opted for slow processes of decisionmaking about the eventual politico-legal form of their communities, whether as independent states or autonomous entities linked to the sovereign power of France or PNG respectively. Autonomy arrangements for West Papua have been formulated within Indonesia but not implemented, intensifying frustration in that province. There is a continuing and pointed need to work constructively with desires for self-determination, whether understood as greater local control over or input into government, or as full independence, in New Caledonia, Bougainville, and West Papua. The latter, however, is the only one of the three that continues to be the site of serious violence. In Jason MacLeod's assessment in Chapter 8, West Papua is "one of the most protracted, complex, and volatile conflicts in the Pacific."

In contrast to MacLeod's discussion of West Papua, Paul de Deckker's and Nic Maclellan's chapters on New Caledonia explore positive steps taken to work against violence, while dealing with some of the causes and the effects of the violent self-determination struggles of the 1980s. In Chapter 6, de Deckker examines efforts to counteract the marginalization of the indigenous population through increased economic and political integration, while in Chapter 7, Maclellan looks at the contribution of the conflict management traditions of indigenous society. In Chapter 5, Anthony Regan examines the complex relations between development and violent conflict in Bougainville, and suggests that "the reconstruction and redevelopment activities associated with the peace process have been the source of further tensions and conflict." However, Regan considers that shared norms valuing peace have emerged during the ten years of protracted violence in Bougainville that significantly reduce the danger of such tensions erupting into renewed violence. People in Bougainville and PNG learned from aspects of the peace process in New Caledonia; this raises the question of whether Indonesia may be able to utilize aspects from both experiences to work with the challenges posed by West Papua.

Fundamental questions about the form of government or constitutional arrangements are also unsettled in a number of independent states. In Chapter 13, Lopeti Senituli examines Tonga's slow movement toward increased democratization, looking particularly at the use of the court system in working toward profound change. Tongans have been drawing on strategies (petitions, boycotts, strikes, marches, and political parties) that are relatively new for them. At the same time, they have also drawn on more traditional approaches that place great value on retaining the integrity of relationships. The combination ensured the peacefulness of this gradual revolution until a riot broke out in the capital in November 2006. The riot and the responses to it within Tonga do not yet suggest, however, that future political life will be characterized by violence. In Chapter 10, Steve Ratuva explores the history of constitutional change in Fiji, through which the population has sought, with mixed results, to manage relations between indigenous Fijians and settler Indo-Fijians. Ratuva examines the role of Fiji's developing economic and political structures in embedding two distinct ethnically identified communities and later efforts to untie the consequences of that process. The complex role of the military forces in Fijian national political life is also discussed.

Some of the negative consequences of government that is only weakly linked to citizenry and community are outlined vividly in Chapter 11, Graham Hassall's account of elite politics in Vanuatu. Hassall argues that elite maneuvering and weak, fractious government constitute Vanuatu's principal source of insecurity, while scarce national resources are diverted from the work of government into political contest. Turning to Nauru in Chapter 12, Max Quanchi outlines a state unprepared by colonization for the complex tasks of government. Nauru offers an exemplary study of how to lose a lot of money in massive financial mismanagement. Previous Nauruan governments did not have the capacity to manage sudden, large influxes of funds, leading *The Economist* to declare the small state "one of the world's most dysfunctional" on the basis of its economic management.[15] Nauruan society, however, has not fallen into violence, but remains intact, if stressed, while the government may now be facing its predicament more realistically.

Of all the Pacific Island states, the Solomon Islands and PNG are at present the most vulnerable and most beset by problems of leadership and governance. Analyses of both countries in this volume point to the role of what is often the gulf between governments and populations, or state institutions and social values and practices, in this predicament. In Chapter 2, Marion Jacka considers that "the mismatch between the adopted Western political and administrative systems and the social and cultural realities of Papua New Guinea's diverse societies" underlies the problems of political instability and poor governance. She suggests that what is failing in PNG is not the state, but approaches to development and modernization, while emphasizing the need for development and state building that are grounded in local aspirations and initiative. Both Chapter 2 and Chapter 9 underline the centrality of community to Pacific Island life and stability.

In Chapter 9, Clive Moore discusses the desire of many Solomon Islanders for significant political change to "localize" state institutions. Reflecting on international intervention in the Solomon Islands in response to that country's long-standing political crisis, Moore suggests that international agencies are not engaging with Solomon Islanders in the radical rethinking of the relationship between governments and ordinary citizens that he argues is necessary for real resolution of the violence and unrest that beset that country:

> The hopes [for the 2006 national election] that a new style of Solomon Island government—one that listens to its people, involves all sectors of the community, and charts a new course—were dashed. The conflict resolution, human security, and development initiatives that have emerged so far are not sufficiently radical to redress the current instability of the Solomon Islands central government. Modern liberal democratic governance structures are not aligned with indigenous systems of power and authority, and so far neither the elected representatives of the people, nor the international agencies involved with rehabilitation, have implemented the central issues of reform.

Addressing Bougainville in Chapter 5, Anthony Regan outlines the complex cultural and social realities that external agencies, in this case mining and plantation companies, often fail to appreciate. In Chapter 4, Abby McLeod develops this point further in her discussion of the different ways

Papua New Guineans and Australians understand the role of conflict and violence in social order and the implications of that difference for police reform in PNG. McLeod argues that "external attempts to promote development and 'peace' in Papua New Guinea will succeed only when local notions of social order are accommodated (if not accepted)." McLeod's work underscores both the need to accommodate local understandings and life practices in any form of development work, if it is to be effective, and the deeply challenging nature of that accommodation.

As McLeod details the need for external agencies to engage with the values of local communities, so Orovu Sepoe calls for greater engagement on the part of local societies and governments with international principles and values. In Chapter 3, Sepoe considers that domination of and violence against women are fundamental to insecurity and development failure in PNG. In making this argument, she seeks both to uphold community life in PNG and to critique it; she appeals both to the values of community life and to the values set out in international instruments on women and human rights. Sepoe envisages a dialogue of values underpinning development: "A continuing and peaceful discourse in ideas and experiences should pave the way for more and better understanding of the diverse cultures of our people."

■ The Colonial Legacy: State and Society

Colonization has left a complex legacy in the region. Moreover, despite decolonization and the emergence of independent states, it is clear from the region's history that the process of forming a state that works, for its own population and in terms of the international environment in which it must make its way, is necessarily slow and is itself, in important ways, a struggle for self-determination.

While metropolitan powers were present in the region from the sixteenth century, it was not until the late nineteenth century that most of the Pacific Islands were progressively annexed.[16] By the beginning of the twentieth century, no part of the Pacific was outside European and US spheres of power. In common with experiences elsewhere, colonization (and decolonization) globalized the form of the modern state, but was no preparation for modern statehood. Colonization offered forms of coercive authoritarian rule, where the local society, and any "development" within it, were run largely to serve the economic or strategic interests of the colonial power. The borders defining colonial territories—borders later inherited by the decolonized state—were determined by the occupying power, often arbitrarily. The border separating West Papua from PNG, and the inclusion of Bougainville and Buka in PNG (rather than the Solomon Islands), are both examples of this—both borders have been sensitive, due to self-determination movements in West Papua and Bougainville.

The introduction by colonial powers of indentured labor from within and beyond the region to work plantations and mines—notably Indians into Fiji and Indo-Chinese into New Caledonia—led to tensions over land that have not been subsequently resolved. Efforts at economic "development" were sporadic, and unequal patterns of development entrenched unequal access to power and resources, often between kinship groups or different communities.[17] Colonial rule was dominated by cost-cutting imperatives, and education and social welfare were the province of missionaries.

Independent statehood in the region (for those territories that are independent) was achieved relatively recently, with most states becoming independent around the 1970s. In general, there was little preparation for statehood in terms of the institutions of government, the education of citizens, or the economic capacities that underpin the structures and services that make up the state. Of these, perhaps citizenship was—and arguably remains—the most neglected and one of the most important. Colonial rule left populations with almost no experience in democratic processes. In Fiji, for example, indigenous Fijians did not have the vote until the 1960s. "When independence came in 1970, the majority of the Fijian people had only a very limited experience of those practices normally associated with democratic institutions."[18] State forms were essentially "delivered" to the Pacific Island region, on top of what was mostly dispersed networks of semiautonomous communities.

Most of the region's people had no traditions of national identification. Few countries shared one indigenous language, a common culture, or any precolonial history of unitary rule; colonial rule was itself fragmentary in important respects. As a result, many peoples in the region had little lived experience of nation and citizenship. People thus tend not to hold their formal leadership or political and economic institutions to account, or they hold them to account in terms of clan or custom expectations. While clan relations and churches form strong patterns of community association and connection, community organizations that might foster active citizenship are not as widespread. While their presence is growing, civil society organizations that could work as an avenue between social life and political institutions are still very recent throughout much of the region. A sense of citizenship, as the fundamental interface of society and the state, has received little focus or assistance. As a result, it is taking shape in a slow and faltering way.

Party politics have translated uneasily into Oceania. Leadership has traditionally been exercised through the lineage or the language group (*wantok*, or "one talk"). Despite the formal introduction of representational democracy along party lines, obligations to and expectations of *wantok* and lineage remain in many respects more powerful than the abstract concept of a party, or obligations to a parliament. This has resulted in very weak party

systems, a high turnover of parliamentarians, and at times unworkable parliaments, particularly in the Solomon Islands, PNG, and more recently
Vanuatu. Dysfunctional political processes weaken governments' ability
either to distribute services to the population or to act as a conduit for people's concerns to the decisionmaking processes in the capital. At best, this is
a serious obstacle to the emergence of active democratic life; at its worst, it
can generate "disillusioned, powerless and poor communities."[19] The breakdown in the provision of services can itself act as a kind of disenfranchise-
ment, and in some areas has been severe.

In Melanesia, lack of party discipline, together with the *wantok* system,
has provided a context of conflicting obligations and systems of accountability that encourages corruption and are open to exploitation by political
entrepreneurs. The state centralizes certain kinds of decisionmaking power,
including over resource use. Particularly in the resource-rich states of
Melanesia, such centralized power can become a prize to be captured. The
Solomon Islands and PNG have experienced the most extreme examples of
this negative dynamic, where "unhealthy codependencies" between politicians and segments of the population can undermine democratic process,
accountability, and appropriate resource allocation, create conditions for
stagnant public and private sectors, and generate crime and cronyism.[20]

Wantokism (clan or cultural affiliation and its obligations), however,
should not be simply equated with corruption, even if the interaction of
wantokism with Western modes of accountability can have that effect.
Within community life, it operates as a form of social welfare. Commenting
on law in PNG, Abby McLeod notes in Chapter 4 that "*wantokism* provides
a particularly strong example of the disjunction between the formal (and
supposedly impartial) legal justice system and Papua New Guinean sociality." The conflict between Western cultural and legal modes of accountability, and custom obligation, is not limited to parliaments and political life, but
is pervasive. At worst, the interaction can work to degrade both, by allowing or even requiring people to play the two forms of accountability against
each other, or by reframing customary solutions in contexts that utterly
change their meaning. The availability of high-powered weaponry has profoundly distorted the dynamics of semi-ritualized traditional warfare in
parts of the PNG Highlands, for example, resulting in a pervasive gun culture.[21] Violence in parts of the Highlands is now no longer under the control
of either customary or state authority; the author of a recent PNG government report has warned that illegal guns pose a threat to elections in 2007
and threaten social and political stability.[22] High-powered weapons also
undermined traditional compensation processes in the Solomon Islands,
intensifying intercommunal conflict. "The demand for money with menaces
bears little resemblance to the voluntary handing over of customary goods
as a gesture of thanks or request for forgiveness."[23]

While decisionmaking in Pacific Island societies is often participative, it is consensual rather than reliant on majority voting or competitive politics. In societies without traditions of competitive representative elections, electoral processes can generate the conflicts that they are meant to contain. Competitive electoral processes can elevate existing social and economic divisions. These divisions can become a source of conflict if the institutional mechanisms devised for containing them prove inadequate to the task. These conditions have generated localized violence in PNG, the Solomon Islands, Vanuatu, and Fiji.

Economic Pressures

Questions of economic fragility, the basic sustainability of small island economies, financial mismanagement, and poor economic growth rates coupled with high population growth have fueled concerns about regional security in donor governments. In discussions of Oceania's economic health and its implications for security and development, it is important to be aware of the existence of both the formal cash economy and the informal exchange or subsistence economy, interacting with each other in complex ways. Growth rates and other indicators are not available for the subsistence economy. Nevertheless, the subsistence economy supports most of the population to varying degrees, even though it is coming under increasing strain. The economic figures available to us, then, provide only a partial insight into the economic life of the countries involved.

Formal economies across much of the region have experienced a lengthy downturn in growth, although there have been signs that some regional economies, including PNG's, are improving. This is particularly significant, as PNG has been one of the weakest performers and is the biggest economy among the independent states.[24] The long economic trough, however, intensified debate over appropriate economic directions for the region, particularly around whether contemporary models of economic liberalization are the answer to the region's economic woes, and need to be pursued more vigorously, or whether these models are contributing to conditions for deeper insecurity and violence. Key aspects of this debate turn on the ways in which the unmeasured subsistence economy is valued and in which the cash and the subsistence economies interact. The strong tradition of communal landownership in the region, upon which the informal exchange or subsistence economy rests, is a particular focus; questions of land tenure are discussed later.

Economic growth rates have fluctuated markedly since the independence decade of the 1970s, reflecting both internal factors and vulnerability to international commodity prices and other economic movements, such as the Asian financial crisis of the mid-1990s. Overall, as economist Stewart

Firth has pointed out, "per capita GDP in the Pacific Islands has increased by 0.5 percent per annum since 1975, by contrast with a decline of 0.9 percent in sub-Saharan Africa."[25]

However, such modest economic growth has been significantly outstripped by high population growth rates across the region. In terms of fertility and mortality rates, the region appears to be comparable with many Asian states of the 1950s and 1960s. Life expectancy in the Pacific has increased and infant mortality rates have fallen. While this is wholeheartedly positive, combined with continuing high fertility rates it means that population growth, at an average of over 3 percent per annum,[26] is well ahead of economic growth in the formal sector. Approximately 40 percent of the populations of PNG, Vanuatu, the Solomon Islands, Tonga, and Nauru are aged fifteen or under.[27] Such growth rates overreach the likely capacity of subsistence agriculture and traditional family-based support networks. They also put extraordinary pressure on the formal economy to expand sufficiently to absorb the large number of new faces looking for work, and to fund education and health services.

Rapid population growth also fuels increased urbanization, as young people move to urban centers or large resource developments looking for work. Urban drift has been characterized by a weakening of traditional kin ties to home districts. Since such ties operate as the principal normative device for social control, their loss is significant and is associated with increasing crime rates in urban centers, with Port Moresby, the capital of PNG, the most notable example. Squatter settlements, unemployment and poverty, prostitution (including child prostitution), sexually transmitted diseases including HIV/AIDS, and social violence have been the negative consequences of population growth, outstripping the capacity of either the formal or the subsistence economy to absorb it. High concentrations of unemployed youths can also be vulnerable to manipulation by those with interests in political conflict, or contribute to an environment in which social unrest or confrontation can more easily intensify into violence.

Pacific Island economies are vulnerable in other ways. Intraregional trade is slight. The formal island economies are small, open, and largely dependent on the export of primary commodities—minerals, timber, copra, palm oil, coffee, and sugar. Their export bases are narrow, leaving Pacific Island states highly exposed to fluctuating prices over which they have no control. As the global economy liberalizes further, at least some of these primary commodity prices can be expected to drop, potentially causing great stress for Pacific Island countries. The region suffered from the reduction of commodity prices in the 1980s and the Asian economic crisis of the 1990s. This intensified economic uncertainty almost certainly contributed to increased political volatility in PNG. A sharp decrease in Fiji's income and employment from sugar and textiles is expected to flow from phasing out preferential trade agreements incompatible with the World Trade Organization. Given the sugar industry's high employment of Indo-Fijians, a drastic decline of the sugar industry will pose a challenge for intercommunal relations.

All the Pacific Island economies are reliant on foreign aid and import more than they export. Australia is the major aid donor to the region as a whole, although not to each individual country. The other major donors, in descending order, are Japan, New Zealand, the European Union, the United States, France, the United Kingdom, and Canada. (The economies of New Caledonia, French Polynesia, and Wallis and Futuna are tied to and supported by France—one of the arguments against full sovereignty.) China is of increasing importance in the region, as a source of aid and investment, but also through its destabilizing competition with Taiwan (discussed briefly in the last chapter).

Migration has also operated as a safety valve for stretched resources and employment for some states; more Samoans, Tongans, and Nuieans live elsewhere, such as New Zealand, than in their native land. There is an increasing demand from Pacific Island governments, made through the Pacific Islands Forum, for access to the labor markets of Australia and New Zealand through extended but temporary working visa arrangements. Remittances have become increasingly important for Samoa and Tonga, and more recently for Fiji. Fijians are well represented in the British armed services, and have also supplied labor for a number of private security companies operating in Iraq. This represents employment, and the Fiji military has a strong record of international peacekeeping service, as Steve Ratuva notes in this volume. Nevertheless, significant numbers of experienced fighters can be a dangerous and unpredictable resource, as the Fijian mercenaries training a con-man's private militia in Bougainville indicate.[28]

Low capacity to manage exportable resources, which often results in resource predation, is a further source of economic and social vulnerability for Pacific Island states. Environmental, financial, or other controls common in developed economies may not be put in place or not applied, as Max Quanchi's discussion of Nauru in this volume makes clear. The Solomon Islands is being stripped of timber by Asian logging companies. Fish breeding stocks are not well policed and are under pressure by trawlers from beyond the region. Governments seeking foreign exchange and investment can be susceptible to pressure and manipulation from parties outside the region, whether companies or governments, supporting inappropriate commercial ventures that leave them prey to bankruptcy and destabilize financial systems.[29] Lack of pressure for public accountability has meant that areas of government have become embroiled in corruption around the export of resources. In other schemes, Vanuatu and Nauru run tax havens, while other Pacific Island countries offer flags of convenience to shipping companies;[30] some governments have shown a willingness to use their vote in international agencies of one kind or another as leverage for aid packages. Competition between China and Taiwan for diplomatic recognition across the region has resulted in often destabilizing "bidding" for support, using aid, investment, or (in the case of Taiwan) just straight cash payments to critical decisionmakers.

There is an argument that microeconomies are simply not viable. A comparison of Pacific Island with Caribbean economies undertaken in 1996 by Te'o Fairbairn and DeLisle Worrell, however, indicated that microeconomies can be dynamic and self-sustaining.[31] Some microeconomies in the Pacific have managed well. Samoa, for example, has an active local business community, built around tourism, service industries, and a small but viable export industry in electrical equipment and semiprocessed foodstuffs. Small, locally managed enterprises could also contribute to local self-reliance.

As with the lack of fit between introduced and indigenous political and social governance, so tension between indigenous and international economic dynamics is an underlying factor encouraging insecurity and conflict. According to Yash Ghai, writing about intercommunal conflict in Fiji, "the root of the troubles is the pace of economic and technological changes, which have seriously disrupted traditional values and structures, destabilized societies, and reduced their economic and political self-sufficiency."[32] These tensions, which complement the lack of fit between customary and introduced political governance, need to be recognized and consciously engaged across the region.

A number of chapters in this volume emphasize the importance of diversifying economic development projects and approaches, and of placing increased emphasis on small, rurally based enterprises that are compatible with community structures and the informal economy. Ideally, this would mean modest increases in growth and greater participation in the formal economy, while sustaining the nature of community life. While jobs need to be generated for city dwellers, efforts could also be made to stabilize urban drift and take the reality of rural livelihoods more seriously into account. As Marion Jacka and Clive Moore suggest in this volume, if over 80 percent of the Pacific Island population lives in rural areas, undertaking subsistence food production and exchange, economic development efforts also need to be more significantly located there. Large resource developments and urban developments need to be at least complemented by many smaller enterprises and industries compatible with local rural communities and able to be managed by them—tourism, infrastructure, and community industries that support community structures while also providing greater economic and employment alternatives within them.

Such an approach would have economic and social benefit, but could also be understood as a form of conflict prevention. Viable community-based enterprises, supported by infrastructure that, for example, provides access to markets, offer a mechanism for responding to rural hardship and generating income and employment. Greater employment opportunity and variety can make a positive impact on urban drift. Moreover, local rural enterprises can also be a way of engaging the tensions between traditional values and economic change, and thus contribute to managing the conflict generated by economic change.

Land

If there is to be a process of mutual accommodation and evolution between international economic exchange and local customary exchange, then the question of land is at the heart of the interface and the friction. For indigenous Pacific people, land is a source of livelihood not only for the individual or family, but also for the lineage, stretching across generations. Land is at the heart of community, customary, and spiritual life. In Melanesia, land is the element by which relationships are patterned. It thus acts as a source of strength and community cohesion, as well as a source of dispute.

There is considerable tension between patterns of customary land tenure and the use of land for investment and commercial development. Custom land tenure does not fit well with the demands of the market, yet local commercial enterprise and foreign investment are vital for economic growth and diversification. Misunderstandings between people applying custom and market approaches to land are common.[33] Anthony Regan's discussion of Bougainville in this volume gives some insight into the potential for highly destructive violence generated by economic activity that does not fully comprehend the range of sensitivities regarding land in the Pacific. The effort to find constructive ways of both respecting the place of land in Pacific life while enabling commercial economic activity is critically important to ways forward that support and build on the sources of resilience in Pacific society.[34]

The failure of many development projects due to the lack of understanding of local relationships between people and land has been discussed by the Australian Senate Committee on Relations with the South Pacific (2003), particularly in terms of how these relationships, and the informal economies they sustain, challenge the dominant World Bank development template: "The modern formal cash economy devalues the traditional economy because, being money-based and reliant on production for cash, buying and selling and earning wages, it cannot comprehend or measure production for consumption, reciprocity, sharing and communal work without wages."[35]

Some commentators, however, are urging substantial reform or abandonment of communal land tenure as an essential, if contentious step in the path to growth in the formal economy. Economist Helen Hughes argues that no country in the world has developed from a base of communal landowner-ship.[36] The World Bank notes that lack of security of tenure for investors, as a result of customary communal tenure, acts to deter investors, especially those interested in large-scale investment.[37] Conflict around these issues is not simply academic—in 2001, reference to land registration in a World Bank draft agreement in PNG sparked widespread protests in which three people were killed.

Land is central both to questions of development but also to questions of security for Pacific people. The Australian senate committee discussed options to enable investment in the Pacific, proposing techniques such as land registration and lease/lease-back arrangements. These approaches remain problematic, however. The committee noted that processes such as land registration can be highly provocative, and called for greater imagina-tion on the part of financial institutions and donors about ways in which "development can be financed at the local level without individual land reg-istration so that communities can remain in control of their land."[38]

Questions of land have played a significant role in many major con-flicts in the region. If the interaction of security and development is to be given genuine weight, then the linkage between communal landownership and the satisfaction of fundamental social and food security needs to be rec-ognized. These outcomes are of extraordinary value, even if they pose sig-nificant complexities for commercial dealings. The resilience of social life in the region rests to an unclear but profound extent upon customary rela-tionships with land. These relationships may be gradually evolving; to undermine them, however, would be counterproductive to regional security. Efforts to improve economic growth that seriously undermine social cohe-sion are not likely to have the desired consequences over the medium to long term.

Resource exploitation may bring conflicts regarding land into sharpest focus. Mining has a particularly fraught history; with logging, it brings together environmental and resource security concerns—both major sources of division within communities. Pointing to Ok Tedi (PNG), Panguna (Bougainville), and Freeport (West Papua), Nic Maclellan argues that meth-ods of natural resource extraction "can devastate ecosystems and destroy indigenous cultures and livelihoods." In response, landowners fight back, leading to governments relying "on police and military forces to control these enclave resource developments, sparking a cycle of repression, con-flict and further militarization."[39]

Self-Determination

Questions of self-determination remain significant and highly contentious in any consideration of security and development in the region. Self-determination has been, and will likely continue to be, central to episodes of serious violent conflict in the broader region. The current conflict in West Papua, which has already destroyed lives and communities, could escalate, with tragic consequences. Escalation could also bear significant negative effects on Indonesia and on relationships between Indonesia and its neighbors. This problem needs attention and support from the international community.

All of the three territories considered here in the context of self-determination—New Caledonia, Bougainville, and West Papua—are mineral-rich.[40] In all three territories, mining has brought massive impacts on land, environment, and culture, and has raised questions of who controls and profits from the wealth brought by resource extraction, and who bears the destructive consequences. In these cases, conflict over self-determination has also been grounded in questions of control of resources, land, and culture, and of collective self-direction, at least as much and perhaps more than in matters of sovereignty and statehood.

As Nic Maclellan points out in Chapter 7, during the 1980s it was New Caledonia that was at the forefront of anxieties about security in the region, as the independence struggle generated violent conflict with the very real threat of rapid escalation. Since intense confrontations in the 1980s for New Caledonia, and the 1990s for Bougainville, the populations of both territories have deferred the question of full independence, enabling a gradual approach to the tasks of political resolution. They have yet to finally resolve the question of what form of self-determination they want, and their stability remains finely balanced. In the meantime, the effort to approach the dilemmas involved gradually and nonviolently makes it possible to hope that constructive ways forward on the challenges of self-determination will be found. In the face of an emphasis on the problems of the region, these outcomes say much about its strength.

The West Papuan conflict threatens to have repercussions not just for Indonesia but also for PNG (with which West Papua shares a land border), Australia, and New Zealand, which may face a humanitarian crisis and refugee outflow if violence escalates. There are efforts in both Jakarta and West Papua to find nonviolent solutions acceptable both to the Indonesian government and to communities in the province. The Indonesian military constitutes a third party, however, with powerful and divisive interests of its own. This situation could deteriorate significantly, with tragic consequences for all parties.

Women

Helen Hakena (who runs a rape crisis center in Bougainville) has noted that for women, the war in Bougainville has not ended.[41] Many of the men, traumatized by the violence, became addicted to a particularly potent home brew during the crisis years, leading to exceptionally high rates of indiscriminate violence against women. Neither the traditional nor the formal policing and justice mechanisms have been able to cope with the social dilemmas generated by the violence, or with the quantity of cases. This is an extreme example, following the chaos of protracted conflict, yet the position of women and the level of violence against them in many parts of the Pacific are troubling. It is a form of deep insecurity directly affecting many people in the region.

Writing of PNG, Orovu Sepoe argues in Chapter 3 that the subordination and vulnerability of women's position in society itself undermines the potential for broader development. "Given both that the female population constitute nearly half of the total population, and the fundamental role that women play in the life of the community, it is no wonder that [the insecurity and restricted life chances of women are] reflected in the overall low level of human, social, and economic development for PNG." The United Nations Children's Fund (UNICEF) agrees, stating that "rape has become a major threat to social stability and economic development and seriously impedes the full and active participation of women and girls."[42] At the same time, Sepoe believes, the insecurity and marginalization of women signifies and continues the pattern of lopsided development and systematic exclusion that she considers as characterizing much development in PNG. The more inclusive a society, she suggests, the less likely it is to resort to violence. Sepoe calls for more participatory, consensual, and reconciliatory decision-making in public and private life—models that have a strong cultural basis in the Melanesian context.

There is considerable variation in the role of women across the region, with some matrilineal societies providing them greater influence. Nevertheless, the Australian Senate Committee on Relations with the South Pacific noted that, regionwide, "women do not only face direct violence, but higher rates of illiteracy, poverty, unemployment, poor health, discrimination, heavy daily workload, . . . and low participation in the political process and decision making at all levels."[43] There is moreover a widespread belief in parts of the region that violence against women is increasing. UNICEF's 2005 report on children and HIV/AIDS in PNG stated that "rape and sexual assault have reached epidemic levels" in PNG, while twice as many women as men aged fifteen to twenty-nine are infected with HIV/AIDS.[44]

There is debate within the region on the extent to which the often vulnerable position of women represents traditional values, or is a deterioration of such values. While the subordinate role of women is rooted at least in part in custom, the interplay of custom with introduced political and economic dynamics is complex, and the pressures of rapid change are intense. Anthony Regan points out in Chapter 5 that the plantation economy in

Bougainville, for example, undermined "the previously preeminent economic roles of women (through men taking control of the new forms of wealth emerging from the cash economy)," and because administration officials did not understand matrilineal ownership. Poverty and social fragmentation also play a role, with "marginalized men work[ing] out their frustrations on the women."[45]

The leading role of women in conflict resolution and peacebuilding in Bougainville and the Solomon Islands and Fiji has been clear, and has had an impact on debates around the broader role of women in those states. This has been recognized by the new Bougainville constitution, through which women have been allocated a minimum number of seats in the autonomous region's parliament. It has not, however, transferred into political leadership roles for women in the Solomon Islands.

Development projects can have complex and unintended impacts on gender roles and benefits do not automatically flow to women. Access to markets is a leading issue for rural women, however. Gender-sensitive support for community enterprises may be one important way of contributing to the security of women and communities.

■ Conclusion

The pressures and problems outlined briefly in this chapter, and others not explored here (including AIDS and other health issues, environmental degradation, climate change), represent serious challenges for the region. It is critical that these problems be recognized and that Pacific Islanders and the international community, particularly those states and agencies closely associated with the region, work together to overcome or manage them. While recognizing problems, however, it is equally important to see the strengths and resilience of Pacific Island states—those factors that work against social disintegration, violence, or widespread poverty. If we see only the problems, the responses devised to them will be unable to draw from local strengths and capacities. Worse, there is a danger that the responses will compound the original problems by further undermining the strengths of local societies—producing economic development projects that significantly erode social cohesiveness, for example, or strengthening governance that fails to engage with local political aspirations and values, or security responses that fail to confront the causes of instability.

Since 2003, there has been repeated concern within some donor states about state failure in the region. This focus does at least draw attention to the urgency of some of the problems with which the region is struggling. But there is a real danger that a focus on state failure at least partially misdirects responses to these problems. The category of state failure does not seem conducive to recognizing the region's positive capacities. Moreover, it can suggest that the best response to weak states is to strengthen the transfer of liberal state institutions—a transfer essentially from "us" to "them." Within this approach, however, local societies are not understood or engaged as a source of solutions. Strengthening central institutions in line with good international practice is unquestionably important. However, if this becomes the primary driving response, it threatens to further alienate local societies by rendering them passive, and weakening both a sense of local responsibility for working to overcome problems, and local ownership of solutions.

By contrast, an emphasis on emerging states and their problems allows the focus to shift to the relationship between government and community, questions of legitimacy, and the gradual development of citizenship. These approaches will be discussed briefly in the concluding chapter. A focus on emerging states can also provide a better platform for acknowledging the region's strengths. Valuing the region's social resilience and cohesiveness is a vital place to start discussions of security and development in the Pacific. If we are serious about avoiding protracted violent conflict, understanding sources of resilience, not damaging them, and where possible encouraging such resilience, is an essential step. Grasping the real strengths of the region enables us to work with those strengths and not against them. For development agencies outside the region, recognizing strengths within it can also enrich relationships with Pacific Island partners, enabling stronger collaboration and mutual respect as a creative basis for good development.

Pacific Islanders are responding in a variety of sometimes conflicting ways to the forces and changes generated by colonial and postcolonial practices and global capitalism. It is an extraordinarily demanding but also potentially creative period for the region, one marked by the challenges of grounding the institutions and processes of government in societies, of bringing together what in some places is an extraordinary range of social, cultural, and linguistic diversity within one national community, and of exploring coming together as a "community of peoples"[46] across the region. Working constructively with Pacific responses to these challenges turns on understanding security and development as part of each other. Both need to be understood broadly. Security is an integral part of fundamental safety, of relations of trust, of shared well-being, and of the basic legitimacy of political, economic, and justice systems. In turn, development in the Pacific Islands region is not primarily the delivery of products, but a process that deeply engages with the evolution of indigenous solutions to the problems of how to construct government and governance processes that are meaningful to Pacific societies. Equally, working effectively with Pacific Islanders on economic development demands establishing economic activities that support societies, not destroy them.

Consistently asking how we can support development that works against violence, that does not embed the inequities or dispossession that often lead to violence and that supports communities who are avoiding or managing sources of potential violence, involves a genuine shift of perspective. It involves being aware of and working with the strengths of communities. In the same way, we can ask how to support security in ways that are able to acknowledge the different structures of legitimacy, authority, and justice in play, and that build on and extend local sources of resilience.

▓ Notes

1. The term "Pacific Islands" often does not include Papua New Guinea, although "Pacific Islands region" does. Throughout this chapter, "Pacific Islands" is also intended to include Papua New Guinea.

2. As West Papua is part of Indonesia, it is not a part of the Pacific Island region in a formal political sense. However, it is predominantly ethnically and culturally Melanesian, and shares the same island as Papua New Guinea and so is often included on that basis. By contrast, New Zealand is a Pacific island, with significant geological similarities with the rest of the region, and is often included in discussions of the Pacific; however, it is an industrialized state with a strongly predominant settler rather than indigenous population and cultural life, as is Australia. Neither is understood in this discussion as a "Pacific Island state," although both are members of the region's leading political body—the Pacific Islands Forum—and are very active in the region.

3. Hau'ofa, *A New Oceania.*

4. For example, see Crocombe, "Enhancing Pacific Security," p. 3, which notes "ethnic tensions . . . , land disputes, economic disparities, and a lack of confidence in governments' ability or willingness to solve . . . problems" as the leading causes of overt conflict in the region.

5. UNICEF, *Children and HIV/AIDS in Papua New Guinea,* p. 1.

6. Maclellan, "Creating Peace in the Pacific," p. 526.

7. Firth, "The Impact of Globalisation on the Pacific Islands," p. 8.

8. Greg Sheridan, "Danger on the Doorstep," *Weekend Australian,* 24 March 2001, p. 14.

9. Wainwright, *Our Failing Neighbour,* p. 29.

10. Dobell, "The South Pacific."

11. Alpers and Twyford, "Small Arms in the Pacific."

12. Maclellan, "Creating Peace in the Pacific," p. 530.

13. Notably, see Dinnen, "Lending a Fist?" p. 6.

14. Solomon Mamaloni, quoted in Wainwright, *Our Failing Neighbour,* p. 20.

15. "Nauru: Mystery Island," *The Economist* (366), 8 March 2003, p. 66.

16. Britain occupied Fiji formally in 1874, Papua in 1884, the Solomon Islands in 1893, and Vanuatu (made a naval commission by both France and Britain) in 1888. New Guinea was colonized by Germany in 1884; the United States and France took possession of Polynesian, Micronesian, and the remaining Melanesian islands. The Dutch claimed West Papua in 1848. The two world wars led to further changes, with German colonies being divided between Australia and New Zealand.

17. Maclellan, "Creating Peace in the Pacific," pp. 528–529.

18. Lawson, *The Failure of Democratic Politics in Fiji,* p. 71.

19. Pitts, *Crime, Corruption, and Capacity in Papua New Guinea,* p. 94.

20. Ibid., p. 94.

21. Garap, "Struggles of Women and Girls."

22. Jerry Singirok, chair of the National Guns Control Committee (PNG), interviewed by Caroline Tilman, *ABC Radio Australia,* 28 June 2006.

23. Care, "Off the Peg or Made to Measure," p. 211.

24. Gross domestic product (GDP) grew in 2004 by 2.6 percent (after a marginally better performance in 2003), and there were indications of a broadening base to growth. "The budget was in surplus, inflation fell, key interest rates eased and public debt fell relative to GDP." Warner and Yauieb, "The Papua New Guinea Economy." Vanuatu also enjoyed an estimated economic growth rate of 6 percent in 2006, as a result of improved tourism and agricultural production.

25. Firth, "The Impact of Globalisation on the Pacific Islands," p. 2.

26. Hughes, "The Pacific Is Viable."

27. UNDP, *Pacific Human Development Report.*

28. Maclellan, "Fiji, the War in Iraq, and the Privatisation of Pacific Island Security."

29. Peebles, *Pacific Regional Order,* p. 23, for example, discusses a case from the Cook Islands: "In 1987, the government guaranteed a loan taken out by an Italian construction company. The company was to build a luxury hotel to promote tourism to the islands. The result was that A$60 million disappeared through crooked Mafia dealings with a few years. 'The project was 80% complete when the insurance company cut off funding to the builders. The country's finances were crippled as the governments liability ballooned to A$122 million. The issue of who owns the hotel has been stuck in the courts for years.'"

30. Tonga and Tuvalu have both had problems with ships registered under their flag trafficking in arms or drugs.

31. According to the study, tourism appeared to have made the greatest contribution to Caribbean economies. The study indicated that, at the time it was undertaken, growth rates, income per capita, distribution across the economy, and basic services were better in the Caribbean. Fairbairn and Worrell, *South Pacific and Caribbean Island Economies.*

32. Ghai and Pao, *News Archives.*

33. A key difficulty is that, in broad terms, Melanesian notions of land tenure "only allow for the multiplication of claims (through marriage, exchange etc), not their extinction or resolution, [whereas] developed states rely upon legal principles of free, simple ownership and permanent transfer of title." Polomka, *Bougainville,* p. 2.

34. This question was a key focus of the PIF's draft Pacific Plan: "Models for land ownership, tenure and associated legislative frameworks, to support the use and management of natural resources, will be developed for countries to use or adapt (perhaps on a sub-regional basis), based on traditionally accepted norms and revising/removing current inappropriate legislation, to help minimise social tensions and maximise economic opportunities and resource conservation."

35. Keith Barr, Ecumenical Center for Research, Education, and Advocacy, Fiji, in Commonwealth of Australia, *A Pacific Engaged,* p. 54.

36. Hughes, "Aid Has Failed the Pacific."

37. World Bank, *Enhancing the Role of Government in Pacific Island Economies,* p. 15.

38. Commonwealth of Australia, *A Pacific Engaged,* p. 58.

39. Maclellan, "Creating Peace in the Pacific," p. 528.

40. French Polynesia and the Marshall Islands, the latter of which is in association with the United States and a site for US missile tests, are also experiencing tension around levels of self-determination.

41. Unpublished address to the Amnesty International conference "Human Rights in the Pacific: Perspectives and Partnerships," Brisbane, September 2004.

42. UNICEF, *Children and HIV/AIDS in Papua New Guinea,* p. 4.

43. Commonwealth of Australia, *A Pacific Engaged,* p. xxv.

44. UNICEF, *Children and HIV/AIDS in Papua New Guinea,* p. 1.

45. Boege, *Conflict Potential and Violent Conflicts in the South Pacific,* p. 83.

46. See http://www.pacificplan.org/tiki-download_file.php/?field=41 (accessed 1 February 2007).

2

Local Solutions: Security and Development in Papua New Guinea

Marion Jacka

MUCH OF THE academic and media commentary on Papua New Guinea is overwhelmingly negative, presenting a picture of economic decline, political instability, and a breakdown in law and order. Such representation is part of the broader portrayal of Melanesian countries as failing states.[1] "The common theme is that the nation-state is on the edge of a precipice, facing a complete breakdown. The perception of crisis has taken on a life of its own, with most people . . . accepting perception as reality."[2]

Such negative portrayals of Papua New Guinea give only a partial picture of the situation, overlooking the many ways in which Papua New Guineans are working to find solutions to the challenges facing them. This chapter affirms the importance of international development assistance in Papua New Guinea, but questions whether current approaches are sufficiently aimed at addressing the underlying causes of the social and economic challenges facing the country.

The views of Papua New Guineans on these challenges are explored, and specific attention is given to issues concerning economic development, law and justice, politics, governance, and the state. It is argued that increased attention should be given to rural development, improved livelihoods, human security, and community-based development.

■ Papua New Guinea's Place in Development Debates

The question facing development theorists when considering the situation in Papua New Guinea is how to explain what is seen (by many) as the "failure of development." This question is not specific to Papua New Guinea—there have been major debates worldwide about "development," as donors and development practitioners have struggled to find explanations for continuing (and often deepening) poverty and disadvantage in many developing countries.

What Is Development? A Papua New Guinean Perspective

The term "development" is itself highly contested. It often connotes a desirable and necessary progression from some inferior state of underdevelopment to a Western-style economic and political system. Issues of development are presented in mainstream debate as the clash between tradition and modernity. As Papua New Guinean writer Regis Stella has said, development is often narrowly defined purely in economic and monetary terms, with traditional culture *(kastom)* viewed as the major cause of failure of progress. For Stella, the proposition that traditional culture is inhibiting development derives from a common fallacy that conceives traditional culture as static: "Culture exists as a living organism, expanding and recreating itself. . . . When development meets resistance from indigenous people it is not always impelled by traditional culture. Sometimes it is because development callously tries to ignore ethical, cultural and social blind spots."[3]

Stella argues that tradition and modernity are not necessarily antagonistic. He points to the need for a broad definition of development, and for strategies "for total and integral human improvement and progression . . . the minimum conditions are equitable distribution of services and resources for the benefit of everyone, ensuring that citizens have adequate opportunities for education, social and economic services, and spiritual development."[4]

Neoliberal Perspective

Much academic and policy discussion of the development record in Papua New Guinea draws on the neoliberal economic framework. The broad argument is that private investment is the key to economic growth and development, and that there are various blockages—such as political instability, poor macroeconomic management, institutional weakness, and poor social capital—that need to be overcome to create the climate for private investment to flourish.[5] The neoliberal approach has been strongly reflected in recent articles published by the Centre for Independent Studies (CIS)—a think tank based in Sydney, Australia.

Political scientist Greg Fry has traced various historical "framings" of the Pacific as enunciated by various authors, and notes that the contemporary view has shifted from either paradise or hell to the "new doomsdayism."[6] This depicts a region marked by grim trends: the failure of development, rapidly rising populations, oversized public services, failing states, and unsustainable resource exploitation. According to the new doomsdayists, the only hope is to follow the policy prescriptions of economic rationalists, which they regard as being based on "certain knowledge" and which require Pacific governments and people "to face the unpleasant facts."[7] To avoid the grim future they predict, the new doomsdayists argue that it is necessary to "open the island economies to the global market, effect structural change, jettison where necessary customary land tenure and inappropriate traditions and connect with the dynamism of Asia."[8] Fry sees the doomsdayists, like earlier Australian framers of the islands, as being engaged in another version of a subordinating ideology that "denies self-determination while claiming to advance it."[9]

In a 2003 CIS article, "Papua New Guinea on the Brink," Susan Windybank and Mike Manning argue that Papua New Guinea shows "every sign of following its Melanesian neighbour, the Solomon Islands, down the path to economic paralysis, government collapse and social despair," and argue for a rethink of Australia's policy approach to aid.[10] The authors point to continuing fiscal crises, poor economic prospects, endemic law and order problems, and clan warfare in areas such as the Southern Highlands. In their view, the blame for this situation lies squarely with the political elite, who have engaged in widespread corruption and used, to their advantage, "windfall mining revenues and generous levels of aid . . . at the expense of investment in roads, education and health."[11] Considerable emphasis is placed on the threat to Australian security posed by the deteriorating situation in Papua New Guinea.[12]

In a follow-up CIS paper, "Aid Has Failed the Pacific," Helen Hughes reiterated many of the arguments of Windybank and Manning, while elaborating on the view that aid is part of the problem.[13] Hughes sees aid as fungible, with governments regarding it as part of recurrent expenditure to be invested in "bloated public sectors" rather than in development projects.[14] While Hughes sees much of the blame as lying with Pacific countries, she also holds multilateral and bilateral donors responsible, and criticizes the International Monetary Fund (IMF) and World Bank for failing to use conditionality effectively. For Hughes, the pace of reform in recent years has not been fast enough. The preferred policy approach for Australia and other international aid donors is (according to Hughes) for all aid to be suspended. However, recognizing the unlikelihood of this, Hughes advocates linking "aid to conditionality under the principle of mutual obligation."[15]

Many of the issues identified by Hughes and her CIS colleagues are generally recognized by development commentators, such as law and order problems, inadequate service delivery, gender inequalities, environmental issues, and the need for rural development. Where many take issue with the CIS approach is with the assessment of the causes of Papua New Guinea's problems, and with proposals about the way forward. Papua New Guineans take offense at the hectoring tone and the representation of their country as being almost beyond hope unless the policy prescriptions outlined are adopted.[16]

Concerns about the CIS analysis include inadequate acknowledgment of the ways in which Papua New Guineans are working to develop their own solutions and the strong elements of "blaming the victim" and of reinforcing notions of inferiority and dependency. In addition, the implication that Papua New Guinea's problems are primarily due to internal factors, such as culture, and misguided government policy, ignore broader historical and global factors. The belief that adoption of the neoliberal policy prescription will automatically lead to economic growth and provide an adequate revenue base for Papua New Guinea governments to deal with the various serious social and economic challenges facing the country is too simplistic. The highly contested nature of certain aspects of the neoliberal agenda, such as abandonment of customary land tenure, calls for a greatly reduced public sector, and privatization is also problematic. Widespread concern about a possible shift to individual land titling has been a major feature of community protests against structural adjustment programs in Papua New Guinea. Customary landownership is the basis of Papua New Guinean society and culture. As with other Pacific peoples, "land is at the centre of life: as a source of livelihood through subsistence activities; a source of power, authority and status; and above all as a source of security and identity."[17] Despite Hughes' assertions to the contrary, there are strong arguments that customary landownership has *prevented* poverty, not caused it. Rural development experts point to the adaptability of subsistence farmers and to the ability of Papua New Guinea to by and large meet its basic food needs, notwithstanding rapid population growth.[18]

Alternative Perspectives

Other commentators emphasize the need to see Papua New Guinea's current situation in a historical and global context. They take issue with the implication that Papua New Guinea's problems have been primarily caused by internal factors, pointing to the colonial legacy, the imposition of Western values and systems on traditional Melanesian societies, and the global nature of many problems facing Papua New Guinea, including the HIV/AIDS pandemic, natural disasters that constrain development, conflicting land interests between indigenous landowners and transnational corporations, youth unemployment, unequal trading relationships, and the impact of privatization and debt.

Sinclair Dinnen points out that European contact with Papua New Guinea's many socially and linguistically distinct communities commenced at the end of the nineteenth century, and for the most remote areas (such as the Highlands) only took place in the 1930s.[19] The country became independent in 1975 after a relatively short and uneven period of colonial administration, and the framework of statehood was established during "an intensive period of institutional modernisation in the twenty years preceding

Independence."[20] In these circumstances and given the country's linguistic diversity, difficult terrain, dual economy, and the attempt to impose a nation-state on stateless, subsistence-agricultural societies, the "development project" was clearly always going to be difficult. The period since 1975 has seen major shifts in the international environment, with globalization leading to intensified integration of the world's economies, dominated by transnational corporations and the major economic powers, unequal trading and investment relationships, and, for many developing countries, growing dependence and poverty.

Papua New Guinean academic Misty Baloiloi regards the deteriorating social and economic position in Papua New Guinea as the outcome of the model of development that has benefited foreign interests and a minority of Papua New Guineans, while marginalizing the majority of the population.[21] The rapid introduction of Western forms of governance, law and justice, commercial enterprise, and resource extraction is seen by many as having major social and cultural costs, with conservation groups in particular mounting vigorous critiques of large-scale resource exploitation.

Some Papua New Guinean commentators also see the processes of globalization and the policies of international financial institutions (IFIs) as playing a major role in the continued dependency and lack of social development in Papua New Guinea. Community activist Julienne Kaman points to the effective abandonment by Papua New Guinea governments of an eight-point development plan drawn up at independence to chart an alternative development model. She argues that instead, the economy has been predominantly geared toward the modern market, which has failed to deliver the "trickle down" benefits its proponents claim.[22] Kaman is highly critical of Papua New Guinea's structural adjustment programs, saying that "the country has been coerced by the World Bank to be further integrated into the global economy in order to . . . repay debts owed to foreign governments and banks."[23] Rising levels of poverty and serious social breakdown, including domestic violence and prostitution, are seen as consequences.

Tim Anderson links Papua New Guinea's various social problems back to the imposed and inappropriate model of development, pointing to the reliance on export-led growth, which he argues has been a "spectacular failure."[24] He states that, notwithstanding high levels of export growth for most of the period from 1965 to the 1990s, ordinary people experienced declining social indicators, increased reliance on imported goods, and declining access to electricity. Anderson points to the negative impacts that have resulted from large-scale resource exploitation, including land alienation, dislocation of families, poverty and unemployment, and breakdown of social systems.[25] The further critique of the export-led strategy is that the economic cross-linkages of mining and logging have been extremely weak. Anderson argues that while investment is needed in Papua New Guinea, it must be appropriate investment, such as in community industries, tourism, and infrastructure that would "support and maintain community support structures."[26]

Development Debates Worldwide

The Structural Reform Agenda

The dominant paradigm in official development thinking during the 1980s was the neoliberal structural reform agenda, as advocated by international financial institutions and major bilateral donors. As initially developed, the so-called Washington consensus called for economic liberalization and a reorientation of the role of the state, which was to abandon interventionist national planning policies and instead create the conditions for market forces to stimulate economic growth.[27] Developing countries were urged to adopt policies of economic liberalization, such as privatization, trade liberalization, and deregulation.

The agenda changed somewhat over the 1990s, as poor growth and poverty persisted in many countries. Increased emphasis came to be placed on the phenomenon of extreme poverty and the issues of governance, seen to explain the disappointing lack of progress in many countries. The "good governance" agenda became a major emphasis of the World Bank and bilateral donors, in response to the perceived weakness of the state in many postcolonial situations. It was considered that "a set of prior enabling public actions" was required, centering on various aspects of the good-governance agenda, including improved macroeconomic management, administrative reform, the state's role in making essential investments in human capital through health and education services, and strategies to make governments more open and accountable. The assumption was that, with the state playing an important but limited role, the conditions would be set for market forces to promote economic growth and social development.

A further shift in official development thinking occurred during the 1990s. This shift incorporated a number of concerns identified by critics of the neoliberal paradigm. It was argued that there was no automatic causal link between economic growth and social development. Aspects of a social development approach, such as the need to address gender and environmental issues and the value of participatory approaches to development and poverty reduction, came to be included in the official development discourse.[28] However, at the core of much official development thinking remains the dominant neoliberal paradigm, with its universalizing theme that, provided governments follow the appropriate good-governance practices, market forces will, in all circumstances, produce development.[29]

Beyond Structural Reform

Two UN bodies, the United Nations Conference on Trade and Development (UNCTAD) and the United Nations Development Programme (UNDP), have been advocating the need to look beyond the structural reform agenda of the 1990s.

UNCTAD's 2004 report on least-developed countries (LDCs) calls for an end to "development pessimism" and for the formulation and implementation of "postliberal" development strategies within the LDCs.[30] Development pessimism has led to the view that the best way to reduce poverty is through ever-closer integration with the world via trade liberalization. International development assistance to the LDCs has increasingly shifted away from the production sectors and economic infrastructure, to supporting basic human needs.

The UNDP, in its 2003 report on human development, likewise argues for a change of course for those "top priority" and "high priority" countries, like Papua New Guinea, that combine low human development and poor progress toward achieving the UN's Millennium Development Goals (MDGs).

The Millennium Development Goals

Papua New Guinea was among the 189 member states that adopted the UN Millennium Declaration in 2000 and thus committed itself to the achievement of the Millennium Development Goals. The eight MDGs represent a partnership between developed and developing countries aimed at creating an environment conducive to human development and the elimination of poverty: eradicating extreme poverty and hunger, achieving universal primary education, promoting gender equality and empowering women, reducing child mortality, improving maternal health, combating HIV/AIDS, malaria, and other diseases, ensuring environmental sustainability, and developing a global partnership for development.

Specific targets are set for each goal to be met in most developing countries by 2015. The Papua New Guinea government has developed a modified set of national targets to be achieved by 2015, in light of current realities. While generally these are far more modest than their global counterparts, they are considered to be "very demanding," given the challenges the country faces.[31]

The UNDP concludes that while the policies identified and implemented during the 1990s "are all necessary to achieve the Millennium Development Goals, they are far from sufficient."[32] This is because the approaches of the 1990s overlook the structural constraints that impede economic growth and human development. These are seen as the root causes of failed development and include barriers to international markets and high debt levels, size and location, vulnerability to climatic shocks or natural disasters, and vulnerability to rampant diseases such as malaria. Papua New Guinea is classified by the UNDP as a "high priority" country and exhibits all of these structural constraints.

The UNDP and UNCTAD emphasize the need for increased international financial assistance for developing the production and trade capacities of poor countries. The UNDP stresses that the market alone will not create the conditions for economic growth—investment in infrastructure, education, health, agriculture, and small-scale manufacturing is required, but poor countries do not have the resources for the necessary investments.[33]

UNDP Policies for Escaping Poverty Traps

The UNDP recommends various policies to help countries break out of their poverty traps: investing early and ambitiously in basic education and health while fostering gender equity; increasing the productivity of small farmers in unfavorable environments; improving basic infrastructure—such as ports, roads, power, and communications—to reduce the costs of doing business and overcome geographic barriers; developing an industrial development policy that helps diversify the economy away from dependence on primary commodity exports; promoting democratic governance and human rights to remove discrimination, secure social justice, and advance the well-being of all people; and ensuring environmental sustainability.[34]

The UNDP stresses that growth must be broad-based, and suggests the following policies to strengthen the links between growth and poverty reduction: increasing the level, efficiency, and equity of investments in basic health, education, and water and sanitation; expanding poor people's access to land, credit, skills, and other economic assets; increasing small farmers' productivity and diversification; and promoting labor-intensive industrial growth involving small and medium-size enterprises.[35]

Alternative Perspectives on Good Governance

A number of commentators have called for a broader perspective to be taken on the term "good governance," extending its meaning beyond the operations of government to all types of organizations in a society. Civil society organizations emphasize the need for governments to be accountable and responsive to people's needs and aspirations, and to respect human rights. The good-governance approach of Australia and the IFIs seeks to address a number of issues of concern to many Papua New Guineans, such as official corruption, security in daily life, unresponsive government, and poor service delivery, but this approach has essentially relied upon structural adjustment policies as the key drivers of economic growth, and there is still a tendency to focus on state institutions. This emphasis is based on an analysis of the integral link between poor governance and lack of economic and social development in the Pacific.

Where this is considered problematic is in the causal connection drawn between good governance and economic growth. Various studies have found that it is difficult to show clear correlations, let alone causal connections, between the two.[36] Peter Larmour points to systematic comparisons between many countries that lead to more tentative conclusions, and concludes that the "link between democracy and economic development is unproven."[37] Nic Maclellan points to the concerns of Pacific critics of the governance agenda, noting that it can be seen "as a way of explaining the disappointing lack of progress which emanates from basic flaws in donor policies." Maclellan further argues that the focus on administrative and policy reform in central government bureaucracies has downplayed the need to focus on rural development programs.[38]

Advocacy of "bottom-up" grassroots development is, according to international and Papua New Guinean community workers, viewed with some wariness in official circles in Papua New Guinea and Australia.[39] At times, this may relate to the fact that community organizations are in conflict with the state, as has been the case in advocacy on environmental and human rights issues. In some quarters, community development approaches, based on recognition of traditional values and culture, are seen as somewhat romantic and utopian, or as overlooking the role of the state in development. These are not well-founded objections. Advocating community development is not to say that appropriate policies and programs at the government level should be abandoned. Indeed, the argument is that state institutions and programs should be geared more to promoting sustainable development and responding to the concerns and living conditions of Papua New Guineans at the grassroots level. Community leaders point to the need to take a long-term approach, and for programs and activities to be culturally relevant. An example is the training and capacity building carried out by the Centre for Leadership (MNCL), a Melanesian nongovernmental organization (NGO) that takes a "best of both worlds" approach, and draws on traditional management practices in addressing issues such as leadership training, organizational development, and program management.[40]

■   **The Pattern of Development:**
From Self-Reliance to Structural Adjustment

At independence, Papua New Guinea had many of the characteristics of other small developing countries, which meant sustained economic development was never going to be easy. These included an open economy that depended heavily on commodity prices over which Papua New Guinea had no control; concentration of foreign investment activity in the extraction of primary commodities for export, to the near exclusion of manufacturing; relative neglect of production for domestic consumption; poor linkages between such export activity and other sectors of the economy; and a small domestic market far removed from the mainstream of world trade.[41]

Notwithstanding these structural constraints, all of which remain today, in the first ten years or so after independence Papua New Guinea experienced reasonable rates of growth, economic management was considered sound, and progress was made on social indicators. However, low levels of gross domestic product (GDP), a decline in the value of Australian aid, high population growth, and "high expectations" began to place major strains on government spending.[42] GDP declined from 1987 and the government, faced with dwindling international reserves and a looming deficit, decided in 1990 to seek assistance from the IMF and the World Bank. The sense of crisis lifted momentarily in the early 1990s, with governments seeing increasing hope in large-scale mining and petroleum prospects, and in logging. However, the revenue from Ok Tedi and other mineral projects only served to fill the gap created by loss of revenue from the closure of the disastrous Panguna mine in Bougainville, and decline in the value of Australian aid.

In the early 1990s, as expenditure grew in excess of revenue, government borrowing expanded, with debt repayment and servicing representing about one-third of government spending by 1994.[43] In 1994 the national currency (the kina) was devalued and subsequently floated. However, continuing fiscal and foreign exchange difficulties led to the government negotiating a further World Bank structural adjustment loan in 1995.

Papua New Guinea's economic problems over this period were exacerbated by natural disasters and external shocks. A widespread El Niño–induced drought in 1997–1998 reduced agricultural production and resulted in a reduction in GDP by almost 2 percent. The financial crisis in Asia reduced demand and prices for a range of Papua New Guinea's export commodities, and the Rabaul volcanic eruption in 1994 and the Aitape Tsunami in 1998, which led to the deaths of over 2,000 people, added to the country's problems.[44]

Since the mid-1990s the story has largely been one of continuing economic problems, and the various efforts of the World Bank and other IFIs (strongly backed by Australia) to prod Papua New Guinea governments into the macroeconomic policies and institutional reform have been seen as necessary for reviving economic growth.[45]

The 1990 structural adjustment package involved an allocation of 410 million kina (K) in two phases, with the first intended to deal with immediate problems and the second involving medium- to long-term adjustment measures including investment deregulation, trade policy reforms, privatization and commercialization of government parastatals, and a shift from direct to indirect tax.[46] The 1994–1995 package was wide ranging and included land registration, removal of most domestic price controls, completion of privatization, a freeze on wages, improved forestry management, higher fees for outpatients and the closure of underutilized health services, and the introduction of a system of fees or loans for tertiary education.[47]

Aspects of structural adjustment have been extremely controversial, with land reform, privatization, and forestry issues particularly contested. The end result has been that, while governments have accepted and implemented many of the conditions, they have resisted others, in particular land reform, aspects of privatization, and World Bank's conditions related to the implementation of forestry regulations.

In 1995, various community organizations formed a coalition to mobilize against the structural adjustment program on the basis that it would "further impoverish the people and would not address the fundamental problems facing Papua New Guinea."[48] While accepting measures that were needed to address the financial crisis, the Coalition for Socio-Economic Justice took issue with a number of aspects of the package, including land reform, health and education fees, removal of price controls on basic foodstuffs, abolition of the minimum wage, privatization, and job cuts in the public service.[49]

On the land issue, the draft agreement with the World Bank made reference to land registration. With at least 97 percent of land under customary ownership, this was seen as a possible precursor of a move to individual titling and land alienation. According to Larmour, it was the land issue, in particular, that "crystallized popular suspicions of politicians, big men and the World Bank."[50] Students and community groups protested in large numbers in Port Moresby, and there were public meetings and demonstrations in the Highlands. In the face of this, government ministers backed away and the conditions relating to land registration were dropped.

In 2001, protests against ongoing structural reform included a rebellion by Papua New Guinea's defense forces in reaction to proposed cuts in the size of the army. The soldiers made explicit connections between their plight and the structural adjustment program, and called for the expulsion of World Bank and IMF advisers from the country. Students, trade unions, and soldiers highlighted corruption in government and the way cost-cutting impacted mostly on the poor. In June 2001, a five-day protest took place against the government's privatization policies, in the aftermath of which four students were shot dead on the University of Papua New Guinea's Waigani campus in Port Moresby by a police mobile squad.[51]

While the government of Michael Somare has maintained the broad commitment to structural reform, it has not been prepared to go "all the way," with reservations in particular about privatization. The Papua New Guinea government takes the view that core assets in the telecommunications, electricity, and transport sectors should only be partially privatized, as full privatization in the absence of effective competition is considered to be against the country's interests.[52]

■ Challenges Facing Papua New Guinea and Its Development Partners

Economic deterioration since the 1990s has impacted severely on service delivery and the provision of infrastructure, and has led to declining social indicators. A variety of social and economic indicators summarize the major challenges for development in Papua New Guinea:[53]

• *Population:* The population of Papua New Guinea was 5.19 million in 2000, compared to 3.01 million in 1980, representing an average annual growth rate over the period of 2.7 percent. It is predicted to double by 2026. In 1990, 42 percent of the population were under fifteen years of age, and the median age was nineteen.

• *Education:* Levels of education are very low. In 1996, approximately 50 percent of children of primary school age did not attend school, and the majority (60 percent) of children who started the first grade dropped out by the sixth grade. On average, the population aged fifteen years and older in 1996 had only 2.9 years of schooling.

• *Employment:* In 2004, less than 10 percent of the population were employed in the formal sector, and waged employment provided less than 300,000 jobs.[54]

• *Poverty:* Given low employment, poverty (as measured by households in which the real value of consumption per adult is below the "upper poverty line") is a significant issue.[55] Based on their comprehensive household survey, John Gibson and Scott Rozelle estimated that in 1996, 37.5 percent of Papua New Guinea's population were living below the poverty line. Using statistical projections from that data, the World Bank later estimated that this percentage had increased alarmingly to 53.5 percent of the population by 2003.[56] In 1996, almost all (94 percent) of the poor were living in rural areas, while 74 percent of the poor were concentrated in the Highland and Momase regions. The same 1996 survey found that approximately 31 percent of all people aged fifteen years and older had no cash income earnings, and poverty was highest in households headed by women (48 percent of such households were below the poverty line). Only 56 percent of women aged fifteen years and older were literate.

• *Wealth distribution:* The wealth that does exist in Papua New Guinea is very unequally distributed. Between 1993 and 2000, wage earners in the lowest income group (30 percent of the population) suffered a 30 percent reduction in real wages, and over the same period the wages of the top income group increased by 74 percent.

• *Health:* Another significant challenge facing Papua New Guinea is health. Six treatable diseases (pneumonia, malaria, diarrhea, tuberculosis, measles, and anemia) contributed to 40 percent or more of deaths of those under age forty-five in 2003. In 1996, only 39 percent of health facilities were operating satisfactorily, and less than 70 percent of rural aid posts were operating at all.[57] It was estimated in 2003 that thirty-three infants were dying each day, the majority from preventable causes.[58]

These indicators are closely connected to a pattern of development by which comparatively few benefit from inclusion in the formal economy, while the majority of the population face a lack of opportunities to earn cash income and access basic services. A fundamental question facing Papua New Guinea is how to find a path toward a pattern of economic development that will avoid the problems associated with the past "enclave" model,[59] and that will place government in a better position to respond to community aspirations for improved livelihoods.

Papua New Guinean Views

The term "poverty" has been controversial in Papua New Guinea. Poverty is a multidimensional concept that means different things to different people across time and place. For Papua New Guineans (and people elsewhere in the Pacific), the term may have negative connotations. With its association with hunger and destitution, it can imply a denigration of traditional lifestyles and the way in which communities have taken care of their members. It has been suggested that "lack of opportunity" and "hardship" are more appropriate terms.

In a participatory poverty assessment survey conducted in 2002 with people from eighteen rural and urban communities of Papua New Guinea, respondents interpreted "poverty" in terms of lack of access to jobs and cash, land, education, healthcare, safe drinking water, and transport and roads. Lack of access to safe drinking water was identified as the most serious problem, followed by the absence of usable roads. Family breakdown was viewed as contributing to poverty through divorce, drug abuse among young people, and crime. Most people believed that poverty had increased in both urban and rural areas over the preceding five years.[60]

While taking issue with the characterization of their country as being "on the brink," Papua New Guineans have deep concerns about the situation they find themselves in, as identified by twenty Papua New Guinean writers:[61] corruption and the crisis in governance, including the lack of political responsibility and lack of financial transparency; the government's increasing inability to provide adequate services, particularly education and health; the widespread alienation of the people, most particularly the rural majority, from the state; the loss of government concern for sustainable and appropriate development that is in harmony with Papua New Guinean culture, and its replacement by a culture of personal greed; the increasing inequity in access to development opportunities and the growing divisions between a few rich urban elite and the growing numbers of rural poor; and gender inequality and the high level of violence against women.

Extensive community consultations were also conducted for the Kumul 2020 project, undertaken in the late 1990s by a committee of Papua New Guinean civil society representatives to develop a vision for the country's economic and social development.[62] Two broad areas of concern emerged: that Papua New Guinea is experiencing a growing spiritual and moral crisis, and that the country's future is being developed on unsustainable foundations.

In the Kumul 2020 project, people identified various symptoms of this spiritual and moral crisis: political instability, law and order issues, a widening gap between the rich and poor, destruction of Papua New Guinea's forest heritage, degradation of infrastructure, and decline in service delivery, with public services seen as inefficient and unsatisfactory. Unsustainable economic development was linked to Papua New Guinea's continued pursuit of a future built on the wrong economic foundations, and to the creation of a low-growth, partially employed economy that, due to forces arising from the country's history and geography, has inadequately utilized available natural and human resources. People (and in particular the rural majority) believed that the economic development strategy had failed to realize the potential of Papua New Guinea.[63]

Uneven Development in Papua New Guinea

There are significant disparities in wealth and income across individuals, provinces, and regions. These relate to the dual nature of the economy, with, on the one hand, a "formal sector" comprising the government sector and a small, mainly export-oriented private sector, and on the other hand, a large informal sector that includes subsistence and small landholder cash-cropping and involves most of the rural population. Also in the informal economy are those in urban and peri-urban areas who, in the absence of employment opportunities in the formal sector, struggle to make a living from various small-scale income-generating activities.

Less than 10 percent of the population are employed in the formal sector, with waged employment concentrated in a small number of public- and private-sector jobs. Most significant, it has been estimated that employment in the formal sector has not increased substantially since independence, despite the population having doubled in the same period.[64]

Regional Disparities

Regional disparities in opportunity and outcomes affect many aspects of life in Papua New Guinea.[65] The most significant disparities are between rural and urban areas, but there are also disparities across provinces. The rural poverty rate of 41 percent in 1996 was 2.5 times the urban rate (16 percent).

In 2000, infant and maternal mortality and life expectancy figures differed substantially across regions. The rural infant mortality rate, for example, was estimated at 69 deaths per 1,000 live births, compared to 29 deaths in urban centers. Infant mortality ranged from 105 per 1,000 deaths in Sandaun province, to 22 in the National Capital district. Life expectancy was 53 years in rural areas, compared to 60 in urban centers, and maternal mortality in the Highlands was double that in the coastal provinces.

Education opportunities also vary widely between regions. In 1996, most (79 percent) of the urban population aged older than five years had attended school, compared to less than half (47 percent) in rural areas. In the Highlands, less than half of primary school–aged children attended primary school, compared to 70 percent and 68 percent in the National Capital district and New Guinea Islands, respectively.

Infrastructure and services are necessarily affected by, but also influence, the disparities. Electricity, for example, was available to only 3.2 percent of rural households in 1996, compared to 59.2 percent in urban areas. In 1999, approximately 58 percent of the rural population did not have access to safe drinking water, and only 4 percent of roads were paved.[66]

The Enclave Resource Sector: Mining, Forestry, and Fisheries

The export-oriented sector comprises mining and petroleum and the non-mineral resource sector (agriculture, forestry, and fisheries). From the point of view of many in the community, it was the embrace by successive governments of large-scale resource exploitation (dating from the 1980s) that led to growing alienation between government and most rural people.[67] Once viewed in mainstream circles as the catalyst for economic growth, more recently there has been growing acknowledgment that mineral exploitation has not realized the high hopes held for it. Various reports point to the "enclave" nature of the mineral sector, which has relatively limited direct linkages with the rest of the economy.[68] The mining and petroleum industries are capital-intensive and create relatively few jobs. Revenues have not translated into sustainable development on a national scale, due to a number of factors, including, according to some accounts, "rent-seeking" by members of the political elite, and a failure to invest in infrastructure and promote diversification in the economy.[69]

The disastrous impacts of some large-scale mining operations in Papua New Guinea are now well known and include loss of land without proper compensation, loss of sustainable livelihood, and degradation of the natural environment.[70] The most notorious examples are the now-closed Panguna mine in Bougainville and the Ok Tedi mine in Western province.

The connection between Panguna and Bougainville's tragic civil conflict is discussed in Chapter 5. The mine dumped about 150,000 tons of waste rock and tailings into the Kawerong River on a daily basis, leading to loss of fish through the Jaba River watershed, declines in coastal fish stocks, declines in local wildlife populations, and loss of land for agriculture.[71]

The Ok Tedi mine has also caused considerable environmental damage through the disposal of untreated tailings in rivers. In 1994, a lawsuit undertaken by landowners living along the Ok Tedi and Fly Rivers resulted in an out-of-court settlement of US$28.6 million for the damage caused by the mine's tailings. A World Bank assessment commissioned by the Papua New Guinea government in 1999 found "significant and unacceptable" environmental impacts much greater than originally anticipated, and predicted that the impacts downstream would be felt long after mine closure. The government declined to pursue the best environmental option—mine closure—on the grounds of impact on national and provincial economies and on affected communities. In 2002, Ok Tedi provided about 10 percent of Papua New Guinea's gross domestic product and nearly 20 percent of its export income. Ok Tedi Mining Limited has since set up a trust fund to help build local infrastructure and create sustainable development projects for local communities.

Despite some earlier assessments of the mineral sector being in decline, large-scale mineral and oil exploitation will clearly continue. While acknowledging the enclave nature of the mining and petroleum industries, the Papua New Guinea government sees this as an important source of revenue into the future, and is seeking to boost investor confidence. Two major new oil and gas projects are under development, with oil and gas exploitation regarded as less environmentally damaging than mining.[72] Since the establishment of the Panguna and Ok Tedi mines, responsibility for monitoring operations was transferred from the Department of Mining and Petroleum to the Department of Environment and Conservation. There is also an emphasis in the Environment Act of 2000 on a "cradle to grave" approach, meaning all phases (exploration to postclosure) will be subject to environmental controls. However, the department has extremely limited resources and capacity to administer these responsibilities.

Panguna was operated by an Australian company, and Australian companies have interests in the Ok Tedi, Porgera, Misima, and Lihir mines. The Australian government and other international development partners could do much to assist the Papua New Guinean government to develop and implement a mandatory code of conduct for internationally funded mining operations, in accordance with internationally accepted environmental, employment, health and safety, and human rights standards. One suggested avenue for effective assistance from international partners in strengthening the regulatory regime is through provision of risk insurance to mining companies on the condition that an internationally acceptable code of conduct be met in return for provision of insurance.[73]

Current concerns about unsustainable mining in Papua New Guinea include mining exploration in protected areas (e.g., the Crater Mountain Wildlife Management Area), and mining impacts on high-conservation-value forest and important wetlands.[74]

Development and security can be promoted in the resource sector by international companies, aid partners, and the Papua New Guinea government working together to ensure that social and environmental impacts are thoroughly investigated, monitored, and maintained within acceptable limits. As Community Aid Abroad has emphasized, certain principles must be observed for development to be sustainable: companies must commit to the principle of obtaining the prior, free, and informed consent of landowners as a precondition for their exploration and mining and forestry activities; and companies must ensure that all affected groups and individuals (not just landowners, but also their affiliated kin networks and neighboring groups) are fully informed of the proposed use of the land and the likely environmental and social impacts, and that detailed agreements be negotiated between communities and companies, covering the terms on which projects will proceed.[75]

In addition, such consultations and negotiations provide opportunities for planning and conducting training workshops on broader community-strengthening and state-building issues, encompassing environmental and cultural heritage values, gender issues, governance, and restorative justice. By integrating these principles into the design and conduct of development projects, international companies and development partners can directly assist the Papua New Guinea government to promote stability and a more secure environment for foreign investments and international aid projects through the long term.

The Nonmineral Export Sector

The agriculture, forest, and fisheries sectors have been a smaller but still significant source of export earnings and internal revenue, comprising approximately 30 percent of GDP in 2001.[76] However, large-scale commercial logging has also caused the most significant and irreversible damage to forest biodiversity, having serious impacts on lands and local communities.[77] From the perspective of Papua New Guinea NGOs and others, the foreign-owned logging industry has been the major contributor to corruption in Papua New Guinea.

Pressure on the government during the 1990s to bring unsustainable logging operations under control led to the development of the Forestry and Conservation Project, to be funded by the World Bank and the Global Environment Facility. With the change of government in 2002, negotiations with the World Bank broke down and the project was put on hold. The government's position is that it wishes to see a continuation of commercial logging, from which it receives a return of K110 million per year, and to determine if there are ways of ensuring sustainable timber production.[78] It remains to be seen what will emerge from a government review of existing logging projects. For many, sustainable small-scale logging carried out by local communities is seen as the way forward. This is included as an aspirational goal in the government's medium-term development strategy for 2005–2010.

Agricultural production for export is divided between large-scale, mostly foreign-owned operations, and cash-cropping by small landholders. The main export crops are coffee, palm oil, coconuts and coconut products, and cocoa.[79] More recently there was a vanilla boom, the result of rising international prices associated with the sharp drop in supply from Madagascar due to a cyclone in 2000. In the Sepik in particular, local farmers responded to this and received significant revenue from the high vanilla prices. However, vanilla prices for PNG growers have since dropped, as supply from Madagascar and elsewhere recovered.

The overall assessment is that, since the 1990s, the nonminerals sector has been neglected: "PNG has allowed its non-minerals sector to wither, particularly its transport infrastructure and agricultural services."[80] In 2001, Michael Baxter pointed to limited growth since 1990, with constraints including low prices, limited market access, and limited demand.[81]

Importance of the Informal Rural Sector

Most rural Papua New Guineans grow or harvest food crops for their own consumption, with some also selling surplus crops. While many rural households are self-supporting in food, people need cash for school fees, clothing, transport, kerosene, medical treatment, soap, and other basic household items. For many, the most important income source is local food sales or remittances from people employed elsewhere in Papua New Guinea, generally in the formal economy.

Rural-urban interdependence is particularly strong. Some 80–85 percent of the population live in rural areas, the majority of food consumed is grown domestically, and many people unemployed in urban areas survive through informal employment in rural areas. "Rural societies also play key roles in the welfare of the unskilled, underemployed, and resource-poor and as the cultural lodestar of the nation."[82]

The Rural Crisis

In his 2001 report "Enclaves or Equity?" Baxter argued that rural Papua New Guinea was in a serious social and economic crisis, and that this was a national crisis, given that 85 percent of the population lived in rural areas, and given the links between rural and urban areas. In addition to the factors cited above, Baxter referred to remoteness from urban markets, low and declining levels of public and private investment, population pressures, the growing HIV/AIDS epidemic, law and order and governance problems, and environmental pressures.[83]

Community workers and academics consulted for this chapter support his assessment.[84] Sarah Garap stresses the links between gender and rural development, given that women are the principal participants in informal activities that generate income, through food production, fisheries, and small-scale commodity production. However, women's activities in the informal sector are severely constrained by lack of market facilities and infrastructure, security issues, and limited access to financial assistance.[85]

In Baxter's assessment, the rural crisis is due to economic priorities and management as well as structural aspects of the economy. He noted that economic management has given priority to ensuring that the country "is open to the trade and investment on which the export-oriented resources sector depends."[86] While rural people will take up much of the responsibility for their development, it is clear that they need a public policy framework and government-led investment to ensure that basic resources are available to start promoting growth and reducing poverty.

The Rural Response

> Rural communities have shown "considerable initiative and fortitude in addressing the social and economic conditions they face."[87]

Historically, subsistence farmers have demonstrated great facility in adapting new food crops.[88] The resulting intensification of production has meant that food production has kept pace with rapid population growth. The ability to step in and fill the gap in the international vanilla market was an initiative of local farmers with no assistance from government or donor-supported agricultural programs.[89] A positive outcome of the declining value of the kina has been the growth of the internal market for food, with those producers able to access urban markets, responding to the greater demand for local food crops due to the increased cost of imported food items.[90]

Most significant, various communities have realized that there is little point in waiting for government, and are undertaking innovative livelihood and community-building activities, as the following examples demonstrate. A Southern Highland community is engaged in rice farming through which people are reportedly being empowered and gaining hope and self-confidence.[91] The Domil community in the Western Highlands is maintaining its road system, is marketing its coffee directly to an international agent, and has set up its own police, schools, and health centers. The community is organized along the traditional *Hauslain* system ("houseline"—where extended families live together in lines of houses) and is supported by the Nazarene Church.[92] The Wide Bay Conservation Project, in East New Britain, was started by a resident of Teimtop village, who sought assistance from East New Britain Sosel Eksen Komiti and Conservation International to protect clan lands from unsustainable logging. The project has involved extensive consultation and community development training over a period of more than seven years, with workshops concerning environment, land rights, Papua New Guinean history and culture, court proceedings, and the constitution of Papua New Guinea. Gender training was carried out to encourage equal participation in development options. Participants were encouraged to look further into the roles and responsibilities within and outside their families in relation to past and present situations. Other workshops were conducted on starting up small businesses and carrying out participatory rural appraisals. Several opportunities for enterprise were identified, such as a guesthouse, vanilla and rice projects, individual ventures, and nontimber forest products.[93]

■ Rediscovery of the Rural Sector

There is some consensus emerging from the government and from other observers about the nonmineral resources sector being the key to future economic development in Papua New Guinea.[94] Baxter stressed the need for long-term development to be based on economic transformation of the rural sector, based on the sustainable development of agriculture, forestry, and fisheries. He argued that the decline in the minerals sector and the urgent rural situation "provide an opportunity to rethink the development choices confronting Papua New Guinea."[95] The Papua New Guinea government's medium-term development strategy for 2005–2010 places considerable emphasis on rural development and agriculture, pointing to the scope for the cultivation of a wide range of crops for domestic consumption and export markets.[96] The strategy also points to the potential of fisheries, and the potential of the country's tropical rainforest, which is characterized by valuable timber resources and high reserves of biodiversity.[97]

There are many questions surrounding this apparent consensus for a renewed focus on rural development. A major one is the issue of balance between the export sector and the informal rural sector. While the Papua New Guinea government's strategy relates in large part to enhancing export-oriented agriculture, there is also an emphasis on growing internal markets and supporting the informal sector. The question is whether this commitment can be translated into action and resourced, given donor preoccupations with macroeconomic stability, public sector reform, and institutional strengthening.

Alternatively, will the emphasis be primarily on export-oriented, foreign-investment-driven production, as has occurred in the past? Papua New Guinea *will* have to engage in export-oriented production, and foreign investment will undoubtedly be needed. However, as has occurred in the oil palm and tuna processing industries, there will continue to be issues around the terms on which this investment occurs, and the employment and environmental practices adopted by foreign companies.[98] Given the decline in the mineral sector and the country's budgetary constraints, a major reliance on large-scale export production could see a continuation of the enclave model (with limited benefits flowing through to local people), but with governments keen to embrace large-scale agribusiness projects, given the prospects of boosting government revenue.

A key issue is whether the interconnection between gender issues and rural development will be recognized, given that women in rural areas are suffering the greatest social and economic disadvantage, while also bearing heavier burdens in child-rearing and supporting their families. It is clear that unless development projects specifically target women, they will not automatically or equally benefit from them, and this will greatly hinder the development of communities and society as a whole.[99]

A further issue relates to the nature of international trading relationships. Like other countries that rely on the export of primary commodities, Papua New Guinea is vulnerable to fluctuating prices for export crops. UNCTAD's reports continue to point to the close connection between poverty and dependence on a narrow range of primary commodity exports.[100] Papua New Guinea is part of the Group of 90, which has been pushing for reform of global trading arrangements in the context of the World Trade Organization's Doha round of agriculture negotiations. The extent to which export-oriented agriculture contributes to genuine development in Papua New Guinea will presumably depend, to a considerable degree, on the outcome of those negotiations.

Finally, there is the vexing land issue. The possibility of a shift from customary land tenure to individual titling is a major concern for Papua New Guineans, given the crucial cultural and social role of land. If development of land is to occur in a way that promotes security and aims to prevent conflict, then financial institutions and donors need to find ways of financing development without requiring individual land registrations or other changes likely to be perceived as undermining customary land tenure.

■ **Law and Justice**

Law and order issues in Papua New Guinea need to be understood in the broader context of uneven development and rapid social and economic change in the colonial and postcolonial periods.[101] Sinclair Dinnen's analysis[102] shows that violence and disorder do not apply uniformly across the country. In many parts of the country, there are few law and order problems, and "those that do occur are managed successfully by local communities." The spread of lawlessness has tended to follow the larger patterns of development, as shown by "the concentration of organised crime in urban centres, armed hold-ups along the arterial highways, and inter-group conflict in the vicinity of large-scale resource development projects." Dinnen points out that while commentators tend to focus on the impact on private investment and the personal security of foreign workers, there are serious impacts on the security and safety of ordinary Papua New Guineans, in particular women, the poor, the old, and the very young. The close connection between *raskolism* (a Papua New Guinea Pidgin word for "juvenile gang crime") and lack of economic opportunities is highlighted.[103] Perceptions of corruption and increasing inequality have also provided a rationalization for the "ostensibly 'equalising' activities of street criminals."[104] Problems of law and order are found also in some rural areas, a consequence of growing rural poverty and the weakening of informal controls.

While there are links between crime and lack of opportunity, there are deeper social questions about masculinity, identity, and socialization among the rapidly growing youth population. Torn between village life and the promise of modern urban living, and frustrated with their effective exclusion from the latter, many young men turn to antisocial and destructive activities.[105]

A Shift in Approach to Law and Justice

> The outstanding challenge today is to develop appropriate strategies for enhancing the capacity of the formal and informal sectors and linkages between them.[106]

Many law and justice issues are difficult to resolve, because of the misfit between the Western system of law and justice and traditional approaches to conflict resolution. In the preindependence nation-building period, traditional approaches were marginalized in the formal justice system (which essentially involved the transplanting of the Anglo-Australian model). Despite some postindependence interest in integrating Western and Melanesian legal traditions, the Western model remained dominant.[107] As law and order issues have emerged, official responses have been essentially reactive, with governments anxious to appear tough on crime, turning to curfews, longer prison sentences, and other punitive measures. At the same time, police numbers have not matched the rapidly expanding population, and police have been poorly resourced. The combination of reactive approaches and lack of capacity has meant that many Papua New Guineans "have little faith in either the efficiency or fairness of the formal justice system."[108] Particularly in the rural areas, people often draw on other mechanisms for minor disputes. For the rural majority, the formal system is often remote, and the most important forum for resolving disputes are the village courts and informal mechanisms that include negotiation or mediation by kin, traditional leaders, or church officials; village moots; or the decisions of local committees *(komitis).*[109]

At the policy level, the debate has focused on the issue of declining state capacity. Practical proposals have concentrated on strengthening the formal sector, with the role of informal institutions "seen as peripheral at best."[110] Supported by "substantial levels" of Australian development assistance, successive governments have aimed to build the capacity of the police force and other institutions of the formal system, "with mixed results," as discussed further in Chapter 4.

More recently, there has been increasing recognition of the way Papua New Guinean communities have been using or adapting traditional mechanisms for resolving conflict, and of the need to promote the restorative justice approaches that have emerged. The Papua New Guinea government's national action plan for law and justice policy marks a significant change in approach. The third pillar of the policy has a focus on crime prevention and restorative justice. It recognizes the informal system as a complementary part of the law and justice system and seeks to strengthen the capacity of informal community-based and other nongovernment structures to prevent and resolve conflict at local levels. The other two pillars of the action plan are improved functioning of the formal law and justice agencies, and improved sectoral coordination.

Restorative Justice

Whereas "retributive justice" is organized around the process of identifying and punishing individuals, "restorative justice" provides a major role for the community and those most directly affected by an offense or dispute. An important objective of dispute resolution is seen as the restoration of balance and harmony in the community affected, and the healing of relationships damaged by wrongdoing or conflict. Some examples of restorative justice approaches, outlined below, operate independently of the state, while others involve linkages or partnerships between state and nonstate entities.

Mass surrenders. Groups of criminals are surrendering themselves and their weapons at public ceremonies. Surrendering groups ask for forgiveness for their deeds, and ask for assistance with their rehabilitation strategies. Mass surrenders are often brokered by church groups or individual pastors. Brokers aim to persuade criminals to renounce crime and, in return, offer help in securing access to legitimate economic or educational opportunities. Where court proceedings eventuate, magistrates are likely to take the fact of surrender into account.

Dispute mediation in an urban setting. In Port Morseby's Saraga settlement (a large, multicultural urban community of approximately 4,000 people from various parts of Papua New Guinea), disputes are mediated by a local committee. Established in 1997, the committee draws on conflict resolution techniques developed by Peace Foundation Melanesia, which provides training in conflict mediation, project planning, and restorative justice methods. Drawing on this, committee members add aspects of their respective cultural ways of settling disputes, conducting mediations within their own particular cultural groups. From 2000 to 2003, the committee conducted more than 200 successful mediations.[111]

Integral human development programs. Raim village in East New Britain has seen radical improvements to peace and security in community life since the establishment of the Raim Youth and Sport Association. The association is undertaking integral human development programs that encompass leadership, religious studies, youth training, "personal viability" courses, cultural programs, music, counseling, management skills, and finance. Through this and previous efforts, community skills have developed to the extent that there was a mass surrender of guns from Raim-Gunanur and nearby villages. There is now a low rate of law and order problems in the village. The Raim sporting clubs have developed, and increased numbers of youth are now involved in church activities and community programs. In achieving this remarkable turnaround, the Raim community has received support from provincial and local government and community organizations such as the East New Britain Sosel Eksen Komiti.[112]

■ Politics, Governance, and the State

Political instability in Papua New Guinea is related to the lack of a sense of national identity, and the mismatch between the adopted Western political and administrative systems, and the social and cultural realities of Papua New Guinea's diverse societies.[113] While it was assumed that political parties would develop to match the adopted Westminster parliamentary model, the reality has been quite different. What has emerged is "a highly fluid and unstable political system, with weak political parties, personalised and parochially based political parties and intense political competition."[114] In this context there is considerable resistance to the state.

With its hundreds of semiautonomous tribal and linguistic groupings, Papua New Guinea was, on the imposition of colonial rule, essentially a stateless society. It is not surprising that a sense of national identity is weak and that "the primary allegiances and identities of most Papua New Guineans remain firmly implanted in local kin-based associations."[115]

Notions of a "failed or collapsed state" are of little value in explaining state-related issues in Papua New Guinea. As Sinclair Dinnen points out: "They are based on an assumption that at some point there was a well functioning centralised state. . . . It is probably more accurate to say that the main problem with the state in Melanesia (including Papua New Guinea), is not so much that it is falling apart but that it has yet to be properly built."[116] Patrick Regan proposes a further alternative perspective to the "failing state" paradigm, suggesting that elements of the unnatural colonial state may be crumbling as Papua New Guineans start to rebuild systems of governance more suited to their culture and situation.[117]

Attempts are being made to deal with issues of politics and governance in various ways, with a significant proportion of the international aid program directed at this area. Reforms to the political system have been introduced in an attempt to deal with the weakness of political parties, and with the first-past-the-post voting system, which has seen candidates elected with a very small number of votes.[118]

In 1995 the government of Papua New Guinea enacted an organic law on provincial and local-level government as the legislative basis for establishing a policy of decentralization in decisionmaking, with the transfer of responsibilities and funds to the lower levels of government. The aim was to improve delivery of services, but there have been ongoing problems with implementation and inadequate financial resources, particularly at the provincial level. A frequent observation is that public servants in provincial areas have great difficulty carrying out their functions, due to the lack of resources for essentials such as office equipment and gasoline to visit communities.

There is a vigorous debate within the country around issues of politics and governance. At various levels—national, provincial, district, and community—Papua New Guineans are working for change with the aim of building systems of governance that are more responsive to people's needs and to Papua New Guinea's situation. An approach that is gaining some ground in the law and justice sector appears to be applicable across other areas: recognizing indigenous structures of governance and the need to build on these and strengthen the links between them and the formal sector.

Charles Lepani, a prominent Papua New Guinean public policy analyst, has suggested a rethink of the approach to decentralization, arguing for more autonomy to be given to those provincial governments that have performed relatively effectively, freeing up national government to focus on the less well-resourced provinces. He also argues for a greater focus on district-level administration and that "entities based on common linguistic heritage, cultural and traditional trading linkages, should be considered . . . as vehicles . . . for decentralised development."[119]

> We Papua New Guineans have accumulated a substantial body of experiences and a collective institutional memory in attempting to build a nation state. We should be able to say that some of the building blocks are either not suitable or defective. . . . The national government with its myriad of responsibilities cannot wait for all provinces to develop equally. . . . It has taken us 30 years to realise that effective district level administrations remain the focus of development and the link our people needed to sustain PNG as a nation.[120]

The government is aiming to address three key issues of decentralization: the demarcation of responsibilities across the various levels of government; institutional capacity; and the introduction of a new funding system "which is both affordable and more closely attuned to the transfer of responsibilities."[121]

■ Conclusion

The role of development aid is a hotly debated topic, with arguments mounted from various perspectives about its effectiveness in the Papua New Guinea context. The situation is more complex than suggested by those who argue that "aid has failed." A more realistic assessment of the impact of aid is that it is a "mixed bag." There are positive examples, and there are examples of unsuccessful programs. It is clear that in the context of Papua New Guinea's budgetary constraints, development aid has played an important role in maintaining health and education services and in maintaining some infrastructure such as roads. Other positive examples include an innovative program for the law and justice sector, and programs aimed at strengthening civil society and community development.

Valuable lessons about how meaningful change occurs in the Papua New Guinea context can be learned from developments at the community level. While various community development initiatives may have a particular starting point, such as working with *raskol* youth, addressing tribal conflict in the Highlands, or undertaking agricultural projects, they tend to take a holistic approach to community needs. They involve community rebuilding and thus point to possible ways of resolving in the longer-term issues associated with the relevance of the state in its current form. In contrast to the "top-down" approach of much donor assistance (pumping in technical assistance to get the state to function better), the "bottom-up" community-strengthening approach involves organic models developed within communities, often with minimal resources.

Accepting the notion that the state has still to be built, support for such community rebuilding must logically provide the way forward. Rather than trying to engineer change, it is important to consider ways of facilitating the efforts being made by Papua New Guinean communities to tackle their issues at the local level. This raises challenging questions about how this can best be done. A lot will depend on the skill and sensitivity of outsiders, whose role should be to assist and facilitate Papua New Guinean community organizations without dominating them, and without imposing their own agendas.

Notes

1. The term "failing states" is regarded by many Pacific Islanders as derogatory. The Australian Agency for International Development (AusAID) has recently used the term "fragile states," for example in AusAID, "Australian Aid," p. 17.
2. Kavanamur, Yala, and Clements, *Building a Nation in Papua New Guinea,* p. 1.
3. Stella, "PNG in the New Millennium," p. 15.
4. Ibid.
5. This position is taken by Australian National University economist Satish Chand in his article "Papua New Guinea Economic Survey." Chand argues for the following priorities in improving investor confidence and promoting growth: political stability, fiscal sustainability, reducing the costs of doing business, and the completion of reforms, including privatization, public sector reform, and trade liberalization.
6. Fry, "Framing the Islands," p. 305.
7. Ibid., p. 309.
8. Ibid., p. 306.
9. Ibid., p. 336.
10. Windybank and Manning, "Papua New Guinea on the Brink," p. 1.
11. Ibid.
12. Ibid., p. 10. Susan Windybank and Mike Manning point to possibilities such as Papua New Guinea attracting transnational criminals, people smugglers, drug and arms traffickers, and terrorists. The threat to Australia's security is seen as arising because Papua New Guinea is unable to effectively monitor its land and sea borders or control parts of its territory.
13. Hughes, "Aid Has Failed the Pacific."
14. Ibid., p. 25.
15. Ibid., p. 26.
16. For example, in the *Papua New Guinea Post Courier,* 15 July 2004, Foreign Affairs Minister Rabbie Namaliu described a similar follow-up article by

Helen Hughes, "Can Papua New Guinea Come Back from the Brink?" as "ill-informed and out-of-date" and ignoring government efforts to tackle the country's problems. Alan Patience, professor of political science at the University of Papua New Guinea, also responded to Hughes in the *Post Courier,* 17 July 2004, describing Hughes' "simplistic argument" as "deeply worrying" and presenting "poor and underprivileged people as losers who don't deserve compassion and help."

17. Nic Maclellan, cited in ACFOA, *Australia and the Pacific,* p. 41.

18. Baxter, "Enclaves or Equity?" p. 34.

19. Dinnen, "Building Bridges."

20. Ibid., p. 2.

21. Baloiloi, "Kumul 2020."

22. Kaman, "Peace Studies as a Process of Peace Building," p. 316.

23. Ibid., p. 317.

24. Anderson, "A Grand Deceit." Tim Anderson is a political economist and member of AID/WATCH. His paper was written for the Australian Conservation Foundation and the Center for Environmental Law and Community Rights in Papua New Guinea.

25. Anderson, "A Grand Deceit," pp. 21, 49. Anderson's criticism of export-oriented resource exploitation applies not only to the minerals and forestry sectors, but also to agribusiness, in particular the oil palm industry. Contrary to some other assessments, Anderson considers that the oil palm industry has had significant social and environmental costs, with limited benefits to local people.

26. Anderson, "A Grand Deceit," p. 24.

27. Jacka, "Australian Aid," p. 2.

28. McGee, "Participating in Development," p. 93. Rosemary McGee's assessment is that the convergence between the mainstream development agenda and alternative participatory approaches should be seen as a sign "of the success of the transformative project of participatory development," rather than as "a triumph of the former over the latter."

29. Kothari and Monogue, *Development Theory and Practice.*

30. UNCTAD, "UNCTAD Calls for End to Development Pessimism," p. 1. Development pessimism is founded on various views, including "that past development policies and international development assistance have failed; that if national development strategies did work they cannot work once a country has undertaken trade liberalization; that the globalization of production renders national development strategy impossible; or that WTO rules leave no room for promoting development . . . weak state capabilities are added as a further ingredient, reinforcing the view that development promotion simply cannot be done."

31. Government of Papua New Guinea and United Nations, *Millennium Development Goals,* p. 2.

32. UNDP, *Human Development Report, 2003: Millennium Development Goals,* p. vi.

33. Ibid., p. 11.

34. Ibid., p. 4.

35. Ibid., p. 6.

36. Jacka, "Australian Aid."

37. Larmour, *Governance and Reform in the South Pacific,* p. 5.

38. Maclellan in ACFOA, *Australia and the Pacific,* p. 8.

39. C. Emery, Pacific officer, Save the Children Fund Australia, interview with author, 16 April 2004; S. Garap, director of Meri I Kirap Sapotim (Women Stand Up: Support Them), interview with author, 3 March 2004.

40. M. Sete, "NGO Capacity Building PNG," discussion in "Good Governance and Civil Society" workshop, Australian Council for International Development annual council, September 2004.

41. "Waigani Seminar."

42. May, "From Promise to Crisis," p. 64.

43. Ibid.

44. United Nations, *Papua New Guinea Common Country Assessment, 2001.*

45. ACFOA, *Inquiry into Australia's Relationship with Papua New Guinea,* p. 10. Structural adjustment programs in Papua New Guinea have been part of the broader approach of donors to economic and development issues in the Pacific. The international financial institution and donor agenda for economic and policy reform in the Pacific was first developed in the early 1990s with a series of key World Bank reports and policy workshops funded by the Australian Agency for International Development and other donors on private sector development, public sector reform, more effective government, and reform of government finances.

46. Kavanamur, "The Politics of Structural Adjustment in Papua New Guinea."

47. Muwali, "South Pacific"; World Bank, "Papua New Guinea." A further World Bank loan was negotiated in 2000 to support "broad-based policy reform" in governance, through better fiscal transparency and accountability and steps to combat corruption; budget and debt management; public sector reform; improved service delivery in health and education; better forestry management; and improved provision of financial services, including banking and pension reform; as well as through a comprehensive privatization program.

48. "Please Support PNG Group's Challenging the World Bank's Structural Adjustment Programme," *The Ecologist,* 27 October 1995, available at http://www.hartford-hwp.com/archives/24/024.html (accessed 31 January 2007).

49. Ibid.

50. Larmour, "Conditionality, Coercion, and Other Forms of Power," p. 253.

51. ACFOA, *Australia and the Pacific.*

52. Commonwealth of Australia, *A Pacific Engaged,* p. 262. Partial privatization involves public-private partnerships, but with government retaining the controlling position.

53. Unless otherwise stated, sources for facts and figures are Government of Papua New Guinea, *Medium Term Development Strategy;* Baxter, "Enclaves or Equity"; and Gibson and Rozelle, *Results of the Household Survey.* Most reports on poverty in Papua New Guinea have quoted or extrapolated from the original data collected by John Gibson and Scott Rozelle in the latter survey (1996), because there has been no subsequent household survey as robust and comprehensive.

54. Estimates vary—one source refers to 65,000 public sector jobs and 70,000 private sector jobs, making a total of 135,000; AusAID, "Poverty Reduction Analysis." Government of Papua New Guinea, *Medium Term Development Strategy,* estimates formal private sector employment to be around 190,000. Adding public sector employment would give a total of 255,000 jobs.

55. The figure of 37.5 percent relates to an "upper poverty line" established in the 1996 study by Gibson and Rozelle *(Results of the Household Survey),* which is widely cited as a reliable measure of poverty in the Papua New Guinea context. The upper poverty line is based on a "food poverty line" plus an allowance for the consumption of basic nonfood items. The 1996 study estimated that 17 percent of the population were below the food poverty line. A 2002 World Bank study cited in Chand, "Papua New Guinea Economic Survey," p. 1, similarly showed 37 percent of the population to be in poverty.

56. World Bank, "Papua New Guinea: Interim Strategy Note," cited in Asian Development Bank, *Country Strategy and Program Update.*

57. World Bank study cited in AusAID, "The Contribution of Australian Aid to Papua New Guinea's Development" p. 9.

58. Government of Papua New Guinea, *Medium Term Development Strategy,* p. 1.

59. The "enclave" model refers to large-scale, foreign-dominated resource exploitation, with limited linkages to the rest of the economy.

60. Asian Development Bank, *Priorities of the Poor in Papua New Guinea.* Baxter concluded in "Enclaves or Equity?" that there was little improvement in the day-to-day living conditions of most Papua New Guineans from the mid-1980s to 1996. Other accounts point to the position worsening since the mid-1990s. AusAID in its "Poverty Reduction Analysis," p. 9, estimated the standard of living, as measured by income per person, declined by 14 percent in real terms between 2000 and 2002.

61. Development Studies Network, "Discussion," pp. 4–5.

62. Baloiloi, "Kumul 2020," p. 1. The process was initiated by a Papua New Guinean government minister who felt that planning had been primarily government-driven and that there should be greater involvement by civil society and the private sector in the process. The committee was chaired by Misty Baloiloi of the University of Papua New Guinea, and comprised representatives from rural communities, local business, academia, the public sector, media, nongovernmental organizations, and the churches.

63. Baloiloi, "Kumul 2020," pp. 9–10.

64. AusAID, "Poverty Reduction Analysis."

65. Baxter, "Enclaves or Equity?"; Government of Papua New Guinea, *Medium Term Development Strategy.*

66. World Bank, *World Development Indicators, 2001*, pp. 143, 299.

67. Cox, "Appropriate Development."

68. Baxter, "Enclaves or Equity?"; Government of Papua New Guinea, *Medium Term Development Strategy.*

69. AusAID, "Poverty Reduction Analysis," p. 6.

70. World Bank and National Research Institute, *Papua New Guinea Environment Monitor,* p. 15; Oxfam Community Aid Abroad, "Submission to the Senate Foreign Affairs, Defence, and Trade References Committee."

71. World Bank and National Research Institute, *Papua New Guinea Environment Monitor.*

72. M. Otter, manager of international programs, World Wide Fund for Nature Australia, personal communication, June and September 2004; World Bank and National Research Institute, *Papua New Guinea Environment Monitor.*

73. Otter, personal communication.

74. Ibid.

75. Oxfam Community Aid Abroad, "Submission to the Senate Foreign Affairs, Defence, and Trade References Committee."

76. Baxter, "Enclaves or Equity?" p. 3.

77. World Bank and National Research Institute, *Papua New Guinea Environment Monitor.*

78. 2003/04 Review Team, "Towards Sustainable Timber Production."

79. The oil palm industry, which operates along the nucleus estate and smallholder model, is often held out as an example of a highly successful export industry, recording growth of around 11 percent per annum since 1980. See Government of Papua New Guinea, *Medium Term Development Strategy,* p. 14.

80. AusAID, "Framework: Australia's Aid Program to Papua New Guinea," p. 2.

81. Baxter, "Enclaves or Equity?"

82. Ibid., p. 3.

83. Ibid., pp. x, 30. Baxter estimates that, based on current trends, there will be 73 percent more rural dwellers in 2020 than in 2000. Population pressures are particularly strong in the Highlands, where average rural density is 32 people per square kilometer (83 people per square mile), with higher rates in some specific areas. Average population density across the country is 11 people per square kilometer (28 people per square mile).

84. Personal communications with M. Bourke, Department of Human Geography, Research School of Asian and Pacific Studies, Australian National University, 22 April 2004; C. Emery, 2004; S. Garap, 2004; R. May, Department of Political and Social Change, Research School of Asian and Pacific Studies, Australian National University, 5 March 2004. May referred to the difficulty of getting pharmaceutical kits from provincial centers to local aid posts in the Sepik, a task falling to local people, who face high transportation costs. Bourke discussed how people in remote poor areas are unable to get to aid posts or hospitals when they become sick, also due to high transportation costs. He and others mentioned the high cost of education—800–1,200 kina, depending on the level—for rural families with limited income-earning opportunities.

85. Garap, "Gender in PNG."

86. Baxter, "Enclaves or Equity?" p. 2.

87. Ibid., p. 35.

88. Ibid.; Bourke, personal communication.

89. May, personal communication; C. Malau, visiting fellow, Burnet Institute, Melbourne, personal communication, 15 April 2004.

90. Bourke, personal communication; Baxter, "Enclaves or Equity?"

91. Okole, "Insights from the DWU Symposium."

92. S. Dinnen, Department of Political and Social Change, Research School of Asian and Pacific Studies, Australian National University, personal communication, 22 April 2004.

93. Meava, "Wide Bay Conservation Project."

94. Government of Papua New Guinea, *Medium Term Development Strategy;* Chand, "Papua New Guinea Economic Survey."

95. Baxter, "Enclaves or Equity?"

96. Government of Papua New Guinea, *Medium Term Development Strategy,* p. 3. The development strategy points to the amount of underutilized land—of the 30 percent of Papua New Guinea's land area suitable for agriculture, only half is currently cultivated—and to generally fertile soils and good rainfall.

97. Government of Papua New Guinea, *Medium Term Development Strategy.*

98. Anderson, "A Grand Deceit," pp. 23–24. The Philippino-owned RD Tuna wharf and cannery operation at Madang has generated controversy. According to Anderson, the land for the wharf facility was allocated without proper agreement with the traditional owners, the Papua New Guinean government waived taxes on the operation, wages are extremely low (US$1.50 a day), and discharges from the ships are damaging the marine environment of the Madang lagoon.

99. Garap, "Gender in PNG," p. 5.

100. Oxfam Community Aid Abroad, "Submission to the Senate Foreign Affairs, Defence, and Trade References Committee."

101. Dinnen, "Building Bridges"; Dinnen "Restorative Justice"; Dinnen, *Law and Order in a Weak State.*

102. Dinnen, "Building Bridges," pp. 2–6.

103. Ibid., p. 3. Dinnen cites a 1998 survey that showed that 18 percent of the Port Moresby population relied on crime as their principal source of income: "Raskolism has become the largest occupational category in the informal economy of the national capital where 40% of recorded crime occurs."

104. Dinnen, "Building Bridges," p. 2. Dinnen says: "Contrary to their depiction in popular stereotypes, gangs are often well integrated into their local activities. As well as ties of friendship and personal association, *raskols* engage in selective acts of redistribution, providing benefits to their neighbors in often the poorest and most socially deprived urban communities."

105. Dinnen, "Building Bridges," p. 4.

106. Ibid., p. 6.

107. Ibid., p. 22. The exception was the village court system, a hybrid institution established in the postindependence period. Village courts are presided over by village leaders as magistrates, and are intended to provide an accessible forum for dealing with minor disputes. The system has been weakened by the fact that many village court officials have not been receiving their allowances since the 1995 handover from national government to provincial and local government. There has also been some criticism that village courts reinforce the subordination of women and girls. Dinnen considers that this could be overcome with better training and supervision.

108. Dinnen, "Building Bridges," p. 6.

109. Ibid., pp. 4–5.

110. Ibid., p. 6.

111. Ivoro, "Conflict Resolution in a Multi-Cultural Urban Setting," pp. 11–12.

112. Oxfam Community Aid Abroad, *"The Raim Story."*

113. May, "From Promise to Crisis"; Okole, "Institutional Decay in a Melanesian Parliamentary Democracy"; Standish, "Papua New Guinea Politics."

114. Okole, Narakobi, and Clements, quoted in Baker, "Political Integrity in Papua New Guinea," p. 8.

115. Dinnen, "Building Bridges," p. 2.

116. Ibid.

117. A. Regan, comments made at the "Good News Workshop," Divine Word University, Madang, 24–26 November 2004.

118. Standish, "Papua New Guinea Politics"; Baker, "Political Integrity in Papua New Guinea."

119. Lepani, "Perspective," p. 52.

120. Ibid., pp. 51–52.

121. Government of Papua New Guinea, *Medium Term Development Strategy,* p. 8.

3

Power, Gender, and Security in Papua New Guinea

Orovu Sepoe

> The empowerment of women . . . is crucial to our efforts to combat poverty, hunger and disease, and to stimulate development that is truly sustainable. And it is essential to the promotion of justice and peaceful resolution of disputes.
>
> —*Kofi Annan*[1]

Unequal and asymmetrical power relations lie at the heart of conflict and insecurity in society. This chapter looks at some of the critical gender issues that impact on the total well-being and long-term security of society, and provides some insight into developing a theoretical and policy framework for addressing development-security issues in the Papua New Guinea context. The central themes of this chapter are threefold. First, strategies to effectively address security issues must, by necessity, focus on the *total* well-being of the individual person: hence, integral human development is the key to security and peace in society. Second, there needs to be a shift away from perceptions of development that prioritize economic growth in terms of materialism and increasing individual wealth, toward thinking of development in terms of more ethical, culturally relevant, humane, and environmentally sensitive forms of livelihood, particularly for a rural and subsistence-based society like Papua New Guinea. Third, hierarchical power relations that generate destructive and violent behavior, as do gender relations in contemporary Papua New Guinea (and many other societies), fundamentally compromise both development and security in society as a whole.

▇ Integral Human Development: A Brief Review

At the dawn of statehood for Papua New Guinea in 1975, the founding leadership had the wisdom and foresight to adopt *integral human development* and *equality and participation* as national goals. The national constitution, in its preamble, states these as follows:

1. Integral Human Development—We declare our first national goal to be for every person to be dynamically involved in the process of freeing himself or herself from every form of domination or oppression so that each man or woman will have the opportunity to develop as a whole person in relationship with others. We accordingly call for—(1) everyone to be involved in our endeavours to achieve integral human development of the whole person and to seek fulfilment through his or her contribution to the common good, and (2) education to be based on mutual respect and dialogue, and to promote awareness of our human potential and motivation to achieve our National Goals through self-reliant effort; . . .

2. Equality and Participation—We declare our second goal to be for all citizens to have an equal opportunity to participate in, and benefit from, the development of our country.[2]

Yet three decades later, by all social and human development indicators, Papua New Guinea has made little, if any, progress on a path to achieving integral human development and equality. According to the UN's Human Development Index, in 1999 Papua New Guinea was ranked 129th out of 174 countries; and by 2003 it had dropped to 137th out of 177 countries.[3] By regional standards, Papua New Guinea has the lowest Human Development Index (HDI) score among Pacific countries. Furthermore, Papua New Guinea's score on the UN's Gender-Related Development Index is lower than its overall HDI score, demonstrating that women have lower levels of literacy and education than do men, and much lower levels of income.[4]

The deteriorating economic and social conditions for the majority of people living in Papua New Guinea have been clearly described by Marion Jacka in the previous chapter, showing that the majority of the population (80–85 percent) living in rural areas are facing serious hardship, with very limited access to basic resources and services. In addition to the regional disparities in economic opportunities, there is glaring gender inequity. In both rural and urban areas, women are facing greater economic and social disadvantage, while also carrying heavier burdens in sustaining their families and communities.

■ Gender Issues in Papua New Guinea

While only 10 percent of the adult population are employed in the formal sector, by far the majority of those are men.[5] Abby McLeod's discussion of women in Papua New Guinea's police force, in Chapter 4, makes clear the discrimination that women face in the workplace. Likewise, in political and decisionmaking forums and institutions, women remain marginalized. There is currently only one woman in parliament. In the informal sector, women are the foundation of much of the economic life that sustains the population: women work the vegetable gardens and are the mainstay of much food production, as well as of much small-scale commodity production. It is women who are most directly held back by lack of access to markets, as well as to loans, and by their vulnerability to very high rates of male violence.[6]

In societies such as Papua New Guinea, where a large percentage of people are based in rural villages, and where customary laws dictate much of their lives, formal laws against domestic violence are simply ignored or unknown. Domestic violence continues unabated in spite of church presence or religious influences, which are widely recognized as gatekeepers of ethical behavior. The prevalence and persistence of domestic violence seem to be sanctioned by traditions and customs that can be questioned, both for their genuineness as well as for their incompatibility with Papua New Guinea's national goals and with human rights standards elsewhere in the world.

Sexual violence against women, such as rape and wife beating, reduces their personal security and abuses their human rights in a fundamental way. This, combined with limited access to education and other basic services, creates ongoing experiences of insecurity, restricting women's opportunities, choices, and capacities. Given both that the female population constitutes nearly half of the total population, and the fundamental role that women play in the life of the community, it is no wonder that this insecurity is reflected in the overall low level of human, social, and economic development for Papua New Guinea.

Prostitution as a survival strategy has become increasingly common for poor women, especially in urban areas. Basic economic hardship traps women in a vicious cycle of violence and poverty, leaving them few opportunities to exercise choice or control over their circumstances. Julienne Kaman has noted that, "faced with the hardship of struggling to make ends meet, the poor are turning to fast money schemes, poker machines, begging, illegal prostitution, bribery and con artistry coupled with increased levels of brutal violence."[7]

These factors partly explain why women and girls have become more vulnerable to the HIV/AIDS epidemic in Papua New Guinea compared to men and boys. The United Nations Children's Fund (UNICEF) reported in 2005 that twice as many Papua New Guinean women as men in the fifteen- to twenty-nine-year-old age group are HIV positive.[8] Given the serious threat that the HIV/AIDS epidemic poses for development prospects in Papua New Guinea, the need to understand the causes of unequal gender relations and their destructive impact is an urgent national priority.

An audit report by the United Nations Development Programme (UNDP) on Papua New Guinea's HIV/AIDS strategy identified the highly unequal nature of sexual partnerships in the country as a major factor contributing to the greater proportion of women among those infected with HIV/AIDS. The report noted that dominant ideas and attitudes in Papua New Guinea about masculinity encourage men to have multiple sex partners, and to conform to the "predatory" view of male sexuality by subjugating women through coercive sex.[9] The consequences include very high rates of cross-generational sex involving younger women and older men. In this context, marriage does not generally protect women from domestic and sexual violence. Unequal gender relations and biased gender norms also prevent women from freely gaining access to information, obtaining treatment for sexual infections, and negotiating safer sex.[10] If Papua New Guinean society as a whole is to develop, there is clearly an urgent need for dialogue to question dominant, destructive values, and to consider more humane values and attitudes within the culture that can provide a model for more equitable relations between women and men.

■ Power, Gender, and Security: Opening a Dialogue

At the heart of violence against women and other forms of insecurity suffered by women is male power and domination. Statistics from research as well as anecdotal accounts and everyday observation bear out the fact that perpetrators of violence against women are mostly men, and that these acts of violence are instigated and perpetuated by those who seek to control women with whom they have close personal relationships or social interactions. The demand to exercise "power over" another person demonstrates a dominant-subordinate relationship. These hierarchically ordered human interactions pave the way for continuing insecurity in the lives of women and filter into public affairs of the state and public institutions. The exercise of power in this manner is evident in the national political life of Papua New Guinea (the public sphere) as well as in marital and other informal social relations (the private sphere).

Power that is exercised as "power over" others is detrimental to integral human development and all other related forms of positive development. Nondomineering and nonhierarchical power relations that value equitable partnerships between various (sometimes contending/competing) stakeholders, and that value mutual respect, are more in accord with Papua New Guinea's national goal for all citizens to have equal opportunities to participate in and benefit from development.

As long as power relations remain significantly hierarchical and unequal in both the private and public realms of life, current high levels of disorder and instability will continue to cause problems for development and security in Papua New Guinea. At the domestic, community, and national levels of society, a shift is needed to a more participatory, consensual, and reconciliatory model of decisionmaking. Such models of decision-making have a strong basis in the Melanesian context.

Achieving integral human development presents the challenge of reconstructing the Papua New Guinean national identity in a fast-changing world. This will involve maintaining aspects of traditional culture that Papua New Guineans value and that are compatible with global standards for humanity, as envisaged in all the universal human rights principles.[11] This does not mean an uncritical acceptance of all external and global concepts and philosophies, but rather means being flexible and open-minded in meeting this challenge. Problems that emerge from this process should be seen as further challenges with which Papua New Guineans need to constructively engage. A continuing and peaceful discourse on ideas and experiences should pave the way for better understanding of the country's diverse cultures. A holistic approach to life, valuing both the human and the natural environment, is the essence of integral human development. Material and technological progress, for instance, should be carefully considered, its advantages and disadvantages weighed against values that people themselves choose to adopt.

If Papua New Guineans are to engage in discussion about and activity in the direction of development and security, and the values underlying them, it should occur not only in parliament and the national press, but also in local communities. If more participatory, consensual, and reconciliatory models of decisionmaking, based in Melanesian practices, are to be fostered, there must be engagement in local communities, where people have at least some access to decisionmaking.

■ Promoting Women's Participation in Decisionmaking

Appalling underrepresentation of women in decisionmaking is an indicator of and a factor contributing to poor governance in Papua New Guinea. Without greater participation of women in governance, their experiences of violence, their views about peace and development, will not be reflected in policies and their implementation. In contrast to the national level, in the villages, where most Papua New Guineans live, it is women who undertake most community development. It is women who to a very significant extent are the victims of violence, who suffer extreme, life-constricting insecurity in ways that certainly affect the bases of development and prosperity of the nation. And it is often women's organizations that are active at the grassroots level, mobilizing against high levels of violence. Affirmative action backed by legal and political reforms to increase the number of women in parliament as well as in the public service is an urgent task for Papua New Guinea. In this regard, Papua New Guinea could learn from the newly formed constitution of the country's Autonomous Region of Bougainville, which, partly in recognition of women's fundamental role in bringing peace to the region, guarantees women three seats in the regional parliament, establishes principles of fair representation for women on all key government bodies, and embeds consultation between the regional government and women's organizations.

In the wider community, more emphasis is required toward reorienting perceptions about gender roles and gender relations. Greater efforts to support female education and literacy would assist here. No doubt this is a daunting task, but "investing in women's and girls' education and health yield some of the highest returns of all development investments, including reduced rates of maternal mortality, better educated and healthier children, and increased household incomes."[12] Unless Papua New Guinea makes a start now, it may never see its first goal—integral human development—come to fruition.

■ Conclusion

Although slowly increasing in numbers, only a small minority of women in Papua New Guinea can effectively exercise real choice and have control over the decisions that affect their lives. Citizenship rights are beyond full realization for the majority of illiterate women, and society as a whole suffers the consequences in the long term, with very limited capacity to improve security and well-being.

Development agencies, international financial institutions, donor agencies, nongovernmental organizations, and other stakeholders in civil society must be cognizant of unequal power relations as the fundamental underlying issue to address in the security and development nexus. Power relations that are based on the principles of inclusiveness, power sharing, and nonhierarchical forms of interaction (in social, cultural, political, and economic terms) are the only basis for finding solutions to reducing poverty in a fundamental way and bringing about security and peace, and more humane and sustainable development.

The underlying issue of unequal power relations, and the failure of respect that is part of it, also needs to be addressed by Papua New Guinean people at every level of society. That is, it needs to be addressed in national leadership and government, by mechanisms such as extensions of the leadership code already in place, but also by opening the way for much greater representation of women in parliament and in government, and by instituting principles of consultation with women's organizations and other civil society organizations. Unequal power relations need to be addressed in the workplace and in education. They particularly must be addressed at the village level, in community development. Investing in community development—safe water, better roads, better access to basic services—will help to empower women in Papua New Guinea, and empowering women will in turn contribute to the basis for development and security.

▓ Notes

1. Kofi Annan, Secretary-General of the United Nations, "Ten Years After Beijing: Call for Peace," address to the Arab Regional Conference, Beirut, 8 July 2004, available at http://www.un.org/apps/sg/sgstats.asp?nid=1017 (accessed 4 July 2006).

2. *Constitution of the Independent State of Papua New Guinea,* Constitutional Laws Library, Port Moresby, available at http://www.paclii.org/pg/legis/consol_act/cotisopng534 (accessed 11 July 2006).

3. The United Nations Development Programme's Human Development Index is calculated using an aggregation of international data measuring factors such as life expectancy, literacy rates, health measurements, school enrollment, and gross domestic product per capita.

4. UNDP, *Human Development Indicators for Papua New Guinea, 2003;* AusAID, "Poverty Reduction Analysis," p. 16; Jacka, "Papua New Guinea," p. 45.

5. Jacka, "Papua New Guinea," pp. 29, 45.

6. S. Garap, cited in Jacka, "Papua New Guinea," p. 45; Toft, *Domestic Violence in Papua New Guinea;* Dinnen, *Law and Order in a Weak State.*

7. Kaman, "Peace Studies as a Process of Peace Building," p. 317. See also UNICEF, *Children and HIV/AIDS in Papua New Guinea.*

8. UNICEF, *Children and HIV/AIDS in Papua New Guinea.*

9. UNDP, *National Strategic Plan on HIV/AIDS in PNG.*

10. Ibid.

11. The Universal Declaration of Human Rights is the global goal and benchmark of human rights. The first paragraph of the preamble to the declaration proclaims: "the recognition of the inherent dignity and of the equal and inalienable rights of all members of the human family is the foundation of freedom, justice and peace in the world." Of the thirty articles of the declaration, Articles 3–5, 16, 18–19, 22, and 25–26 are of direct relevance to the meaning of security and development pursued in this chapter (see http://www.un.org/Overview/rights.html, accessed 30 January 2007). Papua New Guinea is also a signatory to the International Convention on the Elimination of All Forms of Discrimination Against Women (see http://www.un.org/womenwatch/daw/cedaw.htm, accessed 30 January 2007) and is also a signatory to the Convention on the Rights of the Child (see http://www.unhchr.ch/html/menu3/b/k2crc.htm, accessed 30 January 2007). In reality, much remains to be done by the government of Papua New Guinea to fulfill its obligations under these conventions.

12. AusAID, "Australian Aid," p. 22.

4

Police Reform
in Papua New Guinea

Abby McLeod

VARIOUSLY DESCRIBED as a "weak state," a "basket case," a state "on the brink," and a potential "rogue state," Papua New Guinea has long been renowned for its lack of social, economic, and political stability, rendering it a key member of the "arc of instability," which encompasses the "unstable" Melanesian states.[1] Internal media reports confirm external perceptions of a country besieged by crime, reporting on a daily basis tales of social disorder. In addition to problems of generalized crime, Papua New Guinea has already undergone one major crisis, namely the Bougainville civil war (1989–1997, discussed in Chapter 5), and occurrences of tribal warfare are regular in the Highland region.

High levels of disorder in some (though not all) regions of the country enjoy a circular relationship with the operation of basic state and social services. In part, they reflect state inability to provide sufficient health, education, and policing services, and the weakness of the relationship between state and society; but violence also further undermines the provision of those services and can act as a significant disincentive to investment and economic activity. Improving law and order in Papua New Guinea has thus become a priority for those engaged (both externally and internally) in the promotion of security and development.

This chapter examines challenges to police reform in Papua New Guinea—an issue of central importance to the promotion of security and development, and one that demonstrates the complexities involved in the simultaneous promotion of social order and development. Particular emphasis is placed on the disjunction between internal and external perceptions of and responses to conflict, following the argument that external attempts to promote development and "peace" in Papua New Guinea will succeed only when local notions of social order are accommodated (if not accepted).

The chapter begins with a contextual overview of Papua New Guinea, providing background information on law and order in the country, including the dimensions, posited causes, and responses to crime. It next discusses notions of social order in Papua New Guinea, outlining the colonial process and the means through which local ideas of social order were challenged by the imposition of Western notions of right and wrong. The Royal Papua New Guinea Constabulary (RPNGC) is also examined, as are the challenges of police reform in an environment of intense legal pluralism. Finally, the chapter offers suggestions for future action.

▓ Papua New Guinea: The Context

Like other Pacific Island countries, Papua New Guinea is a young state, having obtained independence in 1975. While the Germans ruled the north of the island from 1884 to 1920, the British ruled the south of the island from 1884 to 1904, at which point Australia assumed responsibility for the latter. In 1921 the former German colony of New Guinea became a mandated territory of the League of Nations administered by Australia, and after World War II the two territories were administered jointly until independence in 1975. While the British, and later the Australians, sought to control Papua primarily in the interests of defense, the Germans claimed New Guinea in attempts to expand their empire.

Papua New Guinea is characterized by extreme diversity, with over 800 distinct language and cultural groups. The population is currently estimated at 5.6 million and is widely dispersed over rough geographical terrain, including highland, lowland, and island areas. Approximately 85 percent of people are semisubsistence farmers who live in rural areas, where they produce food and cash crops such as coffee, oil palm, copra, and cocoa on their own land.[2] While living conditions vary greatly throughout the nineteen provinces of the country, in most areas of Papua New Guinea the government fails to deliver basic services such as education and health adequately, nor can it maintain law and order.

Despite the absence of reliable crime statistics, scholarly research suggests that *raskolism* (a Papua New Guinean Pidgin word for "juvenile gang crime") white-collar crime, sexual violence, domestic violence, sorcery, and electoral violence feature frequently in contemporary Papua New Guinean life.[3] In a recent survey of community perceptions of the police, 38 percent of respondents (most of whom were in Port Moresby) claimed to have been victims of crime, the most common crimes being car-jacking and breaking and entering.[4]

While no single explanation can account for problems of crime in Papua New Guinea, rising crime rates have been situated against a background of school dropouts and unemployment, the legalization of alcohol, urbanization, public anomie, and rebellion.[5] Beginning with the Morgan Report in 1983, a causal relationship between modernization and crime has been posited frequently, with urban drift, population expansion, uneven development, unemployment, and the loss of tradition being advanced as explanations for rising crime rates. More generally, proponents of the nationalist perspective have attributed the rise in all types of crime to the inapplicability of foreign laws to the emerging nation and to the inability of the developing state to enforce its political will.[6]

Approaches to law and order in Papua New Guinea have undergone a number of shifts since independence. Most significant, while early approaches to crime-control emphasized "getting tough," since the 1984 release of the Clifford Report, a more central role for the community in the maintenance of law and order has been proposed.[7] This approach has become a key feature of law and order discourse in Papua New Guinea, particularly under Australian-supported programs, and has gained further impetus from the restorative justice movement, which posits a more participatory dispute resolution process for victims, offenders, and their communities. Accompanying the growing awareness of the misfit between "formal" and "informal" mechanisms of social control has been an increasing acknowledgment of the weakness of the state and its consequent inability to effectively maintain social order. Attempts to address the state's inability to maintain social order have been made through capacity building, the strengthening of interagency communication, and sectorwide approaches to operational, planning, and budget coordination, all of which are thought to enhance the state's operational and policymaking functions.[8]

In the twenty-five years following independence, Australia provided Papua New Guinea with 540 million Australian dollars (A\$) for the purposes of institutional strengthening, capacity building, economic reform, and strengthening the rule of law, focusing primarily on the law and justice sector and in particular, the police force.[9] In addition to significant support to the police, assistance has also been provided to the courts, prisons, the ombudsman, and the public legal services, to make their operations more transparent and accountable. While law and justice assistance has been targeted primarily at the state, recently the Community Justice Liaison Unit (CJLU) was established under the Law and Justice Sector Program (LJSP) to help bridge the gap between state and society. Collectively, these activities are perceived as fundamental to the reduction of poverty and the achievement of sustainable development.

In the wake of the 11 September 2001 and 2002 Bali bombing incidents, heightened concerns over regional security resulted in notable shifts in Australian engagements with the Pacific region. Beginning with the Australian-led Regional Assistance Mission to the Solomon Islands (RAMSI), an explicitly interventionist stance replaced the "light footstep" approach that had characterized much recent assistance to the region.

In keeping with the interventionist approach, on 30 June 2004 the governments of Australia and Papua New Guinea signed a treaty establishing the Enhanced Cooperation Program (ECP), committing an additional A$800 million to Papua New Guinea over a five-year period for the police-led initiative. Under this program, it was anticipated that in-line personnel would be placed in central government agencies (including legal, economic, and financial specialists), and that approximately 230 Australian police officers would be seconded to the Royal Papua New Guinea Constabulary, where they would hold line positions in Port Moresby, Lae, Mt. Hagen, the Highlands Highway, and Bougainville. Significantly, on 13 May 2005, the Supreme Court of Papua New Guinea declared the ECP's enabling legislation unconstitutional, leading to the rapid withdrawal of the policing component.

Despite acknowledgment that the reach of the state in Papua New Guinea is limited, the ECP focuses attention once again on the state, rather than the community. Fortunately, the LJSP operates simultaneously alongside the ECP, a central component of which is the previously mentioned CJLU. While these programs will inevitably assist in efforts to reduce problems of social disorder, the issues that have impeded the efficacy of previous attempts to address law and order problems continue, namely that the state is responsible for enforcing laws that contradict the notions of right and wrong held by many state employees.

More specifically, while the modern concept of statehood tasks the state with a monopoly over the use of violence (hence criminalizing the use of violence by nonstate agents), throughout Papua New Guinea violence continues to be seen as a legitimate form of remedy under locally prescribed circumstances—a situation that is slowly changing in response to the gravity of violent acts undertaken with modern weapons, including guns. This disjunction itself cannot be seen as a cause of violence, but it severely undercuts attempts to control crime through the formal criminal justice system. In order to understand this disjunction, a brief overview of local notions of social control and the colonial process is warranted.

▪ Social Order and the Colonial Process

Upon arrival in Papua and New Guinea, colonists were confronted with hundreds of semiautonomous social groups possessing many of the characteristics often attributed to "stateless" societies, namely leaders with influence rather than authority, social orders in which the natural and supernatural worlds were intricately intertwined, and integrated political, social, religious, and economic systems that lacked specialized functions.[10] In the absence of a specialized system of police, courts, and prisons dedicated to the maintenance of "law and order," Papua New Guinean societies lacked the concept of "crime" as a transgression against the state, with wrongs being committed against people, property, and the supernatural order, rather than against an acknowledged authority.[11] As highlighted by Peter Lawrence, the presence or absence of the concept of crime impinges directly on the aims of dispute resolution, with state societies focusing upon the administration of abstract impartial justice, and stateless societies seeking the reparation of social relations.[12]

"Pacification" and "civilization" were necessary prerogatives of the German, British, and Australian administrations, and were similarly pursued via the armed patrol. The armed patrol was led by an officer known as a *kiap* (a European agent of colonization), accompanied by local men who served as carriers, police, bodyguards, and interpreters. In assuming a multiplicity of roles, the *kiap* epitomized the colonial approach, which was generalist rather than specialist.[13] The *kiap* was the executive, judiciary, and law enforcer all in one, exercising administrative rather than legal justice alongside everyday administrative tasks such as census taking, road construction, and political education. "Pacification," which initially entailed the curtailment of tribal warfare and the establishment of the government's monopoly over the use of violence, was said to be complete when the majority of people assisted the police and brought wrongdoers to the *kiap*.[14]

Law was perhaps the primary means through which colonial administrators sought to dominate local Papua New Guineans. Through the imposition of foreign notions of social order, it was believed that with increasing exposure to the administration, locals would eventually progress toward a more "civilized" existence. The notion of "order" imposed by the administration was based upon a homeostatic view of society, in which violence was antithetical to order, and war and interpersonal violence were perceived as dysfunction rather than normality.

The holding of *kiap* courts (assisted by government-appointed local officials) was central to the extension of control, as these courts punished locals for engaging in behaviors that were found acceptable under local custom, and altered existing modes of dispute resolution. Most obvious, self-help mechanisms such as warfare and revenge killings (which were previously activated in response to grievance) were deemed criminal offenses, and those who engaged in these activities were incarcerated, thus acquainting local peoples with the notion of "crime" as a transgression against the administration. The criminalization of violent acts presented the most blatant cleavage between local and administrative approaches to social order, whereby violence was deemed criminal by the administration yet acceptable or unacceptable to local peoples depending on the circumstances and social relationships involved in individual acts. Add to the equation the influence of missionaries, and the situation became one of intense legal pluralism, in which local, church, and colonial rules coexisted.

Criminal offenses were dealt with in accordance with the Queensland

Criminal Code, while less serious offenses were dealt with in accordance with the Native Regulations (1889) in Papua and the Native Administration Regulations (1924) in New Guinea.[15] In both territories, there were dualistic systems of justice, with misdemeanors and conflicts involving expatriate residents being dealt with by a different system of justice. In 1966, the Local Courts Ordinance (1963) was implemented, with a view to creating a unitary and specialized system of justice.

With the move away from informal administrative justice came the formalization of the court system, and the wholesale importation of Western laws and rules of admission and procedure. In particular, Western rules of procedure disallowed the hearing of evidence that was not directly related to the case, ignoring the "traditional" Melanesian practice of "airing the talk" or digging out the root of a problem. In denying litigants the opportunity to fully air their grievances, the local courts failed to offer litigants a true sense of closure, and tensions over the root of problems that came before the courts often remained unchecked.[16] Furthermore, in contrast to local mediation procedures that sought to restore social relations, Western adjudication procedures emphasized the notion that while one disputant wins, the other loses.[17]

Alongside the imported system of courts, Western-style policing in Papua New Guinea began with the Armed Native Constabulary (1890) in Papua, followed by a number of police forces, including the Royal Papuan Constabulary (1939), the Royal Papua and New Guinea Constabulary (1955), and the Royal Papua New Guinea Constabulary (1965). During the colonial era, "native" police provided a strong physical presence on which colonial administrators relied heavily. Local policemen (there were no policewomen until after independence) were selected primarily on the basis of physique and character, receiving training that emphasized physical conditioning rather than scholastic development. With force being the order of the day, local policemen were sanctioned to use armed force where necessary, often for the purposes of expediting submission.[18] Colonial police were hence primarily "pacifiers," operating within a militaristic framework that viewed the community with suspicion.

In response to increasing lawlessness and the desire to overturn several decades of foreign legal domination, law reform achieved great prominence on the preindependence agenda. The Constitutional Planning Committee was established in 1972 to oversee the preparation of the constitution, and the Law Reform Commission was established under the constitution to investigate matters of law reform. The reports and plans of the immediate preindependence period are dominated by nationalistic rhetoric and illustrate the desire of Papua New Guineans to affect a definite break with colonial institutions. Phrases such as "commitment to Papua New Guinean ways," "power from the people for the people," and "homegrown" clearly highlight the direction in which the powers of the day were attempting to guide the people of their country.[19] However, despite vociferous preindependence nationalist rhetoric, the modern nation-state of Papua New Guinea inherited much from its colonial predecessors, including the Western legal structures that were established during the closing phase of the colonial era, namely a formal hierarchical court system (including village courts), correctional institutions, and a police force.

Since independence there has been continuous debate about the appropriateness of these institutions to Papua New Guinea, yet such debate has not been seriously entertained in the context of donor-driven institutional strengthening projects—an admittedly difficult task. Of all law and justice sector agencies, the Royal Papua New Guinea Constabulary has a particularly problematic reputation, despite having received substantial support from the Australian government. As the longest-running bilateral aid project in Papua New Guinea, the RPNGC Development Project provides keen insights into the difficulties entailed in attempting to strengthen an institution that is at odds with the society in which it operates. In particular, the RPNGC Development Project highlights the ongoing relevance of local notions of social order (albeit changing notions) to state institutions, hence providing insights of relevance to public sector reform more generally.

■ The Royal Papua New Guinea Constabulary: Challenges to Reform

The RPNGC, constituted under the Police Act of 1988, is commanded by the commissioner of police and currently has a funded strength of 5,250 members (although the authorized establishment is 6,300). In addition to the regular constabulary (which includes 14 mobile squads), the RPNGC employs reserve police, who are typically part-time employees of other companies. The reserve police, of whom there are approximately 2,000, are paid a small monthly salary to assist the regular police, and posses the same powers and functions. Unlike regular and reserve police, auxiliary police (approximately 3,500) have geographically bound powers and, while initially intended to work in rural areas, they now work in both urban and rural areas. Both reserve and auxiliary police can be found in the employ of private sector organizations throughout the country, for which they provide security services. In addition to police personnel, a handful of civilians (approximately 3 percent of the constabulary's strength) are employed by the RPNGC.

With a population of over 5 million (based on projections), the police-to-population ratio is currently estimated at 1:1,121, substantially under the UN's recommended ratio of 1:450. While many people associate contemporary law and order problems with Papua New Guinea's low police-to-population ratio, the Public Sector Reform Management Unit suggests that "the current number of police is not itself a cause of under-performance. It is the way that the members of the force are deployed, trained, utilized and supported that has the greatest impact on performance."[20] For example, while nearly half of the country's serious reported crimes occur in Port Moresby, only approximately 8.5 percent of police are stationed there, demonstrating the constabulary's failure to adapt to the changed conditions wrought by extensive urban migration. In addition, despite common calls for a more visible police presence throughout the country, approximately a third of regular police are engaged in nonoperational duties.

Government commitment to the RPNGC is minimal, with inadequate annual budgets severely curtailing its ability to fulfill its primary functions. The majority of police members occupy barracks that verge on being condemned, and basic operational costs, such as for uniforms, vehicles, fuel, stationery supplies, and communications, are unable to be met by government funding. Police members receive a regular (albeit inadequate) salary, yet frequently face extensive delays in obtaining allowances and entitlements, as do pensioners for whom the constabulary is responsible. Despite these difficulties, the constabulary's budget for 2005 was approximately 10 percent less than the 2004 budget. This does little to engender improved constabulary relations with other law and justice sector agencies, which are seen as competitors for diminishing government funding.

The RPNGC faces a number of challenges, most of which constabulary members acknowledge themselves. These challenges include cultural misfit, discipline, poor community relations, gender issues, poor work performance, and overreliance on punitive policing, as outlined below.

The issue of cultural misfit between Papua New Guinean notions of right and wrong and the Western-introduced legal justice system lies at the heart of multiple RPNGC difficulties. While sworn officers are fully cognizant of their organizational obligations, RPNGC members are first and foremost Papua New Guineans who hold beliefs that conflict with the criminal code that they are paid to uphold. For example, the notion of "impartial justice" is at odds with Papua New Guinean assessments of wrongdoing, whereby the structural relationship between victim and offender is central to the adjudication of wrongdoing; domestic violence is an acceptable form of punitive action against errant wives; adultery is a more grievous offense than murder; the death of a clansman necessitates retaliation; rape of a woman is a transgression of a man's property rights; the list goes on. Hence, while readily identifiable problems such as lack of resources, poor management, and discipline may be responsible for the constabulary's relatively poor performance, so too is the fact that members of the constabulary are required to enforce laws that conflict openly with their internal beliefs and external (to the constabulary) social obligations.

Wantokism (giving preference to speakers of the same language) provides a particularly strong example of the disjunction between the formal (and supposedly impartial) legal justice system and Papua New Guinean sociality. To outsiders, decisions made on the basis of *wantokism* appear to constitute blatant favoritism, and foreign observers frequently render the *wantok* system synonymous with nepotism, clientelism, and corruption (all of which do occur and are often indistinguishable from *wantokism*). Describing the system as such, however, merely refers to the effects of the system, rather than those aspects of the system that serve to perpetuate its existence. For example, it is important to understand that a host of beliefs motivate Papua New Guineans to favor one's *wantoks* in the workplace, including fear of sorcery, fear of unpopularity among one's own people, and fear of group exile. In policing, the *wantok* system affects not only workplace decisions such as rostering, training opportunities, promotion, and access to resources, but also the ways in which the police interact with both criminals and victims. As the *wantok* system constitutes a social security network for the people of a language group (some of whom are police, some of whom are victims, and some of whom are offenders), it is fundamentally antithetical to the notion of impartial justice. This is a significant impediment to reform and one that is strongly rooted in Melanesian cultures throughout the South Pacific. However, if our interest is reform, it is the causes (or internal logic) rather than the effects of *wantokism* to which we should turn immediately.

The impact of culture on the workplace—alongside other factors such as organizational allegiance and reluctance to "whistle blow"—can also be seen in the constabulary's poor discipline record. Under the Police Act, members of the constabulary can be charged with either minor or serious disciplinary offenses. However, the relationship between decisionmakers and wrongdoers (often couched in terms of *wantokism*) seriously impacts both investigation and prosecution, resulting in few incentives for good workplace performance. The consumption of alcohol on duty, being absent without leave, the misuse of police property (particularly vehicles), and police brutality are among the most common offenses committed by police, with litigation against the RPNGC costing the state approximately 25 million kina (K) annually.[21] A recent report suggested the creation of an external body to monitor police behavior, a call that is supported by the majority of police.[22]

Primarily as a result of poor police discipline, public confidence in the police is minimal. A recent report by the RPNGC Development Project, Phase III, showed that 78 percent of respondents to a survey on community perceptions of the police felt that the police did not act in a disciplined manner while on duty.[23] While 75 percent of respondents claimed that they would report a crime to the police, people cited fear of police brutality, slow response times, bribery, and lack of follow-up as disincentives to reporting.

Furthermore, there is widespread belief that police services are no longer free, with police responding only to complaints for which financial or material recompense is offered (which in some cases is genuinely necessary; e.g., in the case that police vehicles have no fuel).

Reserve and auxiliary police, who often act unsupervised, are claimed to be particularly guilty of disciplinary breaches. Despite the obvious lack of public confidence and trust in the police, it is noteworthy that Papua New Guineans see an ongoing role for the police in the maintenance of law and order, and that they continue to interact with the police, regardless of their reservations. This stands in stark contrast to popular calls for a return to "traditional" ways and rejection of the state.

Gender issues are of concern to both community members and women working within the constabulary. With only 5.4 percent of regular police being women, female members of the public are often reluctant to report to the police for fear of having to deal with a policeman who will not take them seriously (particularly in the case of domestic violence). Within the police force, policewomen are concentrated in the lower ranks, with only six commissioned women officers in 2007. This may be largely attributed to inequitable access to training and promotions, although the introduction of an equal employment opportunity policy and merit-based promotion policy has partially addressed this inequity. Policewomen are denied equal access to major operational duties (such as electoral security) and police resources (particularly vehicles), and suffer from frequent sexual harassment in the workplace. While the position of women in the RPNGC has improved in recent years, attempts to empower policewomen are extremely complicated in light of men's resentment of women's changing social position in contemporary Papua New Guinea, a factor that heavily impacts married policewomen, whose husbands prevent them from work-related travel and punish rather than encourage them for good work performance.

As a result of their inequitable workplace status, policewomen are often poor performers, as are policemen who feel discouraged by the environment in which they work. Generally, morale is incredibly low, a problem that is widely attributed to poor living conditions, lack of incentive for achievement, lack of resources necessary for job completion, lack of management, and lack of disciplinary disincentives. Despite being well trained (as a result of training projects), RPNGC personnel demonstrate little interest in transferring newly acquired skills to the workplace, a reluctance that may be associated with a host of factors, including fear of jealousy (in the event that one performs well), lack of management and supervision, and lack of opportunities. Poor performance is manifest in a variety of ways, most publicly in the constabulary's poor rates of arrest and prosecution. For example, while approximately 80 percent of arrests are for minor offenses, "nationally, there is a better than even chance of not being arrested for a major crime," with an almost two in three chance of not being arrested, providing little disincentive to criminals in Port Moresby.[24]

The constabulary is best known for its highly punitive and reactive methods of policing, which are clearly at odds with the proactive, community policing model (emphasizing positive relations between police and communities) by which it professes to abide. While there is little doubt that the original impetus toward community policing emanated from the RPNGC Development Project rather than the constabulary, there now appears to be some commitment to community policing from within the RPNGC. This commitment, however, is not widespread, and community policing, as in other countries, suffers from internal perceptions that it constitutes "soft policing," hence mitigating members' willingness to employ community policing techniques. In light of resource inadequacies and community calls for community police visits, there is some indication that community policing is gaining favor among members, and there are some areas of Papua New Guinea in which communities and the police are working together relatively well (e.g., certain regions of East New Britain and Central provinces). Community policing, however, has yet to become a constabulary-wide ethos.

The need for police reform in Papua New Guinea has been long recognized. The RPNGC has been receiving Australian support in the form of the RPNGC Development Project since 1989, prior to which Australian police officers were involved in the ad hoc provision of specialist training for RPNGC officers and many RPNGC officers undertook placements with Australian state forces. Conducted in three distinct phases, the last of which concluded in February 2005, the RPNGC Development Project delivered capacity-building and institutional-strengthening initiatives using advisers drawn primarily from the Australian and New Zealand police forces. In addition, the project engaged various civilian advisers in the areas of human resources, information technology, infrastructure support, and gender and development. Advisers provided support and guidance to immediate counterparts and have not held in-line positions, in contrast to the recent interventionist approach of the ECP.

Despite the differing foci of each phase, a number of key areas received consistent attention since 1989, including fraud and anticorruption, prosecutions, community policing (since 1993), corporate planning, information management, human resources, logistics and infrastructure, leadership and management, training, finance, discipline, general duties, and gender. As the various phases of the RPNGC Development Project were designed primarily with reference to outputs rather than outcomes, it is difficult to assess the impact of the project on the RPNGC and on Papua New Guinea more generally. However, some brief comments on the project are warranted.

At the most basic level, the RPNGC Development Project essentially sustained the constabulary for a number of years. Hence, while the performance of the constabulary may be questionable, without the project a number of constabulary functions (e.g., training and recruitment) would have simply ceased to exist. Obviously, the external funding of basic constabulary functions raises the critical question of sustainability and demonstrates the need for long-term partnerships based on a "whole of government" approach (working across the organizational boundaries of bureaucracy), an issue that is partially addressed by the ECP.

In hindsight, it is clear that RPNGC Development Project personnel were severely constrained by lengthy reporting requirements, which prevented them from interacting with RPNGC personnel in a responsive manner. Furthermore, it appears that the discontinuity between phases and the high rates of adviser turnover may have mitigated positive project impacts. Despite these hindrances, however, improvements have been made in most areas addressed by the project. Among other improvements, fraud-case conviction rates have improved significantly, successful prosecutions have increased, a corporate planning process is in place, the position of policewomen has improved, and a standardized system of crime statistics has been implemented.

In the case of the RPNGC, as with other public sector agencies, it would be foolhardy to equate sustainability solely with project design, as sustainability is highly dependent on a host of factors, including improved government support of the RPNGC and the retention of key RPNGC personnel. Clearly, the sustainability of all externally driven change is dependent on local ownership of and commitment to change. In the case of the constabulary, corruption means that high-level personnel stand to gain from the lack of discipline and accountability, hence changes that challenge the status quo will be difficult. Moreover, cultural and institutional misfit, political instability resulting in a high turnover of ministers and commissioners, a high degree of cultural diversity that complicates replication, and the constant transfers of personnel will pose further challenges to ongoing reforms within the RPNGC.

The form of future assistance to the police remains unclear following the completion of the RPNGC Development Project in February 2005 and the removal of the ECP police contingent in May 2005. However, it is apparent that there will be a substantial decrease in advisers dedicated solely to the RPNGC, from approximately twenty-two to less than ten. This will impact heavily on the constabulary, which will lose personnel who have decades of experience; institutional memory will no doubt flounder.

▣ Disentangling Law and Order Reform

Papua New Guinean perceptions of law and order reform differ greatly. Despite popular calls for a return to Melanesian forms of governance and social control, calls for the return of the *kiaps*—the European agents of colonization—are similarly prevalent. Such calls are framed against a romanticized past in which tribal fighting was controlled, medical care and education were comparatively accessible, and roads were constructed and well maintained. This romantic notion, however, when closely examined, is littered by tales of domination and the destruction of "traditional" values. The fluctuation between these ideas about a "golden past" and a period of domination are highly significant in the current context, in which people simultaneously desire and reject the need for Australian intervention in Papua New Guinea.

One could easily interpret the apparent eagerness of some Papua New Guineans for Australian Federal Police (AFP) intervention as an indication that Papua New Guineans and Australians conceive of police reform in a similar way. While it is undeniably the case that Australians and Papua New Guineans seek the same basic outcome, namely improved law and order in Papua New Guinea (albeit for different reasons), experience suggests that the cultural means of achieving that outcome differ greatly. Indeed, conversations with several serving members of the RPNGC suggest that their willingness to work alongside AFP personnel relates not to a desire to be mentored or to benefit from skills transfer, but rather to a desire to access the material wealth that is associated with expatriate personnel.

The provision of donor assistance and the deployment of foreign police personnel certainly assisted in the increased provision of resources while foreign agents were in Papua New Guinea; however, the ability of the constabulary to sustain the provision of resources after their departure is dependent on whole of government reform, rather than on police reform alone. In this regard, the comprehensive scope of the Enhanced Cooperation Program is a step in the right direction, holding promise to effect more lasting changes than single-agency programs. However, unless ongoing attention to local involvement in management and decisionmaking processes is addressed throughout the ECP process, there is little hope of local ownership of reforms and hence of sustainability.

Further complicating the development of appropriate reform strategies, it is important to note that after fifteen years of police assistance, albeit in the form of advisory support, members of the RPNGC are incredibly donor savvy. This has led to a number of external appraisals of the RPNGC being misinformed, which is perhaps most obvious in relation to the purportedly low skill levels of RPNGC personnel. While literacy levels and basic education are low (given the previously minimal entry requirements of the RPNGC), in reality RPNGC personnel are highly trained in multiple policing functions and are highly skilled. The problem is not lack of skills, but rather lack of application due to a variety of circumstances, including logistical limitations, cultural misfit, low morale, inadequate leadership, fear of progressing, and the haphazard transfer of trained personnel into other operational areas. Additional training will only assist in the development of the police force if these problems are simultaneously addressed—a lesson of value to all attempts at public sector reform in Papua New Guinea.

■ Conclusion

The prevention and management of conflict in Papua New Guinea, and the subsequent development of the nation, are difficult tasks indeed. As outlined in this chapter, Papua New Guinea is a diverse country characterized by extreme pluralism of all forms, including legal pluralism. Significantly, in the relative absence of the state in much of Papua New Guinea, state law is the least powerful of many available regulatory systems, with local and church rules and sanctions being more meaningful to the majority of Papua New Guineans. This fact in itself sheds serious doubt on the potential of state-centered reforms, such as the infant police–led Enhanced Cooperation Program, to significantly affect ongoing problems of law and order. At the more particular level, the discussion of police reform illustrates the substantial difficulties of reforming an institution that holds little meaning for much of the country, including the personnel who populate the institution.

Despite the obvious complexities of police (and other) reform in Papua New Guinea, there is impetus for change from both within and beyond the police force. While local and state notions of social order continue to differ, changing social circumstances, in particular the prevalence of guns, have resulted in the reconfiguration of local conceptions of right and wrong. Consequently, while violence remains a socially acceptable means of conflict resolution in some situations, recognition that violence impedes personal and group well-being, as well as the country's development, is increasing, as demonstrated by the proliferation of community groups against violence. Significantly, the people of Papua New Guinea continue to posit a central role for the police and other institutions of the state in the maintenance of social order, while simultaneously engaging in creative efforts to manage conflict at the local level. Inherently, such dual engagements both emphasize and transform the disjunctions between state and society, as people struggle to make the workings of the state more meaningful in the local context.

Discussing the difficulties of Papua New Guinea's law and order situation demonstrates that there is no single formula, structure, or leadership style that can be applied to contemporary law and order problems. Furthermore, it is clear that for reform to be meaningful, the cultural complexities and nuances of both Papua New Guinea and the institutions themselves must be acknowledged. That is, reform must be conceived of as a contextually specific rather than generic enterprise. This necessitates ongoing dialogue among donor agencies, consultants, and recipients, with a view to the continuous modification of practice in response to local circumstances. Ultimately, genuine partnerships are necessary. The aim of development assistance for Papua New Guinea's policing ought not to be to transform the RPNGC and similar institutions into quasi-Australian law and order institutions, but rather to strengthen the structures that aid policing and other law and order functions—be they state or nonstate structures—in such a way that they are sustainable and meaningful to those who will be required to utilize them.

▓ Notes

1. ASPI, *Strengthening our Neighbour;* Hughes, "Aid Has Failed the Pacific," p. 2; Windybank and Manning, "Papua New Guinea on the Brink," p. 1.

2. Hanson et al., *Papua New Guinea Rural Development Handbook,* pp. 11–12.

3. On *raskolism,* see Goddard, "The Rascal Road"; Harris, *The Rise of Rascalism;* Dinnen, "Praise the Lord and Pass the Ammunition." On white-collar crime, see Maino, "Serious Economic Crime." On sexual violence, see Borrey, "Sexual Violence in Perspective"; Zimmer-Tamakoshi, "Wild Pigs and Dog Men"; Banks, "Contextualising Sexual Violence." On domestic violence, see Banks, "Deconstructing Violence in PNG"; Banks, *Women in Transition;* Toft and Bonnell, *Marriage and Domestic Violence in Rural Papua New Guinea;* Ranck and Toft, *Domestic Violence in Urban Papua New Guinea;* Toft, *Domestic Violence in Papua New Guinea;* Garap, "Struggles of Women and Girls"; Counts, "All Men Do It"; Scaglion, "Spare the Rod and Spoil the Woman?" On sorcery, see Knauft, *Good Company and Violence;* Aleck, "Law and Sorcery in Papua New Guinea." On electoral violence, see Dinnen, "Violence, Security, and the 1992 Election"; Dinnen, *Law and Order in a Weak State;* Standish, "Elections in Simbu."

4. RPNGC, "Report on Community Perceptions of the Police."

5. Government of Papua New Guinea, "Report of the Committee to Review Policy"; Biles, *Crime in Papua New Guinea.*

6. Kaputin, "The Law"; Narokobi, *The Melanesian Way.*

7. Clifford, Morauta, and Stuart, *Law and Order in Papua New Guinea.*

8. Law and Justice Sector Working Group, *The National Law and Justice Policy;* Papua New Guinea–Australia Development Cooperation Program, *Law and Justice Sector Review.*

9. AusAID, "The Contribution of Australian Aid," pp. xii–xiii.

10. Lawrence, "The State Versus Stateless Society."

11. Ibid. See also Dinnen, "Restorative Justice in PNG."

12. Lawrence, "The State Versus Stateless Society."

13. Dinnen, *Law and Order in a Weak State;* Gordon and Meggitt, *Law and Order in the New Guinea Highlands.*

14. Downs, *The Australian Trusteeship,* p. 99.

15. Chalmers and Paliwala, *An Introduction to the Law,* p. 97.

16. Strathern, "Legality or Legitimacy"; Strathern, "Report on Questionnaire Relating to Sexual Offences."

17. Roberts, *Order and Dispute,* p. 20.

18. Kituai, "My Gun, My Brother."

19. Government of Papua New Guinea, *Final Report of the Constitutional Planning Committee*.

20. PSRMU, "A Review of the Law and Justice Sector Agencies," p. 63.

21. Ibid., p. 8.

22. RPNGC, "Draft Report."

23. RPNGC, "Report on Community Perceptions of the Police."

24. PSRMU, "A Review of the Law and Justice Sector Agencies," p. 76.

5

Development and Conflict: The Struggle over Self-Determination in Bougainville

Anthony Regan

ECONOMIC DEVELOPMENT can be a source of tension and conflict in many parts of the world, especially where patterns of development are changing, and in the process can have significant impacts on control of scarce resources and power. However, there can be more complex linkages between development and conflict, including differences in perceptions of development and how it occurs.

This chapter illuminates the complexity of the relationship between development and conflict in Melanesia through reference to Bougainville, a reluctant part of the Southwest Pacific state of Papua New Guinea (PNG). Violent conflict occurred in Bougainville from late 1988 to 1997, its impacts including thousands of deaths and the closure of one of the world's largest copper and gold mines, which operated at Panguna, in the mountains of central Bougainville, from 1972 to 1989. The conflict is widely perceived as originating with the rejection by Bougainvilleans of the mine because of, among other things, its social and environmental impacts.

There is an extensive literature on what has become known as the "greed and grievance" debate—about whether political grievances or economic greed (or a combination of them) best explain how civil wars occur.[1] All of these explanations of civil wars are related to questions about the relationships between conflict and development. Grievance theories argue that various forms of resource or political deprivation cause civil wars, while the greed explanation argues that rebels are motivated by the "pursuit of self-interested material gain" derived from resources such as oil, diamonds, or timber.[2] Because differences over a major resource project were involved in the Bougainville conflict, there has been consideration of the relevance of these competing explanations,[3] the main conclusion being that neither explanation on its own was sufficient to understand the origins and course of the Bougainville conflict.

That is not to say, however, that differences related to economic development were not relevant to the Bougainville conflict. Rather, both the origins of the conflict and the way that it developed two main dimensions (a separatist dimension as well as a multifaceted and divisive internal conflict among Bougainvilleans) involved numerous complex and diverse strands. The complexity is such that it cannot be adequately reflected under either the greed or the grievance explanation alone. The diverse strands highlighted in this chapter reflect in part the extremely uneven impacts of over eighty years of economic change in Bougainville after direct colonial administration was established there in 1905. This in turn contributed to tensions and divisions among Bougainvilleans, in part related to growing economic inequality, but also in part to cultural factors and to the existence of quite different perceptions of development. All of these factors, as well as others such as the personalities of key actors, for example the leader of the Bougainville Revolutionary Army (BRA), Francis Ona, contributed to the origins of the conflict and shaped the way that it developed. Further, this is not to say that economic development was the sole factor in the origins of the conflict, an issue about which there are varied views.[4]

Despite the remarkable and continuing success of the peace process that ended the conflict in 1997, the reconstruction and redevelopment activities associated with the peace process have been a source of further tensions and conflict. The chapter concludes by briefly examining whether such tensions point to dangers of new cycles of violent conflict in Bougainville, suggesting that, paradoxically, the experience of violent conflict has encouraged the emergence of shared norms that may significantly reduce the risk of such tensions causing violence in the future.

■ The Context: Papua New Guinea and Bougainville

First settled almost 30,000 years ago,[5] Bougainville is named for the French explorer Louis de Bougainville, credited with being the first European to sight its main island, in 1768. About 1,000 kilometers (625 miles) east of PNG's capital, Port Moresby, Bougainville consists of two adjoining large islands (the main island of Bougainville and the much smaller Buka Island) separated by a narrow passage, and many smaller islands. Its 9,438 square kilometers (3,630 square miles) constitute about 2 percent of PNG's land area, and its approximately 200,000 people constitute about 4 percent of the national population of more than 5 million. Geographically, culturally, and linguistically, Bougainville is part of the Solomon Islands chain, and became part of PNG rather than the British colony of Solomon Islands as a result of the "accidents" of late-nineteenth-century colonial map-drawing.

Bougainville's people exhibit great linguistic and cultural diversity; there are about twenty-one distinct languages and many more sub-languages and dialects,[6] and considerable cultural diversity exists both within and between language groups. Significant differences exist in even the material culture and the diet of groups occupying different ecological niches—especially coastal, valley, and mountain.[7] There are also quite marked differences in culture even within some large language groups, and certainly between such groups. In general, language groups are not the primary basis for group identity, but rather much smaller groups determined by ecological niche, or separation by major physical boundaries.[8] In fact, Bougainville fits PNG's pattern of extreme cultural and linguistic diversity (with over 800 language groups in PNG). Indeed, the main distinction between Bougainvilleans and the people of all other parts of PNG is the much darker skin color of a large majority of the former. A sense of common identity, with skin color the primary marker, developed gradually among the diverse Bougainvillean language and culture groups during the twentieth century.

Bougainville's close contact with the outside world and its integration into PNG are relatively recent, even for Melanesia. A permanent Christian mission and colonial administrative post (under German New Guinea) were first established in 1901 and 1905, respectively, but some mountain groups on the north of Bougainville Island had almost no contact with colonial authorities until after World War II. Australia took control of German New Guinea, including Bougainville, in 1914. Relations between Bougainvilleans and colonial authorities and central government have often been troubled, in both colonial and postcolonial times (the latter starting in September 1975).

From the 1950s, identity politics developed in Bougainville, initially centered on grievances about colonial neglect. As resentment about the social and economic change associated with the imposition of the mine developed, Bougainvilleans increasingly singled out the influx of "outsiders" from elsewhere in PNG as the main cause for their problems. In the turbulent politics of the years leading to PNG's independence, there was increasing talk of secession from the rest of PNG, and considerable mobilization of political support by educated leaders around Bougainvillean identity.[9]

Precolonial social structures in Bougainville were based on small, localized landholding clan lineages that could link in various ways and for various purposes, but normally on a temporary basis. They were stateless societies, where stability was maintained in part by the principle of balanced reciprocity—the constant reinforcing of relationships through balanced exchanges. Most language and culture groups in Bougainville are matrilineal, with descent through females being a key principle of social organization, and with females also being the custodians of lineage land. While a male remains a member of his mother's lineage, upon marriage he ordinarily moves to his wife's land, and so usually makes limited use of his lineage's land. While matriliny contributes to women having relatively high status in most Bougainvillean societies, in many respects these societies are nevertheless patriarchal, with men tending to dominate public and political life. These same social structures continue to be the main social units today, but as we shall see, economic change since colonization has tended to undermine traditional authority and customary ways of doing things.

I have described elsewhere some other key features common to pre-colonial Bougainvillean social structures that help to explain some of the ways in which Bougainvilleans have responded to socioeconomic change:

- Highly egalitarian structures through which inequality can disturb social harmony.
- Balanced relationships through which violence can occur, but that usually result in action to restore balance, often through reconciliation ceremonies involving exchange of shell valuables, pigs, and the like.
- Land as a basis for social organization, with each lineage having a close relationship to its holdings. While there have been many internal migrations in Bougainville's almost 30,000 years of human occupation that have contributed to the complex webs of rights to land, all groups tend to recognize the importance of the rights of descendants of original owners of particular areas of land.[10]

■ Phases of Economic Development in Bougainville

Until the early nineteenth century, when whaling brought the first regular contact with Europeans for some coastal and small island communities, Bougainvilleans relied on a purely subsistence agricultural economy. While today perhaps 90 percent or more of Bougainvilleans continue to live at least semisubsistence lifestyles, a series of economic changes that began even before the establishment of direct colonial administrative rule in 1905 has brought dramatic changes to subsistence life and to precolonial social structures. These impacts have been variable, with people from Buka, the far north of Bougainville, and the central eastern coast around the German and (until 1942 and from the mid-1960s) Australian colonial center of Kieta having much more intensely experienced change, compared to many groups on the remote central and northwestern coast and in the mountains, who continue to have limited contact with the outside world today. It is possible here only to highlight some of the main phases and impacts of such change.[11]

From about 1870, young Bougainvillean men, especially from Buka and the far north of Bougainville, were recruited by "blackbirders"—labor recruiters for plantations elsewhere in the Pacific and in northern Australia,[12] a practice that also affected Vanuatu and the Solomon Islands (as discussed in Chapter 9). Then from the time German New Guinea was established in 1884, young Bougainvillean men—again predominantly from Buka and northern Bougainville—were recruited to work on plantations and for the colonial administration elsewhere in New Guinea. Those that returned to their homes (many who were "blackbirded" did not) were relatively wealthy in goods, and acutely aware of the difference in material wealth of Europeans compared to subsistence Bougainvilleans.

The establishment of the plantation economy in the early stages of German administration in Bougainville from 1905 saw the beginning of the cash economy, and a vast expansion in the range of European material goods available to Bougainvilleans. The numerous plantations, established mainly in fertile and relatively densely populated areas of Bougainville's east coast,[13] employed thousands of Bougainvilleans. They worked in part because of the need for cash to pay colonial "head tax," but also because of increasing dependence on Western goods. The plantation economy had many wider impacts,[14] but particularly the undermining of the previously preeminent economic roles of women (through men taking control of the new forms of wealth emerging from the cash economy), and also of the authority of traditional leaders. Laborers returning with both new forms of wealth and new experiences of a wider world were not always susceptible to such authority, and often competed with traditional leaders for the new forms of administrative and political authority made available by the colonial regime.[15]

It seems certain that the incredible scale of the World War II influx of Japanese, Americans, Australians, and others,[16] with their immense wealth (in terms of equipment and the like), had significant impacts on the Bougainvilleans with whom they came into contact. As most Bougainvilleans did not travel much beyond their area of birth, and so had limited direct experience of Europeans, this sudden and intense contact made many acutely conscious of the difference in material wealth between themselves and people from the industrialized societies. It also contributed to a sense of grievance about the very limited economic development achieved in Bougainville by the Australian administration in the immediate postwar years.

Change did occur, however, after World War II, in part through Australian war reparations, but also through considerable administrative effort to support Bougainvillean small-holder agricultural development. A range of cash-crop activities were promoted from the late 1940s.[17] War reparations, cash-cropping, and other commercial activities were leading to the emergence of some relatively wealthy Bougainvillean businessmen by even the early 1950s.[18]

From the early 1960s, growing income, derived from rapidly expanding village cultivation of cash crops, especially cocoa, brought growing socioeconomic change. By 1989, about 10,000 small-holders were producing over 18,000 metric tons (20,000 US tons) of cocoa valued at about 1,000 kina (K) per metric ton (K900 per US ton). The cocoa income contributed to growing economic inequality, mainly due to the persistence of customary social structures through which people obtained access to land. Evidence from the matrilineal Nagovisi area of southwest Bougainville gathered by Donald Mitchell in the 1970s and early 1980s illuminates how this occurred.[19] Before perennial cash crops were introduced, land was transferred slowly between the landowning clan-based lineages (mainly through mortuary arrangements) in cycles over several generations. At any point in such cycles, a lineage might have many members and be land-poor, or have few members and be land-rich. But so long as land was needed mainly for subsistence agriculture, there was ample land for all. However, the introduction of perennial tree crops, and especially cocoa, tended to "freeze" the traditional cycling of land. Members of small, land-rich lineages had much greater access to land for cocoa than did those of large, land-poor lineages. Indeed, by 1980 some members of lineages in the latter category were cutting down cocoa groves to provide land for subsistence gardens to newly married couples. There were also areas, including Siwai in southwest Bougainville, where a range of factors, including significant internal migration in the past, resulted in sizable populations with limited access to land. Where cocoa was the main source of revenue, such groups had few opportunities. James Tanis talks of wider impacts of the cocoa economy in Nagovisi in the 1980s, including land pressures (often resulting in disputes over ownership), changes in social relations as women sought to limit access of their brothers and their brothers' children to lineage land, and an increasingly individualistic culture, with reducing reliance on customary leadership and ways.[20]

Even greater economic and social change resulted from the activities of the giant Australian mining company Conzinc Riotinto Australia Limited, which in 1972, after eight years of development, began operating the huge, open-cut Panguna mine through its majority-owned subsidiary, Bougainville Copper Limited (BCL). Much has been written about the mine and its impacts,[21] and so only a few key points will be highlighted here.

In its seventeen years of operation (1972 to 1989) the mine had huge impacts on the economies of PNG generally and of Bougainville. For PNG, it contributed 16 percent of internal revenue and about 44 percent of export earnings. For Bougainville, it provided employment (between a third and a half of BCL's average of 4,000 employees were Bougainvilleans), other economic activity (there were about 200 businesses dependent on BCL, a number of them Bougainvillean-owned, and BCL spent tens of millions of kina per year locally on goods and services), and the limited share of mine revenue paid to members of lineages owning land that was subject to BCL's mining-related leases, and also to Bougainville's provincial government.

BCL's mining-related leases cut across the middle of Bougainville, about 50 kilometers (30 miles) from east coast to west coast. They covered 13,047 hectares (32,617 acres), about 1.5 percent of Bougainville, but only about one-third of that land was actually utilized. The leases included land for port and recreation facilities, a port-to-mine access road, the mine itself, and an extensive tailings disposal area. About 4,500 Bougainvilleans lived in the mining-related lease areas in the late 1980s. The land consisted of over 500 blocks, each owned by a local clan lineage.

The mine generated total revenues of K1.754 billion in its seventeen years of operation.[22] The distribution of cash benefits from the mine in the decade ending in 1987 involved "about 60 percent going to the national government (in taxes, fees and dividends) and 35 percent going to foreign shareholders; 5 percent went to the . . . Provincial Government [of Bougainville], and 0.2 percent went to local landowners in royalty payments."[23] Adding about K21 million paid in rents and compensation to owners of land in the mining-related leases, they received about 1.4 percent of total cash generated by BCL operations.

While the mine was the source of a range of grievances in Bougainville against both BCL and the PNG national government (which was itself a 20 percent shareholder in BCL), it also created tensions and divisions among Bougainvilleans. The mine was resented as an imposition for the economic benefit of the rest of PNG, with environmental and social costs for Bougainville, and with little financial return for either owners of land who were subject to mining-related leases or Bougainville as a whole. Environmental damage included destruction of land for the huge open-cut pit, and massive impacts on the river system, into which vast quantities of overburden and tailings were dumped daily. Social impacts included those perceived as flowing from the influx of as many as 15,000 people from elsewhere in PNG attracted by economic opportunities associated with the mine (and also by plantation employment).

The most direct impacts of the mine were on the landowners in the lease areas, especially those in the vicinity of the pit, many of whom had to relocate their villages. Some groups of owners expressed strong opposition to the establishment of the mine in the middle to late 1960s, but as it became clear that the mine would proceed, the main issue became the very low rates of compensation proposed by the colonial administration. Once vigorous protests by landowners had convinced the administration and BCL to pay much-improved land rents and compensation,[24] owners in the lease areas largely acquiesced, but many remained resentful of continuing impacts and the relatively small share of revenues and economic opportunities to which they had access.

Ongoing tensions and conflicts among owners of land in the lease areas were exacerbated by the way the colonial administration recorded ownership, by the quantity of rent and compensation paid by BCL, and by the way payments were made.[25] The implications of ownership by "corporate" matrilineal clan lineages were not understood by administration officials. Public hearings of the Land Titles Commission were held to determine boundaries and ownership of blocks, and whoever came forward at the hearings stating that he or she was the "title holder" was recorded as such if the members of the community present agreed—or acquiesced. The communities in the mountainous area around the mine had been a day's walk from the relatively developed areas on the nearby coast until the mine road was built (in the late 1960s), and very few spoke either English or Tok Pisin (the lingua franca in New Guinea). The process resulted in misunderstandings, and was open to manipulation. These being matrilineal societies, women were regarded as the custodians of lineage land (and still are today), yet many men were recorded as title holders. This was often done on the understanding that the men in question would represent the lineage, but it was sometimes in part the result of misunderstandings about what was involved in being recorded as title holders. In a number of cases, people later disputed the rights of individuals listed as title holders. Further, rent and compensation payments were made to those listed as title holders, in the expectation that they would distribute the money to those with links to the block who had any entitlements. In practice, there were often disputes about such entitlements, and so about distribution of the money. In a number of cases, it was said that senior men listed as title holders favored particular nieces and their families over others, leading to divisions within lineages. Finally, over the life of the mine, the population in the mine lease areas grew rapidly with the birth of many children in the early 1970s; by the late 1980s, the number of adults seeking a share of rent and compensation payments had greatly expanded. With amounts payable not expanding to keep pace with these growing demands, rifts developed between leaders of younger landowners and those of the older generation who were in charge of landowner organizations to which some forms of compensation were paid for long-term investment and limited distribution purposes.

Ironically, while mining-related lease owners were left resentful and divided by the revenue distribution, in other areas of Bougainville there was often resentment of what was seen as their relative wealth,[26] a factor that added to the overall tensions resulting from economic inequality.

■ Some Impacts of and Dynamics Arising from Economic Change

It is possible here only to highlight a few aspects of the varied impacts of and dynamics arising from the changes outlined above. First, people from

Buka, northern Bougainville, and the central eastern coast, all areas with relatively long periods of close contact with and education and employment by Europeans, had considerable advantage over people from more remote areas in terms of taking advantage of opportunities offered by economic change.[27] Second, people from inland valley and mountain areas had less experience of the outside world than did coastal peoples, even in the precolonial period, when coastal people traded often long distances, while inland people tended to stay very close to their place of birth.[28] With plantations, mission stations, and colonial administrative centers generally situated on the coast, inland people developed contacts with the outside world much more slowly than did some coastal people. People in the remote areas of the mountains and the west coast had limited opportunities even to participate in cash-crop activity due to transport and (in the case of high mountain areas in particular) disadvantages of climate. Third, the impacts of the mine on groups owning mining-related lease land were variable, with people from the east coast who had long experience of European "development" apparently more readily absorbing and adapting to the experience (including dealing with tensions resulting from the inequalities of the distribution of mining-related rents and compensation), without the "disintegrative" social impacts that apparently occurred for some mountain communities.[29]

Fourth, the emergence of wealthy Bougainvillean businessmen in the early 1950s, documented by Scott MacWilliam,[30] was the precursor of far more extensive economic inequality that began to develop by the 1980s, resulting from uneven access to land for cocoa plantations, exploitation of opportunities associated with the mine, and even the return in the 1970s and 1980s of retired well-educated people (especially people from Buka) from jobs elsewhere in PNG, who set up local businesses in various parts of Bougainville. Fifth, Bougainville was unique in PNG in achieving almost universal primary school education in the 1980s. At the same time, the availability of secondary schooling (especially the last two years of secondary schooling) was limited, and jobs and other economic opportunities were restricted. The matrilineal descent and landownership system of most language groups meant that young men had little access to land until they married and became well-established in relationships with their wife's lineage. So in the 1980s in Bougainville there was a considerable pool of semieducated young men with little opportunity or social status.

Finally, there was widespread resentment against the presence in Bougainville of large numbers of people from other parts of PNG. In part this came from a sense of difference and superiority related to the increasingly politicized sense of Bougainvillean identity, and to the associated phenomenon whereby outsiders were readily blamed for apparently increasing crime and other social problems. In fact, such problems had more to do with changes to social structures connected with economic change, in particular reduced salience of customary leadership, rather with than any other cause. Resentment of outsiders was also related to the fact that they were seen as competing with Bougainvilleans for employment and other opportunities for economic activity.

However, there was what can best be described as a cultural factor involved in resentment of outsiders. Bougainvilleans increasingly took the view that, just as original owners of land in Bougainville had special status and rights in connection with that land, the people of Bougainville should enjoy special status and rights in relation to the mine and the wealth derived from it. On this view, the customary owners of the mining-related lease areas deserved not only far more than they actually received in rents and compensation, but also more respectful treatment by BCL and its senior staff. They also were entitled to preferential employment and access to other economic opportunities associated with the mine, and after them it was Bougainvilleans more generally who were entitled to preferential treatment. It was a view that also lent support to an argument for a much increased share of mine revenue for Bougainville as a whole. Finally, it was a view that supported the idea that, in general, outsiders should behave with respect and decorum toward Bougainvilleans (as the original owners of the land that the outsiders were visiting)—a view that strengthened perceptions of increased crime and other social problems of the 1980s as being caused by outsiders. These ideas in due course became the basis for the ideology of the Bougainville Revolutionary Army.[31]

Not surprisingly, the varied experiences and impacts of both economic and other forms of change that came mostly in association with colonialism drew varied responses from Bougainvilleans. From as early as 1913 in Buka,[32] and emerging after that in many areas, struggles to come to terms with the outside world included "cargo cults," probably originating in part in Bougainvilleans' own belief systems, involving ideas of a millennium when every wish would be fulfilled, especially in relation to abundance of food and reunion with deceased relatives.[33] However, Bougainvillean "cults" were also often a response to what seemed the severe injustice of the great material wealth of Europeans, and so directed themselves to finding access to that wealth, especially through various kinds of "religious" practices. However, other factors involved an element of resistance to colonial rule and associated assertions of the wish to retain the autonomy of communities and the ways in which change (including economic change) occurred. (Elements of local millenarianism can be found across Melanesia, and can be an important factor in social and political dynamics. Its role in contemporary West Papua is discussed in Chapter 8.)

Similar factors were also involved in the development of a number of rather different movements that emerged after World War II, such as the Hahalis Welfare Society in Buka, which for several years from the late 1950s sought to develop its own path toward economic advancement of its 6,000 members and many more sympathizers. The society refused to participate in the colonial administration's system of elected local government, opposed integration of Bougainville into PNG, and opposed the Catholic Church for failing to assist people's material advancement. Confrontations with police riot squads and mass prosecutions followed.[34] Concern about the impact of Hahalis resulted in development projects for Buka, and greater interest by the Catholic Church in material progress and social justice for its adherents. As James Griffin notes, "The moral for Bougainville was that Port Moresby would only respond when its authority was challenged."[35] Such a perception was later reinforced by the struggles in the late 1960s over mining-related lease rents and compensation, and by the unilateral declaration of independence in 1975, and probably helped drive the actions of Francis Ona and others that precipitated the start of conflict in late 1988.

Hahalis had links with a number of similar movements,[36] including Damien Dameng's Me'ekamui Pontoku Onoring, of central Bougainville, southwest of the Panguna mine. From around 1959, Dameng gradually built support among 10,000 or more people around an ideology based on restoring traditional customary ways and authority, and opposing the mission, the colonial administration, and (from the mid-1960s) the Panguna mine, all because of their undermining impacts on societies anxious to protect their autonomous ways. Dameng was to become a significant figure in the origins and direction of the conflict from 1988.[37]

The distinction between "cargo cults" and social movements seeking their own path to development is not an easy one to make. The cargo cult element seemed to flourish best, however, in less developed areas. Groups seeking shortcuts to wealth who seem to have some resonances with the cargo cult element continue to exist in postconflict Bougainville, as discussed below.

The other main examples of resistance involve the opposition to the mine, and the support for Bougainville's separation from PNG, which emerged at least as early as the 1950s. Intensified by the controversies surrounding the mine, by 1975 separatist sentiment had become a widespread movement that supported a unilateral declaration of independence, made on 16 September of that year. It is difficult now to disentangle the complex mix of factors that resulted in such a widespread degree of discontent with the prospect of remaining part of PNG. The experience of colonial development and of the imposition of the Panguna mine were certainly of central importance, and contributed to political mobilization around a sense of a Bougainvillean identity distinct from the rest of PNG. Secession was of course opposed by PNG, and received no international support. The dispute was resolved in 1976 by agreement with PNG for a constitutional guarantee of autonomy for Bougainville, and payment to its new provincial government of the royalties payable to the PNG government by BCL.[38] The problems in Bougainville seemed resolved—until they emerged again in a more dramatic form in the late 1980s.

■ The Conflict and the Peace Process

The complex origins and unfolding of the nine-year conflict (1988 to 1997) and the subsequent peace process have been discussed elsewhere.[39] For present purposes, it is necessary merely to paint the bare outlines of the conflict and peace process before commenting briefly on the roles played by the various impacts, tensions, divisions, and responses associated with or arising from economic change.

Overview of the Conflict, 1988–1997, and Its Impacts

Violent conflict was precipitated in 1988 by internal disputes among the Bougainvillean owners of land leased by BCL over the revenue share received by younger landowners. Another factor involved grievances of young Bougainvillean employees of BCL, in part related to what they saw as BCL's failure to recognize the rights of Bougainvilleans to preferential employment treatment. In November 1988, leaders of these groups destroyed pylons carrying power lines to the mine. In doing so, they were seeking neither permanent closure of the mine, nor the initiation of a secessionist struggle. Rather, they intended mainly to support unresolved demands for massive increases in Bougainville's share of the financial returns from the mine.[40] However, the explosions elicited widespread violence by police mobile squads, and the conflict escalated over the following months to also involve Papua New Guinea's defense forces. This violence was the catalyst for mobilization of a broad coalition of Bougainvillean interests. Groups of angry landowners, mainly wanting outsiders to leave Bougainville, others that were strongly secessionist, and still other groups like Dameng's Me'ekamui Pontoku Onoring who opposed mining, all actively supported Francis Ona, the leader of the young landowners and the mine employees. Early in 1989 they persuaded him to expand his agenda to make Bougainville's secession his primary goal.

Wide support was quickly mobilized on that basis, and disparate armed groups emerged who by mid-1989 had grouped loosely under the Bougainville Revolutionary Army. Young men flocked to the cause in many areas, often seeking the status until then denied them by limited employment and other opportunities. However, support for the BRA was not uniform. Many leaders in Buka, northern Bougainville, and the central eastern coastal areas, conscious of the advantages of integration into PNG, tended to discourage their people from actively supporting the BRA.

The mine closed in May 1989, and has never reopened. While some, such as Dameng, would have been happy with that as a permanent outcome, Ona and other senior BRA leaders initially anticipated it as a short-term development. They expected that the mine would later reopen under a new fiscal dispensation that would make it the main source of revenue for an independent Bougainville.[41]

During 1989 and early 1990, most non-Bougainvilleans fled Bougainville in fear of actual or threatened violence in what was in some ways a form of ethnic cleansing. In May 1990, after withdrawal of the PNG security forces from Bougainville following a March 1990 cease-fire, Ona made Bougainville's second unilateral declaration of independence. As in 1975, the move did not gain international recognition. PNG responded by imposing a sea and air blockade, at first on the whole of Buka and Bougainville. Then, after PNG forces began returning to Bougainville beginning in late 1990, the blockade was maintained, and continued until the mid-1990s, in relation to areas under BRA control. It caused great hardship in Bougainville, especially in terms of access to medical supplies and health services more generally.

From about mid-1990, localized intra-Bougainville conflict developed in many areas, often associated with preexisting tensions related to economic inequality. Leaders of some communities sought assistance from the PNG security forces, which began returning to parts of Bougainville in late 1990. The process started in Buka, where many (though by no means all) leaders favored integration into PNG, and where semicriminal elements associated with the BRA who came from relatively undeveloped areas of the mountains of northern Bougainville had wrought havoc in some relatively affluent Buka villages in mid-1990. This resulted in deep resentment on the part of many from Buka, and contributed to a long-term ethnic divide between elements of the Buka population and the Bougainville mainland that continues to be a political factor in Bougainville. In other areas, including Nagovisi and Siwai, preexisting localized tensions associated with unequal access to land sometimes influenced bitter local conflict.

From about 1992, diverse armed Bougainvillean elements opposing the BRA at the local level (usually centered on former BRA elements that supported local leaders' requests for return of the PNG forces) began combining into the Bougainville Resistance Forces (BRF). Both the secessionist conflict between the BRA and the PNG national government, and what amounted to a multifaceted civil war within Bougainville, continued until ended by the peace process, which began in July 1997.

The conflict had terrible impacts. For Bougainville, they included perhaps several thousand deaths (at least hundreds in armed conflict, many more from extrajudicial killings on all sides, and an unknown number due to the PNG blockade); deep divisions among Bougainvilleans; destruction of most infrastructure and of private sector productive assets; destruction of the capacity of the local state (the administrative arm of Bougainville's provincial government); and large-scale dislocation of life for huge numbers, with up to 60,000 of the total population of about 160,000 living in refugee camps by 1996. By the time the peace process began in 1997, Bougainville had gone from its preconflict status as the wealthiest of PNG's nineteen provinces, to arguably the most impoverished. For PNG, there were hundreds of combat deaths and many more injuries, massive economic impacts through closure of the mine, and deleterious impacts on state capacity—not to mention on the morale of the security forces, which were in a constant state of crisis from 1989 to 1997.

Overview of the Peace Process, 1997–2005

The peace process, generally regarded as beginning with talks in New Zealand in July 1997, built on many previous peace efforts going back to at least early 1989. The initial talks were between the divided Bougainvillean groups, and they agreed to cooperate in talks with the national government, which began in October 1997. From an early stage, the process was supported and facilitated by the international community, mainly through a regional truce and (later) cease-fire monitoring group, and by a small United Nations observer mission.[42] Until June 1999, the primary focus was on building a process within which the parties could feel secure. Negotiations on the divisive political issues then began, and continued for over two years, concluding with the signing of a peace agreement in August 2001.

The agreement contains innovative solutions to the difficult problems that faced divided and distrustful parties at the start of the political negotiations. It comprises three main elements. First, a high degree of autonomy is made available to Bougainville under constitutionally guaranteed arrangements. Second, the most divisive issue, Bougainville's secession, is dealt with by a constitutionally guaranteed but deferred referendum for Bougainvilleans on independence, to be held ten to fifteen years after the establishment of the autonomous Bougainvillean government.[43] Third, Bougainville is to be demilitarized, through both the withdrawal of the PNG security forces, and a three-stage process of disposal of the weapons held by the BRA and the BRF.

During 1998 and 1999, difficulties in dealing with decisions on sharing power in interim political structures for Bougainville precipitated significant divisions among the Bougainvillean groups supporting the peace process. The prointegration Buka leadership was again prominent, claiming that unless they achieved a significant role, Buka would secede from Bougainville and develop its own relationship with the rest of PNG. But from December 1999, most factions reconciled and then negotiated with PNG on the basis of a united position. Similar concerns about Buka's role were again expressed by some Buka leaders in mid-2005, after government elections for the Autonomous Region of Bougainville, as established under the peace agreement, resulted in a president who had been a major figure in the BRA's civilian government. It is too early to say if such differences will give rise to serious ongoing problems.

One significant group who have remained outside the process, from a very early stage, are supporters of Francis Ona, who believed that Bougainville's independence had already been established under Ona's May 1990 unilateral declaration. In April 1998, Ona announced himself president of the Independent Republic of Me'ekamui,[44] supported by the armed Me'ekamui Defence Force (MDF). Ona and his supporters set up road-blocks to maintain a "no-go-zone" in the mountains around the former mine site, refusing to disarm, though also indicating that they would not actively undermine the process. Ona died in mid-2005, but the Me'ekamui group continue to remain outside the peace process.

■ Impacts of Economic Change on the Conflict and Peace Process

Some aspects of the dynamics unleashed by the ongoing economic change that began with colonization have already been highlighted. Differences in economic interests of the leadership of Buka and northern Bougainville and parts of the central eastern coast, on the one hand, from those of much of the rest of mainland Bougainville, on the other hand, were a factor not only in divisions that occurred early in the conflict and then in the Bougainville civil war, but also in divisions in Bougainville's leadership during the peace process.

The variable impacts of economic development, which left some areas with very little in terms of transport infrastructure, cash crops, or mining, led to tensions between and within groups, during and after the conflict. Relatively affluent villages in Buka and the central eastern coast were sometimes targeted by BRA and other armed elements from less affluent areas, as were relatively wealthy individuals and groups in many areas, especially in the early stages of the conflict.

The desire of young men to find status in the BRA (and other armed groups) has been a constant factor during the conflict and peace process. There has also been, for some, a self-enrichment motive involved. Sam Kauona, the military leader of the BRA, has described what happened after the PNG forces withdrew from Bougainville in March 1990. BRA members and others started "making claims to a lot of materials, including hundreds of vehicles abandoned by the mining company. . . . It was madness. . . . They didn't know how to drive the vehicles but they went from one to another—there were so many. There was virtually no control. They took all the money that was left in the drawers. Because of all the material goods Bougainvillleans started fighting one another."[45] The problems Kauona describes continued beyond early 1990. Large amounts of goods from houses and offices in Panguna and the Bougainville capital (Arawa) were shipped by barge to the Solomon Islands for sale, leading to tensions and conflict among BRA elements. Theft of vehicles and other goods was often a motive in attacks on relatively wealthy individuals and groups in Bougainville.

Resentment of outsiders and the desire for recognition of the special rights of Bougainvilleans as the original owners of Bougainville were factors in both the ethnic cleansing of 1989–1990, and the desire for secession. They also influenced the early hopes of Ona and the BRA for the resumption of mining becoming the basis of as much revenue as possible flowing to mine-lease landowners and to Bougainville as a whole.

The so-called cargo cult influences, combining resentment of the unjust material wealth of the white man and the search for quick access to such wealth, seems to have been a factor in much that happened during the conflict. Many—though by no means all—leaders and members of the BRA had limited understanding of how economic development occurred, and expected that rapid change would simply follow the closure of the mine and the ousting of the PNG forces. Moreover, these leaders initially had little sense of the deleterious impacts of such events as the pillaging of the mine's assets and the destruction of other infrastructure that occurred beginning in 1990. As discussed below, cargo cult influences sometimes seem to be a continuing and surprisingly strong factor in the postconflict situation, a particular instance involving Noah Musingku, the Bougainvillean head of a failed Port Moresby–based fast-money pyramid scheme called U-Vistract.

■ Economic Development in Postconflict Bougainville

In terms of continuity, the main focus of postconflict development activity relates to restoration of the small-holder cocoa sector, and of the transport infrastructure needed to market the cocoa produced. A huge effort by donors (notably Australia and the European Union) saw small-holder cocoa production levels rise in 2004–2005 to record levels similarly attained in 1988–1989, and it is estimated that about 23,000 families now derive income from cocoa.[46] All of the problems arising from the cocoa economy in the 1970s and 1980s are again becoming evident. Some of the problems involved have been highlighted in a 2003 report,[47] but have been given limited attention by either donors or Bougainville's authorities, mainly because there are no obvious immediate alternatives to cocoa in terms of providing access to cash incomes for Bougainvillean villagers.

The situation for young men is another area of continuity, with much the same factors operating to make a new generation of undereducated males with few opportunities feel frustrated and powerless. There is also some continuity in relation to attitudes to outsiders, especially in relation to establishing businesses. There was strong resentment expressed by many Bougainvilleans in 2004 and the first half of 2005 about small businesses being established in Bougainville's urban centers by Asians and by a few businesspeople from other parts of PNG.

In terms of change, there is no large-scale mining, though there is increasing discussion among Bougainvilleans as to whether such mining should be permitted in the future. In mid-2005, the newly elected president of the Autonomous Region of Bougainville, Joseph Kabui, stated that there would be no future mining without endorsement from the people through a vote in a plebiscite. It seems likely, however, that there are limited prospects that either Panguna or a new major mine will be developed in the foreseeable future, given the combination of the massive investment required and the continuing divisions in Bougainville on the issue, including strong opposition from those who supported Ona. On the other hand, there is extensive alluvial gold mining taking place in the mountains of central Bougainville, both in the Panguna mine tailings dumps and down the Jaba River from those dumps, as well as at other sites. The levels of production are not known, as they are occurring in "no-go-zone" areas controlled by Ona's MDF, but are estimated by some Bougainvillean leaders to amount to K25 million or more per year.[48]

The peace process itself has contributed to difficulties in relation to economic development. Donor funding was provided for a range of peace process–related purposes, including humanitarian assistance; support for regional peace monitors and for the small United Nations observer mission; facilitation of the process in a variety of ways (organizing negotiation meetings and transport and subsistence of participants); and development projects. Not all of this funding has had the impacts intended. Indeed, from an early stage there was a series of funding initiatives from parts of the international community that arguably not only had unintended, deleterious impacts on the peace process, but also may contribute to long-term problems in the Autonomous Region of Bougainville in terms of encouraging unrealistic expectations and demands among Bougainvilleans.

Humanitarian assistance to Bougainvilleans provided during the conflict and the early stages of the peace process was in general well-targeted, reducing some of the worst impacts of the conflict (including the PNG-imposed blockade on BRA-controlled areas), and even assisting the BRA in understanding the war-weariness of the people and the need to explore peaceful resolution of the conflict. Small-scale community-based projects in the early stages of the peace process helped to restore health and education services in many areas. More recently, much of the development assistance to Bougainville has been well designed, notably a major Australian-funded project for upgrading and maintaining the main trunk road, under which the international contractor is obliged to develop Bougainvillean contractors and work teams, and thereby build local capacity and spread economic benefits widely.

In terms of unintended impacts, three main kinds of funding require particular mention. First, early in the peace process, aid donors sought to offer what they termed "peace dividends"—mainly small-scale projects (classrooms, healthcare buildings, and small commercial projects) to communities supporting the peace process. The term "peace dividends" was an unfortunate one in these circumstances, suggesting that peace was not necessarily something to be supported because of its inherent value, but rather on the basis of economic returns of some kind. Second, the UN observer mission, the United Nations Development Programme, Australia, and New Zealand all offered allowances and other financial benefits to Bougainvilleans (and in some cases PNG government officials) attending peace process meetings, taking part in awareness activities, and so on. The funds were offered in good faith, mainly because of the lack of income that most Bougainvilleans experienced well into the peace process. But as a result, it quickly became the norm that such payments were a necessary part of peace process activities, with people often being reluctant to take part without some form of recompense. Third, in early 2001, following poor progress toward agreement on a weapons disposal process, Australia offered as incentive a fund of A$5 million (the Bougainville Excombatants Trust Account [BETA]) to provide small commercial and other projects to groups of former combatants from communities where weapons disposal was proceeding—another form of "peace dividends."

All of these well-intentioned initiatives added to overall perceptions that there was an unlimited pot of international funds available to support peace process–related activities of Bougainvilleans, and tended to create a perception for some that the peace process was about money. In a postconflict situation, where people had few avenues for access to income, the flow of funds from the international community became a major consideration. Among other things, it undermined long-established patterns of self-reliance and contributed to both inequality and perceptions of inequality. Unequal access to such funding proved to be a divisive issue for the BRA and BRF leaderships, and in a number of communities. There are also signs that expectations of large payments for participation in government activities will be a problem for the Autonomous Region of Bougainville.

Until his unexpected death in July 2005, Ona in many ways remained consistent on his position in the lead-up to the conflict, in that he continued to explore a range of means of obtaining huge wealth for Bougainville, including supporting a case in the US courts against one of the main BCL shareholders, Riotinto Zinc, and apparently supporting the claims of Noah Musingku. The latter, after fleeing arrest in Port Moresby in 2002 for failure to appear at court proceedings related to his collapsed U-Vistract pyramid money scheme, lived under the protection of Ona and the MDF. He claims to have developed a new international finance system under which Bougainville will no longer need foreign support, and will be immensely wealthy (the head of the world, not the tail). Musingku has persuaded thousands of Bougainvilleans to believe that he will deliver massive payments through his new system (including repayment of sums invested in U-Vistract in the late 1990s, together with the interest promised in the 1990s: 100 percent per month!). Musingku's appeal is in part explained by the desperation of many in postconflict Bougainville to find an easy way to restore their preconflict economic position, and in part by Ona's concern to be the source of great wealth for Bougainville. But it also indicates that beliefs similar to those involved in "cargo cults" about the possibility of finding special avenues to fabulous wealth remain a factor in Bougainville.

Conclusion

This chapter has shown that where rapid economic change is accompanied by economic inequality in a situation of small and previously egalitarian social groups, with few crosscutting links and with diverse understandings of what is involved in development, it has the potential to contribute to conflict in unpredictable ways. Among other things, it can exacerbate ethnic fault-lines—in the case of Bougainville, such fault-lines involved not only Bougainvilleans and people from other parts of PNG, but also opposing groups of Bougainvilleans.

The situation in postconflict Bougainville has many of the same dynamics that helped create and foster the conflict in and beyond 1988, and so the question arises as to whether there are dangers that Bougainville is at risk of a new cycle of conflict developing. While this is undoubtedly a possibility, there are also some significant differences between the situation in 2007 compared to that of the late 1980s. First, the disruptive and divisive impacts associated with the large Panguna mine (including the large influx of outsiders) no longer apply. Second, for now at least, while there is some economic inequality among Bougainvilleans (especially arising from cocoa production), it is minimal when compared to the inequality of the 1980s.

Third, and perhaps most important, the common experience by Bougainvilleans of revulsion against the impact of violence, and their common efforts in support of peace, has brought some important changes. In particular, a strong consensus has emerged among most—if not all—communities that violence is no longer an acceptable means of resolving conflict, especially among themselves. The same experience has also contributed to widely held views about the need for the state—especially the police—to avoid the use of violence in its dealings with communities.[49] This is not to say that violence no longer occurs in Bougainville—it certainly does. Rather, when it does occur, a wide range of pressures tend to emerge from within communities to stop it and to prevent it from occurring again. Norms that have the potential to gradually widen pressures from civil society to limit the actions of the state, and the actions of civil society itself, appear to be emerging not through donor funding from nongovernmental organizations, but through broad-based societal responses to the experience of terrible conflict. This may be the best protection against the risk that new tensions and divisions arising from new cycles of economic change could generate similar cycles of violent conflict.

Notes

1. See, for example, Collier and Hoeffler, "On Economic Causes of War"; Berdal and Malone, *Greed and Grievance;* Ballentine and Sherman, *The Political Economy of Armed Conflict;* Regan and Norton, "Greed, Grievance, and Mobilization in Civil Wars."

2. Regan and Norton, "Greed, Grievance, and Mobilization in Civil Wars," p. 319.

3. Regan, "The Bougainville Conflict."

4. See, for example, those surveyed in Regan, "Causes and Course of the Bougainville Conflict."

5. Wickler and Spriggs, "Pleistocene Human Occupation of the Solomon Islands"; Spriggs, "Bougainville's Early History."

6. Tryon, "The Languages of Bougainville."

7. Ogan, "The Cultural Background to the Bougainville Crisis"; Regan, "Identities Among Bougainvilleans."

8. Regan, "Identities Among Bougainvilleans."

9. For more on the development of Bougainvillean identity and the process of its politicization, see Nash and Ogan, "The Red and the Black"; Ghai and Regan, "Bougainville and the Dialectics of Ethnicity, Autonomy, and Separation."

10. Regan, "Identities Among Bougainvilleans."

11. The focus of this analysis on impacts of economic development also excludes consideration of impacts of other, and in many ways closely associated, changes, including Christian missions, colonial and postcolonial government administration, political ideologies of various kinds, and so on.

12. Docker, *The Blackbirders;* Corris, *Passage, Port, and Plantation;* Oliver, *Black Islanders.*

13. They occupied 3 percent of Bougainville's land, but 10 percent of the areas suitable for plantation agriculture. Oliver, *Black Islanders,* p. 31.

14. See Wesley-Smith and Ogan, "Copper, Class, and Crisis"; Ogan, "Copra Came Before Copper."

15. Oliver, *Black Islanders.*

16. There were about 50,000 Bougainvilleans when World War II began. By early 1944, there were about 130,000 foreigners—including about 65,000 Japanese and 60,000 Americans. Nelson, "Bougainville in World War II."

17. Connell, "Taim Bilong Mani."

18. MacWilliam, "Post-War Reconstruction in Bougainville."

19. Mitchell, "Frozen Assets in Nagovisi."

20. Tanis, "Nagovisi Villages as a Window on Bougainville."

21. There is an extensive literature on the impact of the mine, including Denoon, *Getting Under the Skin;* Bedford and Mamak, "Compensation for Development"; Connell, "The Panguna Mine Impact"; Connell, "Compensation and Conflict"; Regan, "The Bougainville Conflict"; Vernon, "The Panguna Mine"; Togolo, "Torau Response to Change"; Tanis, "Nagovisi Villages as a Window on Bougainville"; and other sources cited in Wesley-Smith, "Development and Crisis in Bougainville."

22. The average exchange rate for Papua New Guinea's currency—the kina—against the US dollar over the period in question was about US$1.1.

23. Connell, "Compensation and Conflict," p. 55.

24. Bedford and Mamak, "Compensation for Development."

25. I have been assisted in understanding the issues discussed in this paragraph by information supplied by a number of people, including Mike Bell (interview, Melbourne, May 2002), Barry Middlemiss, and a number of members of landowning lineages in the mine lease areas.

26. Bedford and Mamak, "Compensation for Development."

27. Regan, "Identities Among Bougainvilleans."

28. Even into the contemporary period, inland people were still setting up their marital residences within a mile or so of their place of birth. Friedlaender, "Why Do the People of Bougainville Look Unique?"

29. Compare the discussion by Filer, "The Bougainville Rebellion," on the disintegrative impacts of the mine on the mountain Nasioi people with the analysis by Togolo, "Torau Response to Change," of the responses of the Torau people of the east coast.

30. MacWilliam, "Post-War Reconstruction in Bougainville."

31. Regan, "Causes and Course of the Bougainville Conflict"; Bougainville Constitutional Commission, "Report of the Bougainville Constitutional Commission," pp. 39–41.

32. Oliver, *Black Islanders,* p. 67.

33. Ibid., p. 62.

34. Rimoldi and Rimoldi, *Hahalis and the Labour of Love.*

35. Griffin, *Bougainville,* p. 11.

36. A number of them are listed and discussed in brief in Bougainville Constitutional Commission, "Report of the Bougainville Constitutional Commission," pp. 32–33.

37. For more on Dameng and his significance, see Regan, "The Bougainville Conflict."

38. Ghai and Regan, "Bougainville and the Dialectics of Ethnicity, Autonomy, and Separation."

39. In relation to the origins and unfolding of the conflict, see May and Spriggs, *The Bougainville Crisis;* Oliver, *Black Islanders;* Ogan, "The Cultural Background to the Bougainville Crisis"; Spriggs and Denoon, *The Bougainville Crisis;* Regan, "Causes and Course of the Bougainville Conflict"; Regan, "Why a Neutral Peace Monitoring Force?"; Regan, "The Bougainville Conflict"; Regan and Griffin, *Bougainville Before the Conflict.* In relation to the peace process, see Wehner and Denooon, *Without a Gun;* Adams, *Gudpela Nius Bilong Pis;* Regan, "The Bougainville Political Settlement and the Prospects for Sustainable Peace"; Carl and Garasu, "Weaving Consensus"; Boege and Garasu, "Papua New Guinea."

40. This statement is based on information provided by a number of former close associates of Francis Ona who prefer not to be identified by name.

41. See Regan, "The Bougainville Conflict."

42. Wehner and Denoon, *Without a Gun;* Carl and Garasu, "Weaving Consensus."

43. The Bougainville negotiating position drew inspiration from the complex provision in respect of deferred referenda arrangements in the 1998 Noumea Accord (discussed in Chapter 6).

44. A word meaning something akin to "sacred land" in the Nasioi language of central Bougainville.

45. "Conflict in Bougainville."

46. Trevor Clarke, personal communication, July 2005.

47. Bourke and Betitis, *Sustainability of Agriculture in Bougainville Province.*

48. From the latter part of the 1990s, the value of the kina dropped dramatically, and in 2005 the exchange rate was approximately US$0.30.

49. Regan, "Clever People Solving Difficult Problems."

6

Development and Self-Determination in New Caledonia

Paul de Deckker

IN MAY 1988, New Caledonia was the focus of worldwide media attention, after twenty-seven French gendarmes were taken hostage on 24 April 1988 by nineteen Kanaks (indigenous New Caledonians) in a grotto on Ouvea Island in the Loyalty Islands. The crisis grew out of an intensifying and bloody four-year struggle for full independence from France on the part of the Front de Libération Nationale Kanak et Socialiste (FLNKS), an independence movement formed in 1980. The FLNKS was opposed by France, as the state power governing New Caledonia, and by the Caldoche (settler New Caledonians), particularly the Rassemblement pour la Calédonie dans la République (RPCR).

French military forces stormed the grotto on 5 May. All nineteen Kanaks and three gendarmes were killed. As well as the shock and distress it caused, this event threatened to deepen already sharp divisions within New Caledonia around questions of self-determination, and plunge the country into more widespread violence.

As the crisis was occurring, France was between two rounds of national presidential elections. In Paris, François Mitterrand was seeking reelection and Prime Minister Jacques Chirac was hoping to replace him. The polls suggested both were potential winners. The hostage crisis became a key element in the presidential election, eventually to the advantage of President Mitterrand. Indeed, it bore all the constitutive elements of French colonial history and forced the two political leaders to take a position vis-à-vis the New Caledonian crisis: Mitterrand favored Kanak nationalists with the left, Chirac favored people loyal to France with the liberals.

In France the news of the military action and subsequent deaths took on overwhelming importance in the presidential election debates. Chirac was perceived as supportive of a colonial situation remnant of the nineteenth century, while Mitterrand, in supporting the FLNKS, presented himself as opposed to the violence. As president of France, however, Mitterrand was the supreme commander of the French army and thus was ultimately responsible for the assault. Since the end of World War II, France had undergone the tumultuous process of decolonizing its overseas possessions in Asia and Africa. The last French colony to gain constitutional independence was the Franco-British Condominium of the New Hebrides in July 1980, now the Republic of Vanuatu, and a neighbor of New Caledonia.

The following analysis will examine the ways that the three negotiating parties—the French metropolitan government, the New Caledonian pro-French loyalists, and the Kanak proindependence parties—acted during and after the crisis. All the parties to the dispute sought to find a solution to the Ouvea conflict; a key path to the restoration of peace was through the construction of a common destiny, shared by all New Caledonians. Remarkably, since 1988, New Caledonia has been stable and peaceful, a position that seemed unattainable in the midst of the *événements* (troubles) of the 1980s. The chapter will also discuss how France, at the end of the twentieth century, became entangled in the Ouvea massacre, and so anachronistically presented the image of a nineteenth-century colonial power. To this end, the historical and socioeconomic background of New Caledonia will be briefly explored and placed in a wider regional and geographic context. In the following chapter, Nic Maclellan discusses the social and cultural impact of the crisis and the contribution of indigenous conflict management approaches to the period of stability following 1988.

This discussion of the crisis over self-determination in New Caledonia is underpinned by some persistent themes in the region, as well as some more particular to New Caledonia. There are tensions over land and competing interpretations of its significance and use, in a society where the indigenous population still operates to a significant extent within a subsistence economy, while the monetarized economy, dominated by mining, is operated largely by multiethnic settler New Caledonians. New Caledonians are undergoing an intensive process of forming the nature of their political community—of "state formation," whether eventually as an independent entity or constitutionally linked to France. As in Fiji, the balance between indigenous and settler New Caledonians is approximately equal, with settlers in this case in a slim majority. This alters the nature of the dilemmas around the formation of political community (or "state building") and around the intersections of customary and introduced forms of governance, while the challenge of creating a sense of common destiny is considerable. Settler New Caledonians are not sustained by the subsistence economy, and cannot rely on semicustomary governance mechanisms in the event of weakening or absent state institutions or services. However, as with many states in the region, and despite its mineral resources, New Caledonia could face serious challenges in economically sustaining the institutions and services of a European- or Western-model state if the territory were to become completely independent of France. These factors have influenced the character of the debates around self-determination in the country.

■ The Legacy of the Past

The main island of New Caledonia, situated 1,600 kilometers (1,000 miles) northeast of New Zealand and 1,200 kilometers (750 miles) east of Australia, is in the shape of an elongated cigar. It is 400 kilometers (250 miles) long, with an average width of 42 kilometers (25 miles). To the east, the four small Loyalty islands fall within its domain, as does the Isle of Pines to the south and the Belep Islands directly to the north. The total land area of this archipelago, a little less than 19,000 square kilometers (7,300 square miles), is similar to the land area of Fiji. New Caledonia is a land of mineral wealth and has the third largest quantity of nickel deposits in the world. Partly as a result, New Caledonia has the highest average income per head in the Pacific Island region, apart from New Zealand and Australia.

The first inhabitants were descendants of Austronesians, whose long migratory journey continued over generations. Departing from Papua New Guinea and traveling by way of the Solomon Islands, Vanuatu, and Fiji, they reached New Caledonia around 1500 B.C.E. This arc is described by the term *Melanesian,* which means "islands of the black-skinned peoples." Later migratory movements westward from the Polynesian archipelagos added to the population of the Loyalty Islands and the Isle of Pines. Today, for reasons of identity and politics, the Melanesians of New Caledonia have claimed the name *Kanak.*[1] There are 333 Kanak tribes and 28 indigenous languages spread over New Caledonia.

The French navy took possession of New Caledonia in 1853 in the name of Emperor Napoleon III, to the great displeasure of Australia and New Zealand, which called for radical action from London to prevent France from establishing a regional presence. Just as in Australia in 1788, New Caledonia became a convict colony; from 1863 until 1897, some 30,000 convicts and deportees arrived to serve out their terms and to use their labor to develop the small settler economy. Penal colonization was the first mode of non-Kanak settlement in New Caledonia. The second was free colonization. At the end of the nineteenth century, the non-Kanak population approached 20,000 people. New Caledonia's principal area of production was agriculture. From 1874, this was overtaken by mining activity following the discovery of significant deposits of nickel, chromium, and cobalt. The mines needed a labor force, drawing a third settler influx from Japan, Indonesia, and other French colonies, including Indochina. The French territory of New Caledonia became a true ethnic melting pot, and rare are the non-Kanak inhabitants who can claim they are not of mixed blood. At the 1996 census, the total population of New Caledonia was about

197,000 inhabitants, comprising 87,000 Kanaks, 67,000 Europeans, 18,000 Wallisians and Futunians, 5,000 Tahitians, 5,000 Indonesians, 3,000 Vietnamese, 2,200 ni-Vanuatu, and 9,800 others. The estimated population in 2004 was about 230,000, with approximately 44 percent Kanak and 34 percent of European descent.

The impact of the French colonization of New Caledonia was similar to that of the British Empire in its colonies. Disputes over land occurred between Kanaks and settlers, along with the displacement of indigenous populations, effectively restricting indigenous culture, language, employment, and movement to particular areas. On the mainland of New Caledonia, especially in the north and around Noumea, 15–20 percent of Kanak people were displaced from their land. World War II, however, brought about drastic changes in the French government's way of thinking about New Caledonia. More than 100,000 US soldiers were permanently stationed on the main island of the territory from 1942 to 1945, and the US wartime influence in the region is often linked by historians to the independence movements of the 1960s and 1970s across the region. European women in New Caledonia were given the vote in 1945, and in 1953, Kanak adults were able to vote in the same constituency as the French settlers, in territorial and national elections. In response to demands for independence from French overseas territories in Africa, Asia, and the Pacific, the French parliament drafted laws to support this movement toward decolonization.

When General Charles de Gaulle returned to power in 1958, however, it became apparent that he prioritized defending French strategic interests. Among other measures, this included the force of nuclear deterrence. Military designs of this kind focused on French Polynesia, and in 1963 Paris decided to halt moves toward independence in New Caledonia and French Polynesia, its two principal territories in the Pacific. As nickel became a strategic material and Polynesia a strategic center, the territories were drawn more tightly under the authority of France, which resumed executive power, reducing the autonomy of local political authorities, who had exercised a certain self-sufficiency prior to 1958. France rapidly came to be considered a regressive country by its Western partners in the region.

At a time when constitutional independence was being achieved in one new nation after another in the former colonies in the Pacific, independence in New Caledonia and French Polynesia dropped from the French agenda.[2] Paris was therefore swimming against the tide even if small steps were taken to give back a small measure of autonomy in some areas. For twenty-five years, from 1963 to 1988, there were repeated efforts to seek political representation balanced between the desire for political independence and the desire to retain fundamental links with France. These efforts were not successful. Kanaks expressed an intention to share power with the French settler "loyalist" community but soon the confrontationist tactics of both sides exacerbated increasingly extreme patterns of behavior.

Within the loyalist community, the time had not yet come to accept a negotiated, collaborative outcome. Because of emotional ties, and economic dependence, the Caldoche (the settler population) felt unprepared for full political independence. They were not alone; 20 percent of Kanak people as well as the great majority of the non-Kanak communities were loyalists. Two opposing positions confronted each other: that of the loyalists, which as noted included some Kanaks, and that of the independence movement, composed essentially of Kanaks. Given the confrontationist approaches, the emergence of the violence that occurred between 1984 and 1988 seemed unavoidable, despite some recognition of the havoc it would cause.

Positioned in the center of a rapidly decolonizing Pacific region, France was decried for its colonial administration of New Caledonia no less than for its nuclear tests in French Polynesia. Critics aimed to hound France from the Pacific Ocean so that its nuclear testing would cease and so the Kanak brothers of the indigenous inhabitants of the other Pacific islands could also gain independence. At this time the ni-Vanuatu chief minister and later prime minister, Walter Lini, led the decolonization crusade and with his Melanesian partners created the Melanesian Spearhead Group.[3] Its main aim was to create the right conditions for its still-colonized Melanesian neighbors to attain independence (Vanuatu remains, at a state level, one of the few international supporters of West Papuan independence). It was also the time when, at the end of his mandate as secretary-general of the South Pacific Commission, Francis Bugotu, from the Solomon Islands, registered with the United Nations the demand that New Caledonia be returned to the list of countries to be decolonized. Paris resisted, arguing that it would not allow small island countries to dictate the French position.

Australia, New Zealand, and independent Melanesian nations took the side of the Kanaks, supporting Kanak aspirations for independence at regional forums. At the time, New Caledonia was thought of as a sort of Rhodesia in the Pacific. Kanak leaders like Jean-Marie Tjibaou and Yann Celene Uregei were welcomed in university circles in Auckland, Wellington, Sydney, and Canberra. The message was clear—New Caledonia must throw off the French colonial yoke. Canberra and Wellington expressed reservations, however, when in 1987 members of the Kanak independence movement passed through Australia to train as guerrillas in Libya with Colonel Muammar Gaddafi. At that time in the New Caledonian bush, deaths mounted on both sides and the violence climaxed with the hostage crisis in Ouvea in May 1988. The deaths, destruction of property, and disruption to civil society throughout the territory became unbearable. All parties finally regarded a peaceful solution to New Caledonia's problems as essential.

■ The Matignon Accord

As the state power, the French government had a fundamental responsibility to ensure peace. French prime minister Michel Rocard was the man to whom Mitterrand entrusted the task of restoring peace in New Caledonia.[4] Rocard brought the two principal opposing groups to a "neutral" negotiating table in Paris and managed to get them to sign the Matignon Accord in June 1988.[5] This had the appearance of a classic negotiated peace settlement, bringing warring parties to a consensus through a conferential system in a "neutral" negotiating environment. Violence ceased and there was optimism that a ten-year interregnum would provide a peaceful solution, even if some years distant. The reality was that loyalist and independence parties remained opposed, and there was a proliferation of subgroups and new parties as people jockeyed for positions in the promised autonomy to come. The accord was symbolized by Jacques Lafleur, leader of the RPCR loyalists, and Jean-Marie Tjibaou, the Kanak leader, shaking hands; a previously unimaginable gesture, given the strength of the opposition between the two sides.

The violence had devastated the territory, and left both settler and Kanak morale in tatters. With the objective of pacifying the territory, the French state resumed direct administration with the promise, outlined in the Matignon Accord, to proceed in ten years' time to a referendum on the question of whether New Caledonia should become independent or remain part of the French republic. The Matignon Accord was put before the people of France through a referendum and approved.[6] However, hostilities continued to simmer and a year later, Jean-Marie Tjibaou and Yeiweine Yeiweine were shot dead on the island of Ouvea by a Kanak who had never accepted that the handshake between Tjibaou and Lafleur symbolized a mutually agreed way ahead.[7]

Underpinning the Matignon agreement were responses by the French government to sources of Kanak grievance. The question of landownership was tackled in a way that attempted to repair the abuses of the past by redistributing land to Kanak communities whose land had been stripped from them. Issues of land and colonization have been a major source of conflict in many Pacific Island states. Jacques Lafleur himself sold a part of his mining interests to the French state, which then ceded it back to Kanak interests in the Northern province. This gesture, also highly symbolic, had as its aim the encouragement of Kanak participation in the economic and financial operations of the mining sector. Finally, from 1988, a policy of positive discrimination looked to provide professional training to 400 Kanak managers in the interests of what was referred to in French as *rééquilibrage,* or creating a more level playing field. This ongoing policy has been widely considered, both in Paris and in Noumea, as successful, although as in many countries, significant income disparities still exist between indigenous and nonindigenous New Caledonians.

In 1989, Michel Rocard traveled to New Zealand, Australia, and Fiji to announce the changes that had been made to French policy in the Pacific. On this trip, he sold the assets of the Indo-Suez Bank to Westpac, an Australian banking company, and some Airbuses. He established the French–New Zealand Friendship Fund to strengthen ties between the two countries through French financing of cultural and scientific cooperation. New Zealand and Australia appeared satisfied with this development. Fiji, Tonga, American Samoa, Niue, and the Cook Islands declared that France held its place in the Pacific by virtue of its territorial entities.

▓ The Noumea Accord

Despite these advances, the pro- and anti-independence factions remained in strong opposition. In this context, it became clear that the proposed referendum about accession to independence would result in new tensions, since one side would have to be the loser. A plan was therefore put in place for a new accord, negotiated by the new socialist prime minister, Lionel Jospin, and officially signed in May 1998 in Noumea by the major political parties. The Noumea Accord established a process of transfer of governmental responsibility leading to the referendum. The referendum on full independence was delayed until at least 2013 (probably 2014), but in the interim there has been a gradual transfer of wide-ranging powers, with the exception of those regarding foreign and defense policy, currency, justice, and public order (the "regalian" powers). The process is both more gradual and more progressive than that envisaged by the Matignon Accord. This is a demonstration of a successful, negotiated conflict resolution, based on the principle of a long-term gestation in which Kanaks could affirm their new political status and improve their socioeconomic position, and in which all sides could engage in a parliamentary process at the provincial level, at the national level (through the Territorial Congress), and in a relationship with the metropolitan power, France.

Since the Matignon Accord, New Caledonia has been split administratively into three provinces—the Islands (20,877 inhabitants in the 1996 census), the North (41,413 inhabitants), and the South (134,546 inhabitants). Each has a provincial assembly where members are elected by universal suffrage according to voting ticket. The congress of New Caledonia numbers fifty-four members drawn from the assemblies of the three provinces.[8] The congress is led by a president, assisted by several vice presidents and two parliamentary administrators. New Caledonia therefore has its own government, which functions in a "collegial" fashion. That is, the executive has representatives from more than one party, and from antagonistic parties, with decisions reached through consensus. It is able to legislate in areas that do not affect the regalian prerogatives of the French state (defense, currency, and justice). The Noumea Accord also set up a customary senate composed of sixteen members, with two members coming from each of the eight customary lands that make up the country. They have only an advisory role, similar to the advisory customary body outlined under autonomy provisions for West Papua, and the role of the Council of Chiefs in Fiji. This interesting intersection of introduced French and customary governance is an important feature of state building in New Caledonia. The processes of state formation in New Caledonia, and indeed much of the Pacific, provide a unique perspective on notions of state building and sovereignty.

Before the French constitutional revision of March 2003, another imaginative compromise was established when New Caledonia became a *pays d'outre-mer* (overseas country), or self-governing entity, within the French republic. This involves wide-ranging self-government within the republic and a system of "shared sovereignty" with France. It was a remarkable outcome in which the dominant partner, France, ceded power gradually to what was previously a dependent colony, though the term "colony" was never used by France to refer to its overseas territories or departments. New Caledonia, no longer a territory nor a department, exercises numerous fiscal, commercial, and regulatory functions, as well as those concerned with air and sea transport and public health. These responsibilities can only increase as new administrative functions are devolved to New Caledonia by the French state as provided for in the 1998 Noumea Accord. Last, the only French citizens eligible to vote in elections relating to New Caledonia are those who can prove ten years' continuous residence in New Caledonia from the date of the signing of the Matignon Accord. These French citizens are equally citizens of New Caledonia and have the benefit of the laws of the country, which protect and favor locals in employment. In relation to French law, New Caledonia is now quasi-independent, and is thus struggling with an unfinished process of state formation that must accommodate both introduced Western and customary systems of law and governance.

■ Assets of the Future

The 2004–2005 electoral results in New Caledonia, as in French Polynesia, radically transformed the political landscape. The Kanak parties did not return a single member to the assembly of the Southern province, which is therefore run exclusively by loyalists. In the Northern province, the assembly is almost exclusively composed of proindependence Kanak members. In the Islands province (comprising Mare, Lifou, Tiga, and Ouvea), the full spectrum of political parties on the ballot was represented in the assembly. New Caledonia undoubtedly became more difficult to govern, as there was no longer an absolute majority in the congress. It has therefore been a question of constantly forming new alliances between the different parties, and of the congress proceeding item-by-item in order to have legislation approved.

Moreover, in an extraordinary outcome, both the FLNKS and the RPCR, the two leading local parties associated with the Noumea Accord, lost representation. The change of the majority in the Southern province, away from the RPCR, can be explained by the erosion of power experienced by Jacques Lafleur,[9] as well as by the emergence of a new generation of politicians who sought to transform the power base by advocating increased social justice, increased equality, and a greater sharing of resources, while keeping strong links with France. Indeed, despite the ongoing social and economic packages brought in under the Noumea Accord, New Caledonia faces the dangers of persistent and deep social divisions between those who have economic power (businesspeople, civil servants, members of the liberal professions, and so forth) and those, mostly indigenous people, who live in poverty on minimum wages (laborers, domestic servants, and those in the mining industry), with limited access to consumer goods as a result.

New Caledonians struggled to understand the remarkable disappearance of proindependence members from the assembly of the Southern province and the simultaneous loss of support for the two partners in the Noumea Accord. However, the relationship between the French metropolis and New Caledonia was not upset by the change in the political situation. If this result appears, at least on the surface, to be a polarization of politics along regional lines, it has not had any appreciable impact on levels of tension or confrontation.

Economy and Finance

In contrast with other French territories in the Pacific—French Polynesia, Wallis, and Futuna—in New Caledonia natural resources, chiefly minerals, contribute significantly to its economic development. For a considerable time, only the Société le Nickel (SLN) treated the ore that it or other mining companies had extracted. The economy of New Caledonia basically revolved around the SLN, which, at the end of the 1970s, employed some 6,000 people. By 2000, the mining sector had changed dramatically, as had Kanak participation in the industry. This might be seen as a deliberate forward-looking policy and overtly economic solution to what were previously seen only as social, cultural, and political problems. Two new mining projects are now being planned. In the Northern province there is a pyrometallurgical project with the Canadian company Falconbridge, piloted by a Kanak semipublic mixed investment company. In the Southern province the project involves a metallurgical factory, Goro Nickel, backed by the Canadian company Inco. These two new factories will triple the production of nickel in New Caledonia and will increase gross domestic product (GDP) by a third.

For several decades, aquaculture has been developing and the export of prawns also adds to GDP. It is now estimated that New Caledonia can produce 50 percent of its total consumption needs in terms of livestock, fishing, and agriculture. Tourism is also a source of income, but is limited by geographical distance and the cost of air travel. Subsistence food production remains important for many Kanaks. In 2004, New Caledonia had a GDP per capita of US$17,538 per person;[10] however, this average figure does not represent the significant provincial, ethnic, and social disparities.

The monetary unit in New Caledonia is the French Pacific franc (CFP): one euro at fixed parity is equivalent to 119.33 CFPs and 1,000 CFPs equates to 8.38 euros. There is increasing talk of giving up the CFP in favor of the euro, which, by devaluing the CFP, would allow the economies of the three French entities in the Pacific, where this currency has been in circulation since 1945, to be stabilized. However, a median devaluation between New Caledonia, French Polynesia, and Wallis and Futuna would need to be found, and this would automatically harm the assets of New Caledonian nationals, for whom the rate of overvaluation is generally estimated at some 5 percent, compared to approximately 25 percent in Tahiti. Such a measure, though, would have the advantage of making New Caledonian exports more competitive. In 2005, French government financial transfers to New Caledonia were approximately US$1 billion. In terms of outlays, New Caledonia's budget increased from US$720 million in 1992 to US$900 million in 2002, while income for the same period rose from US$720 million to US$870 million.

New Caledonia's principal exports, amounting to 90 percent of total exports, are still mining and fishing products, accounting for up to US$315 million and US$1.5 million, respectively. The value of imports rose from US$49.5 million in 1993 to US$71.5 million in 2002. Of this, 39 percent came from France, 13 percent from Australia,[11] 13 percent from the European Union, 5 percent from New Zealand,[12] with the remaining 30 percent shared among Singapore (10 percent), the United States (4.3 percent), Japan (3.3 percent), and other countries combined (12.4 percent). Aside from its two bigger neighbors, New Caledonia conducts some trade with Vanuatu, Fiji, French Polynesia, and Wallis and Futuna. The proposed French-Pacific economic market has yet to come to fruition.

Regionalism

The Matignon and Noumea Accords supported New Caledonia being more firmly grounded regionally in the Melanesian arc. Links with the Republic of Vanuatu, where more than 30 percent of the population speak French, seemed to be a natural development, but the paths to cooperation have not been easy. Agreements for education, training, and economic exchanges were signed, but there have been difficulties putting these into effect, partly due to political instability experienced by Vanuatu since the beginning of the 1990s. New Caledonia also sought to establish itself in the Pacific market, but its exports have had difficulty competing with the price of products from other Melanesian countries also situated in the commercial sphere of Australia and New Zealand. For New Caledonia, its regional trading possibilities lie on a different plane. It is possible that this potential will be realized within the Melanesian arc, but in close partnership with Australia and New Zealand.

There has been a resurgence of concern regarding political instability, poor governance, and the potential for terrorism and organized crime in the region. The Australian government has sought New Caledonian cooperation, from both the police and the military. Noumea has hosted a number of regional security meetings, with the French national police active in the exchange of policing methods, information, and the establishment of regional police networks in the Pacific Island region. In 2006, Australia, New Zealand, and France agreed to take cooperative action against illegal fishing in the region (a serious threat to a key regional resource) and to strengthen joint work on disaster management.

For the past decade, joint military operations have been undertaken by French, Australian, New Zealand, Tongan, Fijian, and Papua New Guinean military personnel, and have been held in New Caledonia every two years or so. The aim is to bring together the military from each of these countries and to organize simulated interarmy commando operations on one of the Loyalty islands or on the mainland of New Caledonia. More than a thousand personnel usually take part. These exercises are intended to establish a common skills base and to prepare for a possible intervention against a variety of internal or external threats related to civil war or acts of terrorism. This regional military collaboration was also demonstrated when field officers and a contingent of soldiers from New Caledonia took part in an Australian-led United Nations operation in East Timor.

Since a low point in the 1980s, Canberra and Wellington have developed a more positive appreciation of France's policies in the Pacific. France has significant means available to foster regional cohesion, while maintaining good terms with the two major Pacific Rim countries.[13] Certainly the page on civil unrest in New Caledonia and on nuclear testing in French Polynesia has now been turned, and the image of France is more positive among its neighbors.[14] Moreover, particularly as Britain has been reducing its presence in the region, France is now emerging as an increasingly significant presence from the European Union, and more broadly the Western Hemisphere, in Oceania.

Finally, in relation to Pacific Island regionalism and the future, it is appropriate to refer to the Secretariat for the Pacific Community, which, in name and function, recently replaced the South Pacific Commission (SPC). This regional body, whose mission is to advance the development of the islands of the Pacific, has been based in Noumea since its creation in Canberra in 1947. In contrast to the Pacific Islands Forum, which is a political body of independent Pacific states, the SPC is a development body with a wide membership. It gathers funds for regional development from the initial, and continuing, sponsorship of Australia, New Zealand, the United States, and France, and new partners such as the European Union and Japan. France has been an important economic and financial partner of this regional organization. At the beginning of the 1990s, amid debates on moving the seat of the regional body to Suva (where the Pacific Islands Forum is centered), France bargained for it to remain in Noumea and offered to finance the construction of new quarters in the most beautiful precinct and bay in the capital. This became an architectural marvel, conceived and realized by a Fijian architect. Although some SPC services are now located in Suva, it seems impractical, in the medium term, for the SPC offices to merge with the Suva-based Pacific Islands Forum Secretariat in order to form a single regional organization. Certain countries, mainly in Melanesia, have been demanding this change since the end of the 1980s.[15] However, there is nothing to prevent the two organizations from working together more effectively or from sharing some of their development programs.

Through a united group of Kanak proindependence political parties, New Caledonia is an observer member at the Pacific Islands Forum. For several years, French Polynesia has also requested this status, without it being granted. Now that the proindependence parties hold the political majority in Tahiti, it is foreseeable that the new president of French Polynesia, Oscar Temaru, will take a seat as an observer. France in the Pacific would then be better integrated into its English-speaking Pacific environment.

Since the Matignon and Noumea Accords, each year the Pacific Islands Forum and the Melanesian Spearhead Group, with the approval of the UN Special Committee of Twenty-Four, on decolonization, send missions to New Caledonia to assess the political climate and to verify that the terms of the two accords are being upheld. At the end of their participation in these missions, some high-ranking Pacific leaders have declared publicly that France has been right to make preparations over the long term for the emancipation of its territories without thereby hastening their accession to constitutional independence in the way that certain other colonial powers have done.

■ Conclusion

The 1970s and 1980s were dominated by the politics of independence in the Pacific Island countries with a majority indigenous population. By comparison, New Caledonia resisted that movement, essentially because settler communities refused to adhere to the idea of a political separation from France. The settlers felt that independence would have a negative economic impact. As we have seen, France provides approximately US$1 billion in annual aid for New Caledonia, and as more and more Kanaks achieve full secondary and tertiary education, get well-paid jobs, and settle in Noumea and its periphery, they insert themselves into Westernized ways of life. At the same time, socioeconomic fractures continue to exist and to expand in the *favellas* (shantytowns) and squats of Noumea's suburbs. This phenomenon is well studied and is certainly not exclusive to New Caledonia. The squats of more than a thousand extended families living in very poor conditions are characterized by violence, be it economic, psychological, or physical. Alcohol and marijuana are the usual sociopsychological compensations, particularly among young people.

Mining projects have been promoted from Paris, both in the Southern province and in the Northern province, and the fiscal arrangements granted to help realize both projects will facilitate better economic growth and wealth distribution. Migration movements from Asia, mainly from the Philippines and China, are possible in order to obtain a semiqualified and less expensive labor force. New Caledonia's economic future seems ensured. With administrative and technical support from Paris, and stable governments with full and equal participation at the provincial and territorial level, New Caledonia should avoid the security and conflict problems generated elsewhere in the region by, for example, ethnic conflict, regional disparities, corruption, money laundering, overmining, and deforestation.

Despite the small population of New Caledonia, the confrontations in the 1980s were an example of how overseas French territories can exert considerable influence on metropolitan politics, leading to efforts to respond constructively to some of the grievances underlying the violence. The conflict within New Caledonia itself over independence has been changed from a violent confrontation to a slower effort to deal more constructively with the very real divisions and disagreements. This slow process of negotiation over the formation of a New Caledonian state that reflects the history of colonization and struggle for independence gives the New Caledonian population a degree of agency and genuine political citizenship in a unique and creative effort at state building. The final choice of remaining fully part of France or to become independent shall be proposed to the New Caledonian people in 2010 to 2015. Voters will have to reconcile the contradictory aspirations of their loyalist or proindependence political trends. Presently, all parties agree that it is healthy to disagree, but that disagreement cannot provide a common destiny.

▨ Notes

1. This is a generic word for "indigenous Melanesian people" in New Caledonia. It is a grammatically invariable word in French according to a political decision taken by Kanak leaders in the early 1990s.

2. Western Samoa became independent in 1962, Nauru in 1968, Tonga and Fiji in 1970, Papua New Guinea in 1975, the Solomon Islands and Tuvalu in 1978, Kiribati in 1979, and Vanuatu in 1980.

3. Set up in 1987 by Vanuatu, the Solomon Islands, and Papua New Guinea. Initially, Fiji refused to join, until Sitiveni Rabuka became prime minister.

4. Rocard was also to repair, once and for all, the shattered relations between New Zealand and France caused by nuclear testing and the Rainbow Warrior affair.

5. The socialist Front de Libération Nationale Kanak et Socialiste (FLNKS, a coalition of parties seeking independence) and the Rassemblement pour la Calédonie dans la République (RPCR, a party described as loyalist in relation to France and therefore anti-independence).

6. The question was: "Do you agree to the law put to the French people by the President of the Republic containing statutory arrangements preparatory to self-determination in New Caledonia?" In response, 80 percent voted yes. Something never before seen in a French national referendum occurred when there was an abstention rate of 63 percent. In New Caledonia, Kanaks voted massively in favor, while more than 60 percent of the other ethnic groups voted no.

7. The assassin had lost family members in the hostage crisis—a likely motivation for exacting revenge on Tjibaou's perceived "soft" attitude toward negotiation with the French authorities. Questions of intercommunal reconciliation are discussed by Nic Maclellan in Chapter 7.

8. Comprising seven out of fourteen members for the Islands province, fifteen of twenty-two for the Northern province, and thirty-two of forty for the Southern province.

9. He eventually resigned from presidency of the RPCR.

10. See http://www.unescap.org/stat/data/statind/pdf/t16_dec05.pdf (accessed 26 June 2006).

11. As an example, the balance of trade between Australia and New Caledonia is negative for the latter (with an export/import cover rate of 20.7 percent in 2002 and a deficit in the balance of trade with Australia of US$73 million). Australia is second largest supplier of goods to New Caledonia after France. Of New Caledonian exports, 6.6 percent go to Australia, which is ranked sixth among countries that import from New Caledonia, behind Japan, France, Taiwan, South Korea, and Spain.

12. The New Zealand trade balance is even more negative. In 2003, New Caledonia imported goods from New Zealand valued at US$38 million, whereas its exports the other way amounted to US$28 million. The fourth-ranking supplier of goods to New Caledonia, behind France, Australia, and Singapore, is New Zealand, which supplies 4.2 percent of New Caledonian imports. The main imports are food products, machines and mechanical appliances, paper and cardboard, and objects made of wood or aluminum.

13. A French offer of immediate military assistance in the RAMSI intervention in the Solomon Island crisis in 2000–2003 was unfortunately not taken. Australia

and New Zealand derive greater commercial benefits from trade with the two French Pacific entities than with other Pacific Island states.

14. Nevertheless, among the bureaucrats stationed in the Melanesian archipelagos, old reflex reactions persist; many still believe that Australians see French diplomats or aid workers as intruders in their sphere of influence, and vice versa.

15. Clearly, economies of scale would be made, redundancies avoided, and a better structuring of development could be brought about. But this is not where the basic structural difficulty vis-à-vis the creation of the sole regional organization lies. Indeed, the Pacific Islands Forum has a political rather than technical mission, while the SPC is essentially a technical body directed toward development. Resistance to the merging of the two bodies is coming more from the Polynesian countries whose economic resources are poor in relation to those of the Melanesian countries. These Polynesian nations have a greater need for development aid from the founding metropolitan members and from the new partners of the SPC.

7

Conflict and Reconciliation in New Caledonia

Nic Maclellan

IN RECENT YEARS, Canberra's policy toward the Pacific Islands has been dominated by concern over "failed" and "failing" states. Politicians and journalists commonly express concern over the so-called arc of instability in the Melanesian islands to the north and east of Australia.

In the 1980s the French Pacific territory of New Caledonia was at the forefront of this concern—driven by French state terrorism in Auckland Harbor, perceptions about "Libyans in the Pacific," and armed clashes between the French state, the independence coalition Front de Libération Nationale Kanak et Socialiste (FLNKS) and the conservative anti-independence party Rassemblement pour la Calédonie dans la République (RPCR).

However, since the conflict of the 1980s, New Caledonia has been presented as a haven of stability in the region, in comparison to neighboring Melanesian countries like Papua New Guinea and the Solomon Islands. New Caledonia has largely dropped off the regional security agenda, with neighboring countries focused on improving trade and economic links.

The current policy focus on crises in the Solomon Islands, Papua New Guinea, and Fiji often ignores a broader historical perspective of the region. However, there are ongoing cultural, political, and social tensions in New Caledonia, and the issues of peacebuilding, reconciliation, and self-determination are just as relevant today for the French dependency as for neighboring independent countries.

During the 1980s, two competing blocs—the FLNKS and the RPCR—dominated New Caledonia's political life. Following the violent conflict in 1984–1988, New Caledonia's leaders have negotiated a series of agreements to bring together these competing political forces to develop a "common destiny" for the Pacific nation. Two decades after the FLNKS's 1984 election boycott, violent clashes have been replaced by a new engagement with electoral institutions, following the 1988 Matignon-Oudinot Accords and the 1998 Noumea Accord. As discussed in Chapter 6, the FLNKS has entered the institutions of government, and Kanak independence leaders serve in a multiparty government alongside their conservative opponents.

However, the introduction of new political institutions—three provincial assemblies, a congress, a multiparty executive government, and a customary Kanak senate—has not ensured an end to political conflict in New Caledonia. The two key political formations of the 1980s have fractured, and the new institutions of governance have created a fluid, multiparty parliamentary system.

A focus on creating peace agreements to end armed violence downplays the need for sustained development programs to address the underlying causes of social and political conflict (the failure of the October 2000 Townsville peace agreement for the Solomon Islands highlights this problem). Rather than short-term negotiations between government officials and armed militias, there is a need for wider, ongoing efforts to address clashes between landowners, government, and transnational corporations over distribution of natural resources; the impact of resource projects on culture and the environment; militarized responses from the state to the demands of landowners, indigenous groups, and movements for democratic rights and self-determination; and social conflicts arising from the effects of economic "reform" programs, with responses from urban squatters, trade unions, or isolated rural communities.[1]

Even though massive French financial transfers have given New Caledonia one of the region's highest per capita incomes, the territory faces challenges similar to those of its Melanesian neighbors: involving the indigenous population in local and national governance; promoting economic rebalancing between the capital and the bush; providing suitable education and jobs for young people; halting the HIV/AIDS pandemic; and managing the wealth of the territory's vast natural resources.

■ The Noumea Accord

The Noumea Accord process, discussed in Chapter 6 by Paul de Deckker, involves some key elements that may have applicability for other regional self-determination struggles:

- New Caledonia has a sui generis status separate from other French territories entrenched by referendum in the French constitution. The constitution, given that it defines attributes for New Caledonia in a separate section, is harder to amend if there is a change of government in Paris.
- New Caledonia has unique political and legislative powers not available to other French "territorial collectivities."
- New Caledonia has a fixed timetable toward a vote on self-determi-

nation to decide its future political status (unlike French Polynesia's autonomy statute, which has no provision or timetable for a referendum on political status).

- The Noumea Accord process involves an "irreversible" transfer of administrative powers from Paris to local authorities and the new congress in New Caledonia (unlike other autonomy statutes, where powers transferred to local authorities can be taken back by Paris).
- The French government has guaranteed funding for the process (in sharp contrast to the Bougainville autonomy process).[2]

■ Community Reconciliation

A focus on civil and political rights and constitutional change downplays the larger question of the underlying causes of conflict, often relating to issues of land, cultural identity, and social and economic rights. As one Pacific activist has noted:

> There is a limit to legislative justice. You cannot legislate away racial discrimination or for peaceful co-existence. Enlightened Constitutions and legislation must be supplemented by social engineering initiatives that are aimed at social cohesion and human security in a multi-ethnic milieu. These must include educational curricula that promote multi-ethnic tolerance and unity. It must include affirmative action or social justice programs that are geared towards rebalancing the inequities in access to educational, commercial opportunities and state services (health, water, electricity) and resources that were inherited from the colonial government. It must include national dialogue between the different racial and ethnic groups to address the "problems of history" relating to the alienation of land and natural resources during the colonial era, and also the place of indigenous peoples in the scheme of democratic governance.[3]

In journalistic shorthand, New Caledonia's conflict is often presented as "Kanaks versus French." But the complexities of reconciliation arise from the complex interplay of class and ethnicity; as in all recent Pacific crises, conflicts within ethnic communities are as significant as those between ethnic communities. There are also political differences between locally born New Caledonians (Kanak and "Caldoche"), public servants and military personnel from metropolitan France (the "metros"), and immigrant communities from other French territories.

New Caledonia's population has evolved through the process of colonial settlement and ongoing immigration, and the indigenous Melanesian population is currently a minority in its own land. Today's political institutions are the latest attempt to recognize the rights of indigenous Kanaks, but also those of the "victims of history"—the descendants of convicts and settlers who have been born in New Caledonia, and those immigrants from other French colonies (such as Wallis and Futuna and the New Hebrides) who have made New Caledonia their home.[4]

A key feature of current political life is the promotion of reconciliation between and within the various communities in the country.[5] But competing political forces in New Caledonia still perceive the Noumea Accord in a different light: some see it as a guarantee that there will be a referendum on self-determination; for others, the question of political independence can be delayed for decades, if not forever.[6]

In Pacific cultures, the public expression of peace and reconciliation is a central element of conflict resolution.[7] Grassroots activists around the region are drawing on a synergistic mixture of Christian and Melanesian values to promote "restorative justice"—for example, in Bougainville, reconciliation efforts emphasize traditional peacemaking processes to promote the reconstruction of social harmony and transcend the "payback" mentality.[8]

Some of the most successful reconciliation processes have involved the often undervalued Pacific traditions of consensus and *la parole*—the power of the spoken word, talking together, shame, and personal pledges of commitment. Custom, ceremony, and a sense of history are a crucial part of postconflict reconciliation, together with the importance of time—allowing people to meet, consult, and decide at their own pace. But not all these processes have been successful, and it is important to compare and contrast experiences across the region.

■ Reconciling Gossanah and the Tragedy of Ouvea

It is worth discussing one example of a long-term reconciliation process led by churches, political leaders, and indigenous groups in New Caledonia, attempting to bring together communities destroyed by the Ouvea crisis of 1988–1989.[9] The crisis has become an important symbol of New Caledonia's conflict, creating political, moral, and social gulfs that are only slowly being bridged by the current mood of reconciliation.

Throughout the conflict of the mid-1980s, Kanak tactics were marked by alternating periods of violence and negotiation.[10] With dialogue impossible after the introduction of the 1987 Pons statute, the FLNKS moved to boycott the May 1988 French presidential elections, and elections on the same day for a new local government. The FLNKS had planned a nationwide mobilization to highlight its opposition to French policy, but the uprising only took place in Canala on the main island of Grande Terre, and on Ouvea in the Loyalty Islands.

As part of the uprising, a local group of Kanak independence activists attempted to take over a police station at Fayaoue on Ouvea on 22 April 1988. In the subsequent melee, three gendarmes were killed and another was mortally wounded.[11] Twenty-seven others were taken hostage and hidden in caves in the north of the island, near the village of Gossanah. The Ouvea crisis led to a major military mobilization on the island, and the torture and maltreatment of villagers by French troops trying to find the location of the hostages.[12] Djubelli Wea, a former Protestant theology student and leading independence activist from Gossanah, was dragged from his sickbed, questioned about the location of the hostages, and tied to a tree. His father, beaten by French troops, later died.

The assault on the caves to free the captured police coincided with a final (and unsuccessful) attempt on the part of then–prime minister Jacques Chirac to glean votes between the two rounds of the 1988 presidential elections. The conservative government wanted to show it would not bow to Kanak demands—Overseas Territories Minister Bernard Pons even discussed use of a 250-kiloton napalm bomb, which would have killed both the hostages and the hostage-takers.[13]

On 5 May 1988, the French government abandoned negotiations and launched a military attack, with elite police and a commando unit storming the cave. Nineteen Kanak activists were killed, with at least three executed after surrendering. Their leader, Alphonse Dianou, was shot in his knee during capture, and left to die.[14] Twenty-nine other men from around Ouvea, including Djubelli Wea, were arrested and transported to jail in Paris. Ouvea was left with a legacy of bitterness and tragedy—men from over half the twenty-seven villages in Ouvea were dead or in jail, and tensions were created with the FLNKS leadership.

The Ouvea tragedy made all parties step back from the brink, and incoming prime minister Michel Rocard proposed negotiations, leading to the 1988 Matignon and Oudinot Accords. The accords included a provision for amnesty for crimes committed before August 1988. After the accords were approved by referendum in November 1988, the French parliament extended the amnesty to those charged with murder, covering both the killers of the four police at Fayaoue, and the police and soldiers responsible for the alleged torture at Gossanah and murder of surrendering Kanaks.

But the legacy of grief and division after the Ouvea massacre contributed to the assassination of Kanak leaders Jean-Marie Tjibaou and Yeiwene Yeiwene. The two FLNKS leaders came to the island on 5 May 1989 to mark *la levée du deuil,* the end of a yearlong period of mourning. At the ceremony, Tjibaou and Yeiwene were shot and killed by Djubelli Wea, who was immediately gunned down by Tjibaou's bodyguard.

These events meant that the people of Ouvea, and especially the community of Gossanah, were isolated politically and morally from many New Caledonians. This included much of the independence movement, because Tjibaou was a charismatic and popular leader of the FLNKS.[15] For many years, the community could not recover from the 1988 Ouvea massacre and the 1989 assassinations, and a sense of isolation, frustration, and bitterness marred their capacity to rebuild links with the FLNKS leadership. The Gossanah community largely supported the "Front Anti-Néocolonialist," made up of various forces opposed to the 1988 Matignon Accord, which led to divisions in subsequent years that were slow to heal.

Journalistic shorthand, which dubs the slain Kanak leaders as "moderates" versus the "extremists" of Ouvea, masks a more complex reality.[16] The reconciliation process—between the Gossanah community; the family, clan, and supporters of the slain FLNKS leaders; and the families and supporters of the four slain police officers—has involved a complex process of trust building that has broader national implications.

I traveled with a delegation to Ouvea in August 1990, just fifteen months after the killing of Tjibaou, Yeiwene, and Wea, and was invited to visit Gossanah. At the time, the community was widely shunned, and some people regarded contact with the militants on Ouvea as a slur on the memory of the two FLNKS leaders. For others, their deaths were seen as part of a more complex whole—on the same visit, I saw a mural to commemorate the "three leaders" painted on the side of a bus shelter near Tiendanite, on the east coast of Grande Terre. The mural, in the style of a Christian triptych, showed Tjibaou flanked by both his lieutenant, Yeiwene, and his assassin, Wea.[17]

On Ouvea, the nineteen slain Kanak activists were buried together at Wadrilla—over time, their graves were transformed into a shrine, with elaborate marble headpieces. The veneration of "the nineteen" was matched by an opposing French campaign to recognize the four gendarmes killed in the assault on Fayaoue on 22 April, and the commandos killed in the assault to release the hostages. In France, the Comité du 22 Avril 1988 à la Mémoire des Gendarmes d'Ouvea—a solidarity committee for the police officers—gained support from the right wing, and maintains a polemical campaign against the French Socialist Party, which granted amnesty to the killers. The committee set about creating memorials around France for the policemen, which were unveiled in 1989, 1992, 1994, and 1995. Every year, they still organize a ceremony to light a flame at the Arc de Triomphe in memory of the Fayaoue gendarmes.[18]

In 1995, an initiative to reconcile the divided Kanak families and clans was initiated by Anselme Poaragnimou, a customary leader who today serves as chairman of the Paicî-Ciamuki customary council. Poaragnimou started traveling from Poindimié to Tjibaou's village, to Ouvea, then to Yeiwene's home on the island of Mare, always using the traditional paths that link clans all over the country, across the mountains and the valleys, across the sea.

The negotiation of the Noumea Accord in April 1998 opened the way for more public gestures of reconciliation. As French political leaders prepared to travel to New Caledonia for the signing of the agreement on 5 May (the ninth anniversary of Tjibaou's death), they felt a need to mark the events in Ouvea. Thus on 22 April 1998, a decade after the attack on the Fayaoue gendarmerie, an ecumenical service was held in a Catholic church on Ouvea to mark the reconciliation of the Ouvea community and the police force.

Further gestures of reconciliation were to follow. In August 1998, France's overseas territories minister, Jean-Jack Queyranne, from the French Socialist Party, traveled to Gossanah and planted a tree in the village. This first visit by a government minister was an important symbol, breaching the tribe's isolation. It also signaled a political shift for key Ouvea activists, from opposition to the 1988 Matignon Accord toward support for the 1998 Noumea Accord. Queyranne later told the National Assembly in Paris:

> I want to recall the memory of an intense moment, one afternoon in mid-August this year in Ouvea. I saluted the memory of the police officers at the monument at the police headquarters at Fayaoue, I was received at the monument for "the 19," and I was the first member of the Government to visit Gossanah. After the traditional welcome and the exchange of customary gifts, the chief and the pastor took the microphone to recall the trauma that the tribe had suffered ten years ago, and welcomed me as a representative of the French Republic. After having affirmed their strong and ongoing commitment to the independence struggle, before me they called on those assembled to vote "yes" in the referendum [to approve the Noumea Accord]. We saw the positive outcome of this in Ouvea on 8 November [date of the referendum].[19]

The central role of the churches is a crucial element in the Kanak struggle and the reconciliation process for Gossanah. Jean-Marie Tjibaou was a former Catholic seminarian; Alphonse Dianou, leader of the Ouvea hostage-takers, trained for the priesthood at the Pacific Regional Seminary in Suva; Djubelli Wea did pastoral training at the Pacific Theological College in Suva; and Jean Wetc and Pothin Wetc, leading Kanak theologians, are originally from Gossanah.

In 2000, the main Protestant denomination Eglise Evangélique en Nouvelle Calédonie (EENC) held its synod in Gossanah. The president of the EENC, Pastor Jean Wete, went on to play a central role in the reconciliation process between the Wea, Tjibaou, and Yeiwene families. Joined by Father Rock Apikaoua (vicar-general of the Catholic Church in New Caledonia), Pastor Wete worked over five years after the Noumea Accord to promote dialogue, face-to-face meetings, and ultimately reconciliation between the wives, then the children, and then the clans of the three central figures of the Ouvea tragedy. Although some family members were reluctant to participate in the process and many tears were shed, this process has been vital in sealing a breach that could not be healed by judicial mechanisms.

Another set of ceremonies was held around the country on 5 May 2001, the thirteenth anniversary of the deaths of Tjibaou and Yeiwene. Then–FLNKS president Rock Wamytan expressed: "The wish that New Caledonian and Kanak collective memory does not forget the sacrifice of its 19 valorous men of Ouvéa, which inspired the intelligence of all parties to come up with the Matignon Accords. May they remember too that the charismatic memory of Jean-Marie and Yéyé has strongly influenced the decision to pursue peace through the Nouméa Accord."

By 2003, even Brigitte Girardin, overseas minister from President Jacques Chirac's conservative Union of Moderate Parties (UMP), felt obliged to travel to Ouvea to mark this spirit of reconciliation. A month later, during his July 2003 visit to New Caledonia, President Chirac stressed the importance of consensus and reconciliation between the territory's different ethnic communities. In a major speech in Noumea's Place des Cocotiers, President Chirac said France and New Caledonia could work together "hand in hand" for the future.

But President Chirac has made no public atonement for his personal role in the events of 1988. When Chirac traveled to the northern town of Kone in July 2003, his visit was marked by protests, with nearly 1,000 members of the proindependence party Union Calédonienne and the Union Syndicale des Travailleurs Kanaks et des Exploités (USTKE; Union of Kanaks and Exploited Workers), a trade union confederation, rallying against the president's visit. Police fired tear gas to disperse the crowd, but the wind blew the tear gas back across the official welcoming party. USTKE spokesman Pierre Chauvat explained: "Remember that when Chirac was Prime Minister between the two rounds in the Presidential elections in 1988, he took the responsibility to murder 19 Kanaks in Ouvea. So we said to him that he had Kanak blood on his hands."[20]

It seems that the spirit of reconciliation only goes so far. In the face of ongoing political differences, the Ouvea tragedy still has vital symbolic power.

▓ Good Governance or Self-Determination?

The ongoing colonial relationship between France and New Caledonia has important implications for the way that systems of governance are created, administered, and reviewed, and the ways New Caledonia engages with neighboring Pacific countries.

In 1986, the UN General Assembly relisted New Caledonia as a non-self-governing territory with the UN Special Committee on Decolonization.[21] While rejecting the involvement of the committee, the French government has acknowledged that decolonization is the solution to New Caledonia's political conflicts, by signing the Noumea Accord in May 1998.[22]

The current academic and policy focus on "good governance"—which dominates Australian policy in the Pacific—largely ignores the question of self-determination. The Pacific Plan (discussed in Chapter 14) does not engage with questions of self-determination or decolonization, even though issues of autonomy and independence remain a central part of political life in the region, from Tokelau to New Caledonia and French Polynesia, from Guam to West Papua and Bougainville.

Current self-determination processes in the Pacific are impacting on the main regional intergovernmental structure, the Pacific Islands Forum. The forum will have to monitor developments around self-determination in all these Pacific nations throughout the coming decade (indeed, the transition processes for both Bougainville and New Caledonia are currently scheduled to culminate at about the same time in 2015).

The forum is currently seeking closer cooperation with the French territories, but this process goes back more than twenty-five years, after the South Pacific Forum put the New Caledonia issue on its agenda at the 1981 leaders' meeting in Vanuatu.

The policy of the Pacific Islands Forum toward non-self-governing territories has been evolving. In April 2004, an eminent persons group (EPG) chaired by Julius Chan, former prime minister of Papua New Guinea, issued a report on the activities and priorities of the forum's secretariat. The EPG report noted:

> There is also a strong view that the Forum needs to better connect with Pacific communities that currently do not have a voice in the Forum process. The key omissions are the French and US Pacific territories. Observer status at the Forum would be a useful step towards enhanced regional inclusiveness and co-operation. We ask Leaders to consider integrating all the French and US territories into the Forum as observers and to be open to approaches from other non-sovereign Pacific territories. New criteria for participation should be developed, grounded in the region's interests.[23]

In response, the Pacific Islands Forum leaders' retreat (2004) resolved to: Encourage closer contacts with non-sovereign Pacific territories, through progressively guaranteeing them observer status at Leaders' meetings and associated meetings of the Forum Officials Committee. New criteria for participation should be developed, *grounded in the region's interests.*[24]

The Pacific Plan, endorsed by forum leaders at the October 2005 forum meeting, proposes closer association with the nonsovereign Pacific Island countries to extend and deepen regional cooperation.[25] (New Caledonia has held observer status with the Pacific Islands Forum since 1999.)[26] Will the Pacific region continue to assist the transition toward a final referendum on self-determination at the end of the Noumea Accord process?

■ Conclusion

In the absence of armed conflict, New Caledonia has dropped from the headlines, an island of stability in the "arc of instability." Australia and New Zealand are developing a booming trade relationship with New Caledonia, but this is not matched by extensive community development programs that assist grassroots peacebuilding (the Australian Agency for International Development does not provide development assistance to New Caledonia, apart from a few student scholarships). There is scope for more active engagement with the people of Australia's close neighbor.

■ Notes

1. For discussion of the regional context to conflict and reconciliation, see Maclellan, "Creating Peace in the Pacific."

2. For discussion, see Faberon, "La Nouvelle Calédonie et la Révision Constitutionelle."

3. Senituli, "Indigenous Peoples in the Pacific Context."

4. The concept of "the victims of history" was invoked at the 1983 roundtable at Nainville-les-Roches in France, where pro- and anti-independence leaders jointly agreed that all residents of New Caledonia—indigenous and nonindigenous—have a part to play in building the country's future. For some Kanaks, this is a compromise on the principle that the indigenous people alone have the right to self-determination.

5. For details, see Maclellan, "Conflict and Reconciliation in New Caledonia."

6. For example, in April 2004, conservative leader Jacques Lafleur told the congress of his RPCR party that a scheduled referendum on self-determination will not happen in 2014. Lafleur told the meeting: "No one will want to go to the referendum. . . . Independence has now become just a word, a dream. . . . So why not let the people dream, why not let them have the feeling that they have not lost, but that we have all won together?" *PacNews,* 20 April 2004.

7. For examples, see Dinnen, *A Kind of Mending.*

8. Howley, *Breaking Spears and Mending Hearts.* See also Thompson, *Breaking Bows and Arrows.*

9. Also see Maclellan, "Conflict and Reconciliation in New Caledonia."

10. Beyond the balance of forces at the time, this was a reflection of customary Kanak modes of warfare, with their "enduring emphasis on restraint coupled with a belief in the psychological value of short, sharp explosions of violence." Douglas, "Almost Constantly at War?" pp. 43–44.

11. *Le Monde* journalists Edwy Plenel and Alain Rollat, in *Mourir à Ouvea,* give key background to the Ouvea crisis. Alexandre Sanguinetti et al., in *Enquête sur Ouvea,* outline evidence of the military's action and breaches of human rights. A Groupe d'Intervention de la Gendarmerie Nationale police officer who was at the center of the crisis has also written an account: Legorjus, *La Morale et l'Action.* See also Weill, *"Opération Victor."*

12. Vivid firsthand testimony from Kanak villagers, detailing beatings and torture by French soldiers, is recorded in two special editions of the magazine *Bwenando:* "Gossanah: Dossier COPIDEC, L'Affaire d'Ouvea" (nos. 109–110, 30 August 1988, and nos. 111–112, 18 October 1988). Chanel Kapoeri, a municipal

councillor in Ouvea, gives his testimony in *Le Mémorial Calédonian,* vol. 9 (Noumea, 1995).

13. Audigier, "L'Affaire de la Grotte d'Ouvea."

14. A photo published at the time shows French troops standing beside Dianou on a stretcher, his knee bandaged, surrounded by the manacled Kanaks face-down on the ground. See "Ouvea: La Verité," *Paris Match,* 10 June 1988.

15. Some of the Kanak leader's writings are collated in Tjibaou, *La Présence Kanak;* and Tjibaou, *Cibau Cibau.*

16. Tjibaou and the Union Calédonienne are often referred to as "moderates," in contrast to the Front Uni de Liberation Kanak and other groups that opposed the Matignon Accord. But it was Tjibaou and Union Calédonien secretary-general Eloi Machoro who planned the "muscular boycott" of the 1984 elections, and Machoro who first traveled to Libya to tweak the French nose, at a time when Colonel Gaddafi was public enemy number one in the Ronald Reagan administration's campaign against "international terrorism."

17. Another tribute to Wea can be seen in the poem "To Djubelly," by Fijian activist Claire Slatter.

18. For details on the solidarity committee, see http://www.gend-ouvea.asso.fr/home.html (accessed 15 September 2004).

19. M. Jean-Jack Queyranne, secretary of state for overseas affairs and acting minister of interior, National Assembly, 1st sess., 21 December 1998, p. 10836.

20. "Protests Follow French President," *Pacific Beat,* Radio Australia, July 2003, available at http://www.abc.net.au/ra/pacbeat (accessed 9 July 2004).

21. After lobbying by the Pacific Islands Forum, the UN General Assembly voted to reinscribe New Caledonia on the list of non-self-governing territories in Resolution 41/41 of 2 December 1986, which "affirms the inalienable right of the people of New Caledonia to self-determination and independence in accordance with resolution 1514 (XV)."

22. Clause 4 of the preamble to the 1998 Noumea Accord states: "Decolonisation is the way to rebuild a lasting social bond between the communities living in New Caledonia today, by enabling the Kanak people to establish new relations with France, reflecting the realities of our time."

23. Eminent Persons Group, "Review of the Pacific Islands Forum," April 2004, available at http://www.forumsec.org.fj (accessed 18 October 2004). The five-person team included former Papua New Guinean prime minister Julius Chan, Australian diplomat Robert Cotton, Samoan ombudsman Maiava Iulai Toma, former Kiribati president Teburoro Tito, and Langi Kavaliku of Tonga.

24. Leaders' decisions, Pacific Islands Forum Special Leaders' Retreat, Auckland, 6 April 2004, available at http://www.forumsec.org.fj (accessed 18 October 2004). Emphasis added.

25. Pacific Islands Forum Secretariat, "The Pacific Plan for Strengthening Regional Cooperation and Integration," Fiji, 2005, available at http://www.forum-sec.org.fj.

26. The potential integration of non-self-governing territories in meetings of Pacific Islands Forum officials and ministers as observers, complements their full membership in other regional development bodies, such as the Secretariat of the Pacific Community and the South Pacific Regional Environment Program. Pacific territories are increasingly integrated through processes such as the European Union's Cotonou Agreement, which includes Pitcairn, New Caledonia, French Polynesia, and Wallis and Futuna as overseas countries and territories, alongside African, Caribbean, and Pacific countries.

8

Self-Determination and Autonomy: The Meanings of Freedom in West Papua

Jason MacLeod

LOCATED ON the western rim of the Pacific, bordering the independent state of Papua New Guinea, West Papua[1] is a land in crisis. A former Dutch colony, Indonesia gained control of the territory in the 1960s. However, the transfer of sovereignty from the Netherlands to Indonesia occurred under highly contested circumstances that included widespread allegations of manipulation, intimidation, and human rights violations. Conflict and violence continue to the present day in varying degrees of intensity, the causes of which appear at once clear and frustratingly complex. It is a conflict within conflicts, wrapped up in Indonesia's transformation from dictatorship to democracy. In this chapter I maintain that any lasting peaceful solution will depend not only on a comprehensive understanding of the root causes of the conflict and the courage to tackle them, but also on an ability to understand and incorporate the deeper meanings of Papuan demands for *merdeka* (freedom) into peacebuilding initiatives.

Without a doubt, the conflict in West Papua is one of the most protracted, complex, and volatile in the Pacific, and one that has become increasingly politicized among Pacific nations and at regional forums. A deep fraternal bond connects the people of West Papua with neighboring Pacific countries, particularly with Papua New Guinea and other Melanesian countries whose people view West Papuans as their kin with the same broad cultural values as their own. There is also a historical link with the Pacific. Prior to incorporation into Indonesia, Papuan delegates participated in regional forums, including the forerunner to the Pacific Islands Forum.[2] While a lasting peaceful and just solution remains elusive, the conflict will continue to have political, social, and economic repercussions not just for Indonesia and for Papua New Guinea, West Papua's immediate neighbor, but also for regional powers Australia and New Zealand, which may be compelled to deal with any humanitarian crisis in the event of further deterioration, such as a refugee crisis like the one that erupted in 1984. The conflict also influences the internal politics of other Melanesian nations such as Vanuatu, whose national Council of Chiefs has shown abiding interest in the political fortunes of their Melanesian kin.

Following an overview of the history of the conflict, the chapter discusses Jakarta's and the international community's policies and activities in relation to West Papua, alongside an outline of Papuan peacebuilding initiatives. Next it analyzes the root causes of the conflict (a mutually reinforcing nexus of historical grievances and direct, structural, and cultural violence), and finally explores the multiple meanings of *merdeka,* highlighting the mismatch between Papuan demands and Jakarta's understanding of those demands: a misunderstanding that often has tragic consequences.

■ The Historical Roots of Protracted Conflict in West Papua

Originally established as a buffer zone to protect the Dutch East Indies Company's lucrative spice trade, well into the twentieth century vast tracts of West Papua existed beyond the reach of "the light hand of Dutch colonial neglect."[3] After Indonesia gained independence, the Dutch retained control of the territory, arguing that West Papua (or "Netherlands New Guinea" and later "Nieuw Guinea") was a distinct political entity from Indonesia with no significant administrative, historical, or cultural connection with the rest of the Indonesian archipelago.[4] This claim was vehemently rejected by Indonesian representatives to the United Nations, who insisted that West Irian (as it was then called by the Indonesians) was part of a united Indonesia that included all the former Dutch East Indies.[5] In doing so, Indonesia was following the successor state principle—that is, the understanding that decolonization would not change the borders established by the colonial power—which for better or worse guided much of the postwar decolonization process.[6]

Few Papuans, however, advocated integration with Indonesia and during the 1950s the Dutch belatedly started to prepare Papuans for self-government.[7] In 1961, Papuans were inducted into a national legislature. On 1 December 1961, symbols of nationalism were formally adopted. *Hai Tanahku Papua* (Oh My Land of Papua) became the national anthem, the name *Papua Barat* (West Papua) was agreed upon, and the West Papuan national flag, the Morning Star, unveiled. Although there was never an official declaration of independence, many Papuans believe this date marks the beginning of West Papua as an independent sovereign state.[8]

In 1961, in a bid to strengthen Indonesian unity and to avert attention away from domestic discontent, notably spiraling economic woes, Indonesian president Sukarno issued the "*Trikora* commands for the liberation of West Irian."[9] More a symbolic invasion to back up diplomatic efforts than a full-scale war, Sukarno's actions, particularly his willingness to court

Russian support in the form of soft loans and a transfer of military equipment, prompted an anxious United States embroiled in the Cold War politics of the time, to intervene. Brokered by the John F. Kennedy administration, the 1962 New York Agreement was signed on 15 August 1962 by Indonesia and the Netherlands under the auspices of the United Nations. Under the New York Agreement, all parties—the United Nations, the Netherlands, and Indonesia—agreed to guarantee Papuan rights to free speech, freedom of assembly, and freedom of movement.[10] The New York Agreement also stipulated that an act of self-determination was to be carried out "in accordance with international practice."[11] Papuans, however, were neither involved nor consulted during this process—leading to a widespread and persistent view among Papuans that the agreement was illegitimate. On 1 May 1963, after a brief seven-month period of UN transitional authority, Indonesia took over administrative control of the territory. From this date, Indonesian nationalists felt that their mission to liberate West Irian was finally complete.

The act of self-determination required by the New York Agreement took place in 1969 and was called the "Act of Free Choice." A cursory inspection of the process shows why Papuans call it the "Act of *No* Choice." Leading up to the "Act of Free Choice," Indonesia—with the full knowledge of the US, Australian, and UK governments—bombed Papuan villages from the air, strafed Papuans with machine-gun fire, detained dissidents without trial, and tortured, disappeared, and executed those who dissented against Indonesian control.[12]

Unfortunately, what "in accordance with international practice" actually meant was not spelled out by the agreement. Jakarta argued that due to the difficult terrain and the lack of political and economic development in the territory, universal suffrage was neither possible nor appropriate. Consequently, 1,025 participants plus one late addition (less than 0.02 percent of the population) were hand-picked by Indonesian authorities. The process of selection of the vast majority of participants for the "Act of Free Choice" was not observed by the United Nations, independent observers, or the international press. In the end there was a series of public forums presided over by the Indonesian military, but no vote. After a few rehearsed speeches, those selected to participate in the "Act of Free Choice" were simply asked to raise their hands if they wanted to remain with Indonesia.[13] All of the participants raised their hands in favor of integration. The "Act of Free Choice" took place amid widespread allegations of violence and intimidation by the Indonesian military.

The acquiescence of the international community was justified with the words of a British diplomat who stated, "I cannot imagine the U.S., Japanese, Dutch, or Australian governments putting at risk their economic and political relations with Indonesia over a matter of principle involving a relatively small number of very primitive people."[14]

In his final report to the UN, Ortiz Sanz expressed a number of reservations about irregularities in the conduct of the "Act of Free Choice." In addition, there was protest from Papuans and some members of the UN General Assembly—notably a delegation of fifteen African states lead by Ghana. However, all this was to no avail. On 19 November 1969, the UN General Assembly "took note" of the results of the "Act of Free Choice," and West Papua was formally integrated into the territory of Indonesia and removed from the list of non-self-governing territories awaiting decolonization.

■ Why West Papua Is So Important to Jakarta

There are a number of reasons why Jakarta identifies West Papua so strongly as part of its territory. Few if any states view with equanimity the prospect of losing territory. Indonesia is a complex archipelago made up of some 17,000 myriad islands and a multitude of different languages and cultures. Capturing and holding this complexity within one state is an extraordinarily challenging task, particularly given that Indonesia is also facing the gamut of difficulties that beset postcolonial states. National unity is commonly seen as inherently valuable and significant, and the risk of fracturing into smaller entities as a very real threat. It is this threat that has been used as justification over the years for the extraordinary and extensive power of the Indonesian military within every level of national life. Still smarting from the "loss" of East Timor, secessionist drives (whether violent or nonviolent) within West Papua resonate in Jakarta as a threat to the viability of Indonesia itself—a possible step toward a deeper unraveling. Unfortunately, Jakarta's fear of disintegration often obfuscates legitimate and deeply seated grievances that fuel demands for *merdeka* (a word that can mean either "freedom" or "independence").

Moreover, for many Indonesians, West Papua represents a place of exile for nationalist heroes who resisted Dutch rule. It was a matter of national pride, therefore, that Sukarno launched a "liberation campaign" for an independent Indonesia that included the entire Dutch East Indies, from "Sabang to Merauke."[15] The "endorsement" of the "return" of the territory by the international community through the United Nations serves to further reinforce Indonesian perceptions of the legitimacy of Indonesian sovereignty over Papua.[16]

For early Indonesian nationalists, the idea of a sovereign state was not related to religion or ethnicity, but was "rather a shared history, suffering, [and] fight against a common adversary."[17] According to the Indonesian argument, it was precisely *because of* the ethnic and religious differences between Papuans and Javanese or other Indonesians that the incorporation of the territory of West Papua became so important—a living demonstration that Indonesia was a political concept and not a state based on religion or ethnicity. Indonesia's maintenance of a multiethnic state is still a source of pride for Indonesian nationalists.[18]

Finally, West Papua is a leading contributor to Indonesia's national economy, generating massive amounts of revenue from its extensive natural resource base for the Indonesian state and security forces. These prevailing historical, ideological, and economic factors reinforce Jakarta's determination to retain West Papua at all costs.

■ The Struggle for Peace and Justice in West Papua

Following the fall of Suharto in 1998, resistance to Indonesian rule in West Papua underwent a dramatic transformation from a struggle led by a numerically small, decentralized, and poorly armed guerrilla army, the Tentara Pembebasan Nasional Papua Barat (TPN-PB; West Papuan National Liberation Army), based in the mountains and jungles of the interior, to a considerably more widespread nonviolent movement based in the cities and towns.[19] Despite decades of military rule and the appearance of acceptance of Indonesian rule—which could also be understood as passivity created by widespread repression—the movement quickly gained popular support. In 1999 a team of 100 civil society leaders traveled to Jakarta to meet President B. J. Habibie. At the meeting with Habibie, however, the leaders of Team 100 declared that they wanted independence from Jakarta. As soon as the word "independence" was mentioned, however, "dialogue stopped right there."[20] Stunned and clearly misinformed about the depth and extent of discontent in West Papua, Habibie put aside his prepared response and appealed to the Papuan delegation to reconsider their desire to separate from Indonesia. Although there was no clear outcome from the meeting, the Papuan struggle had exploded onto center stage and the team returned home to a hero's welcome. A number of Team 100 members immediately went on to begin preparations for a national consultation (*musyuwarah besar,* often shortened to *mubes*) on the causes of conflict in West Papua and strategies to achieve *merdeka.*

The *mubes* attracted thousands of Papuans from around the country, with some highland delegations walking through the mountains and jungles for a month to attend. For the first time, the long-banned Morning Star flag was flown. At the *mubes,* delegates agreed to hold a congress six months later. Delegates to the congress, which was attended by key Papuan leaders living in exile and representatives from every sector of society and region in West Papua, decided to form the Presidium Dewan Papua (PDP; Papua Presidium Council), a kind of parallel government. Under the leadership of Chief Theys Eluay and Vice Chair Thom Beanal, the PDP pledged to pursue independence through peaceful means.

Although dialogue between the West Papuans and the Indonesian government called for by the presidium did not eventuate, the ability of the PDP to mobilize popular support for *merdeka* and Papuan political leaders' explicit and widespread commitment to nonviolence as a means of carrying out a political struggle for independence, constituted a challenge to Indonesian authority and legitimacy that the armed struggle had not. In the face of a persistent and disciplined nonviolent movement and growing international support, Jakarta found it increasingly difficult to justify repression and military operations as a response to the criminal violence of a small minority. Sometime in early to middle June 2000, Indonesian political, military, and intelligence strategists met to discuss how to neutralize Papuan demands for *merdeka*. The Indonesian government's plan for reasserting their authority included improving social welfare, but also decapitating the leadership, military operations to eradicate separatism, and establishing pro-Indonesian militias.[21] By late 2000 it was evident that the brief "Papuan Spring" (a phrase coined by Richard Chauvel) had ended. Five PDP leaders were jailed (but later released) on charges of subversion, and on 10 November 2001 Theys Eluay was assassinated by Kopassus—the Indonesian special forces—after attending a dinner party as the military's guest of honor.

It was in this context of mounting tension that the central government promised special autonomy. Many Papuans publicly questioned Jakarta's sincerity and commitment to resolving the root causes of the conflict, and instead saw Jakarta's offer of special autonomy as a political ploy to avert the threat of independence from the restive peripheries of the archipelago.[22] As the political situation in West Papua rapidly began to deteriorate, however, Papuan moderates seized the moment. Rather than wait for Jakarta to draft a special autonomy package for them, a team of Papuan intellectuals, political leaders, and activists from nongovernmental organizations (NGOs) began a consultation and drafting process of a special autonomy law that reflected core Papuan demands.[23] After a period of bargaining in Jakarta, on 22 October 2001, Law 21, on special autonomy for Papua, was enacted. Although some of the more radical proposals in the original draft did not make it into the legislation (such as caps on migration), special autonomy was a far-reaching proposal that sincerely attempted to address the core causes of the conflict within the framework of a united Indonesian state.[24]

Nonetheless, special autonomy and the political loyalties of those who drafted it were also questioned by many of the political elite in Jakarta. Since special autonomy became law, however, its full implementation has floundered and Papuan aspirations for improvements in health and education in particular have not been realized. The reasons for this are twofold. First, while the central government approved special autonomy, it did so at a time when it was politically weak and the threat of separatism was at its highest. Since then, key political groups in Jakarta (parliamentarians, members of the Badan Intel Nasional [BIN; National Intelligence Organization], and the Tentara Nasional Indonesia [TNI; Indonesian National Army]) have viewed special autonomy with increasing suspicion. Fears are held by many politicians in Jakarta, who often do not seem to realize the extent and depth of discontent in West Papua, that special autonomy represents "the thin edge of the wedge" that will become a lever for eventual independence. There are key players in the TNI who are also not in favor of special autonomy, because it threatens their stranglehold on the economy by giving greater control of West Papua's lucrative natural resources to Papuans.[25] Second, the implementation of special autonomy has been hampered by lack of capacity, mismanagement, and corruption by Papuan politicians and civil servants.[26]

In January 2003, with advice from the BIN, then–president Megawati's administration issued a presidential instruction *(inpres)* to partition West Papua into three separate provinces *(pemekaran)*.[27] While couched in terms of facilitating better provision of public services and bringing the government closer to the people, it is widely believed that the policy was clearly designed with the broader political objective of weakening separatism.[28] In particular, the creation of a new province allowed the TNI to increase troop numbers.[29] Aside from further militarization of the territory, Papuans also feared that the creation of new provinces would intensify the displacement and marginalization of the indigenous population, as new jobs in the civil service (the traditional avenue of advancement for the Papuan elite) would be taken up by migrants because of the lack of skilled Papuans.[30]

Widely perceived as a tactic from Jakarta to "divide and rule," and overwhelmingly rejected by Papuan leaders, *pemekaran* also created widespread confusion because it conflicted with and contradicted special autonomy. Under special autonomy legislation, the Majelis Rakyat Papua (MRP; Papuan People's Assembly), a centerpiece of the legislation, was meant to be the body that approved any attempt to divide the province. Designed to be a Papuan upper house (or senate) of forty-two members, comprised of traditional leaders, women, and religious leaders, the MRP was also charged with the responsibility of assisting with policy development, approving the appointment of high-ranking officials, and safeguarding the culture and traditions of Papuans. However, the establishment of the MRP has been repeatedly stalled by Jakarta and was still not formed when Megawati issued the *inpres*. In the absence of the MRP and given the failure to fully implement special autonomy, there was strong resistance within West Papua to the division of the province.[31] In spite of this and the obvious contradictions between *pemekaran* and special autonomy, the creation of the province of West Irian Jaya went ahead.

In October 2004, Susilo Bambang Yudhoyono was elected president amid promises of supporting the full implementation of special autonomy and nonmilitary solutions to the conflict in Papua. Following a controversial constitutional-court ruling on the division of West Papua, Susilo Bambang Yudhoyono established the long-awaited MRP. However, the original decisionmaking powers of the MRP under special autonomy were removed, leaving the body reduced to a symbolic institution without any real power. Jakarta's emasculation of the MRP and espousal of policies that are inconsistent with the spirit and letter of special autonomy have been seen by many Papuans as being insincere and counterproductive.[32] As West Papua's Dewan Adat Papua (National Council of Customary Chiefs) symbolically handed back special autonomy and other Papuan leaders withdrew their cooperation with the MRP, creating a crisis of legitimacy in the body, Jakarta stepped in to appoint a number representatives loyal to the central government.

Many in the international community continue to affirm their support for special autonomy as a workable and promising solution for conflict in West Papua. However, the implementation of the law has been undermined and obstructed by contradictory and confusing policies from Jakarta, ongoing repression by the Indonesian security forces, and a culture of impunity that protects human rights violators and undermines Papuans' trust in Jakarta.

Meanwhile, Papuan resistance groups are also starting to reconsolidate after the collapse of the PDP, agreeing to put aside their differences and pursue their aspirations for political change nonviolently. The decision to form the West Papuan National Council for Liberation was made at a meeting of West Papuan resistance groups in Papua New Guinea in November 2005. This is the first time in West Papua's four-decade-long struggle that guerrilla fighters from the TPN, political organizations, and civil society groups have come together under one national umbrella organization, marking a significant turning point in a movement that has long been riven by disunity and division. If there is successful consolidation of resistance groups in West Papua around a shared vision, functional and achievable objectives, and common strategy, this could dramatically strengthen the movement's negotiating power.

Civil society groups are also increasingly important in the province and in working for nonviolent political change. Inside West Papua the Christian churches constitute the most prominent civil society group, and are considered by most Papuans to be the only foreign institutions that have become truly Papuan.[33] The Catholic and Protestant Churches in West Papua (with their international partners) run an extensive radio communication network that services a vast network of mission stations linked by airstrips and light aircraft. In many cases, these aircraft are the only way in and out of remote villages, aside from walking. The churches also run health services, support interfaith peacebuilding and human rights work, organize women's groups, and carry out education programs. The United Nations Development Programme (UNDP) and the development arms of the United States, European Union, the Netherlands, Canada, Japan, Germany, Australia, and New Zealand, among others, all make contributions to health, development, education, and governance programs in West Papua. There are also a few international humanitarian, peace, and development agencies with programs in West Papua, including the Red Cross, World Vision, Search for Common Ground, Peace Brigades International, and others, working alongside some 500 Papuan NGOs.[34] The largest injection of international money in Papua, however, comes from transnational companies, particularly in the oil, gas, and mining sector. The timber industry also has a significant impact, particularly the illegal sector, which is rapidly exploiting West Papua's extensive forests (75 percent of the territory is forested) to service rising demand in China and elsewhere.[35] There remains a great need throughout West Papua—particularly in the remote areas—for peace and development programs in the areas of health (with urgent attention to address HIV/AIDS), education, conflict transformation, grassroots economic development, and community leadership and governance.

Despite the obduracy of the conflict in West Papua, Papuan-led peacebuilding efforts have helped work against violent conflict between Papuan groups or between Papuans and settlers by maintaining nonviolent discipline; local efforts have also mobilized an active Papuan peace constituency to address the causes of the broader conflict, and raised its international profile. Relevant movements or efforts here include Team 100; the large *musyuwarah besar* gathering in 2000; the second congress six months later, which saw the formation of the PDP as a parallel governance structure; the development of the special autonomy package by a group of prominent Papuan civil society leaders; the organizing work of the Dewan Adat Papua; the formation of the West Papua National Coalition for Liberation; and the ongoing work of civil society groups, particularly the churches, to make West Papua a "land of peace." These efforts have occurred despite a confusing and inconsistent policy approach from Jakarta, a continuation of military operations, and a lukewarm response from the international community.

■ Root Causes of the Conflict

Both Papuan nationalism and Papuan peacebuilding initiatives have emerged largely in response to a complex interaction of five long-standing, deeply rooted, and mutually reinforcing causes: historical grievances; ongoing military operations and human rights violations; maldevelopment characterized by large-scale projects in the resource-extraction sector that have also resulted in ecological destruction and sociocultural dislocation; displacement and marginalization created by Jakarta's promotion of migration to West Papua; and institutional racism contributing to what Papuans call a "crisis of identity." The root causes of direct, structural, and cultural violence in West Papua all reinforce one another, making the conflict extremely resistant to resolution.

Historical Grievances

Perspectives on how West Papua was integrated into the Republic of Indonesia are so polarized, it is as if the two parties are talking about two entirely different historical events. The issue of the "Act of Free Choice" has become so prominent that it needs to be dealt with in some way. The dominant Indonesian view is that the act was the last stage of a decolonization process involving the transfer of a territory that was always meant to be part of the Republic of Indonesia, and that the result has been officially and democratically endorsed by the United Nations.[36] The dominant Papuan view, on the other hand, is that the whole process was fraudulent, fundamentally violated Papuans civil and political rights, and was backed up by state violence with the full knowledge and acquiescence of the international community. This Papuan view is not just held by activists. The perception that Papuans were betrayed by the international community has been so thoroughly socialized throughout the territory that it is common even in remote villages for Papuans to launch into an animated and in-depth discussion of their political history with outsiders. By the time the "Act of Free Choice" was endorsed by the United Nations, Jakarta believed that justice had finally been achieved, while many Papuans considered that a terrible travesty had just taken place and that their right to vote on their collective future, as promised, had been denied.

Yet a commitment to self-determination and to addressing Papuan's historical grievances may or may not lead to a referendum on independence. Essentially, the Papuan preoccupation with "straightening history" (*meluruskan sejarah),* a key demand of the second Papuan congress, is about Papuans casting off their status as the objects of politics so that they might play a more active role in determining their own politics. It is not about Papuans holding the absolute truth about what happened, asserts Benny Giay (Papuan sociologist, theologian, and human rights defender), but about loosening Jakarta's monopolization of Papuan history.[37]

Ongoing Military Operations and Human Rights Violations

Since Indonesia took control of the territory, Papuans have been subject to ongoing military operations carried out by the TNI. While nobody knows exactly how many Papuans have died, killings by the Indonesian military and related deaths have been on such a scale that most families know relatives or friends who have been detained, disappeared, or killed.[38] A 2005 report by the Centre for Peace and Conflict Studies at the University of Sydney found that military operations in the Jayawijaya regency in the central highlands of West Papua in 2003–2005 resulted in 371 homes burned by the Kopassus; 6,393 internally displaced people; the destruction of pigs, chickens, and food gardens; the burning of churches, schools, and health clinics; the formation of militia groups; extrajudicial killings; rape; intimidation of human rights workers; and indiscriminate assaults against unarmed Papuans.[39] The report also cited serious allegations from Reverend Sofyan Yoman, the president of the Fellowship of Baptist Churches, that funds earmarked for special autonomy have been used for military operations by the TNI.[40] These experiences of gross human rights violations at the hands of the Indonesian state have directly led to deeply held Papuan aspirations for justice, peace, equality, and freedom.

The Indonesian armed forces, particularly the TNI, have been upheld by the Indonesian government as defenders of the unity and territorial integrity of the Republic of Indonesia, and maintain an extensive network of personnel throughout the archipelago to support this role. The TNI's ubiquitous presence extends from cabinet down to the most remote hamlet. This territorial command structure and the TNI's involvement in politics are enshrined in the doctrine of "dual function" *(dwi fungsi),* which protects the military's civilian roles and its commitment to internal defense.[41] The central purpose of the TNI is internal: to defend the territorial integrity of the Indonesian state.[42] In West Papua the TNI's role as the guardian of the state is used to justify widespread human rights violations. For example, after the conviction of Kopassus soldiers for the assassination of West Papuan independence leader Theys Eluay, General Ryamizard Ryacudu, army chief of staff at that time, called his men "heroes." "I don't know," said Ryacudu, "people say they did wrong, they broke the law. . . . But for me, they are heroes because the person they killed was a rebel leader."[43]

In addition to targeted assassinations and military operations, the army is also creating nationalist militia groups, replicating the same strategy of low-intensity conflict interspersed with military operations that was used in East Timor. Members of militias are mainly drawn from the large pool of non-Papuan migrants, with the objective of inciting and waging a proxy war on the state's behalf. For example, an Indonesian militia, the Barisan Merah Putih (Red and White Garrison)[44] has been established in Wamena.[45] Eurico Gutteres, a notorious militia leader from East Timor, was also reported to have established a militia in Timika.[46] There is also evidence of Laskar Jihad, a Muslim militia, being established throughout West Papua.[47] As well as creating nationalist militias, it has become something of an "open secret" that the TNI has a symbiotic relationship with elements of the Free Papua

Movement's National Liberation Army, which it uses to foment conflict in order to justify repression to reestablish "law and order," conduct counterinsurgency operations, and play factions of the armed struggle against one another.[48] A recent Yale University report on genocide in West Papua concluded that, taken together, the Indonesian government and military's acts "appear to constitute the imposition of conditions of life calculated to bring about the destruction of the West Papuans."[49]

Maldevelopment

Since Indonesia gained control of West Papua in 1963, Jakarta has been determined to "modernize" West Papua. To achieve this objective, Jakarta has promoted large-scale projects in the mining, oil, and gas, timber, and fisheries sectors to exploit West Papua's abundant natural resources. Economic growth has been facilitated by a surplus of cheap skilled (non-Papuan) labor, an Indonesian military willing to ruthlessly protect investment, and attractive investment conditions and tax breaks for multinational corporations. These large-scale projects enrich a small percentage of migrants, produce little to no benefit for Papuans, and wreak sociocultural and environmental havoc. Indonesia's development policy in West Papua has also failed to address Papuan poverty and disadvantage. Not surprisingly, Jakarta's development policy has fueled Papuan demands for *merdeka*.[50]

Maldevelopment in West Papua is entwined with the TNI's predatory role in the conflict economy. If the territorial command structure and the TNI's involvement in politics constitute the military's dual functions, its network of extensive business interests is its unstated but vital third function.[51] The TNI only receives 25–30 percent of its budget from the state. Consequently, 70–75 percent of its operating budget is obtained from legal and illegal business activity supported by a network of military/business foundations and organizations.[52] Papua is an extremely lucrative frontier posting for TNI soldiers. The TNI's extensive business interests includes logging operations,[53] the provision of security for mining companies,[54] fishing operations,[55] brothels,[56] and a range of other legal and illegal businesses. Consequently, the TNI has a vested interest in maintaining enough conflict to justify its presence and protect its economic interests, but not so much that it will provoke a domestic and international backlash. The TNI has been an opponent of special autonomy precisely because greater empowerment of local indigenous communities, an increase in the amount of revenue returned to the provincial government, and the ability of the provincial government to develop policy threaten its economic interests.

The giant gold and copper mine run by the US-based mining company Freeport McMoRan and its Anglo-Australian partner Rio Tinto, is a good case in point. Freeport is Indonesia's largest taxpayer.[57] According to Lesley

McCullough, Freeport payments to the TNI included a onetime payment of US$35 million and annual "contributions" of US$11 million.[58] In early 2003, as a result of shareholder questioning in the wake of the murder of two US citizens and an Indonesian citizen (allegedly by the TNI), Freeport admitted that it had paid US$4.7 million in 2001 and US$5.6 million in 2002 to the TNI to "support costs for government-provided security."[59] The *New York Times* claims that between 1998 and 2004, Freeport paid the TNI a staggering US$20 million.[60]

Researchers have documented about 160 killings by the Indonesian military and Freeport security personnel in the Freeport mining concession area since it began operations in 1967, two years before the question of West Papua's sovereignty was meant to be resolved.[61] Nobody has been held accountable. According to Indonesia's National Commission on Human Rights (Komnas HAM), human rights violations around the mine "are directly connected to [the TNI] acting as protection for the mining business of Freeport."[62] The nexus of Indonesia's development policy in West Papua, the failure to alleviate poverty, and the denial of indigenous rights, militarism, and human rights violations have led Papuan theologian Benny Giay to conclude that Indonesia's development policy is simply "killing in the name of development."[63] Yet more large-scale development projects continue to be proposed for West Papua. British Petroleum[64] and BHP Billiton,[65] for instance, are currently in the process of establishing large-scale mining projects in West Papua.

In addition to widespread human rights violations that have gone hand-in-hand with resource extraction, Jakarta's economic development policy has also facilitated cultural and ecological destruction. In the Freeport mining concession area, this has included riverine tailings disposal at the rate of over 200,000 tons per day, which has wiped out over 100,000 square kilometers (38,000 square miles) of rainforest; and overburden, which has filled up two highland valleys with rock waste.[66] The massive open-pit mine that was once a mountain is considered by the Amungme people to be their ancestral grandmother, *Tu Ni Me Ni*. "To the Amungme, Freeport's mining activities are killing their mother . . . on which they depend for sustenance—literally and spiritually."[67]

At the heart of cultural and environmental degradation has been the denial of Papuan's spiritual, economic, cultural, and material attachment to land. Land and military-backed resource theft in West Papua is facilitated by Article 33 of the Indonesian constitution, which does not recognize the existence of indigenous people, let alone indigenous land rights.[68] Opposition to development by acting to protect land and culture, or insistence on participation in decisionmaking, or the right to veto development projects, is seen by the Indonesian state as an act of subversion.

Papuans' experience is that Jakarta's economic development policy has been designed and implemented without their participation. This lack of inclusion, and the detrimental effects on the environment and Papuan culture, deepen feelings of exclusion.[69] This is not a widespread rejection of development. The question is: What kind of development, for whom, and on whose terms? Papuans' experience of modernity has left them estranged, while also eroding traditional institutions and values.[70] Papuans have repeatedly said they want to be able to participate in the design and implementation of development policies in ways that result in tangible improvements in their daily lives. They have also said they want to be supported to reempower local communities to manage their own lives according to their own traditions and "life projects," in contrast to "development projects" that are perceived to be solely in the interests of others.[71] Indigenous-led culturally and ecologically sustainable development also includes the rights of local communities to say no to the development projects proposed by governments and corporations.

According to the UNDP's 2004 Human Development Index, West Papua is Indonesia's second poorest province, after West Nusa Tenggara (although the highlands of West Papua are Indonesia's poorest and most disadvantaged region).[72] West Papua's current status in health[73] and education[74] indicates extreme disadvantage in the territory, "reflecting a systemic failure of the state [and] an ethnic form of state discrimination."[75] The HIV/AIDS situation, at thirty times the national average, is particularly distressing,[76] especially when accompanied by allegations that the rise of HIV/AIDS is a result of a deliberate military strategy of using HIV-infected prostitutes in military-run brothels to facilitate genocide.[77]

Special autonomy was meant to address the need for social and economic development by returning to the provincial government the 70–80 percent of the wealth that previously went to the central government. In 2001 the province's budget increased by 50 percent as a result of special autonomy.[78] In 2002 it increased by 300 percent.[79] Despite these significant increases, the picture on the ground is not promising. For example, special autonomy stipulated that 30 percent of the budget would be spent on education. However, according to an analysis of the 2002 budget, expenditure on education amounted to a mere 7 percent. The promise of free education under special autonomy, contrasted with the reality of no real change for the overwhelming majority of Papuans, has led to persistent allegations of corruption.[80]

Maldevelopment, particularly in the resource-extraction sector, and the contrast between West Papua's abundant natural resources, the significant wealth this generates for outsiders, and widespread poverty in West Papua, is a major source of resentment that fuels Papuan demands for *merdeka*. The nexus between exploitative development projects and the Indonesian military, which provide protection for national and transnational companies and operate a network of legal and illegal businesses, only exacerbates the situation.

Migration

Jakarta's modernization strategy in West Papua, consisting of interlinked development and migration policies, has mutually reinforcing economic and security objectives. "Not only is it meant to boost national development, but such policies have sought to stimulate economic interactions across ethnic and regional lines and thereby promote a sense of belonging to a single nation."[81] After forty years, it is clear that this strategy is not working, and has had the opposite effect. Jakarta's development and migration policy has led to the enrichment of migrants (and in recent years a small number of Papuans) at the expense of the greater impoverishment of the majority of Papuans, particularly those in the rural areas. Migration has also intensified a sense of shared Papuan identity, fanning the fires of greater resentment and resistance. "Far from enhancing national integration . . . the government's policy of modernization has spurred local resistance . . . and undermined the territory's integration into the state."[82]

Two types of migrants settle in West Papua: transmigrants and spontaneous migrants. Transmigrants are predominantly poor Indonesians from the more populous areas of Indonesia, particularly Java, Bali, and Sulawesi, whose migration and resettlement in West Papua is sponsored by the central government. Over 220,000 people transmigrated to West Papua between 1970 and 2000.[83] Transmigration was dramatically scaled back in 1998, but Jakarta is currently considering reintroducing large-scale transmigration to West Papua.[84] Spontaneous migrants are self-funded economic migrants attracted east to Indonesia's frontier in search of a better way of life.[85] The migration rate of self-funded migrants has continued to accelerate since 1998, with the largest percentage of new migrants in recent years coming from Sulawesi.[86] By 2000, over 560,000 self-funded migrants had settled in West Papua, attracted by an improvement in communication, transportation, and the "honey-pot effect" of West Papua's abundant natural resources.[87]

According to the UN's 2004 report on human development in Indonesia, the total population of West Papua is 2.2 million, of which 1.5 million are indigenous Papuans,[88] made up of 7 major, and some 305 smaller, distinct indigenous groups.[89] Migration has dramatically altered the demographic composition of the territory. According to Indonesian population figures in 1971, migrants consisted of only 4 percent of the population.[90] By 2000, 35 percent of the population were migrants,[91] with 66 percent of them settling in West Papua's cities and towns, where they dominated the economy.[92] The vast majority of Papuan's—over 86 percent—live in the rural areas, with most concentrated in the highlands and the south.[93] Massive socioeconomic change wrought by migration has greatly altered the territory's demographics, increasing pressure on land, creating competition for resources, displacing indigenous Papuans, and fueling horizontal conflict.

Migration and resulting competition for land and resources, coupled with clashes of culture, have led to obvious cleavages between Papuans and non-Papuans. In addition, inmigration has exacerbated divisions between Papuans by increasing competition for resources, particularly land and economic opportunities.[94] In other words, migration has in some respects contributed to a sense of shared Papuan identity, but at the same time it has also deepened divisions between Papuans. These fractures are predominantly along class and ethnic lines: between Papuans from the northern coastal areas (who due to earlier contact and Dutch policies generally have better formal education) and Papuans from the highlands; and between Papuans living in the urban areas and those living in the isolated rural areas.[95] Occasionally, conflict between Papuans and settler non-Papuans (particularly those from Sulawesi, who dominate the trade and transport sectors) has led to violence.[96]

Unlike other parts of Indonesia, in Papua the marketplace is not a social connector.[97] The sight of Papuan women sitting in the dirt selling a few vegetables in marketplaces around the towns of West Papua, while migrant traders in well-stocked stalls dominate sales, is a visible daily reminder of Papuan resentment. This reality reinforces the bigger picture of military-backed multinational mining corporations like Freeport enriching migrants and foreigners while Papuans are forcibly displaced, harassed, and impoverished in their own land.

Although many migrants who have been born and raised in West Papua are integrated into the Papuan community, on the whole migration has caused displacement and marginalization of Papuans, fueling demands for *merdeka*. Without a population policy that controls migration coupled with a participatory propoor development policy designed to improve indigenous welfare and protect indigenous culture, it seems very likely that vertical and horizontal conflict in West Papua will increase.

Institutional Racism

The daily experience of Papuans is one beset by racism. It is common to hear comments by non-Papuans that Papuans are "stupid" *(bodoh)*, "lazy" *(malas)*, "drunk" *(mabuk)*, and "primitive" *(primitip)*.[98] "According to Indonesians," says Benny Giay, "Papuans are primitives and backward tribal peoples. They are bearers of stone age cultures holding them back from being able to participate in the whole process of modernization."[99] This attitude gives rise to, and in turn is reinforced by, policies and structures ostensibly designed to "civilize" Papuans but that serve to further exclude them.[100]

While Indonesians from other parts of the archipelago are freely encouraged to incorporate local traditions and culture as part of an affirmation of Indonesian unity, Papuan cultural identity is more often seen as a direct threat to national integration and, in the process, is denied and criminalized. One example of this is the 1984 murder of Arnold Ap and his colleague Eddie Mofu, from the cultural music group Mambesak. Ap and Mofu were killed by Kopassus soldiers because their work of collecting and performing Papuan songs and dances from throughout West Papua, in order to celebrate Papuan culture, was seen as promoting Papuan nationalism.[101]

The task of strengthening Papuan culture and traditions is still viewed as suspect by the TNI. Traditional leaders are regularly regarded as being "subversive," and efforts to restore traditions and indigenous forms of governance are treated with great suspicion by the government.[102] One indigenous elder commented to the US Agency for International Development (USAID) researchers that the government "regards us as the enemy."[103] In fact, the only experience that many isolated communities have of the Indonesian state "comes in the form of men wearing camouflage."[104] For Theo van den Broek, Papuans "have not been treated as human beings but as objects; objects of policy, objects of military operations, objects of economic development, objects of tourism, and so on," which in turn gives rise to Papuan demands for *merdeka*.[105]

Decades of this marginalization have resulted in a variety of social ills such as alcoholism,[106] and encouraged a belief among Papuans that outsiders are needed to save them. Outsiders (whether Indonesian migrants or internationals) need to take this into account when designing development projects. Accordingly, programs are needed that strengthen the capacity of indigenous communities to develop and participate in change processes, to articulate their own vision for the future and a realistic and achievable plan to get there. Traditional Amungme leader Thom Beanal and Benny Giay have concluded that Papuans need to regain their self-belief, and rediscover and reaffirm their own history, knowledge, culture, traditions, religious beliefs, governance structures, and values as a basis for indigenous-led civic reempowerment.[107]

It goes without saying that the task of ending racism is extremely difficult. It is a task that Western countries, in particular, have had little success with. However, the concern for Indonesia, says anthropologist activist Brigham Golden, is that a discussion of racism "is not even on the table."[108]

While the causes of conflict in West Papua appear at once clear and simple—historical grievances and a history of military occupation and gross human rights violations at the hands of the security forces—resolution is made more complex because of the presence of structural violence in the form of maldevelopment led by the resource-extractive industries, the symbiotic economic relationship between business and the military, and the exclusion of Papuans from many of the decisionmaking processes that effect their daily lives. Inequitable and discriminatory social, economic, and political structures in West Papua are further reinforced, legitimized, and justified by the cultural violence of racism. Historical grievances combined with direct, structural, and cultural violence, along with rapidly changing demographics and the presence of large numbers of migrants, have turned West Papua into a tinderbox. Perhaps one hope of avoiding plunging into the abyss lies in facilitating not only a deeper analysis of the root causes of the conflict, but also a deeper understanding of the multiple and layered meanings of *merdeka*. Doing so might help break down the rigid polarization of positions around the question of West Papua's future. Such an exercise might also open up surprising common ground for dialogue, as well as assist in the formation of functional strategic objectives for Papuan peacebuilders.

■ The Multiple Meanings of *Merdeka*

As "self-determination" can be understood in a variety of ways, so Papuans and policymakers in Jakarta frame *merdeka* in critically different ways. For Indonesian nationalists embroiled in a liberation struggle against colonial Dutch rule in the 1940s, *merdeka* was the "battle cry with which the citizenry was summoned to support the cause, the salute with which revolutionaries would greet each other, the cry of solidarity at every mass rally, and the signature at the end of every republican document."[109] This popular understanding of *merdeka* as "independence" is reinforced through symbols and national rituals like Independence Day celebrations, held across the country every 17 August. For Papuans, however, *merdeka* "holds a sublime, almost spiritual significance."[110] Together with the emergence of an emphasis on *adat* (tradition), *merdeka* has become a powerful ideology cutting across class and tribal affiliations.

Despite the fact that Papuan nationalists associate *merdeka* with independence, many Papuan aspirations inherent in the word *merdeka,* such as protection of local community land, resources, traditions, and identity, and the desperate need for health and educational services, do not necessarily point to independence. Issues like corruption, governance, lack of local capacity, and a participatory development policy that simultaneously meets local needs for employment and services, and protects the fragile environment and diverse Papuan cultures, will also not necessarily be resolved by independence. Yet the desire for *merdeka* in Papua has often been represented—with tragic outcomes as the Indonesian military brutally repress Papuan aspirations—as the desire for secession or independence.

Papuan demands for *merdeka* are far more nuanced than the demand for a separate and sovereign state. Papuan understandings of *merdeka* encompass six overlapping and mutually reinforcing meanings. These meanings have their roots in West Papua's long history of Melanesian cultural resistance and in political millenarianism.[111] (Also see Anthony Regan's discussion of millenarianism in Chapter 5.)

Merdeka *as the Struggle for an Independent and Sovereign Political State*

Merdeka is most often portrayed as a demand for a sovereign Papuan state. So, for example, Richard Chauvel notes that, stimulated by a potent combination of injustice and repression, the demand for independence "is stronger today than it was in 1961, when the Morning Star flag was first raised."[112] However, as Eben Kirksey points out, even Papuan demands for *merdeka* as "independence" do not necessarily imply that Papuan nationalists consider that the end point of the struggle is the state. Indeed, many Papuan activists express hopes "for new systems of governance based on indigenous modes of authority" that are other than the state.[113] In a similar vein to discussions in the Solomon Islands about "Melanesianizing" the state, there has been discussion among Papuans of, for example, small self-managing communities for each indigenous group in West Papua, held loosely by guidelines laid out by a national parliament in a highly devolved state.[114]

Merdeka *as Hai*

Papua, along with many areas within Melanesia, has a long history of what anthropologists describe as "cargo cults," or millenarian movements. Instead of the term "cargo cults," Benny Giay prefers to use the Amungme word *hai,* which he describes as the irrepressible "hope" of an oppressed people for a future that is peaceful, just, and prosperous.[115] Giay argues that *hai* is a universal phenomena, expressed whenever popular movements struggle for a more peaceful and just world, free from oppression and domination.[116] However, some of the sociopolitical-religious movements that have emerged in West Papua are also exclusivist in nature, carried out by groups preoccupied with hopes for terrestrial paradise.[117] Often, local *hai* movements fuse Christianity with local belief systems, infusing new religious movements with sociopolitical aspirations.[118] Such movements can inspire unrealistic expectations of what *merdeka* will bring; a time, for example, where everybody will have unlimited wealth and nobody will have to work.[119]

Merdeka *as a Papuan Liberation Theology*

Merdeka has also been described as a kind of Papuan liberation theology, "in which a Christian desire for a world of human dignity and divine justice is finally manifest in Papua."[120] This reflects the role of the church in Papua as an institution that is viewed as independent and Papuan. The church, says Benny Giay, is a "liberating institution . . . , a fortress of last resort, [and] the bearer of a new hope,"[121] whereas the bible "portrays a new world, free from manipulation, intimidation and trauma. It lifts up the eyes of those who are oppressed to a new world. Sometimes people see in this new world a New Papua, an independent West Papua," where freedom from all kinds of oppression and violence are guaranteed.[122]

Merdeka *as Restoration of Local Traditions, Indigenous Forms of Governance, and Identity*

To many Papuans living in the isolated areas, *merdeka* can be understood as an adat-led restoration and recovery of local forms of community governance, traditions, culture, and identity.[123] It means being able to control their own lives, resources, and identities. It also means the right to veto development projects and receive proper compensation when land is appropriated by the state. After years of being marginalized by successive colonial authorities and state-led development schemes, *adat* leaders from the Baliem valley, speaking to a group of USAID researchers studying indigenous governance and the revitalization of *adat,* said they were less concerned about the political status of West Papua and more concerned with being able to meet the needs of their communities.[124]

Merdeka *as Mobu*

In a land where foreign companies make millions of dollars in profit a day but schools remain empty, chronic hunger prevails, and a lack of basic medical care results in widespread morbidity, the demand for basic services necessary for a healthy life animates many Papuans' demands for *merdeka.* The Me people of the central highlands articulate the realization of this desire as *mobu,* which literally translates as "full or satisfied."[125] Theo van den Broek, of the Catholic Office of Justice and Peace in Jayapura (Sekretariat Keadilan dan Perdamaian), says that *mobu* "implies a sense of material and spiritual satisfaction where no-one need suffer from hunger, poverty, or disease."[126] This concept exists among other indigenous groups. Among the Dani, for instance, "the duty of a leader is focused on 'ensuing fertility,' which means that all members of the community should be given the opportunity to develop and have equal access to collective forms of wealth, such as land and resources. Similarly, each member of the community deserves equal right to be healthy and educated. In brief, welfare means that all basic needs of every person, not just a minority of people, are fulfilled."[127]

Merdeka *as a Movement to Restore Human Dignity*

The story of suffering in West Papua is often recounted as a story in which Papuans describe themselves as being treated as if they were less than human, as if they were animals. *Merdeka* therefore is also about an end to the destructive racism that pervades Papuan society. Given the way Papuans have been marginalized and displaced by migration, addressing Papuan disadvantage must include the ability for Papuans to restrict and control migration. Animating culture to direct positive social change, and celebrating and being proud of indigenous Papuan identity, are also seen as an important means of achieving this end.

■ Toward Freedom and Liberation

Although *merdeka* is translated as "freedom" in Bahasa Indonesia, Jakarta equates Papuan demands for *merdeka* with a narrow meaning of freedom as the desire for a sovereign state. In doing so, legitimate Papuan objectives such as a discussion about the history of West Papua, as well as demands for greater equality, participation in decisionmaking, and an end to the impunity of the Indonesian military, are marginalized. For Papuans, however, the deeper and broader meaning of *merdeka* is more akin to "liberation" (*pembebasan* in Indonesian). The problem for Jakarta is that given the history of the past forty years and the lack of trust Papuans have in Jakarta, few Papuans believe that their aspirations for peace, justice, equality, and democracy can be met within the framework of the Indonesian state. The meaning of *merdeka* is often summed up as the desire "to be rulers of one's own land" *(tuan di atas tanahnya),* expressing an understanding of self-determination that has meanings that are at once national and particular, both more and less than the desire for independence. Nonetheless, much of the substance of the wider meaning of *merdeka* inherent in Papuan demands is consistent with the goal of social justice for all, the fifth pillar of *pancasila,* the five principles that articulate the philosophical basis of the Indonesian state.[128]

By only understanding *merdeka* as "independence," security forces and policymakers in Jakarta—as well as outside activists, development practitioners, and policymakers—lump all Papuan aspirations together as a demand for independence or sovereignty, thereby making it difficult to respond to demands for *merdeka* that can be met within a framework that does not necessarily imply support for a political outcome of independence. The polarization of all Papuan demands for *merdeka* as being synonymous with the demand for independence has tragic consequences for Papuans who suffer persistent and horrible human rights violations at the hands of the security forces who have repeatedly responded violently to any perceived threat to the territorial integrity of the Indonesian state. Jakarta's fear of *merdeka* as independence, and its consequent security-based approach to prevent this, ironically pushes Papuans further toward identifying the realization of *merdeka* with the goal of political independence. In the process, the wider meaning of freedom as social justice, equality, and democracy is lost.

As long as *merdeka* is understood by Jakarta only as a threat to nationalist symbols or political sovereignty, the government will ignore and even violate the tenets that could form the basis of mutually satisfying outcomes. If Jakarta continues to ignore the deeper meanings of *merdeka*—the desire for peace, justice, and sustainable development—the Indonesian government will ironically entrench the understanding that *merdeka* can only signify political independence, further encouraging violence and the Indonesian government's nightmare of disintegration.[129]

To facilitate understanding and the possibility of creative and peaceful solutions, it would be helpful if all parties involved in West Papua responded to the deeper and more subtle meanings underlying Papuans' use of the term *merdeka*. For Papuans, this will also mean breaking down the demand for *merdeka* into functional strategic objectives that are clearly defined and achievable. For outsiders, it is also critical to support Papuan-led social justice programs and campaigns, and the efforts of Papuans who are reconstructing indigenous governance structures, that facilitate the realization of the wider meaning of *merdeka*. At the same time, outsiders need to recognize that the meaning of the words "special autonomy" has been lost. For Papuans, special autonomy now means little more than a type of government administration by a power that is viewed through the lens of over forty years of colonialism. To address this problem, Brigham Golden suggests a broad renaming and reframing of political solutions, like the special autonomy legislation, as *daerah independen* (independent region), for example, and consistently implementing the law so that the moral aspirations inherent in *merdeka* are met.[130] In this way, the deficit of trust in the territory might begin to be restored. Perhaps then, says Golden, conflict resolution initiatives such as special autonomy will be seen as encompassing people's longing for *merdeka,* and not in opposition to it.[131]

Conversation over West Papua quickly becomes polarized once it shifts to questions of territory, but remains open if the discussion focuses on other substantive issues, captured by the wider meaning of *merdeka*. By emphasizing the meaning of *merdeka* in the Papuan context as a shared commitment by migrants, Papuans, and other Indonesians in general, to justice, equality, and democracy, it might become possible to start to talk about how to resolve conflict, while in the short-term avoiding the more difficult question of sovereignty and political self-determination.

■ Conclusion

Without reining in the military, devolving genuine power to Papuans, and sustained practical steps that restore trust and meet the moral aspirations inherent in Papuans demands for *merdeka,* there is a real danger that Jakarta will inadvertently push Papuans further down the road to violent struggle for independence.

As John Rumbiak[132] and other Papuans[133] have noted, working for justice and peace in West Papua is not a struggle for the Papuans alone. The international community not only shares responsibility for the causes of the conflict, but has also benefited economically and politically. Consequently, members of the international community need to recognize their own involvement and responsibilities in supporting the emergence of an outcome that meets the legitimate needs of the parties involved. The silence that surrounds the conflict in West Papua needs to be broken. The first step is to open the province to greater scrutiny by the international community.

While understandable, given the Cold War politics of the time, the process of the transfer of power from the Netherlands to Indonesia fundamentally violated international democratic norms, shared concepts of human rights, and notions of natural justice. Moreover, ongoing military activities in the province continue to violate basic human rights, while many Papuans feel marginalized within their own homeland. Eventually, *all* parties responsible—not just Indonesia—will need to sit down and discuss the issue, and ultimately Papuans will need to be returned the right to freely and fairly determine their own political future in a just and creative arrangement that meets Papuan needs for human security, participatory development, and indigenous identity.

The international community can also contribute to ending military impunity and restraining the military's destructive role in the economy by holding the TNI accountable and tying forms of assistance to the TNI to concrete improvements in the area of military reform, human rights investigations, and an end to impunity. In the context of the presence of large resource-extractive companies in West Papua, the international community can also work to ensure that development is culturally sensitive, respects human rights, and recognizes the right of local communities to say no. More specifically, the international community can also support community-led participatory development, work to end illegal logging, work toward implementing extraterritorial legislation that subjects foreign corporations to the same laws in their own country, and support regulation to end corruption, like the Publish What You Pay campaign and the US Foreign Corrupt Practices Act, legislation that prohibits the payment of bribes to officials and imposes more rigid accounting practices on US companies operating abroad.[134]

At its heart, any intervention in West Papua needs to be based on a deep understanding and analysis of the multifaceted and interlinked root causes of the conflict, and designed by Papuans themselves in response to the wider moral meanings associated with Papuan aspirations for *merdeka*. Jakarta's dangerous policy montage of divide and rule, large-scale development based on resource extraction that further marginalizes Papuans, and migration, together with the military's intent on eradicating separatism through violence while maintaining a mafia-like grip on its network of business operations, threatens to exacerbate Papuan demands for independence. These actions also betray ordinary Indonesians' hopes for a better Indonesia than the one left them by Suharto.

▪ Notes

I am indebted to Anne Brown, Greg Poulgrain, Richard Chauvel, Rachael Harrison, Zohl de Ishtar, John Ondawame, Annie Feith, and John Bass for their helpful insights, feedback, and assistance. All errors, of course, are entirely my responsibility.

1. West Papua has been known by many names during its recent history: Dutch New Guinea, West New Guinea, West Irian, Irian Jaya, Papua, and West Papua. To avoid confusion, I refer to the territory as West Papua (including both the province of Papua and the recently established province of West Irian Jaya). For the sake of clarity, I refer to the indigenous people of West Papua as Papuans, while I refer to nonethnic Papuans—in other words, Indonesians from other parts of the archipelago living in West Papua—as migrants.

2. Maclellan, "Self-Determination or Territorial Integrity?"

3. Chauvel, "Essays on West Papua," vol. 1, p. 1.

4. Bone, *The Dynamics of the West New Guinea (Irian Barat) Problem*, pp. 55–57.

5. See, for example, Permanent Mission of the Republic of Indonesia to the United Nations, *Questioning the Unquestionable.*

6. This doctrine is known as *uti possidetis juris;* see Saltford, *The United Nations and the Indonesian Takeover of West Papua*, pp. 8–9. It was in part a result of this principle that the incorporation of East Timor, as a former Portuguese colony, was not seen as consistent with international practice.

7. Chauvel, "Essays on West Papua," vol. 1; Chauvel, "Constructing Papuan Nationalism."

8. Papuan Congress resolution, 4 June 2000, available at http://www.koteka.net/ppc.htm (accessed 1 May 2002). See also Chauvel, "Constructing Papuan Nationalism," pp. 8–11.

9. *Trikora* is an acronym for *Tri Komando Rakyat* (The Three Demands of the People). The first demand was to crush efforts to make Papua a puppet government for the Dutch. The second was to raise the Indonesian flag on West Irian soil. The third was to integrate West Papua into the Republic of Indonesia.

10. Saltford, *The United Nations and the Indonesian Takeover of West Papua.*

11. *New York Agreement,* art. XVIII.

12. See, for example, Saltford, *The United Nations and the Indonesian Takeover of West Papua;* Osborne, *Indonesia's Secret War,* pp. 35–48; Budiardjo and Liong, *West Papua,* pp. 20–32.

13. See Saltford, *The United Nations and the Indonesian Takeover of West Papua;* Osborne, *Indonesia's Secret War,* pp. 46–48.

14. Saltford, *The United Nations and the Indonesian Takeover of West Papua,* p. 94.

15. From Sukarno's Independence Day anniversary speech, cited in Bone, *The Dynamics of the Western New Guinea (Irian Barat) Problem,* pp. 85–86.

16. Permanent Mission of the Republic of Indonesia to the United Nations, *Questioning the Unquestionable.*

17. Chauvel, "Decolonising Without the Colonised."

18. Ibid.

19. International Crisis Group, "Indonesia: Ending Repression in Irian Jaya," p. 3.

20. Rumbiak, "From the Ashes of Empire," p. 5.

21. See, for example, King, *West Papua and Indonesia Since Suharto,* pp. 129–131; Tapol, "West Papua"; Chauvel and Bhakti, "The Papua Conflict," pp. 28–29.

22. Aceh was also offered special autonomy at the same time. See, for example, McGibbon, "Secessionist Challenges in Aceh and Papua."

23. See Sumule, "Swimming Against the Current," for a summary of the process of initiating, drafting, and promoting special autonomy. Richard Chauvel and Ikar Bhakti, in "The Papua Conflict," p. 37, say that this was "perhaps the first time since 1963 in which Papuans actively participated in the making of government policy."

24. Sekretariat Keadilan dan Perdamaian–Keuskupan Jayapura, "Recent Developments in Papua." See also King, *West Papua and Indonesia Since Suharto,* pp. 81–94.

25. See, for instance, Chauvel and Bhakti, "The Papua Conflict," p. 37; Rumbiak, "Human Rights in Papua," pp. 145–146.

26. See, for instance, Sumule, "Social and Economic Changes in Papua," pp. 104–105; "Papuan Students Demand Graft Probe," *Jakarta Post,* 19 July 2005, available at http://www.kabaririan.com/news/msg03405.html (accessed 20 July 2005).

27. International Crisis Group, *Dividing Papua.*

28. Chauvel and Bhakti, "The Papua Conflict," pp. 37–39.

29. Tiarma Siboro, "Army to Station Extra Division in Papua," *Jakarta Post,* 19 March 2005, available at http://www.kabar-irian.com/pipermail/kabar-irian/2005-march/000629.html (accessed 15 April 2005).

30. Chauvel, "Constructing Papuan Nationalism," p. 49.

31. Chauvel and Bhakti, "The Papua Conflict," p. 39.

32. Thom Beanal (Dewan Adat chair), cited in Wing, *Genocide in West Papua?* pp. 46–48. See also "Manokwari Declaration of the Dewan Adat Papua, 4 February 2005," in Wing, *Genocide in West Papua?* pp. 52–53.

33. Timmer, "Living with Intricate Futures."

34. For more on the role of nongovernmental organizations in West Papua, see Bonay and McGrory, "West Papua," pp. 452–453. See also Blair and Phillips, "Peace and Progress in Papua."

35. Telapak and EIA, "The Last Frontier."

36. See, for example, Permanent Mission of the Republic of Indonesia to the United Nations, *Questioning the Unquestionable.*

37. Giay, *Menuju Papua Baru,* pp. 36–37.

38. See, for example, Budiardjo and Liong, *West Papua;* Osborne, *Indonesia's*

Secret War. A death toll of 100,000 is often quoted in the literature, while some Papuans claim that church documents estimate the figure to be much higher.

39. Wing, *Genocide in West Papua?* pp. 19–22.

40. Ibid., p. 19.

41. See, for example, Lowry, *The Armed Forces of Indonesia.* See also Davies, "Indonesian Security Responses to Resurgent Papuan Separatism."

42. Lowry, *The Armed Forces of Indonesia.*

43. M. Rizai Maslan, "The Theys Murder Verdict: The TNI View," 23 April 2003, available at http://www.kabar-irian.com/pipermail/kabar-irian/2003-april/000199.html (accessed 20 July 2005).

44. "Red and White" refers to the colors of the Indonesian flag.

45. International Crisis Group, "Indonesia: Resources and Conflict in Papua," p. 10.

46. "Keberadaan Eurico Guterres di Timika Meresahkan," *Sinar Harapan,* 5 December 2003. For a summary of Gutteres's activities in East Timor, see McDonald et al., *Masters of Terror,* pp. 164–167.

47. See, for example, Elsham, *Laskar Jihad dan Satgas Merah Putih Meningkatan Aktivitas Latihannya.*

48. See, for instance, Tebay, *West Papua,* p. 10.

49. Brundige et al., "Indonesian Human Rights Abuses in Papua," pp. 74–75.

50. Elmslie, *Irian Jaya Under the Gun.*

51. McCulloch, "Trifungsi."

52. Lowry, *The Armed Forces of Indonesia;* McCulloch, "Trifungsi."

53. See, for instance, Telapak and EIA, "The Last Frontier."

54. See, for example, Abrash, *Development Aggression;* McCulloch, "Trifungsi"; Perlez and Bonner, "Below a Mountain of Wealth, a River of Waste."

55. An example is the fish canning factory run by Djarma Aru Limited (Djayanti Group) on Kimaam Island. See Catholic Relief Services, *The Peacebuilding Toolkit,* pp. 23–28.

56. Robert F. Kennedy Memorial Center for Human Rights, "Indonesian Military Brothels Contribute to Skyrocketing HIV/AIDS Rate in West Papua," *West Papua Report,* June 2005, available at http://www.rfkmemorial.org/human_rights/1993_bambang/rfk_papua_report_6_05.pdf (accessed 20 July 2005).

57. Blair and Phillips, "Peace and Progress in Papua," p. 51.

58. McCulloch, "Trifungsi."

59. Dorothy Kosich, "Freeport's Reputation Simmers on the Front Burner, Again," 26 July 2005, available at http://www.kabar-irian.com/pipermail/kabar-irian/2005-July/000678.html (accessed 28 July 2005).

60. For an excellent 2005 expose into the activities of Freeport, see Perlez and Bonner, "Below a Mountain of Wealth, a River of Waste."

61. Abrash, *Development Aggression,* p. 13. For a reference on killings by the TNI and Freeport security personnel, see Perlez and Bonner, "Below a Mountain of Wealth, a River of Waste."

62. Cited in Kennedy and Abrash, "Repressive Mining in West Papua," p. 93.

63. Giay, *Menuju Papua Baru,* p. 31.

64. George Monbiot, "In Bed with Killers," *Z Net,* 2005, available at http://www.zmag.org/content/showarticle.cfm?sectionid=44&itemid=7776 (accessed 5 May 2005).

65. MacLeod, "Gagged."

66. Kennedy and Abrash, "Repressive Mining in West Papua." See also Perlez and Bonner, "Below a Mountain of Wealth, a River of Waste."

67. Abrash, *Development Aggression,* p. 19.

68. Blair and Phillips, "Peace and Progress in Papua," p. 51.

69. Chauvel, "Constructing Papuan Nationalism," p. 12.

70. Blair and Phillips, "Peace and Progress in Papua," p. 74.

71. Blaser, Feit, and McRae, *In the Way of Development.*

72. UNDP, *Human Development Report, 2004.*

73. Dennis Blair and David Phillips, in their report "Peace and Progress in Papua," p. 76, give a snapshot of local health conditions in Papua. They write that local health clinics are understaffed and poorly equipped; over 20 percent of the population in the central highlands suffer from malnutrition and vitamin deficiencies; over 50 percent of children under age five are undernourished; infant mortality is more than double the rate in Indonesia as a whole; the maternal mortality rate in Papua is three times greater in Papua than in the rest of Indonesia; only 40.8 percent of children are immunized, compared with the national average of 60.3 percent; inadequate primary healthcare results in preventable diseases; of infant deaths, 26 percent are caused by pneumonia, 19 percent by diarrhea, and 11 percent by malaria; and the average life expectancy is forty to fifty years (fifteen years below the national average). As well, Rodd McGibbon, in "Plural Society in Peril," p. 26, claims that the reason for such neglect is "an ethnic form of discrimination." For a report into the AIDS/HIV epidemic, see Butt, Numbery, and Morin, "Preventing Aids in Papua."

74. During a two-week walk through the highlands in 2002, I observed that 90 percent of the schools in a remote area in the highlands were empty, mainly due to lack of school funds for teachers and the inability of parents to pay school fees. See also Blair and Phillips's report "Peace and Progress in Papua," p. 75, which states that the literacy rate for women is 44 percent compared with 78 percent in the rest of Indonesia; and for men, 58 percent compared to 90 percent. Only 10 percent of the Papuan people have a high school education, and only 1 percent have graduated from college. See also McGibbon, "Plural Society in Peril," p. 26.

75. McGibbon, "Plural Society in Peril," p. 26.

76. Blair and Phillips, "Peace and Progress in Papua," p. 77.

77. See Robert F. Kennedy Memorial Center for Human Rights, "Indonesian Military Brothels Contribute to Skyrocketing HIV/AIDS Rate in West Papua." See also Wing and King, *Genocide in West Papua?* pp. 8–10.

78. McGibbon, "Plural Society in Peril," p. 43.

79. Ibid.

80. See "Papuan Students Demand Graft Probe," *Jakarta Post,* 19 July 2005. See also Sumule, "Social and Economic Changes in Papua," pp. 104–105. On Transparency International's 2004 Corruption Perceptions Index, Indonesia ranked 137 out of 145 countries; Transparency International, *The 2004 Corruption Perceptions Index.*

81. McGibbon, "Plural Society in Peril," p. viii.

82. Ibid.

83. Ibid., p. 23.

84. Ibid., pp. x, 20–23.

85. Ibid., pp. 23–25.

86. Ibid., p. 23.

87. Ibid., pp. 23–24.

88. UNDP, *National Human Development Report, 2004.*

89. McGibbon, "Plural Society in Peril," p. 31.

90. Ibid., p. 25.

91. Ibid.

92. Ibid., p. 26.

93. Ibid.

94. Ibid., pp. 31–35.

95. Ibid., p. 9.

96. Ibid., pp. 27, 44–45.

97. See, for instance, Abubakar Riry and Mashudi Noorsalim, "Peace Market: Building Trust Through Trade in Ambon," *Inside Indonesia* (82), April–June 2005, p. 15, which describes how a market in Ambon has facilitated relationship building across religious divides.

98. See, for example, Giay, *Menuju Papua Baru,* p. 5–6; Timmer, "Living with Intricate Futures," pp. 278–279; King, *West Papua and Indonesia Since Suharto,* p. 63.

99. Giay, "Against Indonesia," p. 129.

100. See, for example, Giay, *Menuju Papua Baru;* McGibbon, "Plural Society in Peril," Chauvel and Bhakti, "The Papua Conflict."

101. See Alex Rayfield, "Singing for Life," *Inside Indonesia* (78), April–June 2004, pp. 7–8.

102. Howard, McGibbon, and Simon, *Resistance, Recovery, Re-empowerment.*

103. Ibid., p. 23.

104. Ibid., p. 14.

105. See van den Broek and Hernawan, *Memoria Passionis di Papua,* p. 73. See also Golden, "Letter to the Editor," p. 33.

106. Golden, "Letter to the Editor," p. 34. Trade in alcohol is closely controlled by the Indonesian military.

107. Beanal, cited in Giay, *Menuju Papua Baru,* p. 13; and Giay, tape recording of a speech given at the Papua Project Workshop, 12 December 2001.

108. Golden, "Letter to the Editor," p. 34.

109. Reid, *"Merdeka,"* p. 155.

110. Golden, "Political Millenarianism and the Economy of Conflict."

111. Ibid.

112. Chauvel, "Constructing Papuan Nationalism," p. 1.

113. Kirksey, "From Cannibal to Terrorist," pp. 3, 97.

114. Ibid., p. 97. See also Chris Richards, "Challenges for Independence: Governance," *New Internationalist* (344), April 2002, pp. 24–25.

115. Giay, "Hai," p. 6. For another description of *Hai,* see "Towards an Amungme History," p. 3; and Kamma, *Koreri,* pp. 291–292.

116. Kjar, "The Invisible Aristocrat," p. 54.

117. See, for instance, Giay, "Zakheus Pakage and His Communities"; Timmer, "The Return of the Kingdom."

118. See, for example, Giay, "Zakheus Pakage and His Communities."

119. See, for example, Rutherford, "Waiting for the End in Biak." See also Kamma, *Koreri.*

120. Golden, "Letter to the Editor," p. 33.

121. Giay, "Towards a New Papua," p. 9.

122. Ibid.

123. *Adat* is a difficult word to accurately translate. Often translated as "tradition," it also points to indigenous beliefs, customs, culture, and customary law.

124. Howard, McGibbon, and Simon, *Resistance, Recovery, Re-empowerment,* p. 29.

125. van den Broek, "Restoring Human Dignity," p. 11.

126. Ibid.

127. Ibid.

128. Golden, "Political Millenarianism and the Economy of Conflict."

129. Ibid.

130. Golden, "Letter to the Editor," p. 33.

131. Ibid. See also Sekretariat Keadilan Perdamaian–Keuskupan Jayapura, "Recent Developments in Papua."

132. Rumbiak, "A Struggle for Dignity, Justice, and Peace," p. viii.

133. Tebay, *West Papua,* pp. 26–27.

134. On Publish What You Pay, see http://www.publishwhatyoupay.org (accessed 28 July 2005).

9

External Intervention: The Solomon Islands Beyond RAMSI

Clive Moore

BETWEEN 1998 AND 2003, the Solomon Islands went through a serious economic and political downturn. Observers began to describe the island archipelago as a "fragile," "failed," or "failing" state. International commentators considered the situation was dire. An assessment drawn up late in 2002 and published in 2003 by the Australian Strategic Policy Institute declared: "There is no effective Cabinet process, real power and decision making occurs outside the formal political arena. A shadow state has emerged in Solomon Islands—a patronage system centred on the ruling cabal's control over resources. The state has been gutted from the inside, and parliament largely serves as an avenue for access to dwindling resources by political players."[1] Mark Otter, editor of the United Nations Development Programme's 2002 report on human development in the Solomon Islands, went further when he described the situation in May 2003: "Solomon Islands is in a perilous state. . . . The government is bankrupt, development has stalled, investment has decreased and the economy is at an all time low. Lawlessness is rife on the streets of Honiara where "order" is maintained through the barrel of a gun. The police force is incapable and unwilling to maintain law and order. Solomon Islands is a failed state. Its future is bleak."[2]

The image created of a broken-backed state is accurate, but it would be wrong to depict a suffering, desperate people—in the style of an African state like Rwanda during its civil war, or Timor Leste during its separation from Indonesia. The problem was mainly confined to one island, Guadalcanal. The total death toll from the undeniably violent occurrences, mainly on Guadalcanal, was probably no more than 150. However, the loss of health and education services was significant in all communities—unnecessary deaths caused by truncated medical services should be added to the direct deaths through violence, and the retardation of children's education has slowed overall development. There were also 20,000 refugees, and a helpless urban poor in Honiara, the capital of Guadalcanal, who were on the verge of malnutrition. But through all of this, at the level of food and housing, life for the majority of the people across the archipelago went on much as before. What had failed was the introduced modern centralized processes of government and its services, the export-led economy, and the infrastructure of urban life, not the lives of the 84 percent of Solomon Islanders who still live in villages and remain dependent on subsistence agriculture and fishing. They ordered their lives much as before, went to church regularly, and made local decisions based on discussions mediated through both elected and traditional leaders. This is the conundrum that the majority of Pacific Islanders, including Solomon Islanders, have to confront every day: how to maintain their diverse and dispersed rural lifestyles while also being part of a modern nation. Australia and other regional nations saw the deteriorating situation as one that breached international security, would encourage drug lords, gun runners, terrorists, and refugees, and endanger international borders. In the villages of the Solomon Islands, the "crisis" was an event on another island to be talked about at night after a hard day's work in the gardens. In years to come, it will be the subject of stories, enter legends and chants, and be acted out in dance-drama, remembered in the same way as World War II or the achievement of independence from the British in 1978.

What the international community depicted as a collapse in security, was in essence a struggle over adapting introduced concepts and practices to a robust indigenous culture, and a struggle over control and distribution of natural and human resources. There were a number of governance and development issues at the core of the crisis. These concern the manner in which the parliament and public service operated, as well as inequalities both in the development of human and economic infrastructure and in the distribution of the profits from development. These inequalities have clear historical causes, some of which we can trace back to before the British protectorate began.

After eighty-five years (1893–1978) as a British protectorate and approaching thirty years of independence, there is no doubt that the national economy was increasingly mismanaged and that internal social pressures were not addressed. The greed of the elite was faintly recognizable in the nation's first years (1978–1986), grew exponentially during the logging-boom years (1987–1998), was slowed during the crisis years (1998–2003), and has cautiously resumed since. The crucial event of the crisis years was the expulsion of about 20,000 "foreign" Solomon Islanders from Guadalcanal during 1998 and 1999, particularly Malaitan families living around the oil palm plantations and in Honiara. The militants, who purposefully and violently expelled about 15 percent of Guadalcanal's total population, called themselves the Guadalcanal Revolutionary Army (GRA), later renamed the Isatabu Freedom Movement (IFM). The GRA/IFM had close links to the Guadalcanal provincial government through its premier (and former prime minister), Ezekiel Alebua. The resultant turmoil was a major human catastrophe in terms of streams of refugees dispossessed from jobs, land, and homes. This led to the counterformation in early 2000 of the Malaita Eagle Force (MEF), consisting primarily of Malaitans, most formerly resident on Guadalcanal, which, together with elements of the police, took control of the capital city Honiara. The MEF and GRA/IFM militias skirmished and fought with each other over several years in a quasi-military campaign: raids and atrocities became the norm, homes and schools were burned, and no-go zones with road blocks were declared. Although the national government, civil society groups, and the international community attempted to mediate through more than twenty-five peace negotiations and forums, the government found itself increasingly incapable of controlling the situation.[3]

Through a coup in June 2000, the MEF removed the government of Prime Minister Bartholomew Ulufa'alu. The next two governments failed to regain control of the situation, law and order plummeted, the economy spiraled downward, and basic services were no longer delivered. Ulufa'alu and his successor prime ministers, Manasseh Sogavare and Sir Allan Kemakeza, at various times called for outside intervention. Then, in June 2003, the Australian government decided, based largely on fears of deterioration in regional security, to establish its Regional Assistance Mission to the Solomon Islands (RAMSI) in July, initially to restore law and order, and in the longer term to aid the rehabilitation of the nation.[4]

These years, 1998 to 2003, are often depicted as an "ethnic crisis" or an "ethnic tension," as if the substantial cause of the crisis was a long-standing ethnic dispute between the people of two major neighboring islands, Guadalcanal and Malaita. But this perspective ignores close and long-standing kin relationships that bind the people of southeastern Malaita and those of the Marau area of southern Guadalcanal,[5] and extensive trading and marriage relationships that have linked the two islands over many generations, including during recent decades when many thousands of Malaitans lived on Guadalcanal. While cultural differences were one aspect of the problem, its causes were much more complex than simple cultural or ethnic tensions.

Guadalcanal is the largest island in the nation, constituting 5,336 square kilometers (2,052 square miles) and 19 percent of the nation's total land area. During the crisis years, the Guale (the people of Guadalcanal) forcefully argued that they had become disadvantaged on their own island, which was the source of a large portion of gross national product. The capital city was shifted to Guadalcanal after World War II and grew to a population approaching 70,000, dominated by Malaitans in the public service, police, teaching, small business, and tourism sectors. Honiara's urban area expanded decade-by-decade and squatter settlements extended onto customary lands. In the early 1970s, a large agricultural project began on the Guadalcanal plains close to Honiara, Solomon Islands Plantation Limited, the oil palms of which eventually expanded to cover 6,000 hectares (15,000 acres), with expansion plans for another 4,000 hectares (10,000 acres), though the latter were thwarted by the events of 1998–2003. Then, in the 1990s, Ross Mining NL Limited began to develop the Goldridge mine in central Guadalcanal. It began production in 1998.[6] The oil palm plantations had a workforce of almost 1,800 and a wider community of about 15,000, two-thirds of whom were from Malaita. The workers and their families purchased surrounding land and were major market food suppliers to Honiara. They also married into the local Guale community. The mine's workforce was smaller, but the profits were substantial and the dislocation of Guale and their fear of future environmental damage from mine tailings was considerable, although this fear seems to have been largely without substance. Both projects paid compensation and rent to customary landowners, but the rents for the oil palm lands, negotiated a quarter century earlier, seemed inadequate when compared with the more generous compensation paid by the mining company. The real profits went to the companies and to the national government, not to the people or Guadalcanal's provincial government. These urban and economic developments drew ever larger numbers of other Solomon Islanders to Guadalcanal, particularly from Malaita, the most populous province.[7]

By the mid-1980s, the Guale were increasingly frustrated by the lack of economic benefit flowing to their province, and the violent and difficult behavior of some Malaitans, whom they felt were substituting Malaitan customary ways for their own and riding roughshod over the real owners of the land. Guale grievances were economic, social, and political, but at their core they were related to the right to control their own land. Intra-Guadalcanal conflicts were also involved, played out from the formation of the GRA/IFM to 2003 and the final capture of Guale rebel leader Harold Keke. They are still simmering today. Guadalcanal is less culturally homogeneous than Malaita. The people of the northern coast, related to those of neighboring Nggela and Savo Islands in Central province, are depicted by some as not "pure" Guale. When the Moro movement emerged on Guadalcanal in the 1950s, as a back to *kastom*[8] protest against lack of development, the people of the Weathercoast (southern coast) were idealized as the true indigenous people of the island.[9] The GRA/IFM originated on the Weathercoast, because of lack of economic development in that area compared with the northern coast, and old animosities, which always divided the Guadalcanal militants, were played out.

Malaitan justification for their retaliation against the Guale was expressed in terms of the need to protect their people on Guadalcanal, and to stabilize the crumbling national government. Both sides and the government began to apply the mechanisms of customary behavior, which included compensation for insult and injury.[10] The "ethnic crisis" explanation comes from the insult both sides felt to their dignity. While the Guale had clear local grievances regarding lack of compensation, Malaitans failed to voice their frustrations as clearly. Their migration to Guadalcanal after the 1940s had several diverse motivations. Because of Malaita's long, thin, and high topographic profile, quite substantial portions of the island are nonarable. The size of the population meant that there was labor available in excess of subsistence needs. Dating back to the 1870s, Malaita's long-term exploitation as the major labor reserve for the Solomon Islands had established a pattern of migration. And the lack of large-scale economic development in the province forced Malaitans to look further afield for economic advancement. The ethnic disadvantage argument was significant for both sides, but does not explain the sudden taking of arms and use of violence.

Figure 9.1 shows the relative sizes of the populations of Malaita, Guadalcanal, and the rest of the Solomon Islands at the time of the first census, in 1931, and at the most recent census, in 1999. Since 1931, and presumably long before that, Malaita has always been the most populous island in Solomons. The precontact dynamics of interisland relations were disturbed by whalers and traders early in the nineteenth century, which caused headhunting raids into the central Solomon Islands in the 1860s–1880s. Malaitan men, unlike the aggressive New Georgia raiders who had obtained their steel weapons from the whalers and traders, were left with little choice other than to leave their island to seek work in order to obtain the requisite European manufactured goods, which had become the most important trade items. Steel goods, particularly axes and later muskets and rifles, became essential items for safety and prestige. In later decades of the nineteenth century, Malaitans became the mainstays of an indentured labor trade, first to Queensland (1870–1904) and Fiji (1871–1911), and then within the Solomon Islands once copra plantations were developed.[11] From the late 1940s, this internal migration was regularized as wage labor and often involved the migration of families, many of them to Guadalcanal. Honiara subsequently became a Malaitan-dominated city and its hinterland became a Malaitan enclave on Guadalcanal.

Malaitan men became laborers who worked away from their island not through choice but through force of circumstance. Contemporary Malaitans were frustrated by the lack of development in their province, which had forced adult males and their families to leave the island to seek work. Likewise, the Guale were frustrated: northern Guadalcanal, particularly the plains, had been alienated for plantations, mining, and Honiara. The compensation they received in return was meager, and large parts of the island, particularly the Weathercoast, remained underdeveloped.[12] Nonetheless, these grievances were not adequate justification for either side's involve-

Figure 9.1 Solomon Islands Population, 1931 and 1999

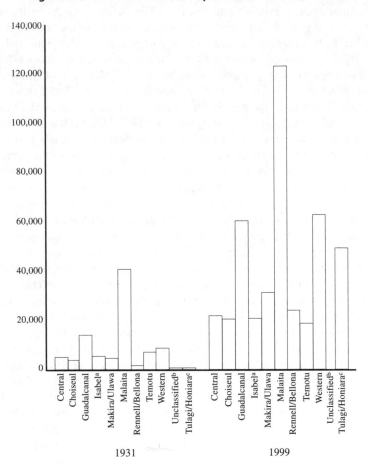

Sources: Solomon Islands Government, *British Solomon Islands Annual Report,* 1931, p. 5; Solomon Islands Government, *National Census, 1999.*
   Notes: a. 1931, includes Russell Islands.
   b. 1931, includes an unclassified category (n = 431).
   c. 1931 Tulagi (n = 50); 1999 Honiara.

ment in a civil war in a nation already precariously balanced economically and politically. The second phase of the crisis developed after the Townsville peace agreement of October 2000 and the handing in of many weapons. The IFM-MEF military confrontation abated, and then changed into anarchy, as those left with weapons, now criminals, formed gangs and terrorized the government, bureaucracy, the general public, and even their own families and *wantoks*.[13] This led to complete breakdown of law and order. Gangs claiming to represent the IFM or the MEF demanded compensation for the slightest offense, raided the bank accounts of government departments, and extorted individuals and villages under threat of violent reaction. If the first phase had its origins in ethnic difference and underdevelopment, the second phase was characterized by criminal opportunism.

The arrival of RAMSI in July 2003 was welcomed by all, and for the first few months there was a honeymoon period that gave way to concern and questioning. RAMSI and the government and people of the Solomon Islands now have to reassess the needs and existing capacity of the regional mission and the nation. This chapter assesses the problems, and suggests some solutions. It also discusses the role of international agencies in resolving local conflict, and the unstable relationship between development, security, and governance.

■ RAMSI and Beyond

The initial strength of the Regional Assistance Mission to Solomon Islands was about 2,000 armed services personnel, police, development advisers, and public servants, the majority from Australia but with token representation from other Pacific Islands Forum countries. They arrived with little more than a blueprint on how to handle the situation. The basic objective was to restore law and order and to assist the proper functioning of the state apparatus. RAMSI was never intended to replace the government, merely to strengthen the government's ability to operate, but this limitation is also at the core of ongoing problems. RAMSI was late arriving—one could argue that the mission was three or four years late, given that all three recent Solomon Island prime ministers pleaded for outside intervention. The problems compounded over these years and are now subsequently harder to solve. Although the assistance mission is sponsored by all Pacific Islands Forum nations, personnel from Australia and New Zealand dominate,[14] and run the long-term agenda. RAMSI consequently must take care not to be neocolonial in its approach. The situation is not unlike colonial powers dealing with former colonies during the lead up to independence and in their first decade as independent nations. There are also financial limits that constrain the operation. Even though Australia is supporting RAMSI at about A$200 million a year, and New Zealand is providing another NZ$16 million per year, RAMSI has limited financial capacity to tackle large projects.[15]

Organizing the surrender of firearms was relatively easy, given the show of military strength. Within weeks, almost 2,500 weapons, including some high-powered military weapons, and 300,000 rounds of ammunition, had been handed in. Most of these were collected around Honiara and on Malaita, but 600 weapons came from Gizo in Western province. Government leaders also divested themselves of their private arsenals: in

August 2003, Alex Bartlett, previously an MEF leader and then minister of tourism, handed in several rifles, two revolvers, and thousands of rounds of ammunition.[16] By late 2003, 3,700 weapons had been surrendered and destroyed, most of their remnants now interned in a grassed mound on the ocean side of Rove police headquarters, a visible memorial to the years of senseless and destructive violence. In November 2004, Peter Noble, then RAMSI's deputy special coordinator, believed that between 100 and 150 high-powered weapons were still extant, hidden mainly in remote areas. At the same time, Malaitans in Honiara claimed there were guns hidden within a few kilometers of RAMSI headquarters. Initially, people were bluffed by RAMSI's claims that they possessed the technology to locate all weapons, but as time went on it became clear to most people that this was untrue and weapons remained buried. Although the initial RAMSI activities were accomplished without loss of life, two RAMSI personnel have since died: an Australian police officer was deliberately killed by a sniper in Honiara in December 2004, and another died through misadventure in March 2005.

More than half of the troops were withdrawn by the end of 2003, and others left in February–March 2004, leaving approximately 200 police, a few dozen armed forces personnel, and senior public servants in "line" positions. The MEF and IFM no longer exist, although in May 2005 there were stirrings in north Malaita from a group calling itself the "Malaita Separatist Movement." Right from the outset, RAMSI has methodically pursued the main corrupt and criminal figures. One of the areas strengthened was the legal system, with improved court facilities and legal experts serving as magistrates, prosecutors, and in the offices of the solicitor-general and public solicitor. By November 2003, over eighty police had been charged, including Manasseh Maelanga, the former commander of the Police Field Force and operational commander for the 2000 coup; his deputy, Patteson Saeni; and two deputy police commissioners, Wilfred Akao and John Homelo. The entire supreme council of the MEF is now in prison or facing charges. Several politicians from the crisis years have also been charged. In jail are Daniel Fa'afunua, minister of communications, aviation, and meteorology and a close MEF confidant; and Alex Bartlett, minister of tourism and one-time MEF secretary-general. Facing charges are Francis Zama, minister of finance; and Andrew Nori, lawyer, former politician, and adviser to the MEF. RAMSI has overseen the trial and conviction of the three main Guale renegades, Harold Keke, Ronnie Cawa, and Francis Lela, with other investigations and trials continuing. Nevertheless, many Solomon Islanders are disappointed that so few senior corrupt politicians, police, and public servants have been detained. They are, of course, unaware of the slow and exacting tasks involved in collecting solid evidence and gaining convictions.

When Prime Minister Alan Kemakeza asked Australia to intervene, he knew that he would be inviting close scrutiny of his own actions. Born in

1951 on Savo Island in Central province, he is unusual among modern leaders in having only a primary school education, supplemented by training from short courses in Australia and the United Kingdom while he was a member of the Royal Solomon Island Police. He became aide-de-camp to the governor-general, then head of the criminal investigation division, senior staff officer to the commissioner of police, and operations officer for Honiara's central police station. He resigned from the police in 1984 and returned to Savo to develop cash crops, before winning the Russell/Savo seat in 1989. He served in two Mamaloni governments as minister of police and justice (1989–1993) and minister of forests, environment, and conservation (1994–1997) during the worst excesses of logging. Out of favor in the Ulufa'alu years (1997–2000), he returned as Sogavare's deputy prime minister, and minister of national unity, reconciliation, and peace, until he was sacked in 2000 for corruptly using compensation funds. He was knighted the same year for his work toward the cease-fire and the Townsville peace agreement, and became prime minister after the December 2000 elections.

Propped up by RAMSI, Kemakeza survived as prime minister until the national elections in April 2006. All members of the cabinet have been closely scrutinized by RAMSI, which undoubtedly has enough evidence to initiate further prosecutions. Rumors persist that Kemakeza will face charges once he loses power. He has accepted senior public servants from Australia and New Zealand as "line" appointments for treasury and finance positions, as well as for positions in the prime minister's office, where they are regularizing the administration. Soon after RAMSI arrived, the prime minister removed eight departmental heads and swapped some key portfolios, in an attempt to improve the efficiency of his government. RAMSI officials quickly helped establish a workable budget, began to manage the national debt, resumed revenue collection, removed "ghosts" from the payroll, and assured public servants (including teachers and police) that they would be paid on time. The next phase included large-scale institutional reform, first of the Royal Solomon Island Police. About one-quarter of the force was removed, including 400 officers, the whole paramilitary division, and all the special constables, and RAMSI officers began working alongside local police. The major task is planning for large-scale economic reform.[17] The third phase will concentrate on sustainable long-term development and strengthening earlier infrastructure reforms.

Exactly how long RAMSI will remain is unclear: the initial estimate was ten years. Because of continuing deep-seated problems, it is clear that it would be counterproductive to withdraw too quickly. However, this will depend on how RAMSI is perceived by the people of the Solomon Islands, the wishes of the new government in 2006, and other international calls on Australia and New Zealand's financial, humanitarian, and security commitments.

▨ Reforming the Constitution, the Parliament, and Public Service

While all of this is exemplary planning, actual implementation is difficult. Speakers representing the Solomon Islands at the April 2005 conference of the University of Queensland's Australian Centre for Peace and Conflict Studies critiqued RAMSI and made suggestions for the future of their nation.[18] It was clear from their analysis that RAMSI initiatives do not always address the needs and reality of the Solomon Islands. Restoring law and order was absolutely necessary, and RAMSI's success was lauded by everyone. However, the rest of the operation is open to criticism.

At a human level, some of the early RAMSI military personnel transgressed local cultural codes by involvement with prostitutes and local women. As well, patience and good manners are an enduring virtue in the Pacific, and RAMSI officials are sometimes a little too brusque in their demands. (This can be a serious matter, as the discussion of the factors leading to conflict in Bougainville, in Chapter 5, also indicates.) RAMSI is also accused of insensitivity in placing foreign advisers into "line" positions when there are Solomon Islanders qualified to hold these offices. However, the situation when RAMSI arrived was dire, and the mission made what were seen as necessary staffing decisions to bolster the government, and would have been negligent if it had not. Generally, many Solomon Islanders feel uneasy about the Westminster system that they inherited from the British, and by what they see as the imposition of first-world values on their Pacific state. They want radical change, but this is not what RAMSI was asked to undertake. Although there is a need to rethink how the Solomon Islands operates as a modern state, RAMSI sees its main task as ensuring the smooth operation of the existing system, not introducing a new one. Solomon Islanders generally, and the panel of speakers at the conference, have high expectations of RAMSI—far too high given that the assistance mission is not the government and does not have bottomless pockets. RAMSI has the unenviable task of guiding a suitable—but also limited— reform process for a nation of half a million people spread through nine island provinces and 1,900 islands, by persuading an inefficient, poorly trained, and often corrupt government and public service that reforms are necessary. When history assesses RAMSI, the mission will be seen as having done a good job in very difficult circumstances.

Strengthening the ombudsman's position and creating clear public service accountability and grievance procedures are necessary to build an effective public service. However, making the public service efficient requires more than new procedures. Retraining and putting the best people in positions of responsibility is also a necessary reform. There is also a distinct difference between what Australian and New Zealand public servants regard as corrupt practices and how Solomon Islanders judge the same practices. *Wantokism* (giving preference to kin) and *kastom* (customary way of behaving) are basic to local culture and have to be accommodated—these cultural concepts can be used to advantage or ameliorated, but not ignored. Although large-scale corruption must be condemned, an acceptable amount of "grease" makes the wheels go around in the Solomon Islands. This is not necessarily financial, but as anyone who has dealt with public and commercial organizations in the Pacific well knows, how you make your approach and who you know make an enormous difference to the success of any quest. Access to any leader or person in authority is relatively easy, even by the lowliest citizen. Extended family connections are important, and one would be foolish to ignore them. Some would argue that the next stage of "grease" is corruption, and that any accommodation to local culture is a mistake, but it is unlikely that a totally rules-based administrative system can be implemented. The reality is, as in much of the developing world, that what to Australians or New Zealanders would be low-level corruption, presented in the Solomon Islands as *kastom,* will continue.

Less than 16 percent of Solomon Islanders live in urban areas: just under 64,000 people at the time of the 1999 census, with Honiara accommodating more than three-quarters of the population. The other small urban centers are Noro and Gizo in Western province, Auki in Malaita province, and Tulagi, the prewar protectorate capital in Central province.[19] Urban life in Honiara is a tale of overcrowded housing and incomes that do not cover the necessities of life for extended families. Malaria debilitates everyone and means that efficiency is constantly compromised.[20] When wages are low and many are unemployed, cultural obligations take the place of social services. Public servants often have domestic matters to think about, matters that loom larger than their jobs. Many public servants have insufficient training to perform properly, and "time-servers" with no work ethic are blocking better-qualified graduates who remain unemployed. Despite RAMSI, the same elite (minus a few now languishing in Rove prison) are still running the administrative and parliamentary processes. The most corrupt of these individuals hope their past misdeeds are too minor to interest the busy prosecutors, and they are not likely, if the past twenty years are any indication, to institute major changes that may affect their own livelihood, or uncover past misdeeds. Politicians and senior public servants are not interested in the cultural reconciliation that the churches and the civil society movement have advocated (along the lines of South Africa's Truth and Reconciliation Commission), because it is too volatile and unpredictable a process. Yet, without it, given the cultural dynamics, there will never be closure and feuding will continue, possibly over generations.[21]

The new wave of leaders, bureaucrats, and academics in Solomon Islands have clear ideas on the way to improve the efficiency and honesty of the parliamentary process and the public service. First, the constitution could be amended to declare vacant the seat of any parliamentarian who changes parties between national elections, ensuring that they face an immediate by-election. One of the characteristics of the political process is that ideologies are not strong and that new alliances form constantly, often based on the lure of better positions or "invisible" financial baits. While this could mean a more expensive electoral process in the short term, in the long term fewer political realignments will occur in between national elections, facilitating a more stable parliamentary process. Second, there must be mechanisms to bring more women into positions of consequence, and particularly into parliament. During the crisis years, women played an important part in defusing tensions and negotiating peace, and many do not want to step back to a purely domestic role.

In the entire history of the national political system, there have only been two women members: Lily Ogatini who was a member of the legislative council in the 1960s, and Hilda Kari, who was elected as a member for eastern central Guadalcanal (1989–2000) and served as a minister.[22] There are fifty parliamentary seats, and women should occupy many more of them, but the position of women in Solomon Island societies is extremely complex. Table 9.1 shows that for 40 percent of people (Central, Guadalcanal, Isabel, and Western provinces), land inheritance is matrilineal, and for another 40 percent it is cognatic or mixed (Malaita and Makira/Ulawa). Women in many Solomon Island societies are depicted as the guardians of the land, but there is no necessary connection between matrilineality and women's political power, and in some Pacific societies matrilineality and matrilocality serve to strengthen male power. Males have always made most decisions in regard to land usage and politics, and the contemporary male elite have hijacked politics and resource deals, to the detriment of women.[23]

The 2004 draft federal constitution rather vaguely suggests that within

Table 9.1   Traditional Land Inheritance Systems, Solomon Island Provinces

Province	Dominant System
Central	Matrilineal
Choiseul	Patrilineal
Guadalcanal	Matrilineal
Isabel	Matrilineal
Makira/Ulawa	Matrilineal and patrilineal
Malaita	Cognatic with patrilineal bias
Rennell and Bellona	Patrilineal
Temotu	Patrilineal
Western	Matrilineal

Source: Government of the Solomon Islands, *Provincial Development Profiles, 2001.*

three years of the constitution coming into force, a law should be passed to "ensure a fair representation of women in parliament."[24] By comparison, the new constitution of Papua New Guinea's Autonomous Region of Bougainville is much stronger and guarantees women three seats in the new parliament, calls for fair representation of women on all constitutional and other bodies, and requires the government to consult women's organizations on all important matters, such as any future amendment to the constitution.[25] One way to ensure that women hold elected political positions is to encourage each political party to nominate a reasonable proportion of women as candidates in all elections. Having women contesting seats, however, does not guarantee representation: of the 24 women among the 453 candidates standing in the 2006 election, none was elected. Both men and women need to realize that the modern political system is not a male preserve and will function better with maximum participation.

A third suggestion is to Melanesianize the system by devolving more government funds to the level of individual electorates, dispersed by individual politicians but through applications from community groups and with sufficient accounting and advisory procedures. The present political culture is largely self-serving and based on personal aggrandizement, not any clear political ideology. While there are political parties and a Westminster system of government, politics in the Solomon Islands has become a type of business out of which personal profit is expected, with little sense of loyalty to the nation. Politicians have become a modern form of Pacific Bigmen and chiefs, and like all successful *kastom* leaders they need to accumulate wealth to distribute to their kin. Modern politicians on salaries cannot legally accumulate enough wealth to satisfy the demands placed on them, but if they do not satisfy their electorates they will not be reelected. The turnover of politicians at each election is about 50 percent, which although cleansing, does not usually remove the politicians whom parliament can best do without. Corruption has its rewards and honesty does not.

In recent years the use of electoral development funds has become institutionalized both in Papua New Guinea and in the Solomon Islands, but with very little control over their disbursement. Much of the money is squandered or corruptly misappropriated.[26] The Rural Constituency Development Fund, when properly administered, serves the purpose of delivering project aid to grassroots communities and allows politicians to claim personal credit. However, there needs to be proper accounting through the public service, with punishment enforced for misuse of the funds. One of the most successful local-level initiatives during the crisis years was Australia's Community Peace and Restoration Fund, which directly funded village-level health, education, and water supply projects in disadvantaged communities. This same pattern, if applied to the electoral development funds, can benefit the people and gain credit for individual politicians. But there should be no expansion of the system until accountability is tight. There is no point in increasing corrupt distribution of these funds.

Fourth, there is no mechanism by which the government can monitor public opinion. Investigative journalism, polls, and letters to the editor are useful but minor players. There needs to be a permanent means by which the cabinet and parliament can listen to the voice of civil society. The churches and other civil society organizations were the only institutions that continued to operate and deliver services to the bulk of the people during the crisis years. Civil society groups were involved in peace negotiations and arguably were more important than the aggressive male militants in achieving peace and reconciliation. Women were an integral part of this voice. Parliamentarians will argue they were elected to run the nation, but Solomon Islanders have also clearly signaled their discontent with the inherited Westminster process.

Two quite different suggestions have been made on how to modify the political system to ensure greater levels of consultation. One is to introduce a house of chiefs, similar to Vanuatu's Malvatumauri, to give advice on matters of traditional custom, to try to ensure that whereever possible modern government does not conflict with customary ways. The second suggestion is to institute an executive advisory committee to the cabinet that includes representatives of the five major churches (Church of Melanesia, Catholic, United, the South Seas Evangelical Church, and the Seventh-Day Adventist Church), the National Council of Women, the Civil Society Network, the ombudsman, the chairman of the Public Service Commission, and perhaps all past prime ministers and governors-general (presuming that they were not in the parliament). It could be chaired by the governor-general and include this broad range of nominated representatives of the people, along with members of cabinet. Such a committee would have no legal power, only the power of moral persuasion, but it would be broadly representative of a larger public voice and be able to offer guidance to the parliament. This advisory structure could be reviewed after a decade and if it was felt worthwhile, incorporated constitutionally in some way.

The 2004 draft federal constitution, if implemented, would change the Solomon Islands into a federal republic and turn the present provinces into states. One constant complaint has been that the central government has paid insufficient heed to the opinions, needs, and finances of the provinces. In 1978, the nation began with seven provinces: Central, Guadalcanal, Isabel, Malaita, Makira-Ulawa, Santa Cruz, and Western. They were based around the main islands or island groups, and varied in size from Malaita, with a 1999 population of 122,000, to Rennell and Bellona, with only 2,377 people. The 1978 national constitution had a centralized power structure with the flexibility to accommodate greater regional autonomy and future expansion or contraction of the provincial system. This occurred when Choiseul province separated from Western province in 1992, and when Rennell and Bellona province was carved out from Central province in 1996. There have been several reviews of the government structure. The 1977 Kausimae Committee led to the Provincial Government Act of 1981, and in 1987 the premiers recommended a federal system to the Constitutional Review Committee. The next year, Guadalcanal province petitioned unsuccessfully for the introduction of state government. In 1996, Prime Minister Mamaloni introduced a new provincial government act that restructured the provincial system so that chairpersons of area councils automatically became the district representatives in provincial assemblies, but this was challenged by Guadalcanal province and ruled unconstitutional.[27]

Immediately after the June 2000 coup, all provinces began to make claims for increased autonomy. Some went as far as to declare themselves to be independent nations. Early in 2002, the parliament began moves to revise the constitution and allow more provincial autonomy. A task force drew up a new constitution—the 2004 document now under discussion. The provinces wanted more devolution of central government funds and power; and Guadalcanal and Western provinces in particular, both major centers for export industries, demanded a more equitable split in revenues.[28]

Advocates of a federal system base their arguments on micronationalism and the obvious failure of central government. They shy away from the financial consequences that the duplication of functions would undoubtedly incur. They ignore the example of Papua New Guinea, where provincial governments were found to be inefficient and the system was modified by abolishing the premiers' positions in 1995, making the national parliament's provincial seats into governors' positions, and linking provinces directly into the national parliament.[29] There has been extensive discussion of the draft Solomon Island constitution without a clear result. Indications are that the present national government does not want the new constitution to be adopted, but that the people see the federal system as their salvation.

Decentralization is very necessary to balance the future growth of the nation, and unless provincial urban growth is encouraged, Honiara will continue to dominate and eat further into Guadalcanal customary land. The inequitable allocation of resources between the central and provincial governments needs to be resolved, and the provincial system should be enshrined in the constitution and not be at the whim of the national government. Provinces should also be able to make their own appointments to key positions. Under the present system, the Ministry for Provincial Government, a national ministry, appoints officers such as provincial secretaries, treasurers, and education officials: when positions are not filled for political or financial reasons, provincial administration is paralyzed. The Solomon Islands could also follow the Papua New Guinea precedent and include the provincial premiers in the national parliament, either using the present electoral system or by introducing provincial seats into the national parliament. Adding nine provincial seats (and another for a governor of Honiara as a national capital district)[30] would enlarge the parliament to sixty seats, but would alleviate many of the present tensions between the regions and the national government.

The constitutional saga demonstrates the difficulty of negotiating future directions and restoring grievances, and creating conflict resolution mechanisms, when there are geographic, cultural, ethnic, and historical issues that override any sense of nationalism or common purpose.

■ Managing Development

The second and third phases of the RAMSI conflict resolution model involve institutional and economic rehabilitation. The Solomon Islands has rich-enough natural resources on land and at sea to enable the half-million population to survive, even without access to government support or overseas aid funds. During the crisis years, the people who lived in rural areas were able to continue living much as before. The family remained the basic economic unit, producing subsistence agricultural crops from communally owned land. Sweet potato and cassava are the basic crops, supplemented by yam, taro, and pana, as well as banana, sugar cane, and betel nut. The main livestocks are pigs and poultry, with some cattle. Fish and shellfish are other important food items in most households. Over several decades, growing population pressures and a tendency to move to large coastal villages have reduced shifting cultivation cycles, which in turn has decreased the size of tuber crops. Even with these limitations, there was no famine or large-scale human catastrophe when central and provincial governments broke down. The delivery of health, education, and communication services was affected, but as many of these services have always been maintained by Christian denominations, the effect was never as severe as often depicted.

Once dependent on copra production, in the decades before the crisis years the Solomon Island export economy was based on tuna fish, cocoa, palm oil, hardwood timber, and, for a short period, gold from the new mine on Guadalcanal.[31] Excessive and unsustainable export of timber in the 1980s and 1990s depleted reserves to the extent that all easily exploitable first-growth forests are expected to have been felled by 2010. In the mid-1990s, 20 percent of national revenue and 50 percent of export earnings came from unprocessed round-log exports. As the economy recovered, logging continued at the old unsustainable levels, with a record 1 million cubic meters (36 million cubic feet) of logs exported in 2004, three times the sustainable rate.[32] Since the 1970s, tuna fishing, now based around a cannery at Noro in Western province, has provided substantial employment, and in 1998 the commercial catch was 94,129 metric tons (104,587 US tons), worth an estimated 203 million Solomon Island dollars (S$) (US$40.6). The fishing industry is reviving again, and Western province now has a substantial stake in the main company. In May 2005 the government announced that the Goldridge mine, which for a short time in the late 1990s produced close to 30 percent of the nation's gross national product, will be reopened by Australian Solomons Gold Propriety Limited, 47.5 percent of which is owned by Michelago Limited.[33] The future of the Guadalcanal plains oil palm plantations is less certain. Neglect during the crisis years means all plantations have to be destroyed and the palms replanted. Landowners are also disputing the original arrangements over payments for land alienation. Although New Britain Palm Oil Company (a subsidiary of a Malaysian company) has signed an agreement to reopen the plantations, it is not clear, despite optimistic forecasts, where the labor force will come from. Malaitans (once 60 percent of the workforce) were evicted from Guadalcanal and show no desire to return.[34]

The nation's economic problems arose from uncoordinated development strategies, overexploitation of a limited number of resources, poor government practices that did not collect sufficient revenue, and overgovernment, with the government tending to take on functions that should have been left to private enterprise. Prime Minister Ulufa'alu was attempting to deal with many of these issues when he was removed from power in 2000. The final straw was the collapse of the central government, which not only failed to collect revenue but also gave away millions of dollars of tax exemptions and squandered aid and reserve funds. The result was a bankrupt treasury and a national economy that fell so low that the central bank was able to maintain only a minimum import/export cover to protect the currency from total collapse. The financial edifice of the state had crumbled.

Despite the subsistence safety net, the declining situation plainly could not continue; the financial structure and development plans had to be resuscitated. Sufficient new building blocks were in place to create a new framework, and provincial and constituency development profiles, prepared in the late 1990s and early 2000s, can be called on to guide reform. The October 2003 national plan for economic recovery reform and development (2003–2006) as well as the Australian government's 2004 report on rebuilding the economy of the Solomon Islands are more recent examples of modeling and policy documents. Together they provide sufficient framework for directing the economy.[35] One source of rational advice continued to operate throughout the crisis years: the central bank stood firm, offering the only stable economic opinions, even though it was seldom heeded. Late in 2003, under pressure from RAMSI, the ten-year contract of the bank's governor, Rick Houenipwela, was renewed, which provided continuity. However, as the central bank and the Asian Development Bank warn, no credible economic analysis and forecasting is possible while the statistics office is moribund. Until 2005, the Department of National Reform and Planning lacked any driving force, but the recent change of minister, returning Fred Fono to his old portfolio, plus "line" Australian appointments in key areas of government, may provide the ministerial direction needed to rejuvenate the treasury and bureaucracy.

As expressed at the beginning of this chapter, the distribution of economic and human development has been poorly managed over many decades. Development has been very uneven, and as Table 9.2 shows, has little relationship to the size of the population in any region. Historically, economic development has been centered in Western, Central, and Guadalcanal provinces. The depletion of the hardwood forests of the nation—the tax revenue from which floated the national economy in the 1980s and 1990s—fell most heavily on Western province and latterly on Isabel and Choiseul provinces.

Although recent development planning has concentrated on Guadalcanal and Malaita, there are substantial inconsistencies in the development of the seven other provinces. After Guadalcanal, the next most important province to the economy is Western province. A base for whalers and traders before the protectorate began, Western province has the largest land area in the Solomon Islands—5,500 square kilometers (2,115 square miles) spread over several islands. Once the site of major commercial copra plantations, 20 percent of the land is now alienated. The province has been heavily logged, unsustainably in recent decades, with little reforestation. It has provided just over 50 percent of the nation's timber exports. Western province is the center of the nation's tourist industry, and Solomon Taiyo also operates from the province, with its cannery at Noro. A substantial number of workers have been attracted here from other parts of the Solomon Islands.

Central, Choiseul, and Isabel provinces have similar size populations. With a total land area of around 615 square kilometers (236 square miles), Central province includes Nggela, Savo, and Russells Islands, the latter island the site of early extensive copra plantations that are still important today. Malaitans were a major part of the plantation workforce and many have settled on Nggela and Russells Islands. Choiseul province, a long, narrow island covering 3,295 square kilometers (1,267 square miles), has no major plantations, and logging did not begin there until 1990, after which the province provided about 13 percent of the nation's logging exports. With few roads, apart from rough logging roads, subsistence agriculture and cash crops dominate the economy; 95 percent of the land is still under communal tenure, and 92 percent of land with agricultural potential is unused. Isabel province has a total land area of 4,156 square kilometers (1,598 square miles), population density is low (five persons per square kilometer; thirteen persons per square mile), and only a small percentage of the land

Table 9.2 Population, Transportation, and Economic Data, Solomon Island Provinces, 2001

Province	Population	Population Annual Growth Rate (%)	Land Area (km²)	Population Density (per km²)	Population Under Age 15 (%)	Roads (km)	Log Exports (m³, 2000)	Alienated Land (%)
Central	21,577	2.0	515	35.1	41.0	103	5,084	20.0
Choiseul	20,008	3.0	3,208	5.0	43.9	25	61,415	4.5
Guadalcanal	60,275	1.5[a]	5,336	11.0	42.0	296	14,109	10.
Isabel	20,421	2.6	4,156	4.9	42.0	35	111,070	16.0
Makira/Ulawa	31,006	2.7	3,230	10.0	42.4	114	16,115	20.0
Malaita	122,620	3.3[b]	4,225	29.0	44.9	248	15,968	8.0[c]
Rennell and Bellona	2,377	2.2	1,154	2.1	41.0	107	0	10.0
Temotu	18,912	1.9	835	22.6	41.1	70	0	17.0
Western	62,739	3.2	5,500	11.4	40.5	208	319,916	20.0
Honiara (capital city on Guadalcanal)	60,000	n.a.	n.a.	n.a.	n.a.	148[d]	n.a.	n.a.

Source: Government of the Solomon Islands, Provincial Development Profiles, 2001.
Notes: a. Lower than normal, due to outmigration in 1999.
b. Higher than normal, due to immigration in 1999.
c. Estimated by lands officer, Malaita province, 13 May 2005.
d. Sealed and gravel roads.

has been alienated. Self-employment in the subsistence sector dominates, supplemented by copra and cocoa as cash crops. In the late 1990s, loggers began to exploit Isabel, producing 111,070 cubic meters (4 million cubic feet) in 2000, the second largest volume in the Solomon Islands.

The two southernmost provinces are Makira-Ulawa and Temotu. Makira-Ulawa province covers 3,230 square kilometers (1,242 square miles) and has some of the largest coconut plantations in the country, on Three Sisters Islands and at Waimamura. However, subsistence cultivation and fishing now dominate the economy, supplemented as in other provinces by cash crops. Temotu province, in the south on the border with Vanuatu, has a mixed Melanesian (82.1 percent) and Polynesian (17.4 percent) population, and the smallest land area—835 square kilometers (321 square miles). The population density is well above the national average; on some islands it is extraordinarily high and causes internal migration.[36] Like Malaitans, Temotu people have a reputation for working elsewhere in the nation as laborers, and are heavily dependent on subsistence lifestyles. There is no longer any logging, because heavy logging in the 1970s removed all commercial forests. Rennell and Bellona province, the second smallest province in land area, and the one with the lowest population, comprises two raised atolls inhabited by Polynesians. The people depend primarily on subsistence agriculture and fishing, with little scope for commercial agriculture and no logging.

The crisis years ensured that the development needs of the rest of the country became subservient to those of Guadalcanal and Malaita. Malaita province, covering 4,225 square kilometers (1,625 square miles), has the third largest land area and is home to 30 percent of the nation's people, averaging twenty-nine persons per square kilometer (seventy-five persons per square mile), the greatest population density in the country, exacerbated by the thousands of Malaitans who returned to the island after the 1999 expulsion from Guadalcanal. The province comprises the main island (actually split into two by a narrow sea channel) and some small outliers. While very little of the land has been alienated, for 130 years Malaita has been exploited mainly for labor and remained underdeveloped, which caused the movement of Malaitans off the island, latterly to Guadalcanal—one of the prime causes of the crisis years. A considerable proportion of Malaita's population lives inland, and the province depends on subsistence agriculture, with copra and cocoa as the main cash crops.

The national government is well aware of the need for more economic development in Malaita province, which would lead to greater work opportunities in the province and less migration elsewhere. In 2005, Malaita province was estimated to have a population of 140,000 people. The income per capita was S$21, which (not unsurprisingly) was one-fifth of the average income on Guadalcanal, and Malaita's per capita grant from the national government was the lowest of any province. As Malaita's premier Reuben Moli told the Pacific Islands Forum's Eminent Persons Group when it visited the province in May 2005: "The absence of socio-economic development on Malaita is a major catalyst that sent Malaitans to seek employment, commercial and social activities in Honiara and other parts of the country."[37]

The 1999 Honiara peace agreement agreed that substantial development funds were needed for Malaita province, as did the 2000 Townsville peace agreement, but nothing eventuated until Malaita's mid-2004 economic development plan (2003–2005), worth S\$447 million, half of which was earmarked for agricultural expansion. In January 2005, the cabinet approved a budget of S\$1.5 million to begin preparatory work on a large-scale oil palm project for the Aluta and east Fataleka areas, which had the potential to be larger than the oil palm plantations on Guadalcanal plains. In recent decades, other pilot projects and plans for large developments have been drawn up: an international airport and fishing industry at Manakwaia (Royal Harbour); a free port at Bina Harbour, south of Auki; and a deep seaport and possible bait ground and fish cannery at Wairokai in western 'Are'are district. All of these projects depend on the agreement of local landowners. The Bina Harbor project stalled due to local land disputes, and the Aluta-Fataleka project is likely to meet with the same fate.

A key issue for all Solomon Islanders is ensuring their continuing relationship with land. In the 1980s, Aliki Nono'ohimae Eerehau, former Marching Rule leader[38] and paramount chief of 'Are'are district, on Malaita, stated the relationship of his people with the land: "'Are'are people do not own the land. The land owns 'Are'are people. The land owns men and women; they are there to take care of the land."[39]

Few Solomon Islanders would disagree with Eerehau. Overwhelmingly, they still live in descent-based groups in small territories, each related to the other by descent from primary ancestors in an established hierarchy. Inheritance rights vary, as do usage rights, but primary rights over the occupancy of land are superior to secondary rights that are activated only with permission of the primary landowners. Modernization theorists argue that the solution to underdevelopment is to remove social formations that conflict with development understood as economic growth, and that customary land tenure is a stumbling block to development. The argument has been explicitly stated in relation to the development of Papua New Guinea, which has the similar style of land tenure to that in the Solomon Islands.[40] The British Solomon Island protectorate built an economy based around coconut plantations on alienated land, mainly in Western, Central, and Guadalcanal provinces, worked by labor from within the protectorate. Missions also controlled quite large areas, and by 1913 about 65,200 hectares (163,000 acres) had been alienated, about 4.5 percent of the total land area. Between 1919 and 1923, a land commission investigated claims that plantation companies, particularly Levers Pacific Plantations Limited, had unfairly gained control of large areas through dubious purchases and declarations of land as waste and vacant. Levers returned 40,000 hectares (100,000 acres) to the government, but in return arranged for large timber-cutting concessions that led to the exploitation of the protectorate's hardwood rainforests.[41]

In other districts, communal landowning systems remained largely intact. District officers, mostly British and Australian, tried to understand and record the complex customary systems of acknowledging rights to land tenure and use. During the 1950s, a number of options were suggested in response to the land tenure problem: to devise a customary land code based on reconstructing custom as it existed in 1893; to extinguish the customary system and introduce a modern land policy; or to take the original system into account but guide land tenure toward a modern system that would mesh with economic development. The latter amalgamated system was chosen, based on adjudication and registration of individual titles within corporate territories.[42] Roger Keesing, an anthropologist who worked on Malaita from the 1960s until the 1980s, lamented this missed chance: "Had the planners understood the rich complexities of customary land tenure, they could have built on its strengths and encouraged the compilation and local legitimation and recognition of genealogically documented corporate land titles, long before the present outbreak of land disputes, with concomitant litigation and violence."[43] The post-1978 government followed the British precedent and allowed the great diversity of customary tenure systems to continue, often frustrating implementation of large development projects.

Solomon Islanders insist that contemporary land tenure systems are integral to maintaining *kastom,* which they are inclined to depict as based on old preprotectorate traditions. In fact, much of today's *kastom* has been arrived at over the past century (especially over the past fifty years). Christianity, a dominant element in modern Solomon Island society, has altered the relationship between the people, the spirit world, and land. Modern messianic and political movements have also altered the basis of power relations. Directly post–World War II, on Malaita, the postwar Marching Rule movement led to written codification of lines of descent and inheritance, and on Guadalcanal the Moro movement preserved a vision of customary ways to behave that had at least some effect on the recent crisis on the island.[44] And the nationwide population movement toward the coasts and into larger villages has meant that some descent-group territories are now uninhabited or have been take over by secondary owners. Families living outside their territories owe their places of residence to the influence of church pastors and other nontraditional leaders. All of this is extraordinarily complex and cannot be legislated into uniformity nationally, or even in any one province, given the possible gradations from one end of an island to another.

RAMSI planners and a series of postindependence governments have not fully appreciated that the strength of the Solomons lies in its villages and its complex local land tenure systems. Large projects will emerge, but not necessarily when and where governments and aid donors desire, and increasing exports is not the only answer to development issues. Subsistence self-sufficiency augmented by selective cash crops has been the mainstay of rural economies for decades, and will remain central to livelihoods. To bolster this inevitability, improving rural transport systems should be a major priority. The Solomon Islands depends on a ramshackle collection of interisland vessels, supplemented by fiberglass and dugout canoes around the coasts and on rivers. More reliable coastal services would encourage villagers to produce cash crops for local urban markets as well as exports. This is certainly the case on the neglected Weathercoast of Guadalcanal, where the ethnic tension practically halted air service to all three airstrips primarily because of the hijacking incident at Mbabanakira airstrip and the deteriorating conditions of the runways. Despite the absence of a road link to the capital city on the other side of the island, it took until mid-2006 to reopen Mbabanakira and Marau airstrips, while Avuavu is still not reopened. Without economic development on the Weathercoast, the same alienation and underdevelopment issues will well up again. A sensible development would be to concentrate on building more main roads and feeder roads into the mountainous interiors of all islands, which would encourage people to stay within their territories, but move closer to the road system. Figures for 2001 (see Table 9.2) suggest that the entire Solomon Islands has only approximately 1,278 kilometers (800 miles) of gravel roads, supplemented by around 200–300 kilometers (125–190 miles) of logging roads and tractor tracks.[45]

In Oceania, new villages have historically developed along main or feeder roads. For example, in Rennell and Bellona province, 80 percent of all settlements are now along the roads. The same has occurred along the northern coast of Guadalcanal from Aola to Lambi, and along the tractor trail from Avu Avu to Marau, as well as along the other major road systems on Vella Lavella, Kolimbangara, Gizo, New Georgia, and Makira. On Malaita, ever since the northern road was extended to Malu'u in 1966 and around the north of To'ambaita to Lau Lagoon in the 1970s, a pattern of migration has emerged in response to the new transport system, which has enabled the movement of cash crops to markets in Auki and Honiara. When the road across central Malaita from Dala to Atori was completed in the late 1970s, it opened up central Kwara'ae, and as the feeder roads developed on the eastern coast in Kwara'ae and Fataleka in the 1980s and 1990s, they became lifelines for the movement of produce and people. Old village sites have often been abandoned, and new villages built along the roads. The worst-served provinces are Isabel (20,421 people and 35 kilometers [22 miles] of gravel roads) and Choiseul (20,008 people and 25 kilometers [16 miles] of gravel roads). Northern, central, and southern Malaita now have a good rudimentary ring-road system, although it is in a constantly bad state of repair. The biggest disgrace is Guadalcanal, where the most sophisticated road-making machinery is located, but only a tractor road links Marau to the Weathercoast, and there is no link to the extensive northern road system. If the inland areas were easier to access, communities would not cluster around the coast, the fallow cycle could be longer, crop quantities would improve, and a larger range of cash crops could be planted in the higher-altitude areas. To date, except at Guadalcanal's Goldridge mine, almost all economic projects have been around the coasts. In the future, as population increases, inland areas will begin to be opened up for development, and forward planning is required to build more extensive road systems and to upgrade the roads from gravel, which has to be repaired every year, to bitumen.

Forecasts based on the 1999 census and current growth rates, even if slowed by family-planning programs and HIV/AIDS, suggest that by 2025 the Solomon Island population will have doubled to around 800,000, and will reach 1 million by the middle of the twenty-first century. The future of the Solomon Islands is in the hands of the 42 percent of the population now under fifteen years of age; on Malaita they make up almost 45 percent.[46] The vast majority of this young population still live in rural villages. While the bright lights of urban centers will continue to lure migrants from rural areas, it is unlikely that an urban workforce will absorb large numbers. The village sector is where development has to take place. Planners also have to remember that the women and youth sectors of the nation constitute a formidable percentage of the national population. As John Roughan noted recently: "Men are only 3 out of every 10 persons. They are a minority and they must stop acting as if the nation belongs to them. Our Social Unrest years not only brought the nation to its knees, this period of distress made it clear that unless women and youth become the new force of change, then the country will be once again run into deep trouble."[47]

■ Conclusion

The Solomon Islands, ostensibly in a postconflict phase and buoyed by international support, could still return to violence if underlying problems are not addressed. The government failed its people in 1998–2003, and is now undergoing a process of resuscitation. Elsina Wainwright, the main author of the Australian Strategic Policy Institute paper that provided the justification and a partial blueprint for what became the RAMSI operation,[48] assessed RAMSI's progress in 2005 and reported fairly negatively. Wainwright correctly noted that national identity building must remain outside the brief of any state-building operation, but other issues must be made more central to reform:

> In Solomon Islands, issues of land tenure, reconciliation, and centraliza-
> tion versus decentralization all need to be addressed. But RAMSI has
> decided that these issues are outside its remit: they are for Solomon
> Islanders to decide upon. What RAMSI seeks to do is give the community
> a secure environment in which to debate important national issues, and to
> provide Solomon Islands with effective state machinery as these issues are
> discussed.
>
> And statebuilding operations can only do so much without local
> momentum for reform. For lasting change to take root, there is a need to
> work with local reformers to build that momentum. RAMSI makes much
> of the fact that it operates in partnership with the Solomon Islands
> Government and people, and that continued local political will is neces-
> sary for the reform to continue.[49]

While still not well enough appreciated by the Solomon Island government, aid donors, or RAMSI, three conclusions are clear. First, the village is
the key to understanding development in the Solomon Islands. Second, civil
society (including the churches) is increasingly an important part of the
nation, alongside the formal government structure. Third, now is the time to
radically rethink the role of central and provincial governments and their
relationship with ordinary citizens.

Unfortunately, the colonial elite have become the modern elite, with
too many vested interests to encourage any radical departure from the old
pattern. Corruption has been moderated but still exists. Three years after
RAMSI, and its attempts to improve administration, the public service is
still remarkably inefficient. The larger overseas aid donors are nations
with unadventurous agendas that follow the patterns of the World Bank
and the Asian Development Bank. RAMSI, supposedly a Pacific regional
intervention mission, is actually driven by an Australian, and to a lesser
extent, a New Zealand agenda. The riots following the 2006 national elections demonstrated the despair felt by many citizens when the old guard
were returned, and the former deputy prime minister was elected prime
minister. The hopes that a new style of Solomon Island government—one
that listens to its people, involves all sectors of the community, and charts
a new course—were dashed. The conflict resolution, human security, and
development initiatives that have emerged so far are not sufficiently radical to redress the current instability of the Solomon Island central government. Modern liberal democratic governance structures are not aligned
with indigenous systems of power and authority, and so far neither the
elected representatives of the people, nor the international agencies
involved with rehabilitation, have implemented the central issues of
reform.

▪ Notes

I am indebted to Sam Alasia, Max Quanchi, David Akin, John Roughan, and Terry Brown for perceptive comments that have informed my views, and to Anthony Yeates for his research assistance. Research for this chapter was funded by the Australian Research Council.

1. Wainwright, *Our Failing Neighbour,* p. 24.
2. Otter, "Is the 'Solomon Islands Paradox' an Australian Responsibility?" p. 1.
3. Moore, *Happy Isles in Crisis,* p. 113.
4. Ibid.; Moore, "Australia's Motivation and Timing for the 2003 Intervention"; Fraenkel, *The Manipulation of Custom;* Government of Australia, *Solomon Islands.*
5. Naitoro, "Solomon Islands Conflict," p. 4.
6. Moore, *Happy Isles in Crisis,* pp. 73–75, 83–88.
7. Fraenkel, *The Manipulation of Custom,* pp. 44–52.
8. Custom and tradition are described by one word, *kastom,* a Pijin English derivative of "custom." *Kastom* refers to ideologies and activities that empower traditions and practices. It is a living cultural mechanism that varies island by island, and incorporates both what are seen as fixed cultural characteristics from the past, and changes that have occurred in more recent decades. *Kastom* has become a symbol of cultural autonomy and resistance, something to be preserved while also accommodating the modern needs of the democratic state and capitalism.
9. Davenport and Coker, "The Moro Movement of Guadalcanal."
10. Moore, *Happy Isles in Crisis,* pp. 27–28.
11. Over the period 1870–1911, 24,865 Solomon Islanders worked in Queensland and Fiji; over the period 1911–1940, 54,071 worked on plantations within the Solomon Islands. During these periods, Malaitans constituted 58 percent of the workers in Queensland and Fiji and 67 percent of those within the protectorate. Price, "Origins of Pacific Island Labourers in Queensland"; Shlomowitz and Bedford, "The Internal Labor Trade in the New Hebrides and Solomon Islands"; Frazer, "To'ambaita Report," pp. 59–62; Bennett, *Wealth of the Solomons,* pp. 150–191.
12. Bathgate, *Fight for the Dollar;* Bathgate, Frazer, and McKinnon, *Socio-Economic Change in Solomon Island Villages.*
13. Literally "one talks," speakers of the same language.
14. The first special coordinator, Nick Warner, completed his tour of duty in August 2004, and was replaced by another Australian diplomat, James Batley, a previous high commissioner to the Solomon Islands (1997–1999) who has recent experience in Bougainville and East Timor.
15. Government of Australia, "Australian Agency for International Development (AusAID)," *Budget Papers, 2004,* pp. 133; *Solomon Star,* 17 May 2005; Wainwright, "How Is RAMSI Faring?" p. 7; Government of Australia, *Solomon Islands;* Government of New Zealand, *NZAID Annual Review, 2003/04.*
16. Solomon Islands Broadcasting Corporation, 20 August 2003.
17. Wainwright, "How Is RAMSI Faring?"; Government of Australia, *Solomon Islands.*
18. The panel speakers were Ashley Wickham, Gordon Nanau, Joseph Foukona, George Hoa'au, Karlyn Tekulu, Paul Roughan, and RAMSI special coordinator James Batley.
19. Government of the Solomon Islands, *Report of the 1999 Population and Housing Census,* pp. 6–7.
20. Ibid., pp. 190–194.

21. Moore, *Happy Isles in Crisis,* pp. 215–219.

22. A few women have been elected at the provincial level.

23. See Pollard, *Givers of Wisdom, Labourers Without Gain,* particularly Chapter 5, "Rethinking the Solomon Islands Government's Women and Development Division," pp. 83–95.

24. Government of the Solomon Islands, "Draft Federal Constitution of Solomon Islands," clause 88.

25. Bougainville Constitutional Commission, "Brief of the 2nd Draft of the Bougainville Constitution."

26. Moses Pitakaka, former chairman who oversaw the leadership code and former governor-general, has called for the Rural Constituency Development Fund to be abolished, precisely for these reasons. *Solomon Star,* 31 May 2005.

27. "Petition by the Indigenous People of Guadalcanal," 1998, app. 1; Fraenkel, *The Manipulation of Custom,* pp. 189–196.

28. Moore, *Happy Isles in Crisis,* pp. 156–158; 193–194.

29. Okole, "Enhancing Nation Building."

30. At present, Honiara is not designated a national capital district like Canberra in Australia or Port Moresby in Papua New Guinea. Totally excising Honiara and environs from Guadalcanal province may be the best solution for dealing with this growing urban area. Its mayor could then become a governor with a seat in the national parliament.

31. Moore, *Happy Isles in Crisis,* pp. 68–92.

32. Interview with Ishmael Wore, manager, Department of Economics, Central Bank of the Solomon Islands, 18 November 2004; BBC Monitoring Asia Pacific, 13 May 2005, available at http://global.factiva.com/en/ach/pront_results.asp (accessed 17 May 2005). See Bennett, *Pacific Forest,* for the best analysis of the timber industry.

33. The Goldridge mine was once the principal asset of Brisbane-based Ross Mining, which was taken over by Delta Gold. The company plans to spend S$400 million over two years to reopen the mine, which is expected to produce 220,000 ounces of gold per year. *Post-Courier,* 13 May 2005; Alex Wilson, "Michelago," Australian Associated Press Financial News Wire, 16 May 2005, available at http://global.factiva.com/en/arch/print_results.asp (accessed 17 May 2005).

34. Moore, *Happy Isles in Crisis,* pp. 85–87; *Solomon Star,* 14 May 2005.

35. Government of the Solomon Islands, *Provincial Development Profiles.*

36. Tikopia and Anuta are the most densely populated (224 people per square kilometer [582 people per square mile]); the Reef Islands are densely populated as well (189 people per square kilometer [491 people per square mile]).

37. *Solomon Star,* 1 May 2005.

38. An anticolonial movement in the late 1940s and early 1950s.

39. Coppet, "Land Owns People," p. 81.

40. Curtin, Holznecht, and Larmour, "Land Registration in Papua New Guinea"; Hughes, "Can Papua New Guinea Come Back from the Brink?"; Hughes, "Aid Has Failed the Pacific"; Hughes, "Helping the Islands to Help Themselves"; Windybank and Manning, "Papua New Guinea on the Brink."

41. Ruthven, "Land Legislation from the Protectorate to Independence"; Ipo, "Land and Economy"; Bennett, *Wealth of the Solomons,* pp. 323–324; Bennett, *Pacific Forest.*

42. Allan, "Customary Land Tenure in the British Solomon Islands Protectorate"; Hughes, "Tenure Conversion in the Solomons."

43. Keesing, "A Tin with the Meat Taken Out," p. 49.

44. Laracy, *Pacific Protest;* Davenport and Coker, "The Moro Movement of Guadalcanal."

45. There are, of course, bitumen main roads in Honiara. These road figures are deceptive in two ways: first, canoes traveling along rivers and around the coasts provide much of the transport system (for instance, 92 percent of the people of Temotu province live on the coast); and second, many of the roads are poorly maintained, only fit for truck or four-wheel-drive traffic. Government of the Solomon Islands, "Temotu Province Development Profile," in *Provincial Development Profiles,* p. 4.

46. Government of the Solomon Islands, *Report on the 1999 Population and Housing Census,* pp. 221–246; Government of the Solomon Islands, *Human Development Report,* vol. 1, pp. 9–11.

47. John Roughan, "Guale Politicians Blew It!" *Scoop,* 9 May 2005, available at http://www.scoop.co.nz/stories/hl0505/S00105.htm (accessed 18 January 2007).

48. Wainwright, *Our Failing Neighbour.*

49. Wainwright, "How Is RAMSI Faring?" p. 10.

10

The Paradox of Multiculturalism: Ethnopolitical Conflict in Fiji

Steve Ratuva

IT IS GENERALLY ASSUMED that the conflict in Fiji is very "Melanesian" in character—that is it can be understood within the same conceptual and analytical framework as conflicts in other Melanesian states such as Papua New Guinea, the Solomon Islands, and Vanuatu.[1] But conflict in Fiji is shaped by different sets of dynamics and manifests itself in different ways than in other Melanesian countries. While what is tagged "ethnic conflict" in other Melanesian states is by and large between two or more Melanesian groups, in the case of Fiji, conflict has, to a significant effect, been between a diaspora group from the Indian subcontinent and a Melanesian indigenous group. The historical, political, and socioeconomic forces that shape the relationships between Fijians and Indo-Fijians,[2] and the role of the colonial and postcolonial state in these, are substantially different than in other Melanesian states.[3] The parallels drawn between conflict in Fiji and other Melanesian states are often positivistic in nature, and fail to take into consideration the different contexts and forces at play.[4]

Fiji became a British colony in 1874 and an independent state in 1970. Under the colonial administration, political representation was divided along ethnic lines and the political culture and institutions evolved along these same lines. After independence in 1970, Fiji was ruled for thirteen years by the Alliance Party under Ratu Sir Kamisese Mara, an Oxford-educated Fijian chief who during the 1987 election lost to the newly formed Fiji Labour Party under Timoci Bavadra, a commoner. Due to its Indo-Fijian parliamentary majority, the new government was perceived as posing a threat to Fijian interests and as a consequence there was widespread public demonstration by Fijians, culminating in two coups in 1987 by the predominantly Fijian military. This was followed by a series of Fijian-dominated governments until 1999, when for the first time Fiji had an Indo-Fijian prime minister in the form of Labour Party leader Mahendra Chaudhry. A year later this government was deposed in a civilian coup and replaced by a

Fijian interim government. Elections held in 2001 returned a Fijian coalition of parties with a strong ethnonationalist orientation to government. The serving prime minister was again returned in 2006. However, 1997 constitutional provisions for multiparty cabinet formation have been activated for the first time, meaning that parties dominated by indigenous interests, and those more closely associated with Indo-Fijian interests, are both represented in government.

In hindsight, the three most "explosive" events in Fiji's contemporary history were the two military coups of 1987 and the civilian putsch in 2000. These events were overtly violent expressions of simmering ethnic tensions that pervaded Fiji's colonial and postcolonial history. Fiji's contemporary history has been a dynamic pattern of latent and overt conflict, violent and nonviolent regime change, and regime maintenance, as well as a syncretic process of both ethnic contradiction and accommodation taking place simultaneously.[5]

To some extent the coups revealed the paradox of Fiji's postcolonial multiracial experiment. On one hand, the policy of multiracialism (also articulated as "unity in diversity"), instituted by Ratu Sir Kamisese Mara and his Alliance Party, advocated people living side-by-side, sharing the same space and tolerating each other's cultures; on the other hand, it encouraged cultural and communal distinctiveness. At one level the two were mutually accommodating, and at another level they were at odds with each other. Multiracialism articulated unity at the level of national symbolism, yet advocated distinctiveness of cultural identity at another level.[6] Cultural distinctiveness, fused with formal political segregation as entrenched in the constitution, embedded in economic life, and fueled by ethnonationalism, created a situation of potential ethnic hostility.

The 1987 military coups broke the democratic shell, which in later years became difficult to mend. The 2000 coup, although a civilian one, was to address some "unfinished business" of 1987. Both were "justified" in terms of the same grievances and shaped by the same ethnonationalist forces. The effects of the coups were profound and long term. The economy struggled to sustain itself as a result of reduced production and investment. There were cases of human rights abuse, religious and racial bigotry, and fractured social relations. Distrust deepened rifts in the political framework of the state. After the 1987 coups, there was a sense of complacency in the Fijian community—that politics would take care of itself and Fiji would in no time return to "normalcy."[7] In contrast, after the 2000 coup there was a feeling of desperation driven by a fear that Fiji could go through the "banana republic" cycle of coups; this sparked widespread political consciousness and a rush to put in place conflict resolution and peacebuilding programs by the state and civil society organizations. But despite the ethnic tension, there was a deeply embedded sense of unity molded by the postindependence multiracial experiment, which has been a powerful catalyst for sociocultural resilience and restraint. This sense of unity and restraint has worked against outright interethnic civil war as has occurred in many bipolar or multipolar states.

This chapter attempts to examine some of the factors that have shaped ethnopolitical conflict in Fiji: the dynamics, configurations, and manifestations of conflict and some of the responses to these. Particular emphasis is given to indigenous Fijian dimensions of the conflict, as the coups were the work of Fijians. Understanding ethnopolitical conflict in Fiji is not easy, because of the complex ways in which tension manifests itself, the different levels of causal variables (more or less directly related to conflict), the different dynamics of conflict at different levels (tension seems to be more pronounced at the level of national political discourse than at the grassroots level), and the diverse consequences, some intended and some unintended. There is a complex interplay between cultural, religious, political, and socioeconomic factors that shape the dynamics and trajectory of conflict in Fiji.

The significance and relationships between these diverse factors needs to be understood. Monocausal approaches to the conflict ignore the multitude of interethnic, intraethnic, socioeconomic, and cultural factors engaging each other at different levels in Fiji's postcolonial milieu and how these manifested themselves during the 2000 coup. Inter- and intraethnic tension take place simultaneously in an oscillating manner at different levels, and to ignore one is to lose sight of Fiji's complex reality and reduce discussion into simplistic generalizations.[8] Intraethnic tension within the Fijian community needs to be understood in the broader dialectics between interethnic and intraethnic politics. This is especially so in light of the ongoing debate within the Fijian community before and during the 2000 coup as to who best represented "Fijian interests" in the face of "threat" from Indo-Fijian "domination." Nationalist Fijians saw moderate Fijians as being "too close" to Indo-Fijians and thus to be purged from Fijian leadership. One way of consolidating and legitimizing one's position in this "power struggle" was to deploy traditional sociocultural systems and kinship loyalty, or *vanua*.[9] Thus while it is true that there was considerable intra-Fijian power struggle during the 2000 coup, this was also linked to ethnic power struggle at another level.

Some also argue that fundamental to the 2000 crisis was the "clash of dynasties," which saw various Fijian traditional power blocks engaged in competition.[10] While it is true that there was mobilization on the basis of traditional loyalty, this was just a component of the broader synergy between interethnic and intraethnic politics. The supporters of the coup were from all around Fiji, and the prominence of the Tailevu traditional "dynasty" in the crisis was due to the support provided by George Speight's relatives (from Ra and Tailevu) and the use of the Tailevu (and Kubuna) traditional politico-traditional establishments to provide legitimacy for the coup. In fact, Kubuna as a confederacy was not collectively behind the coup; rather, in order to legitimize the coup, the coup-makers had to use the name of the Kubuna confederacy. While there was tension between various Fijian political fractions due to ideological and political reasons, there was no evidence whatsoever of a "clash of dynasties" by which various traditional establishments were competing for power. While traditional loyalty is important in understanding Fiji's political conflict, it has not been a leading generator of conflict in this case.

Intraethnic tension within the Indo-Fijian community also has direct synergy with interethnic politics. The political seismic line between the two major Indo-Fijian political parties (the Fiji Labour Party [FLP] and National Federation Party [NFP]) is based on the "Fijian factor," meaning that demonization of each other is based on one's political closeness to the "coup-making" Fijians. The NFP under Jai Ram Reddy was seen to be "too close" to Fijians during the 1999 election (through an alliance with Rabuka, the leader of the 1987 coups), and the FLP under Mahendra Chaudhry used this as a powerful ammunition for communal mobilization leading to Reddy's downfall.

This chapter attempts to move away from monocausal and ethnicized discourses and examines the broad spectrum of factors and their potential linkages—socioeconomic, cultural, political, and sociopsychological—and how they have contributed to shaping the configuration and trajectory of ethnopolitical conflict in Fiji. After a brief historical overview of Fiji and an examination of the relationship between population distribution and political tension, the chapter discusses the institutionalization of ethnic relations through electoral and constitutional mechanisms, some socioeconomic factors that have spawned grievances over the years, the political significance of ethnic stereotypes and the importance of ethnonationalism in driving conflict, and the changing role of the military in ethnic politics and tension. The chapter concludes with an examination of some of the attempts to address ethnic tension in Fiji.

◼ Demography and Ethnopolitics: The Dilemma of Bipolarity

Population distribution itself does not naturally breed ethnic tension in a bipolar society, as some pluralist theorists would argue.[11] What is important is rather how the demographic pattern becomes institutionalized as part of the political culture and process, and when the politics of numerical balance, domination, or marginalization becomes a significant variable in the political equation.

Fiji's total population is about 890,000, distributed as follows: Fijians,

51 percent; Indo-Fijians, 44 percent; and other minorities, 5 percent—largely Europeans, part-Europeans, Chinese, part-Chinese, Pacific Islanders, and other Asians.[12] The demographic pattern has had significant changes over the years (as seen in Table 10.1), and this has had some impact on the dynamics of ethnic politics. For instance, the 1946 census revealed that for the first time the Indo-Fijian population (120,414) had overtaken the Fijian population (118,070). This sent shockwaves through the Fijian community, and to many Fijians the thought of their country being taken over by the "alien" Kaidia became a nightmarish possibility. The 1987 coups, however, raised nightmares of their own for the Indo-Fijian population, leading to significant emigration. As a result, by 1996, the year of the first postcoup census, the number of Fijians again outstripped that of Indo-Fijians.

Religion is closely associated with ethnicity and ethnic tension in Fiji. Most Fijians are Christians, while most Indo-Fijians are either Hindus or Muslims. This sharpens and strengthens the ethnopolitical divide. During the 1987 and 2000 coups, religion was deployed as a means of ethnic mobilization and legitimization. Table 10.2 shows the direct parallel between ethnicity and religion.

Fiji can be described as bipolar. Having two major ethnic groups in political contestation over state power creates an environment for potential instability. Unlike those bipolar states where there are significant minorities to act as a tension absorption "buffer," in Fiji the minorities constitute a mere 5 percent and are largely insignificant in the political numbers game. The two ethnic groups (Fijians and Indo-Fijians) have more or less the same chances of coming to power in an election. On one hand the state becomes the site for power contestation, on the other hand there are mechanisms in the constitution such as communal voting to maintain ethnic "equilibrium" in the face of impending tension. Paradoxically, ethnic power struggle and communal bargaining have somehow contributed to maintaining equilibrium in the ethnopolitical equation.

Population size does not necessarily correspond to political bargaining power. During the early years, Indo-Fijians were more politically assertive, despite their smaller population compared to Fijians. Since the turn of the twentieth century, Indo-Fijians have consistently demanded equal rights with Europeans, including the right to vote. They were finally granted the franchise in 1929, although Fijians were still "represented" by chiefs nominated by the governor and Great Council of Chiefs until 1965, when they were granted the franchise. Indo-Fijians were more demanding in terms of their rights due to their more vulnerable position within the colonial schema. To them, social mobility in terms of education, access to socioeconomic opportunities, and attainment of equal political rights with Europeans were the only means of escaping the humiliating conditions of the cane fields. The Indo-Fijian demands were backed up by strikes, threats of

Table 10.1 Population by Ethnic Origin, Fiji, 1881–1996

Ethnicity	1881	1901	1921	1946	1956	1966	1976	1986	1996
Chinese[a]	—	—	910	2,874	4,155	5,149	4,652	4,784	4,939
European	2,671	2,459	3,878	4,594	6,402	6,590	4,929	4,196	3,103
Fijian	114,748	94,397	84,475	118,070	148,134	202,176	259,932	329,305	393,575
Indian	588	17,105	60,634	120,414	169,403	240,960	292,896	348,702	338,818
Part-European	771	1,516	2,781	6,142	7,810	9,687	10,276	10,297	11,685
Rotuman	2,452	2,230	2,235	3,313	4,422	5,797	7,291	8,652	9,727
Pacific Islander	6,100	1,950	1,564	3,717	5,320	6,095	6,822	8,627	10,463
Other	156	467	789	514	91	273	1,270	810	2,767
Total	127,486	120,124	157,266	259,638	345,737	476,727	588,068	715,375	775,077

Source: Government of Fiji, Bureau of Statistics, *National Census*, 1996, p. 29.
Note: a. Chinese did not come to Fiji until after 1901.

Table 10.2   Religious Affiliation by Ethnicity, Fiji, 1996

Religious Affiliation	Ethnicity			
	Fijian	Indian	Other	Total
Christian				
Methodist	261,972	5,432	13,224	280, 628
Catholic	52,163	3,520	13,637	69,320
Other Christian	76,245	11,767	11,522	99,534
Hindu	864	262,851	458	264,173
Muslim	324	53,753	246	54,323
Other religion/no religion	2,007	1,495	3,597	7,099
Total	393,575	338,818	42,684	775,077

Source: Government of Fiji, Bureau of Statistics, *National Census,* 1996 (unpublished figures).

strikes, refusal to join the war effort during World War II, and whipping up anti-European sentiment. While incremental gains were made by Indo-Fijians over time in response to these, there was also a downside. Fijians saw these demands as evidence of *kocokoco* (selfishness) and *viavialevu* (arrogance) of the Kaidia, who were not to be *vakabauti* (trusted). Distrust of Indo-Fijians (as political leaders, business partners, or even as work colleagues) based on such characterizations remains a significant factor in the political perception of many Fijians.

On the other hand, Fijians felt relatively comfortable under the patronizing and paternalistic care of the British through the policy on natives. Fijian demand for political equality was not considered a necessity, since it would destroy the sense of trust and goodwill with the British under the terms of the 1874 cession deed. Political demands and strikes were considered destructive and alien, and undermined the Fijian way of *veilomalomani* (mutual relations) and *lomavata* (consensus).

These two different approaches to some extent underpinned the continuing ethnic power struggle in political and constitutional negotiations over the years. While Indo-Fijians have consistently demanded a common roll (one person, one vote), Fijians insisted that there should be reserved seats under the communal roll as a way of protecting their political position and rights in the face of Indo-Fijians' numerical superiority. Moreover, while population distribution is important in shaping ethnic tension, it has to be understood also in the context of the dynamics of power struggle and power distribution. The interplay between demographic dynamics and political variables such as the fear of numerical and political marginality, and demand for greater representation in relation to a group's perceived political rights, can be a recipe for ethnic tension.

■ Social Engineering and the Institutionalization of Ethnic Politics

Since Fiji became a British colony on 10 October 1874, ethnic compartmentalization (first between Europeans and Fijians and later involving Indians) has been an integral part of the status quo. Through British colonial rule, small Fijian chiefdoms and larger kingdoms came under centralized rule under the 1876 native affairs ordinance. The new law (which was the basis of the so-called native policy) instituted a number of dramatic changes to Fijian institutions and systems of social relations. These included the imposition of a rigid communal system that locked Fijians into the subsistence sector under the tutelage of chiefs, restructuring of the chiefly system to make it more responsive to the needs of the colonial state (this included the formalization of the Great Council of Chiefs), and the reconfiguration and codification of the landowning system.[13]

The separate system of administration for Fijians (called the Fijian administration) worked well for the British, because it facilitated their "indirect rule" and "divide and rule" policies effectively. While Indians worked as laborers within the commercial sugar sector under exploitative conditions, Fijians remained subsistence village dwellers under very rigid communalistic rules dictated by the native policies.

These sociocultural and institutional arrangements were to have a long-lasting impact on ethnic politics and communal tension. First, the Fijian administration consolidated a sense of homogeneity and collective identity among Fijians. It created a collective sense of "Fijianness" as opposed to the *vulagi* (foreigners). Second, the native policy shielded Fijians and Indo-Fijians from any meaningful interaction at the social, economic, or political level, because the system encouraged ethnic partition through separate economic activities and political representation. Fijians came to distrust Indo-Fijians, and Indo-Fijians developed an attitude of cultural superiority toward Fijians.

Third, through the institutionalization and universalization of chiefly power, chiefly authority became crystallized as a permanent part of the state structure and the centripetal force around which Fijian identity and loyalty revolved. Fourth, the paternalistic native policy bred complacency and distrust for "democratic" means of representation through elections.[14] Under the Fijian administration, Fijian representation to the legislative council was through appointment, until a mere five years before decolonization (in contrast to Indo-Fijians). The colonial system itself was undemocratic and reinforced authoritarian rule. Fijians thus came to see their political rights in relation to the notion of "paramountcy of Fijian interests" rather than democratic community; in other words, they had an indispensable special right to rule in order to protect themselves against Indo-Fijian political ambitions.

Fifth, the system helped to reproduce and crystallize ethnicity as the dominant political ideology. The native policy institutionalized ethnic differentiation as a political norm. Ethnicity became the major mobilizing factor for political party membership and the basis on which political ideology and policies were formulated. Last but not least, the rigid communal and subsistence system marginalized Fijians from mainstream commerce. Over the years, these factors continued to be a source of ethnic grievances and were used as means of mobilization and justification by nationalists during the coups of 1987 and 2000.[15]

The legacy of the native policy continues to this day. Although it was meant to protect Fijians from the ravages of Western influence and later Indian domination, it had in various other ways reshaped and reconfigured Fijian political culture, communal psychology, and social relations in a permanent way. Under the Fijian administration, a number of Fijian institutions, such as the Great Council of Chiefs, the Native Land Trust Board, the Ministry of Fijian Affairs, and the Fijian Affairs Board, were set up to facilitate and protect indigenous interests within the broader ideological parameter of "paramountcy of Fijian interests." Over time, these institutions became the formal instruments through which Fijians came to define their identity and collective consciousness separately from other communities.

The communal separation created by the Fijian administration has been part of the dilemma faced while trying to create a collective national consciousness over the years. On the one hand there have been efforts to mobilize a collective identity around the state (civic nationalism). On the other hand was the need to maintain a distinctive ethnic identity, drawing on political and ideological mobilization around ethnocommunal markers (ethnonationalism).[16] The tension between civic nationalism and ethnonationalism is a common phenomenon in many multiethnic states. In Fiji it assumes a syncretic character—that is, there is a dynamic process of tension and accommodation taking place simultaneously between civic nationalism and communal nationalism. At one level there is accommodation between them and at another level there is tension. Paradoxically, this syncretic relationship has provided a climate for both conflict and restraint.

Although the Fijian administration was designed as a protective mechanism, it has also turned out to be communally divisive. Apart from this, Fiji's constitutional provisions for elections have also played a vital role in socially engineering ethnic compartmentalization.

■ Constitutional and Electoral Engineering: Maintaining the Equilibrium

The constitutional changes in 1964 and 1965 saw Fijians granted full democratic representation (following Indo-Fijians by thirty-five years). Under the 1965 constitution, there were to be thirty-four elected members of the legislative council, and of these, twelve were to be Indo-Fijians, twelve were to be Fijians, and ten were to be Europeans.[17] The population distribution was 42 percent Fijians, 51 percent Indo-Fijian, and 4 percent Europeans, and the seat allocation was a deliberate effort to keep a political balance between Fijians and Indo-Fijians. European overrepresentation was designed to consolidate their colonial supremacy, and also to keep the "Indian threat" in check.

The 1965 constitution was the result of a compromise between Fijian and Indo-Fijian leaders, producing numerical balance in the seat allocation and also a balance in the manner of representation. Thus two systems of voting—"communal" and "common" franchise—were introduced. Communal roll referred to the reservation of seats for communities, while common roll referred to cross-communal voting, commonly referred to as "one person, one vote." The Fijian leaders promoted a communal electoral system to avoid political domination by Indo-Fijians, while Indo-Fijian leaders favored common roll, which would give them greater political voice due to their numerical superiority.[18]

The first full election under the 1965 constitution was in 1966. What later became the multiracial Alliance Party grew out of this election. The Alliance Party was an umbrella organization for a number of ethnic-based political groups: the Fijian Association, for Fijians; the Indian Alliance, for Indo-Fijians; and the General Electors Association, for Europeans, part-Europeans, Chinese, and Pacific Islanders.[19] The other major political party was the Indo-Fijian-dominated National Federation Party, formed in 1963.

While Indo-Fijians advocated independence, Fijians feared that independence could mean possible "Indian takeover." But political negotiations between the leaders of the two communities in London in 1969 paved the way for a postcolonial constitution based on political balance that at the same time provided for protection of various Fijian rights and privileges as a compromise.

The 1970 postcolonial constitution provided for fifty-two seats: twenty-two Fijian seats, twenty-two Indo-Fijian seats, and eight seats for general electors. Twenty-seven of these seats were communal and twenty-five were common. The senate (upper house) was deliberately structured to establish the dominance of Fijian representatives as a way of safeguarding legislation dealing with Fijian matters.[20] The senate compromise was to satisfy Fijians as well as maintain political balance.

The Alliance won the first postindependence election, in 1972, on the basis of an apparently contradictory philosophy. On the one hand was its appeal to tradition and communalism as a way of mobilizing Fijian support, and on the other was its use of multiracial rhetoric to mobilize multiethnic support. The election in 1977 was won by the Indo-Fijian-dominated NFP as a result of a split in the Fijian vote, with a substantial shift toward the extremist Fiji Nationalist Party (FNP), led by the late Sakeasi Butadroka, who advocated the repatriation of Indo-Fijians to India. However, because the NFP could not form a government due to internal bickering, the governor-general, a Fijian high chief, duly appointed former prime minister Ratu Sir Kamisese Mara, the leader of the Alliance Party, to become interim prime minister. The Alliance came back with a bigger majority later in the year, and also won convincingly during the 1982 election.

However, the fortunes of the Alliance Party changed when it lost to the Labour Party–National Federation Party coalition during the 1987 election—both parties having strong Indo-Fijian representation. The 1987 election was the turning point in Fiji's parliamentary democracy. The new coalition government, under Bavadra, was overthrown one month after it came into power, on 14 May 1987, in a military coup led by Lieutenant-Colonel Sitiveni Rabuka. The military, composed almost entirely of Fijians, was responding to the demands by Fijian nationalists for the return of power to Fijians.[21]

The military coup brought to the surface the underlying ethnic tensions that had been characteristic of Fijian politics for a long time. The coup was preceded by nationwide ethnonationalist agitation and mobilization. A second coup occurred on 25 September 1987, when Rabuka felt that an agreement, called the Deuba Accord, meant to set up a Bavadra-Mara government of national unity, would undermine the "aspirations" of his first coup, which was for the Fijianization of the state. Bavadra (a Fijian) was still seen as a political "frontman" for Indo-Fijians.[22]

Following the 1987 coups, the 1970 constitution was abrogated and a new constitution, weighted in favor of Fijians, was put in place in 1990. The 1990 constitution increased the number of seats to seventy, and of these, thirty-seven were reserved for Fijians, twenty-seven for Indo-Fijians, and five for general electors. It also provided that only a Fijian could become a prime minister.[23] The first election under the 1990 constitution was in 1992, which was won by Rabuka's party Soqosoqo in Vakavulewa ni Taukei (SVT). However, national and international condemnation of the constitution as racist led to its review and the development of a new constitution (1997) after nationwide consultation. The total number of seats provided for in the new constitution was seventy-one, and of these, forty-six were communal (twenty-three for Fijians, nineteen for Indo-Fijians, one for a Rotuman, and three for other ethnic groups), and twenty-five were open seats. In addition, a multiparty cabinet was proposed.

The first election under the 1997 constitution took place in May 1999. The ruling Fijian party, the SVT, lost the election and Rabuka lost power. The new government was led by Mahendra Chaudhry of the Labour Party— Fiji's first Indo-Fijian prime minister. Exactly one year later, in May 2000, a nationalist putsch overthrew the government. A new election in 2001 saw the victory of the Fijian party Soqosoqo Duavata ni Lewe ni Vanua (SDL). Following a court battle, the SDL was directed by the Supreme Court to form a multiparty cabinet in line with the constitution, but an attempt to do so with the (Indo-Fijian) Labour Party failed due to irreconcilable differences.

All the constitutions following independence advocated communal representation and as a result, competition over state power naturally became ethnic in nature. The state became a site for ethnopolitical contestation, and this seriously enhanced the possibility of ethnic conflict. All the coups have been preceded by elections that were won by Indo-Fijian-dominated parties. Shifts in the political gravity as a result of the election results, together with the ethnicized political consciousness, created a favorable condition for nationalist agitation and political action.

■ Socioeconomic Grievances

Real or perceived socioeconomic disparity has the potential to inflame ethnic grievances. Debate over whether Fijians are in fact economically disadvantaged has been part of a long-running exchange. Both Fijians and Indo-Fijians make up, roughly equally, the sprawling, poor squatter settlements in the Suva-Nausori corridor, where approximately 10 percent of the nation's population lives. Both groups are well represented among the unemployed and underemployed.

There are three major strands to the economic grievances debate in Fiji. The first is the neo-Marxian political economy thesis, which explains ethnic conflict in terms of competing class-conflict variables. This argument, articulated in various forms, argues that ethnic grievances in Fiji are derived from unequal distribution of resources across ethnic groups.[24] Ethnicity is seen as a mobilizing tool that hides the class interests of the multiethnic ruling class (Fijian chiefs and Indian business elites). Members of both the Fijian and the Indo-Fijian working class are victims of capitalist exploitation, but their class alliance is thwarted by divisions created by ethnicization of politics. A variant of this view contends that Fijian elites and leaders need to be blamed for their inability to deliver more equitable development.[25]

The second view, based on ethnic stereotyping, argues that lack of Fijian socioeconomic development and apparent innovation is caused either by their own "laziness" and inability to cope with internal sociopolitical problems, or by their communalistic orientation. Distribution and consumption are considered more important virtues than accumulation and individual enterprise.[26]

The third view has undertones of the "greed and grievance" thesis. The first aspect of this view puts the blame squarely on the "greedy" Indians, who supposedly conspire and use devious means to dominate business and commerce at the expense of Fijian socioeconomic development.[27] For a number of years, the Fiji Nationalist Party, led largely by small-scale Fijian businessmen, has been singing the same tune to win Fijian political support. The second aspect of the greed and grievance thesis puts the blame on "greedy" Fijians, who through their desire for more wealth and political control contribute to Fiji's problems.[28] These explanations, driven by ideological and ethnicist assumptions in their own particular ways, only partially contribute to explaining the complex dynamics of ethnic conflict in Fiji. The socioeconomic grievances were part of a much more complex process to which class, ideological, ethnocultural, and political variables contributed.

We have seen how, as a result of the native policy, Fijians were left out of mainstream commerce and economics and as a result were left behind in the areas of business and education. Early attempts to reform Fijian institutions to allow for greater flexibility, openness, and individual enterprise were resisted by both British and Fijian leaders on the grounds that they would undermine Fijian unity. Early development projects also often failed, because they still operated within the communal ambit and were controlled by chiefs. Fijians were also handicapped by the communal landowning system, which could not be used as collateral for loans. In the 1960s, for example, Fijians only received 7 percent of the total value of loans. The 1960–1961 figures also show that the average size of the Fijian loans were only half of those of Indo-Fijians, and a tenth of those of Europeans.[29]

Most of the land in Fiji (83 percent) was, and remains, communally owned by Fijians. Of this, arable lands were leased out to Indians for sugar cane farming; the land remaining to Fijians (for subsistence agriculture) was largely mountainous and inaccessible. Freehold land, which was best for agriculture, was dominated by non-Fijians. In the early 1960s, only 0.2 percent of the freehold land belonged to Fijians. During the same period the number of Fijians in selected professions (lawyers, doctors, and dentists) was only two, compared to fifty-eight for Indo-Fijians, one for Chinese, and seventy-six for Europeans and part-Europeans.[30]

After independence, Fijian business progressed but remained well behind other ethnic groups. Prime Minister Mara was blamed by nationalists for forming alliances with the rich Indo-Fijians to enhance his own wealth, and this perception was one of the reasons for the Alliance's downfall during the 1977 election. The same grievances came to the fore during the 1987 coups, prior to which the 1986 census had indicated that Fijians were seriously lagging behind in education and commerce. Many Fijians felt that their economic misery would be worsened by Indo-Fijian political control. In response to the economic grievances, the postcoup state put in place a number of affirmative action measures, among which was the deliberate expansion of the Fijian middle class to counter the dominance of the non-Fijian middle class. The affirmative action policies, however, did not really benefit most ordinary Fijians.[31]

Even the 1996 national census figures showed that Fijians were still lagging behind other ethnic groups in commerce by a ratio of one to six. This statistical disparity was reinforced by the visual manifestation of wealth. Indo-Fijians tend to publicly exhibit more material wealth in terms of shops, businesses, good houses, cars, and other forms of a more affluent lifestyle. During the street riots in Suva during the 1987 and 2000 coups, many of the socioeconomic frustrations were channeled toward Indo-Fijian properties. Ethnic and class cleavages interplayed in an explosive way. Emphasis on ethnicity had diverted people's attention away from their basic socioeconomic conditions. Through institutionalized communalism and ethnic stereotyping, poor Fijians had been made to believe that social mobility was only possible through deployment of means that achieved political supremacy for Fijians. Ethnicity mystified class relations in a dynamic way. Poor, unemployed Fijians involved in the riots saw Indian businesspeople as their class and ethnic "enemies," and saw the physical destruction of the symbols of their wealth and economic power as the only means to get even.

■ Clash of Cultures? Cultural Identities and Construction of Distinctiveness

Differences in culture do not necessarily lead to conflict; conflict occurs when differences are politicized and used as a means of achieving particular economic, political, or personal objectives. The interaction between the various ethnic groups in Fiji has created a new cultural synthesis that has made cultural distinctiveness less obvious than before, although there are still observable differences that have survived over the years. The dynamics of cultural change resulting from internal and external factors have led to either conscious transformation and adaptation, or resistance in the form of "escape" into "tradition."

Fijian cultural identity is based on the notion of the indigenes as the original settlers of the Fiji group. The earliest evidence of human habitation in Fiji is about 3,000–4,000 years ago. For hundreds of years, an Austronesian culture that had aspects of Melanesian and Polynesian cultures evolved, shaped by internal dynamics as well as external links with Tongan and Samoan cultures through trade and warfare. Despite changes imposed by the British colonial system, Fijians still claim primordial origin through various mythologies, appeals to tradition, and certain forms of deeply rooted cultural practices and ceremonies. Christianity has been incorporated as a "traditional" religion and a major component of Fijian identity, while other religions (such as Hinduism and Islam) are considered heathen and thus contrary to Fijian cultural norms (despite arriving not long after Christianity).

The coups of 1987 and 2000 were justified as protecting Fijian culture and Christianity against the forces of *tawalotu* (heathenism). A coup-supporting priest belonging to a Pentecostal group publicly proclaimed while addressing supporters in parliament during the 2000 hostage siege that "Rabuka is the Moses and Speight is the Joshua of the Fijians," liberating them and leading them away from bondage.[32]

While globalization has substantially transformed Fijian culture and identity, it has also contributed to consolidating claims to primordiality. Globalization has increased interaction between various ethnic groups (through the marketplace, pop culture, nightclubs, boardrooms, etc.), but among Fijians it has also intensified fears of weakening Fijian culture in the face of the "Indian threat."

Indo-Fijian identity is more complex given the diverse religions, caste, and subethnic categories. While Hinduism and Islam are the major ethnoreligious categories, other categories such as Sikhism and Buddhism are also represented.

There are two competing discourses around Indo-Fijian identity. The first is based on the view that Indo-Fijian culture has rich primordial roots in the great Indus civilization.[33] There is a romantic feel about how this inheritance has been globalized through the Indian diaspora, as expressed in well-known literary works such as those by V. S. Naipul. The romantic notion of "motherland India" forms the basis for cultural pride and mythological reminiscence about a culture superior in artistic, architectural, commercial, and technological achievements compared to the *jungali* (bushman) culture of the Fijians. Thus, while mythologization of the Indian motherland reinforces a sense of cultural continuity, genesis, and permanence, it also invokes ethnic stereotyping against the "inferior" Fijian culture.

The second strand of Indo-Fijian identity is based on the assumption that India was admittedly the "grandmother" but that now Fiji is the "motherland." The Indo-Fijian culture has a Fijian genesis and thus is an inseparable part of Fiji's history. For many descendants of the indentured laborers, Fiji, not India, is their homeland, the site for their claim to legitimacy. This claim to Fiji as motherland by Indo-Fijians has created a situation of identity contestation with many Fijians, who feel their sense of legitimacy threatened. National Reconciliation Week, organized by the government in October 2004, was an attempt to find space to reconcile these two contending modes of ethnocultural legitimacy.

The boundaries of these two modes of cultural identity are often defined and redefined by ethnic politics. Because of the ethnicized political climate, cultural identity is often subsumed into political identity, and vice versa. Identity boundaries also change as a result of greater globalization, intermarriage, and convergences of economic and political interests. Much of this is happening in Fiji in a dynamic way, and over time may become a stabilizing factor.

Ethnic Consciousness: Stereotypes and Scapegoating

In Fiji, as in other societies, ethnic stereotypes developed as a direct result of the socioeconomic, cultural, and political engagement between Fijians and Indo-Fijians and the way in which this engagement shaped their perceptions of each other. Under the native policy, Fijians lived a rigid communal life in a subsistence setting under the tutelage of chiefs. They were denied the privileges of universal education and participation in mainstream commerce, and lived a rather unsophisticated life characterized by communal labor and reciprocity. Private accumulation was perceived with disdain, and communal reciprocity and redistribution were considered sociocultural assets. On the other hand, Indians lived a regimented plantation life and had to toil from sunset to sundown under a rigid and often violent indentured system.[34] They were much more inclined toward individual accumulation and individual achievement.

These two contrasting sociocultural experiences, enforced by colonial policy and reinforced by compartmentalized ethnic politics, provided the nurturing ground for racial stereotypes that evolved from early in the twentieth century until today. Indo-Fijians perceived Fijians as lazy, stupid *jungalis,* while Fijians perceived Indians as cunning, selfish, untrustworthy, and conspiratorial.

These stereotypes do not only emerge in moments of anger and humor; they have over the years been used at the level of political and parliamentary discourse by politicians and leaders as a means of condemning the other group either explicitly or implicitly.[35] Fijian nationalists used the stereotypes effectively in their mobilizing speeches during the coups as a way of fueling anger against Indo-Fijians. On the other hand, the coups merely reinforced in the minds of Indo-Fijians the violent "barbarity" of the Fijian character.

Ethnic Conflict and the Changing Role of the Fiji Military

Understanding the role of the military in ethnic conflict in Fiji is crucial because of the military's role in the past as an agent of Fijian nationalism and as an arm of the Fijian establishment. This was to find expression when the military intervened on behalf of the Alliance Party and Fijian nationalists during the 1987 coups. This is not to say that the military was the root cause of the coups but rather that it was an instrument of its execution.

Since its establishment in the 1800s the military had been part of the broader Fijian establishment and had been closely aligned to the Fijian leaders. It was almost inevitable for the military to intervene when the Fijian establishment, organized around the Alliance Party, was threatened. When the Alliance Party lost the election to the Fiji Labour Party in 1987, the military under Rabuka staged a coup and deposed Bavadra's government. Rabuka later "civilianized" himself by becoming an elected prime minister in 1992.

After 1987 the Fijian state was heavily militarized in a number of ways: a record number of military officers became government ministers; as part of the affirmative action policy, a significant number of military officers were given important and powerful public service and government corporate positions, and scholarships for overseas studies, especially in law; the size and budget of the military was increased significantly; military cadetship was introduced into schools; and military surveillance of the public through the Fijian Intelligence Service (headed by a military colonel) increased tremendously.

The militarization of the state was significant because it helped to consolidate the ethnonationalist-inclined state. The militarization and ethnocratization of the state took place simultaneously and reinforced each other in a mutually embracing way. The military became the guardian of ethnonationalism, and ethnonationalism became the legitimizing mechanism for consolidation of the military.

The military-ethnonationalist alliance went through various stages of transition as a result of the changes in the general political climate in Fiji, review of the constitution, change in leadership of the military, and external pressures from foreign donors and neighbors. After the 1987 coups, the military's overseas reputation took a nose-dive and a number of countries such as Australia, the United States, and New Zealand withdrew their links and aid. The Fijian military are also sensitive to UN views, as the army is a significant contributor to UN peacekeeping operations internationally, and is thus both exposed to UN positions and somewhat reliant on peacekeeping as a source of income. These pressures led to internal transformation in the form of reprofessionalization and image repackaging of the military. When Commodore Frank Bainimarama took over, he instituted further changes in the structure, and more interestingly, in the ideological orientation of the army. The military's culture and ideology was progressively depoliticized and deethnicized, with the aim of the military no longer operating as a Fijian institution, but as a national institution to protect national interest.[36]

This process of transformation was severely tested during the May 2000 civilian coup. On the one hand a breakaway group of elite soldiers belonging to the Counter-Revolutionary Warfare Unit helped coup leader George Speight take members of Chaudhry's government hostage. On the other hand, when all the state institutions were handicapped, the military as an institution intervened by asking the president to step aside, abrogated the constitution, and declared martial law. This quelled lawlessness in the streets and enabled the army to deal with the coup makers entrenched in the parliamentary complex. However, some legal opinions considered these military actions illegal. The courts also later found the abrogation of the constitution invalid and reinstated it.

There were conspiracy theories that the military more broadly was a party to the coup, but there has been no evidence of this at all, except for "evidence" such as the deposing of the president, abrogation of the constitution, and the fact that a Fijian nationalist party was once again appointed as interim government (going on to win the postcoup election). The commander of the Fiji military responded to these allegations, saying that he had asked the president to step aside on 20 May 2000 "to stabilize the country and to protect the president whose life was under threat," adding that stability was needed "so that soldiers do not have to shoot."[37]

Moreover, the military has taken a consistently strong stance in bringing those involved in the coup (including those who took part in the 2 November 2000 mutiny to topple the commander) to justice. This created significant tension with the government. Until its dissolution in early 2006, the Matanitu Vanua Party (MVP) was in coalition with the SDL government. The MVP was an extremist nationalist party of which coup leader George Speight was a prominent member—although in jail. Other prominent former members of government jailed for their part in the coup include the former vice president, the deputy speaker, and a senator who is also a high chief who instigated the mutiny. Others are serving either life or shorter sentences, and still others are being investigated. The MVP has pushed for a "slowdown" in the investigation and prosecution of those implicated in the coup. Laisenia Qarase, the SDL leader and prime minister until the coup in December 2006, tried to appease the MVP nationalists and coup supporters as a way of maintaining their support for the government, because with six seats, they literally held the balance of power.

The military, on the other hand, was adamant that all coup-makers, mutineers, and planners should be prosecuted and punished if found guilty. In late 2004 the government suggested that they were not going to renew the army commander's contract, hinting that he was a big barrier to speedy "resolution" of the postcoup problems. The commander's contract was eventually renewed, but the tension between the government and the military continued. The military was alleged to be interfering in the selection process of the new vice president, while the military was concerned that the vice president could become president and so commander in chief of the army, and thus they insisted on someone not implicated in the coup, unlike the former vice president.

In mid-2005, the government proposed legislation it claimed was aimed at "reconciliation" and that prominently included granting amnesty to coup-makers if they could establish that their actions were politically, rather than criminally, motivated. However, it became clear that Commodore Bainimarama indirectly threatened to remove the government if the legislation was passed. This stand by the military commander demonstrates the contradictory position of the military in contemporary Fiji and indicates both the degree to which as an institution it has moved away from ethnonationalist alliances, but also the degree to which it remains a key player in Fiji's ethnopolitical drama.

The military has been trying to establish itself as a body that belongs to everyone, rather than to any particular ethnic group. It has also been trying to make this point to the public, particularly the Fijians. As part of this role it has sought to become a reconciliatory and mediating force between the two major contending ethnic groups.[38] The military is thus working to become a guardian of civic identity and civic nationalism, compared to its former role as guardian of Fijian ethnonationalism only. However, the role of the commander at least became dangerously paradoxical in this context, as he was threatening the elected government with removal in order to uphold the civic nationalism represented by the constitution.

■ Responses to Ethnic Tension: Toward Conflict Resolution

Since independence ethnic tension has been taken for granted. It was often considered a "normal" phenomenon that would somehow sort itself out. The multiracial schema of the early postcolonial era seemed to have been working admirably, in that while there was some ethnic tension, the general atmosphere was cordial and stable.

The possibility of a major flare-up or a coup was a far-fetched idea, although tension came to the surface in various ways, most notably in 1977 when the Alliance Party lost the election narrowly to the Indian-dominated National Federation Party. It was only after the 1987 coups that people began to sit up and take stock of the diverse and unpredictable possibilities in Fiji politics. To the Fijian establishment and ethnonationalists, the only way to contain any further conflict was to ensure perpetual Fijian dominance of politics and affirmative action in the area of commerce and economics. After the 2000 coup there was a deeper realization that something had to be done and that the stability, security, and trust necessary to deal with the complexities facing Fiji politically, economically, and socially would not happen automatically. As a result, programs were put in place both by the government and civil society organizations to address the conflict.

Following the 2000 coup, UN agencies, the Commonwealth Secretariat (an important body in Fiji), the European Union, and bilateral donors (particularly Australia, New Zealand, and the United States) also pressed the interim government to uphold the 1997 constitution, hold elections, and pursue justice for those responsible for the coup. This external effort supported and accompanied the work of Fiji's key legal bodies (the courts, the human rights commission, the law society) and civil society organizations.

The Paradox of Constitutional Engineering

The 1970 postcolonial constitution was meant to provide political balance between the Fijians and Indo-Fijians. It was a "consociationalist" constitution of sorts that resulted from a behind-closed-doors agreement between leaders of the two major ethnic groups during the 1969 constitutional talks in London. The two groups had fundamental differences in perception and expectations. Nevertheless, a compromise was reached between the Indo-Fijian demand for a common electoral roll, and the Fijian insistence on communal voting, which they believed would guard against political domination by the Indo-Fijians (who by then constituted about 51 percent of the population) and entrench their own political supremacy. Provision was made for an equal number of seats for Fijians and Indo-Fijians in the lower house (representatives), while Fijians would have the majority in the upper house (senate). In addition it was agreed that changes to laws relating to Fijian land and rights would only be made through a vote of two-thirds majority. Because of Fijian dominance in the upper house, this would be deemed difficult.[39]

This constitutional balance, it was hoped, would ensure stability as long as the status quo (that is, Fijian political dominance) was maintained. The first test for this constitutional equilibrium was in 1977, when the Alliance Party lost the election, but because the NFP could not form a government in time, the governor-general reappointed the former prime minister. This diffused a volatile situation. At the moment of political uncertainty following the 1977 election, there was talk within the military circles of a possible military takeover.[40] For failing to ensure perpetual Fijian rule, the 1970 constitution was abrogated and, unlike the 1997 constitution, was never allowed any chance of resurrection. Instead, an alternative constitution that would provide for Fijian political supremacy and thus "stability" was promulgated in 1990.

The logic behind the 1990 constitution was that political control by Fijians would balance out economic domination by Indo-Fijians and thus would contain ethnonationalist grievances; in such analyses, these grievances were seen as the main threat to stability. The underlying fear was that political control by Indo-Fijians would undermine indigenous interests because both political and economic power would shift toward Indo-Fijian hands. But the 1990 constitution was condemned by many as "racist" and as not conforming to internationally accepted norms of governance and equity, although the framers argued that it was in line with the principles of the UN Draft Declaration on the Rights of Indigenous Peoples of 1993. Nevertheless, the constitution was reviewed and changed as a result of international and local pressure, and a new version came into force in 1997.

The new 1997 constitution provided for protection of various Fijian rights and privileges as well as provision for affirmative action under the social justice section. It was a much more rigid constitution that attempted to socially engineer ethnic integration through such provisions as a compulsory multiparty cabinet and an alternative voting system.[41] Both these provisions failed to achieve their constitutionally prescribed aims, at least in the time before the next coup. The political culture built up over the years was at odds with the mechanistic provisions of the constitution. Institutional innovations introduced by the constitution, such as a human rights commission, did, however, assist in dealing with some of the impact of the coup. Despite the fact that the 1997 constitution was hailed as "one of the best in the world," it could not avoid the 2000 coup, and may have directly led to it.

Constitutional attempts to socially engineer ethnic integration have not led to the desired results. Stability was not delivered by constitutions that continued entrenched ethnic division, nor was integration achieved by purely legal and constitutional means. Part of the reason was that the constitutional mechanics failed to take into consideration the dynamics of political culture, in particular the sociocultural complexities of Fijian ethnonationalism. The assumption was that people and their cultural dispositions must adapt to the written word rather than the written word being configured to respond to the social dynamics. Legalism and constitutionalism have so far not fulfilled expectations (although the multiparty cabinet, formed in 2006, represented an effort to breathe further life into the 1997 constitution).

Social Engineering Through Affirmative Action

Affirmative action became a large-scale state policy after the 1987 coup. It was justified by the ethnonationalist government on the grounds that equitable distribution of resources and opportunity was the only way to satisfy Fijian socioeconomic grievances and pacify the rising tide of ethnonationalism (the tide that it had ridden to office). Prior to 1987 there had been a number of programs, under the colonial administration or after independence, specifically targeted at Fijian socioeconomic advancement. For a variety of reasons, success was mixed, and many programs operated within the ambit of communal life, outside mainstream commerce.

After the 1987 coup, the government introduced affirmative action policies in the areas of commercial loans, financial investment, taxi licensing, education, and civil service recruitment. The aspiring Fijian middle class took advantage of the opportunities to further their social mobility and gained entry into areas previously outside Fijian participation. The small Fijian middle class was supportive of the postcoup state because it provided the enabling political environment for them to be able to compete with the Indo-Fijian middle class, who dominated commerce, the professions, and posh residential areas. Ethnonationalism was a convenient means through which they could counter Indo-Fijian commercial hegemony and advance their own individual interests.

The next ten years saw a dramatic and unprecedented expansion of the Fijian middle class, who clearly benefited from the affirmative action policies of the government. By the time of the 2000 coup, the established Fijian middle class had consolidated and entrenched their economic position in a significant way. Unlike in 1987, they mostly opposed the 2000 ethnonationalist coup on the grounds that it had the potential to undermine their economic gains. The new Fijian middle class thus became a stabilizing force in the face of ethnonationalist agitation. In this case, although affirmative action only benefited the Fijian middle class rather than the grassroots people, it pacified a significant category of Fijians, who in the future will continue to be a stabilizing force.

Affirmative action policies for Fijians are ongoing, and have the goal of achieving a fifty-fifty parity in commerce by 2020. The affirmative action plan is based on the assumption that addressing socioeconomic disparity is a way of addressing the "root causes of political tension in Fiji and as such, serves as an integral component of national reconciliation and confidence building."[42] The broad thrust of the affirmative action policies is still to increase Fijians' share of the business sector, rather than to reduce the numbers of unemployed youth open to mobilization during political turmoil. Moreover, affirmative action has been seen by Indo-Fijians as discriminatory and an affront to human rights. The government, in response, started allocating scholarships to poor Indo-Fijians.

Significant economic hardship is suffered by both communities, particularly unemployment and underemployment. The coups themselves had serious negative effects on the economy and have contributed to this hardship. Moreover, Fiji's major export, in addition to tourism, is sugar, the industry for which the Indians were brought to Fiji in the first place. The World Trade Organization, however, is phasing out the preferential trading arrangements that supported this export, over three years beginning in July 2005. This has meant a dramatic revision downward of government growth predictions, and will mean real hardship across the country. Indo-Fijian sugar farmers and millers, however, will bear much of the direct brunt. Working with the reality and the perception of economic grievance is important. However, development policies need to actively benefit both communities, and need to be seen as doing so if they are to promote reconciliation and improved trust between them rather than entrench resentment.

Resilience and Peacebuilding

Despite years of political tension and ethnic competition, including coups, Fiji has been able to show a remarkable degree of resilience. There are a number of reasons for this. The multiracial experiment since 1970 has created a framework for intercommunal ethnosocial relations that even the continuing competition over state power by the elites could not completely undermine. The coups were driven more by nationalist elites who were able to mobilize wide-ranging socioeconomic grievances rather than being a spontaneous expression of anti-Indianness by Fijians. Indeed, while causing much destruction, deep hurt, and alienation, the coups have also galvanized elements of indigenous Fijian society, in particular, to build bridges with Indo-Fijians as fellow citizens and work actively for a more unified Fiji. Fijian culture possesses powerful norms of restraint and absorption of tension that held many Fijians back from involvement in anti-Indian violence. Local chiefs in some areas worked with religious leaders to restrain community members from joining the coup supporters. Indo-Fijians have also held back from vigilantism and have rather pursued legal avenues for redress. Emigration, particularly of well-educated Indo-Fijians, may have also acted as a safety valve of sorts.

A number of civil society organizations, including church groups, nongovernmental organizations (NGOs), and trade unions, have been involved in very extensive nationwide or locally based conflict resolution and peacebuilding programs. Many of these organizations have specialized in various issues such as conflict transformation and resolution, development, gender equality, poverty, constitutional awareness, human rights, voter education, and counseling. For example, one such organization, the Ecumenical Center for Research, Education, and Advocacy (ECREA), counsels individuals, works with groups and communities on discrimination and human rights, and works with rural communities on the underlying causes of the violence, its effects, and their own role in it. Many organizations and groups learned from the experience of the earlier coups in 1987. In particular, networks had formed across different groups and sectors (linking church organizations to NGOs to trade unions) and across ethnic groups to combat ethnic polarization. Strong coalitions were formed soon after the coup to press for a return to democracy and observance of rights. There is a strong range of civil society organizations, as well as some government bodies, upon whose expertise and advice external agencies wishing to support peacebuilding in Fiji can draw.

The courts as well as some government instrumentalities and agencies have also been actively seeking and promoting responses to the underlying conflict within their own ambit of operation. Fiji's human rights commission, for example, has used legal and educational means to seek redress for human rights violations and emphasize the value of respecting rights. The SDL government created a new ministry for multiethnic affairs and reconciliation, whose responsibility was to coordinate national reconciliation to help heal the wounds and fractures between communities resulting from the 2000 coup. The government organized nationwide programs for reconciliation between communities affected by the 2000 coup. In October 2004, a national reconciliation week involved various ethnic groups, the government, the traditional Fijian establishment *(vanua)* and the various religious organizations. Fijians generally welcomed the idea of a reconciliation week, but many Indo-Fijians did not support it. The Indo-Fijian-dominated Fiji Labour Party, ousted by the coup, boycotted the reconciliation week on the grounds that reconciliation was only meaningful if based on a strong, clear, and primary commitment to legal justice.

What reconciliation means, and which interests or spectrum of interests define the terms by which it will be conducted, are still very much being worked through in Fiji. While there are commonalities on what enables the resolution of the conflict, there are also differences in expectations that could lead to further tension. As noted earlier, the reconciliation legislation discussed by the Qarase government, for example, linked proposals for a reconciliation commission and for compensation for injured parties with amnesty for coup-makers if they could demonstrate that they were engaged in or actively supporting political, rather than criminal, violence. However, the amnesty provisions were vigorously opposed by a broad cross-section of civil society organizations from across the ethnic communities, as well as by the ethnically Fijian-dominated military.

Until the 2006 election, the Fiji Labour Party repeatedly boycotted conciliation talks with the government, including the *talanoa* sessions, organized by the East West Center in Hawaii. FLP leader Chaudhry was accused of being "arrogant" and boycotting goodwill gestures by the government for political gain. On their part, prior to the 2006 election, government parties failed to include the Labour Party in cabinet, as required by the constitution, while Prime Minister Qarase had been identified with a frankly ethnonationalist position. This rift at the level of elite party politics has not stymied a range of formal and informal reconciliatory efforts, but it was a clear indicator of the ongoing need to create paths toward political reconciliation. Following the 2006 election, the provision in the 1997 constitution for inclusion of any party with more than 10 percent of parliamentary seats in a multiparty cabinet was for the first time upheld. Returning prime minister Qarase included nine FLP members in the new cabinet. The multiparty cabinet, and the two parties themselves, will now need to manage party differences to avoid further political conflict.

Despite the tensions, conflict management in Fiji has been successful in many ways. The economy has recovered better than might have been expected, law and order have been restored, and efforts at reconciliation are ongoing. However, how to engage with the underlying conflict, in a way that steps beyond a cycle of coups and satisfies enough of the major ethnic communities' concerns, remains an ongoing challenge.

■ Conclusion

It is not accurate to categorize ethnic conflict in Fiji as being "Melanesian" in nature, as some have suggested. The manifestations and dynamics of conflict in Fiji are very different from those of conflicts in other Melanesian countries. In fact, comparison with Malaysia is much more appropriate, given its political, historical, and demographic similarities.

There is no singular cause of conflict in Fiji, but rather a variety of forces at play, some more direct than others. Some factors create conditions for potential conflict while others further reinforce these conditions. The socioeconomic factors have to be understood in relation to the historical interface between subsistence life and the new capitalist mode of production. The colonial policy on natives locked Fijians into a rigid subsistence sector and marginalized them from mainstream commerce and education, so that by the time of independence Fijians were lagging far behind economically. This was a direct cause of grievances that later found expression in ethnonationalist agitation and was mobilized by elite interests. In addition, the compartmentalized political structure, based on ethnic representation and competition, provided favorable conditions for ethnic tension, as it polarized the communities and forced them into direct competition for political power. The ethnicized ideological and social discourses in the realm of political and everyday interaction were conducive to tension, but it was the shift in the political gravity away from Fijian political dominance that sparked off the coups in 1987 and 2000. Fijian fear of Indian domination has been an important factor and to many Fijians, loss of political control to an "alien" ethnic group was simply not tolerable.

Ethnic tension in Fiji has led to three violent coups and the consequences in terms of undermining and violating human rights, the damage to political and economic life, loss of property, loss of jobs, and personal hurt have been significant. The coups and the associated conflicts have caused considerable harm, but at the same time they can be seen as part of the growth of a small postcolonial and multiethnic state. The emerging contradictions that we see in Fiji are typical of many postcolonial states. The tensions also provide the opportunity for political, social, and human transformation. The nationwide attempts at conflict resolution perhaps show the growing desire for unity in a tense, culturally diverse society. In a televised public reconciliation program during National Reconciliation Week, one of the leading Fijian chiefs who was a coup supporter in 2000 tearfully hugged an Indo-Fijian community leader saying: "You belong to this country and I will not do anything again to harm you and the Indian community."[43] These words echoed the sentiments of the week, but the question remains—how deep and how sustainable is reconciliation? How strong is the commitment to work toward a genuinely shared understanding of reconciliation? Moreover, how do different groups within Fiji understand the relationship between reconciliation and justice?

Fiji's capacity to absorb tension is highly likely to be tested. Fiji's economy suffered as a result of coups in both 1987 and 2000, but has managed to recover relatively well. Unemployment and underemployment remain problems. However, changing arrangements for international trade in sugar (and to a lesser extent textiles), upon which Fiji is heavily reliant for export income, may mean a considerable drop in economic growth from 2006. This will directly affect Indo-Fijians, who dominate the sugar industry, but it will indirectly affect Fijians and increase unemployment across ethnic groups. Economic contraction and unresolved political tension is a challenging mix for any country. While affirmative action can be valuable, it is also important that development orientations do not embed resentment by ignoring need and overwhelmingly favoring one community at the expense of another.

Perhaps one of the biggest potentials for peacebuilding in Fiji lies in its syncretic nature. While there is tension, there is also accommodation; those forces that invoke conflict are the very same forces that have been used to maintain peace. For instance the chiefly system was widely used as a mobilizing tool for nationalist agitation, but at the same time it was used as a restraining force. The same could be said of religion—on one hand it was an instrument for bigotry, and on the other hand it was used as a vehicle for peacebuilding. Local peacebuilding efforts support these tendencies toward accommodation by generating intercommunity dialogue and understanding. Interestingly, while negative stereotypes exist, there are also positive perceptions. As an example, Fijian parents are sending their children to Indo-Fijian schools as a way of assimilating values of hard work and industriousness. There is generally a sense of resilience as Fiji continues to work with its destructive past.

■ Editor's Note: The 2006 Coup

On 5 December 2006, the commander of Fiji's armed forces, Commadore Bainimarama, took executive power from the government of Laisenia Qarase in a bloodless and remarkably slowly and publicly executed coup. While a number of issues apparently motivated the coup, a key factor was the deep division between the military leadership and the government over the question of what constitutes appropriate reconciliation and justice in the aftermath of the 2000 coup and mutiny attempts. As noted earlier, the government was pursuing amnesties that were unacceptable to the military leadership. Despite flowing directly from the earlier coups, the 2006 coup was thus sharply different in character and motivation, as the above discussion of the changing nature of the Fijian military makes clear. However, the questions the 2006 coup raises about how political processes in Fiji can deal with serious division remain at least as pressing.

▥ Notes

1. The distinction between Melanesia, Polynesia, and Micronesia has been taken for granted, but increasingly these categories are posing analytical difficulties. The lines that "separate" them are too blurred to be useful. These categories were first invented by French explorer D'Urville in 1830, and since then they have stuck. Categorizing Fijians as "Melanesian" is highly problematic because of the diverse cultural influences that have shaped the Fijian culture.

2. The use of ethnic labels is politically contentious in Fiji. I have used "Fijian" for the indigenous and Indo-Fijians for those of Indian ancestry. The term "Indian," as generally used, is misleading, because it normally refers to someone of Indian nationality. See Ratuva, *Participation for Peace,* for a comprehensive assessment of ethnic classification in Fiji.

3. In fact, ethnic conflict in Fiji has been compared to ethnic conflict in Malaysia. This is because of the tense relationship between a diaspora and indigenous population, similar colonial and postcolonial state policies to mediate ethnic conflict, and the configurations of conflict. See Ratuva, "Ethnic Politics, Communalism, and Affirmative Action in Fiji."

4. Journalists, policymakers, and some academics often paint a broad brush of "Melanesia" as a homogeneous entity without understanding the specific differences between the different states. Terms such as the "arc of instability" have been applied to Melanesian states as categories that assume this homogeneity.

5. See Ratuva, "The Paradox of Multi-Culturalism."

6. The multiracial and multicultural approach has been referred to as the "saris, samosas, and steel-bands syndrome," because it merely focuses on the "superficial manifestations of culture" and ignores the fundamental power and legitimacy structures, which are responsible for domination. See, for instance, Donald and Rattansi, *"Race," Culture, and Difference.*

7. See Ratuva, "Storm in Paradise."

8. Many academic analyses of Fiji, as of other postcolonial states, have not escaped from ethnic biases. Academic analyses by Indo-Fijian or Fijian academics often take an ethnic slant.

9. Ratuva, "Anatomising the Vanua Complex."

10. See, for instance, Fraenkel, "Clash of Dynasties and Rise of Demagogues"; Lal, "Chiefs and Thieves and Other People Besides."

11. See Premdas, "Constitutional Challenges."

12. The official ethnic classifications in Fiji (as reflected in the constitution and official documents) are Fijians, Indians, and "others."

13. For details, see Ratuva, "Ethnic Politics, Communalism, and Affirmative Action in Fiji."

14. See Lawson, *The Failure of Democratic Politics in Fiji.*

15. See Ratuva, "Ethnic Politics, Communalism, and Affirmative Action in Fiji."

16. Stavenhagen, *Ethnic Conflict and the Nation State;* Erickson, *Ethnicity and Nationalism.*

17. See Government of Fiji, *Constitution of 1965.*

18. See Ali, *Plantation to Politics.*

19. The "multiethnic" structure of the Alliance Party was based on the Malaysian consociationalist arrangement in the 1960s. The Malaysian Alliance consisted of the United Malays National Organization; the Malayan Chinese Association, and the Malayan Indian Congress. Mara copied this arrangement and used it as basis for the structure of the Alliance Party.

20. See Government of Fiji, *Constitution of 1970.*

21. For details, see Ratuva, "Storm in Paradise."

22. Ibid.

23. Government of Fiji, *Constitution of 1990.*

24. See Howard, "State Power and Political Change in Fiji"; Naidu, "State and Class in the South Pacific"; Durutalo, *The Paramountcy of Fijian Interests and Politicization of Ethnicity;* Sutherland and Robertson, *Government by the Gun.*

25. Sutherland, "State and Capitalist Development."

26. These responses are based on my interviews of a number of Indo-Fijians.

27. Ravuvu, *The Façade of Democracy.*

28. See, for instance, Lal, "Chiefs and Thieves and Other People Besides."

29. Sutherland, "Globalization, Nationalism, and the National Agenda."

30. Narayan, *The Political Economy of Fiji.*

31. Ratuva, "Addressing Inequality?"

32. Radio Fiji, 30 May 2000.

33. Nandan, *Requiem for a Rainbow.*

34. Naidu, *Violence of Indenture.*

35. In a parliamentary debate a Fijian government minister referred to Indians as "weeds," because "they grow everywhere and destroy other plants," an analogical reference to the perceived selfishness and cunningness of Indians. The leader of the Indian-dominated Fiji Labour Party once caused controversy when he told Fijians to wake up and get away from their "backward" situation.

36. Colonel I. Naivalurua, personal communication, 2003.

37. *Daily Post,* 11 December 2000, p. 5.

38. Colonel M. Saubulinayau, personal communication, 2004.

39. Norton, *Race and Politics in Fiji.*

40. Denoon, *Rabuka.*

41. Government of Fiji, *Constitution of the Republic of Fiji.*

42. Government of Fiji, *20 Year Plan.*

43. Fiji TV, 11 October 2004.

11

Elite Conflict in Vanuatu

Graham Hassall

M ATAS KELEKELE, in his first televised address to the nation following his inauguration as president of Vanuatu in 2004, warned that
political and parliamentary instability threatened to destroy the country.[1]
Although the new head of state was referring to the political crisis of the
day—the controversy that followed Prime Minister Rialuth Serge Vohor's
decision to attempt to switch the state's allegiance from China to Taiwan—
the political, legal, and constitutional dynamics of the episode followed a
recurrent pattern exemplifying the fragility of this style of governance.
Tenuous party allegiances have led to frequent no-confidence votes in parliament, disrupting governance at the national level, and leaving the court to
uphold the rule of law and protect the constitution, while obliging members
of parliament (MPs) to carry out their legal obligations and public responsibilities.[2] The persistence of this pattern since independence suggests that
"elite conflict" is the biggest threat to the security of the state.

Although such political maneuvering does not appear at first sight to
have direct impact on the lives of people at village level, it produces a "governance deficit" with significant consequences. Few governments have
served a full parliamentary term, and this disruption of the life of a parliament implies disruption of programs of legislation, policy oversight, and
scrutiny of the performance of the executive. In brief, the proportion of the
nation's human and material resources devoted to resolution of political
contests determines the resources available to the nation for other governance imperatives. In a microstate of just over 200,000 citizens and with
limited revenue and low human development indicators, efficient use of
public goods, including leadership, becomes imperative. In 1993, William
Rodman described Vanuatu as "a weak state with a local people who have
responded to the challenges of the colonial and postcolonial era by actively
seeking control over their own destiny."[3] Questions of why Vanuatu's political life is marked by a debilitating level of elite contest and weak formal

governance have been discussed from a broader regional perspective in Chapter 1. Vanuatu is an emerging state where relations between state institutions and society are relatively undeveloped. The issue at the present is how "the people" are faring in strengthening their state and society in ways that count.

As an archipelago of majority Melanesian peoples, Vanuatu has achieved an admirable sense of national identity and coherence in the two decades since independence. This may be due to the unfortunate irony that ni-Vanuatu nationalism was forged in the context of the inadequacies of the joint British-French colonial presence in their New Hebrides[4] "condominium." From the late 1970s, a group of young educated New Hebrideans, with Anglican priest Walter Lini in the lead, were able to galvanize the people into effective and successful anticolonial and proindependence action.[5]

In the first decade of independence, this leadership maintained a quasi-revolutionary atmosphere that mostly attributed the young state's inadequacies to the intervention of outsiders. In the second independent decade, the challenges of leadership and state building taxed the abilities of the new elite considerably, and in the process removed any illusions about the speed with which this small Pacific Island state could move toward prosperity. In the contemporary period, the inability of the governance system to meet expanding social and economic expectations for advancement and to reform itself has rendered the performance of the state the principal source of instability and a major threat to the long-term sustainability of the nation. Issues of most concern include the quality of political leadership (and corruption in public office), the instability of the executive branch of government, effective oversight of the public sector and delivery of services (particularly health and education), and economic growth and multiplication of employment opportunities. There is a lack of articulation between government and the customary governance mechanisms that continue to carry considerable weight in ni-Vanuatu society. This cursory summary of the postindependence period suggests a transformation in risk from conflict based on clash of political aspirations, which took place in the lead-up to independence, to risk of conflict generated by failure of the system as a whole to meet the nation's developing needs.

While the New Hebrideans struggled to achieve independence, there were threats to national unity during the final phases of the passage to independence.[6] On the northern island of Santo, the Nagriamel movement attempted to declare its own republic,[7] and there was also agitation toward autonomy and/or independence on the southern island of Tanna.[8] These conflicts, plus the later violent independence struggles and repression in neighboring French-controlled New Caledonia (discussed in Chapters 6 and 7), prompted an earlier phase of international anxieties about Melanesian insecurity.

As it turned out, the young state was able to marshal sufficient domestic and international support to suppress these separatist movements and ensure state unity. The attainment of independence in July 1980 brought to an end the Anglo-French "condominium"—the form of joint government established in 1914.

While the majority of the population is Melanesian, there are small minorities of Polynesians, Chinese, Fijians, Vietnamese, Tongans, and Europeans. Domestically, ni-Vanuatu people identify themselves with their home island—whether Santo, Malekula, Tanna, Pentecost, and such—more than they do with the label "ni-Vanuatu." However, whereas ethnic diversity has often been identified as a trigger for political conflict, this has not been the case in Vanuatu. Conflict is not structurally embedded in relations between ethnic or linguistic communities, though differences in culture[9] and religion[10] have been a source of conflict in the past.[11]

■ Sources of Conflict

Land, Economy, and Finance

Ownership of land, and land usage, go to the heart of access and privilege and have the potential to give rise to future conflicts.[12] As Spike Boydell has commented, land tenure systems are defined socially; they are constructed to accommodate a particular way of life.[13] The formal market economy and the resulting commodification of land are driving alternative forms of land tenure and land use. There is both confusion and tension around a wide variety of interactions between customary and commercial land usage; these are not simply economic interactions and tensions, but also concern changing and competing forms of power and social definition. At independence, all freehold ownership of land was returned to customary owners, and a system for long-term lease was established. In subsequent years, those with best knowledge of the law have been able to convert leases for their beneficial use. This has also led to the establishment of some nouveau riche new "millennia chiefs" (successful capitalists who hold economic power without the benefit of customary titles). Such social change has to some extent challenged customary authority and thus challenged the traditional systems of arbitration in land dispute resolution.

Moreover, land in the urban and peri-urban environment of the capital, Port Vila, is subject to particular demographic pressure and could be the focus of significant friction. These factors combine to suggest that whereas land issues have not been a trigger for significant conflict since independence, current practices relating to legal title, and the pressures of urbanization, will become issues of concern in the not too distant future.

In a land-related issue, management of the environment and the sustainability of logging practices have not become as problematic in Vanuatu to the extent that they have in neighboring countries, such as Papua New Guinea and the Solomon Islands, where logging "has amounted to nothing short of the rape and pillage of their national heritage and has, all too often, come hand in hand with corruption. Local officials and landowners have discovered, too late, that clear felling leaves them not only without their forests but without even the subsistence living on which they have relied for thousands of years."[14]

A major concern for Vanuatu, as for the other "small island developing states" of the Pacific, and a potential catalyst for social unrest, is the slow development of Vanuatu's economy and its inability to meet the aspirations of citizens in both village and urban areas. In 2002 the UN's Human Development Index (HDI) for Vanuatu was assessed at 0.57, placing it in the "medium human development" category of nations, at the same level as Cambodia and Botswana.[15] The scale of the challenges facing the country give added significance to the "governance deficit" already noted.

High population growth and slow rates of economic development, especially in the outer islands, are yielding negative economic growth. An Asian Development Bank (ADB) study released in 2004 reported annual growth in gross domestic product (GDP) at 0.8 percent, against a Pacific average of 0.9 percent, and annual population growth at 2.6 percent, slightly higher than the regional average of 2.4 percent. Put together, this amounts to a negative annual GDP per capita growth rate (1.7 percent).[16] In the long term, this situation must be addressed by some means. Other volatile and potentially destabilizing social conditions flow from or are exacerbated by weakness in the formal economy. High levels of youth unemployment intensify the demand for economic growth and generate urban drift. At the same time, urbanization places stress on land tenure arrangements around towns (particularly the capital, Port Vila) and weakens traditional mechanisms of social control, leading to increased social violence, social alienation, and risky behavior.[17]

In 2004 the ADB assessed the country as having a range of good prospects, but in the context of an unstable and at times fragile policy and legal environment: "Although Vanuatu has good growth prospects due to abundant natural resources and increased tourism potential, its growth was hampered in 2003 by frequent shifts in policies, the high cost of doing business, and difficulties in enforcing contractual agreements. The country suffers from low adult literacy and primary and secondary school enrolment rates and from poor access to health and social services."[18] The ADB's strategy seeks to improve economic management and governance, reduce poverty, and create an enabling environment for private sector development. Vanuatu's economy is dependent on international trade and is vulnerable to shifts in world market prices. Tourism and an offshore banking center are two of the major sectors of the economy. Together with legitimate banking and investment ventures, the country has gained a reputation for less reputable financial practices.[19] In 2004 the Australian Securities and Investments Commission took legal action to control the activities of "investment clubs" registered in Vanuatu but operating in Australia in ways that contravened legislation on corporate activity.[20] The presence of a moderate-size tourism industry has not proven conflictual to date, but given the importance of the tourism industry to the state's economy, any signs of discontent with tourism-related issues that do appear, will have to be taken seriously.

Labor disputes are also a potential source of conflict.[21] The country's first general strike, in February 1994, in support of public servants who had been seeking a wage increase, resulted in sporadic violence, sackings, and suspended sentences. This long-running strike affected the postal, health, and agricultural sectors badly. The government dismissed all daily-rate workers, suspended all strikers (approximately 1,200), and reportedly prohibited state-owned media from airing union views.[22]

The Governance System

Both state and nonstate elements of governance are highly relevant to discussion of Vanuatu. The constitution of Vanuatu establishes a "modified Westminster" form of government, comprising an elected parliament, from which the prime minister is in turn elected and the executive government is formed, and an independent judiciary. The head of state is a president who holds mostly ceremonial powers and who is elected by the parliament plus the heads of the provincial bodies. The members of parliament are determined by the people at regularly scheduled general elections. The constitution of Vanuatu allows parliament to make laws for village or island courts;[23] seven such courts have been established.[24] Each consists of three lay justices, one of whom must be a chief. The body of decisions of the island courts provides "guidance" for new cases, but not precedent. Settlements may be based on custom, as far as the Supreme Court. Lawyers have no right to appear, and there are no technical rules (e.g., for evidence).

The national constitution recognizes custom chiefs but does not define their role in decisionmaking about nontraditional matters. Many ni-Vanuatu, however, regard custom leaders as the "moral anchor" of the nation (although even the notion of "chief" itself is not uniform throughout the archipelago).[25] There is a national council of chiefs (Malvatumauri, created at independence), but its role is not clearly determined. Its members are elected every four years under supervision of the national electoral commission.[26] Custom chiefs are appointed to local government councils on the instruction of the minister of home affairs.[27] Although chiefs traditionally had a role in what are now demarcated as penal and civil jurisdictions, they now only possess an advisory role, and need specific rules to guide them. In some instances, chiefs are sitting as courts at village level, and hearing cases beyond their jurisdiction. In 1997, custom chiefs from four villages on Ambae established their own sixteen-page constitution to protect and safeguard the general welfare of their people, to protect and promote traditional values, and to resolve disputes and disagreements. Tanna chiefs have also attempted to codify "Tanna law." Chiefs on the southern island of Aneityum have also been seeking greater constitutional recognition.[28]

The recognition of *kastom* (custom) is not without complications.[29] Naturally, not all traditional leaders view the nation's problems in the same way, and there has been division within the Malvatumauri. Additionally, tradition in most ni-Vanuatu societies accorded greater rights to men than to women, and this imbalance, while addressed in modern law, has not been altered much in everyday practice. Women's groups, such as the National Council of Women, are therefore engaged in ongoing struggle with such traditionally patriarchal structures as the Malvatumauri, in order to give the rights of women equal status. This is often regarded in Vanuatu as a tension between international norms, such as the Convention on the Elimination of All Forms of Discrimination Against Women, and customary values.

In structural terms, the constitutional system satisfies most descriptions of "democratic societies."[30] Detailed investigation of the system in operation, however, provides insight into to a range of issues that have given rise to conflict.

Executive Instability

The executive has rarely been stable since independence, and governments have fallen through use of the no-confidence option on multiple occasions. Box 11.1 outlines the pattern of executive instability that has persistently deprived the state of clear political leadership due to parliamentary fluidity triggered by weak party affiliations and use of the no-confidence motion.

For the first decade or so following independence, Vanuatu's politics were grouped around an anglophone group (the Vanuaku Pati [VP]) and a francophone group (the Union of Moderate Parties [UMP]). More recently, however, executive government has often been formed by a dominant group *within* one of these parties, in association with cooperating groups *within* the group who are otherwise in opposition.

The following sequence of events illustrates the kind of political maneuvering that characterizes parliamentary politics in Vanuatu. When the government of Edward Natapei (a subgroup of the VP) expelled the UMP from its coalition in 2003, the opposition, led by Serge Vohor, twice moved and then withdrew a motion of no-confidence seeking to win back executive power. The Natapei government replaced the UMP with the National United Party, the Greens, and independents. Notwithstanding this, UMP member Maxime Carlot Korman crossed the floor in December to join the ruling coalition. In June 2004, Prime Minister Natapei dissolved parliament rather than face a no-confidence motion (his party, the VP, was split, and three senior members, including a former prime minister, Donald Kalpokas, signed the no-confidence motion). Following the subsequent snap election, the National United Party and caretaker prime minister Natapei boycotted the first sessions of the new parliament in an effort to stall the vote for the next prime minister as long as possible: they now lacked the numbers to prevent the UMP and other supporters from electing Serge Vohor as the next prime minister, and several weeks passed before the parties completed negotiations that finally resulted in Vohor's election to the post.

But the identification of a new government did not complete the cycle. The defection of three government MPs one week after the election in protest at not getting the portfolios they had been promised triggered the filing of a motion of no-confidence by then–opposition leader Ham Lini. Within two weeks, Lini's party had joined the Vohor government, and on 26 August 2004 the parliamentary speaker agreed to Lini's request for withdrawal of the motion. The remaining opposition parties petitioned the court to order the reinstatement of the motion on the basis that it had the requisite number of signatures—an argument with which Chief Justice Vincent Lunabek concurred. All of this is, to be sure, quite complex to the outside observer. Parliament was ordered to meet on 1 September 2004. By November, with the government of Serge Vohor itself now in jeopardy (Vohor's failed attempt to switch the state's recognition from China to Taiwan is described below), an attempt was made to alter the constitution in yet another attempt to nullify the effect of a no-confidence vote.[31] This effort was to no avail and on 11 December 2004 parliament elected Ham Lini as the next prime minister.

The extent of the ineffectiveness of parliament that has resulted from this partisan maneuvering has never been adequately assessed.[32] One argument suggests that firmer control of political parties will provide stability to the party system; in Vanuatu—as elsewhere in the Pacific—active measures have been attempted to counter the effects of party-hopping. The Members of Parliament (Vacation of Seats) Act of 1983, for instance, attempts to thwart the problem of party defections by providing that an MP vacates his or her seat if "having been a candidate of a party and elected to parliament he resigns from that party" (sec. 2[f]). The act also requires parliament's standing orders to "make provision for the identification and recognition of the leader in parliament of every political party and for otherwise giving effect to this section" (sec. 4[5]). Whereas such rules limit transfer between

Box 11.1   Patterns of Political Instability in Vanuatu

1980
30 July: Independence from France and UK. Independence constitution.

1988
16 May: Riots in Port Vila.

December: President Ati George Sokomanu attempts to dissolve parliament, is charged with sedition by Prime Minister Walter Lini, and jailed.

1991
September: Donald Kalpokas replaces Lini as Vanuaku Party (VP) leader and prime minister.

2 December: General elections. Coalition formed by Union of Moderate Parties (UMP) and National United Party (NUP); Maxime Carlot Korman becomes prime minister, but party associations are fluid; of 46 total seats: UMP 19, NUP 10, VP 10, Melanesian Progressive Party (MPP) 4, Tan Union Party (TUP) 1, Nagriamel 1, Friend 1.

1994
2 March: J. M. Leye elected president.

1995
November: Fourth general elections, with the UMP divided in the lead-up. When none of the three main parties obtains sufficient votes to form a government, intense lobbying takes place and two UMP groups maneuver separately to form coalitions with other parties. Korman forms a negotiating committee to discuss a new coalition arrangement with other parties. Rialuth Serge Vohor claims this is against the UMP constitution and applies to the Supreme Court to have Korman suspended from the coalition. At issue is whether the party president or the party's national executive has the power to suspend a party member. Meanwhile, six other UMP members ally with Donald Kalpokas's Unity Front and gain office with Korman as prime minister. A petition against the government's legitimacy fails in the Supreme Court.[a]

(continues)

21 December: Serge Vohor replaces Korman as prime minister.

1996

February: President Leye considers dissolving parliament, but the conflict is resolved according to constitutional rules.

8 February: Eight members of the ruling UMP side with the opposition Unity Front; Vohor resigns after forty-eight days to avoid facing a no-confidence motion filed by an opposition party and eight dissident members of his own party. Vohor subsequently revoked his resignation, arguing that parliament had not met to endorse his decision and that neither the constitution nor standing orders are specific on such details.

20 February: Vohor's party boycotts an extraordinary session of parliament, which is adjourned until 23 February, when Vohor's predecessor, Korman, regains the premiership.

August–September: In August, a no-confidence motion signed by twenty-seven of the fifty members of parliament is submitted, to be debated at a special session of parliament on September 6. Korman's government boycotts the extraordinary session of parliament and invites leaders of opposition groups to join the government. The Supreme Court accepts a petition from the opposition ordering that parliament sit, and on 25 September Korman is defeated in a no-confidence motion (twenty-seven votes to twenty-two).

October: Vohor regains the prime ministership. Barak Sope becomes deputy prime minister and minister of commerce. Twenty-five days later, Vohor sacks Sope and his allies Lava, Boulekone, and Ravutia.[b]

1997

20 May: Korman withdraws a no-confidence motion after negotiating with Vohor to recombine their UMP factions and after the formation of a coalition with the Melanesian Progressive Party. Vohor thus remains prime minister. His 29-member coalition government comprises 20 UMP members, 5 MPP members, 3 NUP members, and 1 Free Melanesian Party member. A week later, the VP, now dismissed from Vohor's coalition government, lodges a no-confidence motion.

November: Vohor resigns. Parliament proves unable to resolve the issue. President Leye dissolves parliament and orders general elections.[c] President Leye's order is later challenged in the Supreme

(continues)

(Box 11.1 continued)

Court, but in January 1998 the Appeals Court rules the order valid. Ambae chiefs write a constitution for their island.

1998
6 March: General election; seats in the 52-member parliament are won by the VP (18), the UMP (12), the NUP (11), the MPP (incorporating Fren Melanesian Party) (6), John Frum (2), independents (2), and the Vanuatu Republican Party (1). Donald Kalpokas becomes prime minister.

1999
November: Kalpokas's government falls; Barak Sope becomes prime minister. Presidential election is held, with Father John Bennet Bani becoming president after several attempts to secure the constitutionally required two-thirds majority.

2001
13 April: Sope's government falls; Edward Natapei becomes prime minister.

2002
2 May: General election.

2003
December: Maxime Carlot Korman crosses the floor of parliament and joins the ruling coalition, less than a week after the opposition had abandoned another attempt to gain a vote of no-confidence. Prime Minister Natapei now has the backing of 34 out of 52 members of parliament.

2004
June: Natapei's government opts for dissolution of parliament rather than face a no-confidence motion.

July: General election. Serge Vohor becomes prime minister. *September 10:* Vohor visits China and reaffirms the "One China" policy.

November 2: Vohor signs a document establishing diplomatic relations with Taiwan.

(Box 11.1 continued)

December: A no-confidence vote removes Vohor. Ham Lini is elected prime minister.

> *Source:* Updated from Hassall and Saunders, *Asia Pacific Constitutional Systems.*
> *Notes:* a. David Ambrose, "A Coup That Failed? Recent Political Events in Vanuatu," *Journal of Pacific History* 31(3), 1996, pp. 53–66.
> b. Pauline Swain, "Vanuatu Politicians Revel in Power Games," *The Dominion* (Wellington), 29 August 1996, p. 8; "Vanuatu: Turmoil Endemic," *New Zealand Herald,* 2 October 1996; "Premier Serge Vohor Revokes Resignation," *Radio Australia External Service* (Melbourne), 20 February 1996; "Sope, Three Allies Sacked," *The Courier-Mail,* 28 October 1996; "Vanuatu Turmoil," *The Courier-Mail,* 26 October 1996, p. 33.
> c. This was a time of intense rivalry between former prime minister Korman and UMP president and then–prime minister Vohor. Korman established a new political party, Ripabliken Paty Blong Vanuatu, to contest the March 1998 elections separately from the Union of Moderate Parties.

parties, the prevalent practice has been movement of parties between coalitions, rather than movement of individual MPs between parties.

■ Impact of Political Contest

Head of State

While the presidency is essentially a ceremonial position, each incumbent since independence has played a significant role in political crises. In 1988 the president unconstitutionally dissolved the government of Walter Lini and appointed an interim government, but this failed, whereupon he was arrested on Lini's orders and subsequently convicted for sedition.[33] In 1991 a different president was instrumental in ending Walter Lini's time as prime minister.

Even more dramatically, in 1996 a group of soldiers abducted President Jean Marie Leye to discuss with him a long-standing dispute concerning payment of salaries. Although the president was returned safely to the capital from the island of Malekula, almost half the defense force was arrested and charged with kidnapping, carrying weapons, and unlawful assembly. The prime minister informed parliament that the soldiers had planned to establish a military government, suspend the constitution, and impose martial law. Struggles between the presidency and the legislature marked 1997.

Elections of presidents have also at times been torrid, with boycotts by opposition members of parliament (1994) and discovery of a past history of criminal convictions of the successful candidate, leading to disqualification and a lengthy period of confusion. The election of the successor in this case required several sessions before the new president—Kalkot Matas Kelekele—emerged with the required majority.

The Judiciary

In Vanuatu, perhaps more than elsewhere in the Pacific, the courts have been relied on extensively to adjudicate what have been essentially political disputes.[34] While in one sense this can be viewed as the normal constitutional role of the judiciary in any state, its too-frequent use can lead to friction between constitutional bodies, to the detriment of national stability and integrity.

The role of the courts in determining the scope of executive power can be illustrated through an example from the 1990s, which though vividly suggesting the scale and frequency of judicial involvement in the settlement of political disputes, also points to the ways in which judicial and other legal actors have become excessively entangled in these disputes. At the same time, judicial involvement in conflict resolution in Vanuatu also points to the resilience of the court system and to its stabilizing role in the constitutional order.

The Supreme Court is repeatedly drawn into disputes between parliamentary factions. Following the chief justice's rejection in March 1996 of an application by former prime minister Serge Vohor that he be reinstated to office, the court ordered that Vohor and other members of his former government return all government property in their possession, and pay the costs of the case. The then-government faced a no-confidence motion the following September in which the opposition parties (Vohor allies) were sure to hold the numbers. After the government canceled a parliamentary session, opposition MPs once more petitioned the Supreme Court, this time to order parliament's resumption.

Although the court ruled that parliament should sit, the parliamentary speaker defied the order and canceled the session, arguing that for technical reasons, the court's ruling was incorrect. Opposition MPs petitioned the Supreme Court to order its resumption.[35] Opposition leader Willie Jimmy threatened to prosecute the speaker for contempt of court and called on the country's police and paramilitary mobile force to obey the Supreme Court rather than the government.

The fate of the chief justice was thereafter dictated by political events. In late 1996 the judicial services commission found him guilty of "serious misconduct" (he issued arrest warrants for the military leaders who had abducted President Leye and stood accused of trying to undermine an agreement ending their pay revolt). President Leye terminated his appointment as a judge in the Supreme Court, and he was ordered to leave the country.

Although the chief justice appealed his dismissal, and the Supreme Court ordered the government not to attempt deporting him until completion of the hearing, the former chief justice was gone before the end of October.

Constitutional Review

There have been several attempts at review of the constitution of Vanuatu. Although these have not been specifically targeted at reducing political instability or preventing violent conflict, they have focused on areas of great relevance to potential conflict: relations with custom authorities, centralization and decentralization, and more careful administration of democratic processes. There have been moves to increase and give greater constitutional clarity to the role of custom and the authority of chiefs and to restrict the activities of religious groups, but these have not eventuated. Some fundamental changes have been made to the system of government, however. In 1994 the country's eleven provincial councils were replaced with six local government regions.[36] Although there has been some resistance to these amalgamations, this level of government appears to be growing in significance. The new arrangements have also required elaborate provisions for the administration of democratic processes, with, for example, the establishment of an electoral dispute committee set up to review complaints about provincial elections.

The Security Forces

Vanuatu has no regular military force, though the national police force includes a 300-strong paramilitary mobile force. The security forces have at times become embroiled in the country's political conflicts. The training of military personnel in Libya in the 1980s can be regarded as a political statement as much as it concerned the development of security capacities and prompted considerable concern in Australia. As outlined earlier, the mobile force kidnapped the president in 1996—an action that could also be construed as an attempted coup—and provoked riots in 1998. It is worth noting here that those riots were quelled by the traditional chiefs. According to Carmody, the mobile force demonstrates the "classic problem" of training security forces in an image of the West without due regard for the cultural and political environment in which they operate.[37] Anthony Regan's discussion, in Chapter 5, of the impact of police mobile squads in significantly escalating the conflict in Bougainville, is another example of the destructive potential of inappropriate armed police behavior.

More recently, police commissioner Robert De Niro Obed was suspended in September 2004 following his attempt to arrest Prime Minister Vohor. Although the commissioner was acting on a warrant issued by the public prosecutor to arrest the prime minister for contempt of court, the prime minister managed to negotiate replacement of the arrest order with a court summons. The Supreme Court dismissed the charges against the prime minister on grounds that his comments were made under parliamentary privilege; nevertheless, the prime minister established a commission of inquiry to determine who had laid charges against him and placed considerable political pressure on the office of the public prosecutor. This episode, occurring at the same time as other elite conflicts in 2004, illustrates yet another dimension that interferes with the flow of governance activities in Vanuatu.

Elections and Democracy

The people voted in general elections in Vanuatu seven times between 1980 and 2004. The composition of governments from 1998 to 2004 demonstrates a particular Melanesian political style, characterized by many political parties and independent members in parliament (see Table 11.1). While each of the elections since independence has marked a crucial phase in the nation's development, and some have been held in the midst of considerable political turmoil, they have not been a source of violent conflict, with one relatively minor exception.[38]

Corruption in Public Life

The active presence of an ombudsman in Vanuatu has resulted in considerable exposure of abuses in political and public offices, and has had a visible impact on political life in the country.[39] An ombudsman act was passed in 1995, and a leadership code in 1996. Marie-Noelle Ferrieux Patterson, appointed ombudsman in 1994, vigorously reported abuses throughout her term of office.[40]

However, criminal conviction or other forms of sanction have not followed in equal numbers. While this pattern of exposure without conviction may indicate a lack of legal capacity, it may also indicate a lack of public consciousness of the situation. For example, in July 1996 the ombudsman

Table 11.1 Changes in Government Composition, Vanuatu, 1998–2004

Election	Number of Parties	Number of Candidates	Number of Independents
March 1998	10	216	62
May 2002	15	257	68
July 2004	18	235	73

reported that the prime minister and the finance minister, Barak Sope, signed letters of guarantee worth twice the island country's annual budget— US$100 million.[41] This put political pressure on both, and Sope was dropped from cabinet and so moved into opposition.

In November the ombudsman recommended that Barak Sope never again be considered for public or ministerial office. The struggle between the two intensified, moving into the courts. In November 1997 the parliament passed an act seeking to abolish the ombudsman, but the president refused to sign it into law. The ombudsman was at the time calling on the prime minister and foreign minister to resign over the sale of passports to a number of Asian businessmen. Other reports by the ombudsman were impacting on additional areas of public life. In January 1998 a report on the preferential treatment of politicians by National Provident Fund officials provoked riots at the fund's Port Vila headquarters and prompted the government to declare a two-week state of emergency.

Of the key public figures mentioned in these reports, only Sope was removed from office through sentencing. In 2002 he received a three-year jail term for forging signatures on government guarantees worth almost US$50 million dollars when he was prime minister in 2000. Four months into his sentence, however, Sope was released through a full presidential pardon on grounds of poor health. This gave him time to recontest—and win—in November 2003 the Efate rural seat he had been required by his conviction to vacate. Following the 2004 snap election, Sope was briefly foreign minister in the Vohor government. This incident, particularly Sope's reelection, also illustrates the lack of public demand for accountability in public office. It indicates the need not just for improved probity in the political elite, but also for greater understanding by the population of the role of political leaders, and for the emergence of a more informed and active citizenship.

International Relations

The political leadership in Vanuatu has always voiced its concern at the influence of foreign advisers and foreign interests within the country. All the while, these same leaders have formed close alliances with foreign political forces most suitable to them. International relations of most significance to Vanuatu have been those with Australia, Britain, France, China, the United States, and other Pacific countries. Vanuatu is one of the major champions of West Papua's independence movement.

Relations with the United States have been framed in recent times by Vanuatu's inclusion in a list of countries that qualified for access to a "millennium development fund"—an initiative of the George W. Bush administration announced in 2004.[42] This unsolicited inclusion on the list, to a country that has repeatedly expressed its concern at the efforts by foreign actors to influence its domestic affairs, produced a somewhat quizzical response: while any country would welcome the promise of large-scale development assistance, there is no guarantee that Vanuatu will act rapidly or in the ways required to benefit from this program. The deportation in October 2004 of a French citizen who had been advising the Green movement and subsequent parliamentary party since the 1990s demonstrated the government's concern about the intervention of foreigners in domestic politics. The deportation was intended as "a warning to other foreigners who have no genuine intentions to stay in Vanuatu." The state had "information on many others who have been manipulating the situations in the country," who would be "expelled if the situation demanded it."[43] This call for review of foreign influence in the country struck a cord with many ni-Vanuatu, since an Asian Development Bank–designed comprehensive reform program (1997–1998), aimed at reducing public expenditure, had the effect of eliminating public service positions while seemingly increasing opportunities for expatriate advisers.

The China-Taiwan contest. Due to economic vulnerability, a number of small Pacific Island states have shown a willingness to "trade" diplomatic support over one issue or another in exchange for what is hoped will be generous aid (e.g., see also the discussion of Nauru, in Chapter 12, in this regard). This is perhaps most evident in relation to formal recognition of the People's Republic of China or of the Republic of China (Taiwan). The Solomon Islands, for example, recognizes Taiwan, but allegiances may shift. The political contest between the People's Republic of China and Taiwan has also included a Vanuatu chapter. Notwithstanding the fact that China had established good relations with Vanuatu over two decades since independence, then–prime minister Serge Vohor made secret visit to Taiwan—in addition to his state visit to China—soon after taking office in September 2004. The new prime minister appears to have calculated that a shift of recognition from China to Taiwan would attract an aid package from Taiwan significantly greater than that offered by China. He miscalculated, on the other hand, the reactions of China and his cabinet alike. Not having taken his cabinet or senior public servants into his confidence, and provoking the inevitable response from the parliamentary opposition and from China, the Vohor government was immediately destabilized. Seeking to justify his actions, Vohor claimed that Vanuatu was not gaining sufficient benefit from its partners and that Taiwan was offering much-needed financial assistance.[44] Media reports suggested that the Vohor government was anticipating Taiwanese aid of US$28 million in 2005,[45] and that improper payments had been made to ni-Vanuatu politicians to facilitate the diplomatic switch.[46]

Vohor's action provoked a strong response from the Chinese, who did not entertain the proposition that Vanuatu could recognize both China and Taiwan.[47] China and Vanuatu established diplomatic relations in 1982, and many in the ni-Vanuatu government and public sector had formed good relations with the Chinese over a period of two decades.[48] Vanuatu's parliament building was provided through Chinese aid. Although there were indications that Vohor's Council of Ministers had convinced him to dissolve the proposed relationship with Taiwan, the political damage had been done, and his government lost a motion of no-confidence in November.

Relations with Australia. Although Australia is one of Vanuatu's most significant partners in trade and development aid, political relations between the two countries have often been tense. During the short-lived Vohor administration of 2004 described above, tensions were attributed on the Australian side to the Vanuatu administration's lack of commitment to principles of transparency and accountability in governance, and on the ni-Vanuatu side to Australia's apparent interference in matters of national sovereignty and respect for cultural differences.

Upon his appointment as foreign minister in the Vohor administration, Barak Sope swiftly called for a review of the position of Australian and New Zealand advisers and ordered Australian Federal Police officers out of the republic. He argued that the police officers had interfered in the country's internal affairs, but also candidly admitted the move was part of his revenge agenda.[49] The repercussions grew larger with the passage of time: Prime Minister Vohor intervened to allow the police officers to return; Sope was removed from the foreign affairs portfolio in a matter of months; and the incident added to Australia's resolve to press upon the government a more disciplined approach to good-governance principles of transparency and accountability.[50] Australian representatives were dispatched to Vila to impress on the government the gravity of the situation from the Australian perspective, an act interpreted by some members of the public as further evidence of Australia's belligerent stance toward the Melanesian states.

Civil Society and the Media

Given the turbulence in Vanuatu's political life at national level, the resilience within ni-Vanuatu society is all the more noteworthy. Ni-Vanuatu people have by and large been spectators of these conflicts rather than protagonists. Such detachment from government, however, means that the elite conflicts continue largely unchecked; the UN's 1996 report on human development in Vanuatu expressed concern at the lack of community engagement in governance, especially at local and provincial levels—particularly since ni-Vanuatu society is based on communities that are well able to express their needs and are well placed to partner with government agencies.[51]

Access to accurate information is essential to decisionmaking by all actors. As with other small Pacific Island nations, civil society agencies in Vanuatu, including professional associations, the media, and nongovernmental organizations (NGOs), are steadily strengthening their capacities and activities, while at the same time being subjected to considerable pressure from state agencies. In this scattered island nation, the reach of these organizations remains limited, however; in 2004, Transparency International estimated that radio reached only 40 percent of the national population.[52] Moreover, the government has traditionally exercised considerable control over the media, whether privately owned or national. Threats to revoke the work permits of journalists, or the licenses of publications, have been noted in surveys of human rights practices. On the other hand, the Pacific regional news agency *(PacNews)* operated freely from headquarters in Vanuatu from 1994, until its recent amalgamation with the Pacific Islands News Association (PINA).

A range of NGOs have been established since the formation of a human rights forum in 1994, and some collective interests are overseen by the Vanuatu Association of NGOs (VANGO). International social movements, religious groups, and intergovernmental organizations also actively participate in development projects in Vanuatu.[53] The Vanuatu chapter of Transparency International has recently developed a prominent profile in the country, educating the public and members of agencies about the values and practices of good governance, and strongly critiquing government practices.[54] When the Vohor government sought swift passage of constitutional amendments, for instance, Transparency International quickly publicized the constitutional requirement to hold a referendum.[55] Strengthening of the capacity of NGOs and other elements of civil society is an important aspect of strengthening the governance capacity of the country as a whole, since experience suggests that a responsive and principled civil society presence provides an additional accountability mechanism for government. Programs that enhance not only civil society capacity but also relations between civil society and the state may prove most beneficial, since the idea of public officials reaching into the community and establishing policy networks (and even implementation networks) is not currently widespread.

■ Conclusion

I have argued in this chapter that instability in the structure of the executive branch of government is one of the main threats to the security of Vanuatu's system of governance. Much of the conflict afflicting public life in Vanuatu occurs at the elite level, among holders of constitutional offices. This pattern of conflict is in contrast to social and political contexts in which conflicts emerge primarily at grassroots levels, and are manifest at higher levels through interest representation. Such is not the case in Vanuatu: the conflicts between Vohor and Korman, Sope, Kalpokas, Kilman, and Lini, cannot be said to represent conflicts among the peoples or communities of Efate, Tanna, Malekula, Santo, Pentecost, or other islands or tribes. For this reason they are described here as conflicts among the elites. Their impact on grassroots communities comes through the neglect of public responsibilities by focusing on political struggle rather than on improving governance. However, the weakness of government also means that complex issues facing Vanuatu, around land tenure, the need for economic growth, and management of the social volatility inherent in high youth unemployment, rapid urbanization, and the fast pace of social change, do not benefit from effective government leadership.

The resilience of Vanuatu society still stems from the continued allegiance to "custom," which provides a strong sense of culture and tradition for the ni-Vanuatu people as they make progress with nation building. Michael Morgan, citing the sentiments of a chief from the island of Erromango, points to the emergence of growing disaffection at the local level concerning the inability of the national government to plan for and deliver services effectively: "Before Independence, the chiefs held power and everything worked correctly. Immediately after Independence it was the Vanua'aku Pati which rules. Then the government split and everything deteriorated. Unity doesn't any longer seem possible with politics. Now we must go back to the chiefs and enable them to sort out how we can again find the pathway to unity."[56]

There have been assessments of Vanuatu's parliament, but not of the constitution as a whole.[57] On the basis of the evidence presented above, any future review could well examine the suitability of a Westminster-style legislature and party system to microstates such as Vanuatu, in addition to seeking ways to strengthen articulation between the coexisting traditional and modern governance systems.

This chapter has suggested that the major source of instability in Vanuatu stems from the operation of the governance system itself. In the lead-up to independence, separatist aspirations in the northern and southern islands of the New Hebrides threatened the unity of the nation and provided the specter of long-term collective violence of a political nature, but this threat was met. Since then, concern has focused on the ability of the state system as a whole to deliver adequate governance outcomes, in terms of policy and law, economic growth, and infrastructural development. The still-undeveloped connection between government and communities is both a consequence of but also a contributor to the weakness of the formal governance system. Stronger engagement between government and communities is an essential element of improved governance. Such engagement is likely to draw more systematically on the participation of customary authorities, as well as other community actors. There also needs to be greater recognition of the equal status of women, and of the need to ensure their education and participation in public life. There are few women serving in municipal or village councils, churches, or chambers of commerce. More broadly, there is need for reconsideration of some aspects of the constitutional system, in ways that stabilize the framing of executive power, and encourage more effective implementation of state services. Emerging civil society and community actors can play a facilitating role in educating the public and leaders alike in such good-governance values as accountability, transparency, and responsibility.

▓ Notes

I am grateful to Jeannette Bolenga for providing background information for this chapter, as well as for reviewing the text.

1. "Warning by Vanuatu's President," ABC Radio Australia News, 3 September 2004, available at http://www.abc.net.au/ra/newstories/ranewsstories_1191115.htm (accessed 12 December 2004).

2. A recent description of this cycle is provided in Morgan, "Political Fragmentation and the Policy Environment." See also Muria, "The Role of the Courts and Legal Profession."

3. Rodman, "The Law of the State and the State of the Law," p. 56.

4. Before independence, Vanuatu was called the New Hebrides.

5. Lini, *Beyond Pandemonium.*

6. See Weightman and Lini, *Vanuatu;* Kele-Kele, "The Emergence of Political Parties"; Lini, *Beyond Pandemonium;* Molisa, Vurobaravu, and Van Trease, "Vanuatu."

7. Shears, *The Coconut War.*

8. Doorn, *A Blueprint for a New Nation;* Kolig, "*Kastom,* Cargo and the Construction of Utopia on Santo."

9. MacClancy, "*Vanuatu* and *Kastom.*"

10. Niditauae, *Pastors in Politics.*

11. A chief from Santo obtained publicity in 2004 for deciding to reject Christian belief and return to custom. There was, too, conflict on Tanna in 2004 between the adherents of the Jon Frum movement and the Prophet Fred. The media reported "a bloody encounter with knives, slingshots, axes and bows and arrows, Jon Frum believers clashed with the members of a breakaway Christian sect led by a softly spoken villager Fred Nasse, who calls himself Prophet Fred. Six houses and a thatched Presbyterian church were burnt down during a battle that involved 400 islanders." N. Squires, "Vanuatu Villagers in Bloody Cult Clash," *Sun-Herald,* 9 May 2004, available at http://www.smh.com.au/articles/2004/05/08/1083911455208.html?from=storyrhs&oneclick=true (accessed 24 January 2007).

12. Larmour, "Land Policy and Decolonisation in Melanesia"; Lindstrom, *Achieving Wisdom;* Van Trease, "The History of Land and Property Rights in Vanuatu"; Van Trease, *The Politics of Land in Vanuatu.*

13. Spike Boydell, "Coups, Constitutions, and Confusion in Fiji," *Land Tenure Centre Newsletter* (80), Fall 2000, pp. 1–7, 10.

14. J. Garrat, "Pacific Island Economies: Can They Make a Go of It?" *Charting the Pacific,* Radio Australia, available at http://www.abc.net.au/ra/pacific/places/jemima.htm (accessed 18 August 2005).

15. UNDP, *Human Development Report, 2004.*

16. Asian Development Bank, *Responding to the Priorities of the Poor.*

17. Bakeo, *The Crisis of Post-Independence Development in Vanuatu.*

18. "A Fact Sheet: Vanuatu and ADB Data as of 31 December," 2003, available at http://www.adb.org/documents/fact_sheets/van.asp (accessed 12 December 2004).

19. Van Fossen, "Financial Frauds and Pseudo-States in the Pacific Islands."

20. "ASIC Looks Into Vanuatu Clubs," *The Age,* July 15, available at http://www.theage.com.au/articles/2004/07/15/1089694476364.html?oneclick=true (accessed 20 August 2004).

21. Prasad, "Industrial Relations in Vanuatu."

22. US Department of State, *Vanuatu Human Rights Practices.*

23. In the instance of the Ambrym Island courts, established in October 1988, the Islands Court Act 10 of 1983 delimits the courts' criminal jurisdiction offenses under the penal code, offenses against the joint regulations, and offenses against Ambrym regional laws. In its civil jurisdiction, the court is limited to disputes concerning ownership of land irrespective of value of the land; claims in tort and contract up to 50,000 vatu; civil claims under Ambrym regional laws up to 50,000 vatu; applications for maintenance made under Joint Maintenance of Children Regulation 13 of 1966.

24. Efate, Tanna, Malekula, Ambrym, Sheppard, Banks and Torres, and Santo. The chief clerk has a role in uniting the island courts, working with the chief registrar and the chief justice to unify solutions. Although there are never sufficient funds to bring the administrators and justices of island courts to the capital for meetings or training, lay justices receive a sitting allowance, and receive training *in situ.*

25. Bolton, "Chief Willie Bongmatur Maldo and the Role of Chiefs."

26. Elections in 1993 returned chiefs from Banks and Torres (2), Santo/Malo (2), Ambae/Maewo (2), Malekula (2), Pentecost (2), Ambrym (2), Paama (1), Epi (1), Shepherd (2), Efate (2), and TAFEA (Tanna, Anatom, Futuna, Erromango, and Aniwa) (4) (the latter including Tom Numake, Isaac Napuati, Roel Yameli, and Henri Naulita).

27. In Order 7 of 1988, under Decentralization Act 11 of 1980, the minister appointed four custom chiefs, two women and two youth, to membership of the Santo/Malo local government council; *Republic of Vanuatu Official Gazette* (9), 28 March 1988. Appointments in similar proportions were made at this time to the Efate and Pentecost local government councils.

28. Tepahae, "Chiefly Power in Southern Vanuatu."

29. Tonkinson, "Vanuatu Values."

30. See, for instance, the interesting analysis provided in Anckar, "Westminster Democracy."

31. The proposed changes, ostensibly to promote political stability, sought to prevent members of parliament from changing political affiliations; to increase the term of government; and to restrict the times at a motion of no-confidence could be introduced. The proposed changes were gazetted without the constitutionally required referendum, and were subsequently struck out by the Supreme Court. "Vanuatu MPs Prepare to Vote on Constitutional Change," *PacNews* (1), 19 October 2004.

32. There are, of course, passing references to parliamentary effectiveness in Howard Van Trease's important edited work *Melanesian Politics.*

33. Sokomanu, "A Presidential Crisis."

34. On 4 August 1991 the Supreme Court dismissed an appeal by Lini to have a congress of the Vanuaku Party scheduled to be held in Mele ruled illegal. In August 1992, Vanuatu's chief justice, Charles Vaudin D'Imecourt, ruled unconstitutional a proposed business law that would have given the minister of finance power to grant or revoke business licenses without fear of a court challenge. D'Imecourt had yet to consider whether he or the president had the power to remove the offending clause, or whether it had to be referred back to parliament.

35. "Outside the court, jubilant opposition supporters honked their car horns as opposition leader Willie Jimmy predicted his group would now be able to topple the government." BBC Summary of World Broadcasts, 5 September 1996.

36. TAFEA: Tanna, Anatom, Futuna, Erromango, and Aniwa; SHEFA: Efate, Shephards Islands, and Epi; MALAMPA: Malekula, Ambrym, and Paama; PENAMA: Pentecost, Ambae, and Maewo; SANMA: Santo and Malo; and TORBA: Torres and Banks.

37. Carmody, "The South Pacific."

38. This took place in Tanna following the general election of July 2004, when aggrieved supporters of an incumbent member of parliament burned ballot boxes after he lost his seat. Thirteen Tannese were charged and received two-year suspended sentences. In September 2004, fire destroyed government buildings on Tanna, with the loss of twenty-four years of records overseeing the affairs of the province's 30,000 residents. Police suspect the fire was linked to the burning of ballot boxes, and the resulting criminal trials. "Fire Destroys Government Buildings," available at http://tvnz.co.nz/view/news_world_story_skin/445546%3fformat=html (accessed 12 December 2004).

39. Crossland, "The Ombudsman Role."

40. These include Office of the Ombudsman, Port Vila: 1998, "Public Report on the Vanuatu Fire Service Failure to Put Out the Fire on 6 May 1998 at Paris Shopping"; 1999, "Public Report on the Discriminatory Criteria of the Vanuatu National Examinations Board for Admission to Year 7"; 1999, "Public Report on the Illegal and Unconstitutional Discrimination in the Citizenship Act"; 1999, "Public Report on the Improper Procedures Used to Extend the Employment Contract of Dr. Trinata A. Manandhar, a Dental Officer at Vila Central Hospital"; 1999, "Public Report on the Mismanagement of the Vanuatu Development Ltd by the Former Manager, Selwyn Leodoro, in 1992–1993, and Illegal Conduct of the Former Chairman of the Board, Tom Kalorib"; 1999, "Public Report on the Maladministration and Political Interference in the Granting of Loans by the Development Bank of Vanuatu"; 1999, "Public Report on the Discriminatory Criteria of the Vanuatu National Examinations Board for Admission to Year 7"; 1999, "Public Report on the Management of the Tender Sale of Ten (10) Deportees' Properties by the Former Illegal Minister of Lands, Mr. Paul Telukluk."

41. Ombudsman Marie Noelle Ferrieux Patterson said that if presented, the guarantees, which were effectively government promissory notes for more than two years' worth of Vanuatu's total foreign reserves, could bankrupt Vanuatu; "Scandal Letters Returned," *The Dominion* (Wellington), 2 December 1996, p. 10. A subsequent report, released in October, recommended that Sope be directed to have nothing more to do with the bank guarantees (In early October he had contacted Scotland Yard to ask for the return of the bank guarantees following his appointment back into the ministry. The ombudsman's report further alleged that Sope broke the law in making a deal over a Cybank proposal, backed by Australian company Oxford Media Group, to set up a type of electronic bank on the Internet. Moreover, the ombudsman's report found that Sope had pressured the Vanuatu National Provident Fund, a worker pension scheme, to pay US$250,000 toward it.

42. Louise Williams, "Cargo Cult Reborn: Once-Stingy America Offers Cash Pot to Deserving Poor," available at http://www.smh.com.au/articles/2004/08/13/1092340468271.html (accessed 12 December 2004).

43. "French National Deported from Vanuatu," *PacNews* (1), 29 October 2004.

44. "Taiwan Considering Financial Aid to Vanuatu," *PacNews* (1), 8 November 2004.

45. Taiwan agreed that a memorandum of understanding had been signed, but that the amount of financial support had not been decided: "Money to Be Given to New Ally Not Yet Set, MOFA Says," *Taipei Times,* available at http://www.taipeitimes.com/news/taiwan/archives/2004/11/07/2003210016 (accessed 8 December 2004).

46. "Politicians, along with family members and associates in Vanuatu have been walking into shops in Vanuatu's dusty capital, Port Vila, and buying goods ranging from food to electrical appliances with wads of USD$100 bills. Some merchants thought it too good to be true and suspected the currency was counterfeit. But this week is different for a number of reasons. One is that a parliamentary no-confidence motion is scheduled to be put next Thursday to oust the Prime Minister, Serge Vohor, who has led a ramshackle coalition since July. But while more than one political grouping could be seeking to grease the wheels of democracy with pay-offs, that does not explain all those large-denomination US notes. The word among foreign diplomats is that the source of the funds swishing around the tiny economy is Taiwan." "High-Stakes Diplomacy in Vanuatu," *PacNews* (2), 29 November 2004.

47. "China Seeks Clarification over Vanuatu's Taiwan Link," *PacNews* (1), 5 November 2004.

48. "PM Urged to Seek More Help From China," *PacNews* (1), 22 November 2004.

49. "Barak Sope Says All Foreign Advisors Should Be Asked to Leave Vanuatu," *PacNews* (1), 8 September 2004.

50. "Prime Minister Says Two Australian Police Can Return," *PacNews* (1), 16 September 2004; "Australia Warns Vanuatu It May Cut Off Aid to the Country," *PacNews* (1), 26 November 2004.

51. UNDP, *Sustainable Human Development in Vanuatu.*

52. "Watchdog Questions Vanuatu's Constitutional Change Process," *PacNews* (1), 22 October 2004.

53. ACFOA, *Inquiry into Australia's Relationship with Papua New Guinea and Other Pacific Island Countries.*

54. "Vanuatu's Legal System Under Attack," available at http://www.smh.com.au/articles/2004/09/08/1094530697620.html?oneclick=true (accessed 12 December 2004). Newton Cain and Jowittt's Vanuatu chapter for Transparency International's "National Integrity System" Pacific Island country studies project is available at http://www.transparency.org.au/nispac/vanuatu.pdf (accessed 12 December 2004).

55. "Watchdog Questions Vanuatu's Constitutional Change Process," *PacNews* (1), 22 October 2004.

56. Chief Mike Yori, quoted in "Politics the Erromango Way," *Port Vila Presse Online*, 28 May 2004, available at http://www.news.vu/en/news/politics/politics-the-erromango-wa.shtml (accessed 24 January 2007).

57. Morgan, *Integrating Reform.*

12

Troubled Times: Development and Economic Crisis in Nauru

Max Quanchi

IN 1907, 11,630 tons of phosphate were dug by hand and shovel on Nauru, lightered out to vessels and shipped to Australia. The first shipment, on SS *Fido,* wrecked on the coast of New South Wales, an omen for the troubled relationship between mining and the Nauruan people that continued for the next century, culminating in the last decades of the twentieth century in public sector mismanagement, the approach of state bankruptcy, parliamentary instability, and internal dissent.

Nauru is a small, raised coral island of roughly 21 square kilometers (8 square miles) in the mid-Pacific near the Equator. Unlike the other countries considered in this volume, Nauru is Micronesian, with one island and one local language (as well as English) spoken among its very small population of 10,000 people (including 2,500 foreign workers).[1] The central drama of Nauru's modern history could be told as a story of phosphate mining, and of sudden wealth and rapid economic decline. Today, "Topside," the central plateau that makes up seven-eighths of the country's land mass, has a large area of unrehabilitated bare coral pinnacles, the legacy of a hundred years of phosphate mining, as well as an open-cut phosphate mine. Phosphate reserves are now largely depleted, however secondary phosphate mining has begun.

In March 2004, Nauru received an additional A\$22.5 million in development assistance from Australia to "stabilise the country's economy and strengthen law and order."[2] This was a huge increase from the A\$3.5 million in bilateral and multilateral aid provided in 2002–2003. The new memorandum of understanding between Nauru and Australia did not specify any particular recent law and order incidents or long-term security problems. Other than training for Nauru's police force, no mention was made of why Nauru needed development assistance to strengthen law and order and to prevent future internal conflicts, outbreaks of violence, or civil disorder. Why was security (understood as law and order) the prism through which development was being defined? The reason may lie in part in the international ramifications of the tiny state's financial "looseness," or lack of fiscal accountability. In part, however, the motive lies outside Nauru and may be traced to the Western perception that Oceania, and especially new nations in the archipelago and islands of the Southwest Pacific, now constitute an arc of instability where governance is unstable, economies are weak, and the possibility of failed states emerging is high.[3] Nauru was called "one of the world's most dysfunctional countries" by *The Economist* in 2003.[4] Added to this is the perception that unstable states might become a haven for international terrorists. The term "failed states" is popular in Western bureaucracies, governments, and the media, but is a faulty construction,[5] similar to the equally misleading phrases of the 1990s that a "doomsday scenario" was looming and the Pacific was "falling off the map," because Western nations in the post–Cold War world, with its easing of tension, had lost interest in the Pacific.[6]

Failed states, as noted by Sinclair Dinnen, are characterized by a combination of six dysfunctions—economic collapse, political instability, breakdown of essential government services, endemic corruption, loss of authority, and collapse of law and order.[7] Of these, only the first, economic collapse, clearly characterizes Nauru. Of the other five criteria for dysfunctional states, Nauru has at times suffered from minor political instability, but only if crossing the floor of parliament, short presidential terms, and continual cabinet shuffling are considered "instability." Corruption exists in the form of misuse of public monies for excessively generous travel allowances to politicians, ministerial conflict of interest, unregistered payments from vendors and bidders, and possibly criminal misappropriation. Nauru does have a poor record in essential services (particularly water, power, external communications, health, and education); however, democratic elections, parliamentary and judicial processes, law and order, and elements of an active civil society continue to operate.

Nauru is not a failed state. Indeed, Nauru was considered such a safe haven that a deal was struck to locate an internment camp for Australia's unwanted asylum-seekers on the island. It does not suffer the common problem of so-called failed states—an identity crisis.[8] Peace prevails and people are happy to remain Nauruans on Nauru. Law and order is maintained and domestic violence, crimes against property, theft, and violent crime are comparable to that in a small rural town in Australia. Sports such as weight-lifting, Australian-rules football, frigate bird–flying, cycling, and walking are popular, and Nauru has won Olympic medals and was scheduled to host the 2001 world weight-lifting titles until it withdrew due to the financial crisis at the time. Absolute poverty is not a problem, although access to quality health services, adequate nutrition, safe water, and housing needs urgent attention. Nauru is also capable of maintaining itself as a member of the international community, although that capacity is declining.[9]

It is sometimes asserted that being small makes countries such as Nauru attractive as a base or conduit for international crime and terrorists. Ben Reilly and Kennedy Graham, for example, claim that "their vulnerability to such criminal networks because of their small size and limited investigative and enforcement capabilities makes them an increasingly attractive arena for criminal networks."[10] The Australian think-tanks—the Australian Strategic Policy Institute (ASPI) and the Centre for Independent Studies (CIS)—have also warned that "instability created by crime and violence in the islands should be of considerable strategic concern to Australia," specifically mentioning Nauru as a danger area.[11] But why Nauru's small size (21 square kilometers [8 square miles]) and small population (about 10,000 people) make it more likely to be a security risk is not clear. Indeed, Nauru has no military capacity of its own to patrol borders, nor has it suffered in modern times from violent disruption, coups, or civil wars. A short bicycle ride around its coastal road or a quick call on one of its 3,500 land-line and mobile telephones would alert neighbors and the police to any strangers arriving on the island, and although it has offshore deep-water anchorages and an international airport, it would be impossible for a malevolent force to train there or launch an attack in the region without attracting notice.

However, Nauru is a troubled nation, destined to rely in the long-term on foreign aid merely to maintain its annual national budget, and it does exhibit worrying trends across several indicators of well-being. There is clear evidence of failed development. The government is unable to provide basic infrastructure—there are empty shelves in the government-run supermarket, a power plant is regularly without fuel, desalination equipment is obsolete, phosphate mining equipment is rundown, seats on departing aircraft are regularly allocated to medical evacuations. Health problems, particularly associated with poor nutrition, keep the national diabetes rate at epidemic proportions, of about 40 percent, and consequently keep longevity at an alarmingly low rate, of fifty-five years of age for males.[12]

David Hegarty, from the State, Society, and Governance in Melanesia Project, has asked for greater depth in analyzing the "arc of instability" proposition. He has called for examination of "what is really happening to the institutions of government," pointing to the need to "situate these developments in historical and political context to determine realistically what threats flow from that analysis."[13] Otherwise, there is a danger that the sources and symptoms of the country's troubles will not be addressed.

▪ Historical Background

Nauru was sighted by the British captain of the *Hunter*, trading out of Sydney toward Hawaii in 1798. He named it "Pleasant Island" and by the 1830s it had become a haven for beachcombers and ship deserters, who often entered into temporary marriages with Nauruan women. The first missionary arrived in 1887. US Protestant missionaries arrived in 1899 and Catholics in 1902. In 1888, a civil war between the original twelve tribes (these are the twelve points on the flag of the independent Republic of Nauru) came to an end when the first German administrator arrived. Germany had been allocated Nauru under the Anglo-German Agreement of 1881, and it became a protectorate under an administration based in the neighboring German protectorate of the Marshall Islands. After Germany's defeat in World War I, Nauru became a C-class mandate in 1919, granted to Australia, New Zealand, and Great Britain, but administered by Australia.[14] Albert Ellis's discovery that a doorstopper in a Sydney office was actually high-grade phosphate is a well-known colonial story. Phosphate mining began in 1907 and developed under an Anglo-German commercial agreement. However, the subsequent Australian, Great Britain, and New Zealand joint mandate over Nauru was a license for unbridled and rapacious mining. Nauru was in effect an Australian colony.

In 1947, Nauru became a United Nations trusteeship and was again jointly administered by Australia, Great Britain, and New Zealand, although once again it was otherwise an Australian colony. The mining of phosphate continued until Nauru, after a sustained history of dissent and protest about mining royalties, Australia's discriminatory colonial attitudes, and failure to act "in trust" for the Nauruan people's benefit, gained independence in 1968.[15]

In 1970, the state created the Nauru Phosphate Commission (NPC) when it bought the mining operation in its entirety from Britain, New Zealand, and Australia. Mining continued under Nauruan control, but now all royalties, and at a much higher world price, flowed into Nauruan hands. The question of rehabilitation was not resolved.[16] Hammer DeRoburt, the founding prime minister of Nauru, noted that "it is the Nauruan contention that the three governments should bear responsibility for the rehabilitation of land mined prior to July 1 of this year (1967)."[17] No rehabilitation occurred despite controversial negotiations, appearances before the International Court of Justice and a A\$55 million out-of-court settlement, and a commitment by Australia to provide A\$2.5 million annually for the next twenty years for environmental rehabilitation. Despite several visiting teams of experts and scoping programs, the Nauru Rehabilitation Corporation has been slow to introduce rehabilitation of the mined area or to carry out tests on whether secondary mining of already-mined pinnacles is worthwhile.

Nauruans have a spiritual and cultural link with Topside, the plateau where the phosphate has been mined. As well as the marks of mining, the raised coral plateau has some housing, a sports field, a rubbish dump, and a small lagoon used for fishing. A part of Topside also became a no-go zone for Nauruans when in 2001 a barbed-wire camp was rapidly constructed for

Australia's unwanted asylum-seekers. Nauruans highlight the moonscape and degraded environment of the significant unrehabilitated parts of the land to the international media, but the physical and aesthetic degradation is minimal in comparison to that in New Caledonia, another Pacific Island with a hundred-year legacy of mining. Most residential housing and social and cultural activity are concentrated on the narrow coastal plain that encircles the island.

Since independence, Nauru has maintained a democratic political structure. It has a long-standing local government structure representing the original twelve chiefdoms, and two new districts and a national parliament of eighteen seats representing 5,000 voters. However, cabinet dismissals and reshuffling have been frequent, and crossing the floor of parliament has been a regular event. There have been ten changes of government in the decade since 1995. Public dissent such as blocking the airport runway to prevent parliamentarians from leaving the island on government-funded jaunts has not been unusual.

Appropriate development policies were not put in place between 1947 and 1968, when Nauru was a United Nations trusteeship administered jointly by Great Britain, Australia, and New Zealand. Notably, education and training in financial institutional management were not provided, and there was little preparation for statehood and effective self-management. Moreover, government processes and bureaucratic monitoring of the phosphate mining by the trusteeship powers (that is, Australia) were not characterized by accountability and transparency—certainly not to the people of Nauru. Since 1969, Nauruans have therefore failed to implement development policies appropriate to their newly independent microstate circumstances. Nauruans themselves have not sought political education or qualifications in the fields demanded by modern governance, and have been unable to fully accommodate democratic institutions or to effectively blend traditional loyalties and tribal identities with introduced forms of authority. Nor did the many postindependence governments of Nauru (up to but not including the current government) introduce principles of accountability and transparency. The result was that by the early 1990s, Nauru was caught in a spiral of declining state revenues, government instability, and financial mismanagement.

■ Where Has the Money Gone?

State revenue from phosphate sales was declining in the latter part of the twentieth century but was still significant. Nevertheless, the United Nations Development Programme (UNDP) revised Nauru's estimated gross national product (GNP) per capita for 1997 from US$29,110 down to per capita US$3,711—an extraordinary reduction.[18] From 1968 to 2001, total mining revenue was A$3.5 billion. Helen Hughes, an observer of Nauruan development over a forty-year period and consultant, calculates that 50 percent of this was spent on salaries, plant, operating costs, and payments to landholders, leaving A$1.75 billion to be added to the reserves, assets, and foreign holdings of the Nauru Phosphate Royalties Trust (NPRT).[19] As well, the Organization for Economic Cooperation and Development (OECD) reported that Nauru received A$24 million in total aid flows between 1970 and 2000.[20] Since then, Nauru has also received other monies, including a loan from Taiwan of A$38 million, A$57 million as an out-of-court settlement (for environmental damage caused by mining), A$2.5 million annually from Australia for mining rehabilitation, A$22.5 million under the latest memorandum of understanding with Australia, an A$1.2 million Christmas "bailout" from Australia to cover the annual royalties payment (known as *ronwan*), A$44 million for hosting an asylum-seeker camp, and a A$38 million loan from General Electric Capital. This is a huge amount of money flowing into a nation of merely 10,000 people. Where has this A$2 billion in revenue, loans, and aid, and A$1 billion from the NPRT reserves, gone?

Even though Nauru's problems have been known since the mid-1990s, the exact dimensions of the decline in national assets, overspending, and mishandling of public funds were never revealed, as there was no systematic budgeting, record-keeping, or tabling of annual reports, budgets, and economic forecasts. There was no public accountability. Without annual audits and parliamentary scrutiny, and without a leadership code to ensure that ministers responsible for finance, treasury, and development reported to parliament on the state of the nation's finances, the practice was for Nauru's democratically elected politicians to keep spending.

Public sector mismanagement (and possibly corruption) occurred on a massive scale, with multimillion-dollar losses on a failed West End London musical *(Leonardo),* on a national shipping line, on a national airline (which at one time ran an extensive regional service with five jets, occasionally requisitioned for Hong Kong shopping jaunts by politicians), and on foreign investment scams. In a typical case of poor judgment, individual corruption, and failed fiscal monitoring, Nauru lost US$12 million from an original US$60 million purchase of bogus letters of credit and bank notes. Corruption and misuse of public monies has allegedly made some Nauruans comparatively wealthy. The A$1.3 billion in reserve in the Nauru Phosphate Royalties Trust in 1990 declined by 77 percent, to an estimated A$300 million in 2004 due mostly to extravagant spending, mismanagement, and misappropriation. The problem was alarmingly simple: a complete lack of conventional fiscal accountability.

Statistics are missing or have not been collected, national budgets are kept secret. The Asian Development Bank (ADB) concluded in 2000 that there was lack of commitment at the political level, an unwillingness to confront harsh economic realities, and an absence of strong leadership within the Ministry of Finance.[21] In 2003, the ADB's opinion was that the government had few options to fund its continuing budget deficits. In the past, loans had been acquired from official external sources, overseas corporations, the local bank (the Bank of Nauru, now insolvent), and drawdowns from the NPRT.[22] An offer in 1999 to use US$5 million in ADB funds and US$1.2 million in technical assistance grants to create a program of sweeping fiscal and financial review and reform was rejected. In 2000, a US$0.3 million ADB technical assistance program designed to strengthen the Ministry of Finance reported that reform had stalled because of "the paucity of up-to-date national statistics and basic economic and financial data." It reported that the Ministry of Finance was unable to implement controls imposed by budgets and had no means to monitor revenue or expenditure.[23]

The failure to ensure that appropriately trained ministers and bureaucrats were monitoring expenditure and reporting to parliament was compounded by the lack of a vocal, critical public. Except on rare occasions of excess, the populace was unable or unwilling to question the traditional leaders they had elected to parliament.

It is estimated that A$25 million is required annually for the next decade to maintain budgets, pay off loans, and restore and develop social and economic infrastructure to reasonable levels.[24] This is despite a 30 percent retrenchment, or 450 Nauruan jobs, from the public sector in 1999. Government jobs are the only alternative form of formal employment to working for Nauru Phosphate Commission. It is estimated that the NPC still employs 1,700 people, far in excess of the 800 it employed when working at five times present capacity in the 1980s.

Stalled Development

Nauru's economy was relying on one export product, and its ability to generate future income was uncertain. Rising phosphate extraction costs and a falling world price suggested that phosphate mining, as mentioned, could not extend beyond 2007. The NPRT and the Bank of Nauru, the government's two borrowing institutions of last resort, were both in trouble. Commentators argued in 2004 that "by international standards the Bank of Nauru is technically insolvent."[25] Nauru had no other natural or human resources to sell, and had not yet examined alternative options such as renting its ocean resources, airspace, or cyberdomains.[26] There were signs that it was prepared to use its vote in international forums in exchange for projects and aid.[27]

In attempts to raise revenue, Nauru sold 1,500 passports, hosted 450 offshore banks at a setup charge of merely US$25,000, sold off its foreign assets and property investments, and signed huge loans on unfavorable terms merely to meet current expenditure. It then abrogated partial sovereignty in a A$44 million cash deal for asylum-seekers with one of its former colonizing powers, Australia.[28] Successive governments pillaged the cash reserves of the NPRT and financed fiscal deficits by borrowing directly from the NPRT in an "unplanned and largely non-transparent manner."[29] Because the People's Republic of China and the Republic of China (Taiwan) compete with aid packages for formal recognition in the Pacific, Nauru established official links with Taiwan and offered recognition in return for a bargain-rate loan of US$29 million, after which it unexpectedly switched official recognition to the People's Republic of China. For a period, Nauru was delisted internationally for money laundering;[30] it also misappropriated regional funds designed to support local coastal environment projects. The US$5 million loan for fiscal and financial reform offered by the ADB in 1998–1999 was closed, with the balance canceled, in October 2002, because of the government's noncompliance with loan arrangements.

Mismanagement has included inflated travel allowances, nepotism, and a bloated bureaucracy. At the bureaucratic level there has been a lack of funds for power, water supply, and wages for government employees, and a serious failure to maintain international telecommunications. Air Nauru, the government airline, has been grounded several times for failing to pay its fuel, maintenance, and other operating costs. The wastage through mismanagement of foreign assets of the NPRT is rumored to be at least US$1.5 billion.[31]

A key issue in mismanagement is the related abrogation of voter responsibility. A solution must be found for what Hughes called "extravagant expenditures and poor investments,"[32] and second there is a need for greater involvement by civil society in the governing processes. The solution must include greater accountability in government, budget stringency, and prudent investment policies for what remains of the phosphate-mining trust funds. It must also include a reform agenda and a government commitment to respond meaningfully to this platform. This was indeed the practical approach undertaken by the government of Nauru in signing the 2004 memorandum of understanding with Australia. A consultant senior financial bureaucrat was soon in place in Nauru, and in late 2004 a reform government was elected, with half the former parliament replaced by younger, well-educated, reform-minded Nauruans. However, political stability, economic growth, and an improvement in infrastructure are not ensured, given that the large ADB project and smaller technical assistance program of 1999–2000 failed to have any impact on financial reform in Nauru.

■ Governance and Security

Human security emphasizes the importance of each citizen's well-being and highlights the need for a security agenda to encompass human rights and development goals.[33] Well-being is difficult to measure, but the absence of want and fear, and access to services, are central issues. Nauruans have some basic food security, through access to subsistence garden plots, horticultural practices tested over time, and in an island environment where they can fish. Nauruans are now relearning traditional fishing techniques (after a partial dismantling of subsistence practices during the high-income years). Overall, nutrition is poor.

The Commission on Human Security's 2003 report calls for acceptable standards in human rights, governance, education, and health; a sustainable, livable natural environment; individual opportunities; and freedom from want and fear.[34] In each case, Nauru has an existing policy, infrastructure, bureaucratic organization, and active elements of civil society, but they are underfunded, inoperative, obsolete, or in decline. Nauru therefore is at least "on the brink." But do a lack of accountability in government and an inability to finance the desired level of services and utilities, along with regular changes in presidential and ministerial leadership and a massive overseas debt, mean that individual and family well-being will decline to the point that reproductive cycles and life generally will be endangered? Extraordinarily bad financial management will not inexorably lead Nauru down a path to internal, intrastate, or international violent conflict, or to a situation where want and fear dominate the lives of Nauruans.

The fascinating characteristic of Nauru's development problems is that it has avoided violent conflict despite a dramatic drop in living standards. Leading characteristics of the ninety-eight violent conflicts worldwide between 1990 and 1996 were that they occurred in countries where agriculture was the main contributor to gross domestic product (GDP); where land degradation, freshwater, and overpopulation were problems; where there was high external debt; where export earnings from primary resources were declining; and where there was vigorous intervention from international agencies (e.g., the International Monetary Fund [IMF] and ADB).[35] This seems to describe Nauru quite well, until we acknowledge that Nauru's smallness, ethnic unity, community tolerance, and social resilience have prevented violent conflict. The strength of individual and family identification with the original twelve districts and chiefly leadership, and a strong sense of respect, tolerance, and reciprocity, have enabled Nauruans to avoid resorting to violence in uncertain times. At the same time, it is possible that this soft response to mismanagement allowed serious failure to escalate at the government level, because ordinary Nauruans were loath to publicly criticize their own political elite (who were simultaneously their neighbors, cousins, and chiefs). It also explains why the arrival of an Australian police presence was welcomed—because accusations of misappropriation, corruption, inefficiency, and poor leadership could be made through a third, neutral, and non-Nauruan avenue.

Financial mismanagement had international ramifications for Nauru, prompting broader regional and international security anxieties. Nauru attracted the censure of international monitoring agencies over its status as a tax haven. In 2003, after finally agreeing to comply with OECD rules, Nauru was taken off the list of "uncooperative tax havens."[36] In 1999, Nauru was blacklisted by the Group of Seven (G7) for laundering Russian mafia and South American drug cartel money, and was more broadly regarded as a serial offender for money laundering. It was blacklisted by the Financial Action Task Force (FATF) and the Financial Stability Forum (FSF) for excessive secrecy, failure to disclose documentation, and an unwillingness to share information with monitoring agencies.[37] In the wake of 11 September 2001, the selling of passports used by terrorists (or other criminals) was a factor in the US embargo, under the post–September 11 Patriot Act, on US financial dealings with Nauru,[38] and in the singling out of Nauru in December 2002 as a "primary money-laundering concern." The US Treasury Department also called for a ban to prevent US financial institutions from dealing with Nauru.[39]

International surveillance and pressure from regulating bodies forced Nauru to close its offshore banking operations and money-laundering loophole, and cease selling "economic passports." Between 1998 and 2002, the sale of about 15,000 passports at US$15,000 each, raised $2.2 million, but this was insignificant revenue at the national level when measured against the government's inability to keep Air Nauru's five aircraft flying (now down to one aircraft), to keep international communications open, and to pay the interest on its foreign loans. In September 2004, Nauru agreed to close its offshore banking and, with guidance from the IMF, to enact new corporate legislation and an anti-money-laundering bill to satisfy FATF monitors.[40] This removed Nauru from the list of possible security risks and freed it from accusations of being a potential aid to terrorism.

Appropriate corrective development policies for Nauru's problems, instituted by Nauruans in association with regional and other foreign agencies, are needed. This process is already under way; it was announced in October 2004 that Nauru would have a "resident representative" at the Pacific Islands Forum Secretariat, the first appointment of this kind in the region. A forum secretariat team had earlier visited Nauru to discuss with leaders of government and civil society the possible remedies for the financial crisis. The Pacific Islands Forum and its regional security declarations (Honiara, Aitutaki, and Biketawa) also provided the framework for the memorandum of understanding signed by Nauru and Australia in 2004. Under the agreement, Australia is providing key assistance in finance and policing worth A$22.5 million.

Three security crisis scenarios, although highly unlikely, can be identified. Nauru demonstrated in 2001 that a portion of its land could be excised and its citizens prevented from offering traditional greetings to visitors, and from developing any social or personal relationship with a large body of foreign persons in an uninhabited part of the island. In exchange for cash, Nauru demonstrated that privacy can be bought. As well as excising a Topside no-go area, Nauru prevented journalists, lawyers, and visiting yachts from entering the country, clearly under pressure from Australia when the latter found itself under international scrutiny for the so-called Pacific solution.[41] The Australian government, by inducing Nauru to host a barbed-wire asylum-seeker camp on Topside, might have created a precedent for any foreign authority, government, or group of individuals to buy space on Nauru in which to privately conduct their activities, free from Nauruan interference or legislation. If Nauru could sell its sovereignty in this way, then Nauru could theoretically sell a similar preferential relationship to any foreign power or seemingly benign organization that is willing to pay. Australia created a potentially dangerous, if unlikely, precedent out of Nauru's desperate fiscal problems, which in malevolent circumstances could develop into a regional or international security risk. Another, also unlikely, conflict scenario might occur if Nauru became an offshore site for dispute in a conflict between the "Two Chinas," due to Nauru's courting of either camp. A third crisis, sparked by an escalation of conflict in West Papua, might be intervention by Indonesia as a result of Nauru's support for West Papuan activists.

■ The Failure of Civil Society in the Postindependence Era

During eighty years of foreign rule, Nauruans protested in many ways, setting up their own shops in competition with expatriate monopolies, sending petitions to the United Nations, seeking to have unpopular resident administrators removed, and in one instance reappointing, and quickly taking political advantage of, the platform provided by the advisory council of chiefs, local government structures, and the legislative council and executive council, established respectively in 1925, 1951, 1965, and 1966. Indeed, one important legacy of the German, Japanese, Australian, British, and New Zealand colonial eras in Nauru (variously from 1889 to 1968) was the propensity of Nauruans to protest, to assert the primacy of tradition, and to question the imposition of Western ways.

After independence, civil society in Nauru was characterized by quiet, subtle maneuvering among the 2,000 or so family groups and twelve districts; more recently it has been characterized by passive resistance through an irregular newsletter, *The Visionary,* which occasionally acts as a watchdog on government mismanagement. Civil society took direct action most famously when women sat on the airstrip to prevent politicians from departing on an expensive rort to see a London musical funded at great loss by the Nauru government; more recently, in September 2004, a noisy demonstration tried to prevent then-president Rene Harris from leaving on a state trip to the People's Republic of China. However, Nauruans were much more active as protesters and unruly subjects when they campaigned for their independence in the 1950s and 1960s. The question of why Nauruan voters, family groups, and traditional leadership have not monitored governance in the same active participatory manner since independence remains unresolved.

One reason might be the inordinate personal wealth and untrammeled consumerism arising from the postindependence largesse of the phosphate royalties. A second cause is certainly due to the lack of political education in the colonial era to prepare voters to assume a full participatory role in responsible, transparent, and accountable government. Although structures were established for participatory democracy after 1968, politics was of little interest to the ordinary voter in an atmosphere of spectacular individual spending power, rampant acquisition of Western goods and foodstuffs, and national flag waving as one of the world's wealthiest and newest microstates. Hughes, as noted earlier a longtime observer of Nauruan development, concluded a recent report by calling on Nauruans to adopt a reformist posture, to establish public accountability of government finances, and to spend less. She even advocated the radical step of returning the remaining mining royalties and trust funds—what remained after several decades of imprudent use and blatant misuse—to family groups, so that individuals could at least access an improved lifestyle.

The failure of civil society—which since independence has been characterized by a high level of passivity and tolerance—may also be part of the social glue that allowed Nauruans to survive the failure of government. The challenge for Nauruans now is twofold. There is a need to generate greater awareness of and attention to the dynamics of the institutions of government. (More problematic is the interaction needed among the citizenry, in this case the twelve chiefdoms, so that greater participation in governance does not undermine social tolerance.) In addition, aid donors will be wary of a "country that has wasted billions of dollars and lacks the political resolve to change its ways."[42] To avoid this fate, Nauruans will need actively to support reform and institutional restructuring, and adjust to a stringent regime and lifestyle in which largesse is replaced by moderation. Political will may need to be generated not only in government, but also more widely in the community.

■ Conclusion

Public education, as a solution to Nauru's problems, was identified in the World Bank and IMF's 2003 poverty reduction strategy. To increase accountability and civil society participation in governance, the World Bank and IMF called for increased knowledge of the links between government policy, human security, and growth. They noted:

> The lack of capacity, and the inability to use existing capacity effectively, remain important constraints to the preparation, implementation, and monitoring of [poverty reduction] in many countries. Not only government capacity, but that of other stakeholders needs to be augmented so that they can engage in policy dialogue. A concerted effort is necessary on the part of both countries and their development partners to increase learning and the dissemination of good practices and to enhance the knowledge base and understanding of growth and poverty reduction.[43]

A political education program in Nauru will be an important first step.

An equally urgent strategy is to convince Nauruans of the importance of secondary and technical education, particularly university and vocational training. For example, only 81 percent of primary-age students attend school, only 55 percent of all potential primary, secondary, and tertiary students are enrolled, and only 7 percent of GNP is spent on education.[44] Similarly, aid efforts to tackle the consequences of poor governance and fiscal mismanagement—including loopholes opened in international financial security regimes—need, where possible, to work with the underlying causes of that mismanagement. Enhanced secondary education and tertiary study and training will eventually provide the human resource expertise needed to create an effective bureaucracy, an active civil society, and an entrepreneurial private sector. Improved primary and secondary general education, but also vocationally oriented to the needs of managing and maintaining a small state, should underpin aid programs that provide direct assistance to financial management agencies in the country.

Five other solutions to Nauru's problems are now in place. First, Nauru has acted to improve its international commitment to financial monitoring agencies. Second, financial expertise is in place to accurately establish Nauru's debts and assets, to develop transparent fiscal policies, and to undertake a full survey of Nauru's actual fiscal condition. Third, Australia seems committed for at least the next decade to meet the estimated A$25 million annually to balance the national budget and meet international debts and commitments. An aid team of eleven Cuban doctors also arrived in September 2004 to reduce the workload of Nauru's small medical staff. Poor health standards, ironically reflecting a dependence on imported but not particularly nutritional food developed during its period of relative wealth, will have a greater chance of improving when the economic situation improves. Fourth, legislative action has been taken in the form of a treasury-fund protection bill, passed too late, but at least designed to stop further improper use of public finances. Fifth, a reformist government was elected in October 2004.

The snap election, not an unusual event in Nauru's troubled parliamentary history,[45] led to nine members of the eighteen-seat parliament losing their seats. This meant that Nauru's political leadership and ministerial responsibility passed into the hands of young, idealistic Nauruans trained in medicine, banking, and economics, and who took fiscal reform as their main task. The current government promises a significant shift in orientation, based on a more realistic grasp of Nauru's difficult circumstances. One of the first motions in the new parliament was the establishment of a select committee to review the constitution. Other reforms included legislation concerning proceeds from crime, to prevent terrorists from operating in Nauru, and a bill mandating greater compliance with international policing agencies.

Another radical suggestion is for Nauruans to abandon their island and move to Australia, or to adopt a dual nationality and dual homeland and enter into a form of free association with Australia, in the same manner that the Cook Islands and Niue have with New Zealand.[46] This is unlikely, as Nauruans showed little enthusiasm for earlier migration schemes. They do not desire to belong to the expanding Pacific diaspora. For the moment, Nauruans are living where they want to be.

Nauru has struggled through a long crisis of financial mismanagement, seen from abroad as a crisis of sovereignty. Other commentators saw events as a challenge to civil society, or a failure of development. But are outsiders asking the right questions? In casting Nauru's problems in terms of security (in the sense of law and order and vulnerability to terrorism), are donors and international agencies denying Nauruans agency in their own destiny and missing the real cause of fiscal collapse? Nauruan society has exhibited resilience and autonomy over a hundred years of imposed mandate and trusteeship rule, and Nauruans have demonstrated a desire to govern their small island according to their own needs and standards. But the close-knit nature and traditional values of Nauruan society may have been a contributing factor, by discouraging criticism and open discussion of governance practices and mismanagement. The lack of education and postsecondary training that would have prepared Nauruans to manage their export industry and economy—to manage their state—was also a fundamental cause why mismanagement assumed such an extraordinary scale. The challenge in the relationship between development and security in the case of Nauru is how to support a capacity for greater understanding of economic management, and more active public discussion of governance, while not undermining those elements of Nauruan life that make for nonviolent conflict resolution, resilience, and connection.

■ Notes

1. In 2002, Nauruans made up 80 percent of the population, with Pacific Islanders and Asians working in the phosphate mines making up the other 20 percent.

2. Government of Australia, "New Memorandum of Understanding Signed with Nauru."

3. Dobell, "The South Pacific." Dobell's influential essay has appeared in several publications, and was a submission to the 2002 joint parliamentary inquiry into Australia's relationship with New Guinea and the Pacific Islands; see *Quadrant,* May 2003, pp. 16–23. On "failed states," see Dinnen, "The Trouble with Melanesia," p. 67.

4. "Nauru: Mystery Island," *The Economist* (366), 8 March 2003, p. 66.

5. Patience, "Failed and Vulnerable States."

6. Fry, "Framing the Islands."

7. Dinnen, "The Trouble with Melanesia," p. 70.

8. "Identity crisis" is identified by Benjamin Reilly and Kennedy Graham as the main cause for internal conflicts in the region; see "Conflict Through Asia and the Pacific," p. 10.

9. Nauru is a member of eighteen international organizations, including the Secretariat of the Pacific Community, the United Nations Educational, Scientific, and Cultural Organization, the World Health Organization, and the Food and Agriculture Organization, and maintains an office at the UN.

10. Reilly and Graham, "Conflict Through Asia and the Pacific," p. 16.

11. Anna Field, "Australia Does U-Turn to Handle Pacific Tensions," *Financial Times* (London), 5 July 2003, p. 4. The ASPI and the CIS have released several recent reports on Australia's relations with the southwest Pacific.

12. In a special cover story in December 2001, *The Economist* (361), p. 73, declared Nauru a paradise well and truly lost and "one of the most cautionary tales of modern development." Helen Hughes, "From Rags to Riches," p. 9, was more brutal, declaring that Nauru's future was to become "a poverty and ill-health stricken Pacific beggar and pariah." See also Helen Hughes, "Sick Phosphate Island in Need of a Remedy," *The Courier Mail* (Brisbane), 20 August 2004.

13. Hegarty, "Through and Beyond the Arc of Instability," p. 51.

14. Thompson, "Edge of Empire."

15. Ellis, *Ocean Island and Nauru;* Viviani, *Nauru,* Hughes, "The Political Economy of Nauru"; Trumbell, "Smallest and Richest"; Williams and Macdonald, *The Phosphateers;* Crocombe and Geise, "Nauru," p. 66; Michael Field, "Exposed: How Nauru Was Ripped Off," *Islands Business,* July 1992, p. 41; Pollock, "Nauru's Post Independence Struggles"; Pollock, "Nauru: Decolonising, Recolonising."

16. Pollock, "The Mining of Nauru and Its Aftermath," p. 289. See also Pollock, *Nauru Bibliography;* Weeranmantry, *Nauru.*

17. Cited in *Pacific Islands Monthly,* March 1991.

18. UNDP and UN Population Fund Executive Board, "Nauru: Earmarking from Target for Resource Assignment from the Core TRAC Line 1.1.1," DP/2001/31, New York.

19. Hughes, "From Rags to Riches," p. 4.

20. OECD, *Development Co-operation Reports.*

21. Asian Development Bank, *Country Assistance Plan: Nauru,* p. 3.

22. Asian Development Bank, *Asian Development Outlook 2003;* Asian Development Bank, *Economic Trends and Prospects in Asia: Nauru,* p. 49.

23. Asian Development Bank, *Technical Assistance to Nauru for Strengthening the Ministry of Finance,* p. 1.

24. Toata, "Keeping the Nauru Economy Afloat," p. 127.

25. Ibid., p. 124.

26. Schoeffel, "The Pacific Islands," p. 4.

27. This is not unusual in the region. For example, though not a whaling

nation, Nauru has joined the International Whaling Commission, and in 2006 supported Japan's bid to increase its scientific whaling cull.

28. In return for housing 782 asylum-seekers for an unspecified time period, Nauru also received eight months' worth of free fuel, two new generators, ten scholarships for Nauruan students at Australian universities, and payment of outstanding Australian medical bills.

29. Asian Development Bank, *Country Assistance Plan: Nauru,* p. 2.

30. Van Fossen, "Money Laundering."

31. Economist Intelligence Unit, "Pacific Islands Economy: Mixed Prospects for Island Nations," EIU ViewsWire, 29 June 2004.

32. H. Hughes, "Fortune Lost to Betrayal," *The Australian,* 22 October 2004, available at http://proquest.umi.com/pqdweb?index=0&did=718479481&srchmode=1&sid=1&fmt=3&vinst=prod&vtype=pqd&rqt=309&vname=pqd&ts=11696 89490&clientid=20806 (accessed 12 September 2004).

33. These points are highlighted by Quinton Clements and the editors in the foreword and introduction to Heijmans, Simmonds, and van de Veen, *Searching for Peace in the Asia Pacific,* pp. ix–xii, 1.

34. Cited in ibid., p. xii.

35. Susan George, cited in Bello, "Globalization, Insecurity, and Overextension," p. 74.

36. *International Money Marketing,* 9 February 2004, p. 27; *OECD Observer* (242), March 2004, p. 4.

37. Jackie Johnson, "Money Laundering and Tax Evasion: Tales from the South Pacific," *Banking and Financial Systems* 115 (2), April 2001, pp. 16–20.

38. Glenn Thompson, "Tiny Pacific Island Is Big Worry for US," *Wall Street Journal,* 16 May 2003, p. A4.

39. Gary Silverman, "War on Terror," *Financial Times* (London), 9 April 2003, p. 14; Economist Intelligence Unit, "Pacific Islands Economy; US Urges Cut in Nauru Financial Ties," EIU ViewsWire, 17 April 2003.

40. "Nauru Parliament to Debate Further Money-Laundering Laws," ABC Radio Australia News, available at http://www.abc.net.au/cgi-bin (accessed 3 September 2004); "Nauru Passes New Money Laundering Laws," ABC Radio Australia News, available at http://www.abc.net.au/cgi-bin (accessed 5 September 2004); Julio Godoy, "Finance; Fight Against Cash Laundering for Terror Is Going Nowhere," Global Information Network, 10 November 2004.

41. The "Pacific solution" was a domestic electoral strategy in 2001 by the Nauruan government, under which Papua New Guinea and Nauru were paid to host, under draconian conditions, asylum-seekers who had entered Australian waters by boat from Asia and the Middle East. Despite the labeling, it was an "Australian solution" to an Australian problem.

42. Hughes and Gosarevski, "Does Size Matter?"

43. World Bank and IMF, *Review of the Poverty Reduction Strategy Paper Approach,* p. 26.

44. UNDP, *Human Development Indicators: Basic Indicators for Other UN Member Countries,* p. 339; UNDP, *Human Development Report, 2003: Human Development Indicators.*

45. For example, founding President Hammer DeRoburt was president four times between 1968 and his death in office in 1992. Bernard Dowiyogo, who died in February 2003, was president on five occasions. Ludwig Scotty, Kinza Clodumar, and Rene Harris have all won and lost the presidency, often briefly and repeatedly.

46. Hughes and Gosarevski, "Does Size Matter?" p. 20; Hughes, "The Pacific Is Viable."

13

Unfinished Business: Democratic Transition in Tonga

Lopeti Senituli

O N 10 NOVEMBER 2004, the king of Tonga, His Majesty King Taufaha'au Tupou IV,[1] gave his subjects the ultimate gift—a role in the selection of the government's cabinet of ministers. By taking this action, His Majesty finally accepted that the people have an integral role to play in the democratic governance of the Kingdom of Tonga. In doing so, he took the mantle and mana of King Siaosi Tupou I ("The Emancipator"), the founder of modern Tonga. In this, he has also kept true to historical tradition, through which reigning Tongan monarchs have voluntarily devolved political and temporal powers to a new dynasty, while retaining spiritual and divine powers for themselves. The Tu'i Tonga dynasty created the Tu'i Ha'atakalaua dynasty, which, in turn created the Tu'i Kanokupolu dynasty. Now, the Tu'i Kanokupolu (His Majesty King Taufa'ahau Tupou IV) is beginning to devolve political and temporal powers from himself—not to a new dynasty, but to the people themselves, the primary repository of political power in any democratic system of government.

Tonga, ruled by a reigning monarch from one of the longest dynasties in the world,[2] stands as an example of political transition, with significant steps being made toward greater democracy in the past few years. There has been an active popular movement for democratization since the late 1980s, and intense debate around particular matters during the first years of the twenty-first century, and recently over freedom of the press. Political transitions are frequently occasions for violence; Tonga, however, has so far managed change and conflict with a notable lack of violence. In the context of this volume, it is an example of development (in this case essentially political development, although this is of course occurring in a context of economic and social change) that could easily generate violent conflict, but that has instead been managed in a way that is sensitive to the security and well-being of Tongan society.

The king's gift came out of the blue. Its public declaration was made by the prime minister, His Royal Highness Prince 'Ulukalala Lavaka Ata, the youngest of the king's three sons. I looked forward to the prime minister's televised declaration to the nation on the evening of 10 November with some trepidation. The last time he made a televised statement (September), it was to rationalize why the former ministers of police; justice and attorney-general; and labor, commerce, and industries were asked to fall on their swords. On top of that, King Tupou had officially closed the Legislative Assembly sessions for 2004 earlier that day; past practice had been that the publicly owned national television and radio stations led their evening news bulletins on such days with an unedited recording of the king's address from the throne. When the national television and radio stations repeatedly advertised that their evening news bulletins for that day would actually lead with an address to the nation by the prime minister (without stating what he intended to say), followed by the king's address, the specter of more ministerial blood on the floor flashed across my mind!

The prime minister's statement began, "His Majesty King Taufa'ahau Tupou IV has graciously agreed to a recommendation from HRH the Prime Minister, for the appointment of four additional Ministers from the elected members of the Legislative Assembly." The historic significance of the prime minister's statement did not register until he said, "Two of the new Ministers will be selected from the nine Noble members of the Legislative Assembly elected by the Kingdom's Nobility. Two will be chosen from the nine elected Representatives of the people." Unbelievable!

The prime minister went on to state he believed that "the widening of Cabinet membership will be a natural progression of the Kingdom's political system," and that it "will be a reflection of the democratic principles of Tonga's Constitution." He also declared that "the changes will be in line with a comprehensive agenda for reform of the Government and the economy and privatization."

He continued, "His Majesty's decision is a departure from usual procedure. He has traditionally chosen Ministers from outside Parliament. They then became members of the House by virtue of their Ministerial positions and do not have to seek election. In this case the new Ministers will be 'Grace and Favour' appointments. They will differ from the current holders of Ministerial office who were appointed by the Sovereign without recommendation from the Prime Minister. Their tenure of office shall be largely dependent on their retention of their mandate from the electorate."[3]

Local kava connoisseurs refer to the political situation in Tonga, in comparison to the rumblings in the regional neighborhood, as a *taupilo,* which on the one hand can be interpreted as a "pillow fight," and on the other as a "farting contest." In my humble opinion, it is neither. Rather, until now, it has been a one-sided political conflict, with those in favor of democratic change winning minor battles here and there, but with no realistic prospect of winning a full frontal war. The conventional wisdom has been that as long as the composition of the thirty-member Legislative Assembly remains skewed in favor of the king and the nobility, the prospect for more democracy is minimal. The Legislative Assembly comprises twelve Cabinet Ministers nominated by the king, nine representatives elected by and from the thirty-three hereditary Nobles of the Realm, and nine representatives elected by the people under universal suffrage. However, recent events in the kingdom suggest that peaceful democratic change is possible; the real question now is whether all the forces in favor of change can work together to achieve it in a systematic manner, or whether change will be allowed to happen haphazardly.

Indonesian academic Arief Budiman, when asked by *The Economist* in July 1997 about the most likely route his country would take out of the political quagmire, replied, with apologies to Samuel Huntington, "'Intervention' as performed by, say America in Haiti, is out of the question. 'Replacement' on the model of the people-power revolution in the Philippines is unlikely. 'Transformation' by the ruling elite as happened in Taiwan is out of the question. The best hope lies in 'Transplacement' a combination of elite-led reform and popular pressure in which the powers that be negotiate a peaceful settlement with the forces of change as they did in Chile."[4]

Tonga too will take a combination of the "transformation" of His Majesty the King (a road to Damascus–type of conversion) and a "transplacement" process where the thirty-three Nobles of the Realm, with the support of the nine people's representatives and the backing of people-power, negotiate a way forward with His Majesty the King (a road to Emmaus–type of dialogue).

His Majesty's gift, as announced by the prime minister on 10 November 2004, appeared as the result of a road to Damascus–type of transformation. The transplacement phase, in my view, began on 16–17 March 2005, when first the Nobles of the Realm, then the common people, elected their representatives for a new look and different Legislative Assembly and the beginning of a new epoch in Tonga's history.

■ Geography

The Kingdom of Tonga comprises 169 low-lying coral and volcanic islands, located just east of the International Dateline in the Central Pacific, and three hours' flight north of New Zealand. Its nearest neighbors are Fiji and Samoa. There are three larger island groups: Tongatapu, Ha'apai, and Vava'u, and three smaller islands, with a total land area of 748 square kilometers (287 square miles), spread over an exclusive economic zone of 700,000 square kilometers (270,000 square miles). Only 36 of the islands are permanently inhabited. The climatic and geological characteristics noted below are shared with many of the islands in the Pacific region.

Tonga falls in a tropical cyclone belt, with an average of one cyclone passing through Tongan waters every year. Cyclones usually develop in Tonga in the period of November to April. Global climate change has triggered more frequent and more severe storms, interspersed with scorching droughts. The El Niño southern oscillation (ENSO) event, caused by regional atmospheric variations, can bring about changes in precipitation and climate patterns. The impact of this unpredictable climate has been harsh on the ecosystems, coastlines, and terrestrial and marine biodiversity. Economically, the impact of global climate change and ENSO has translated into decreased agricultural yield, death of livestock, and variable marine biodiversity.

Nuku'alofa, Tonga's main urban center (on the island of Tongatapu), is vulnerable to many hazards, especially earthquakes, cyclones, coastal erosion, storm surge, and tsunamis. Nuku'alofa lies in the seismogenic zone that results from the convergence of the Pacific Plate with the Indo-Australian Plate. Thus, strong earthquakes have to be expected, due to the city's geographical location with respect to the Tongan Trench (zone of convergence). The last big earthquake, in 2006, measured above 8.0 on the Richter scale and caused extensive structural damage in the outer island of Ha'apai.

■ Population

Tonga's total population is about 98,000 according to the latest (1996) census, with women comprising 49.3 percent. Population growth is low, substantially curtailed by a high and sustained level of international migration, especially to New Zealand, Australia, and the United States. Internal migration flows—motivated primarily by a search for employment, cash income, and education—have led to an unhealthy concentration of people on the main island (70 percent), particularly in the capital, Nuku'alofa. By 1996, 68 percent of the population lived in Nuku'alofa.[5]

■ Economy

Tonga's economy has a narrow export base and a heavy reliance on foreign aid and foreign exchange remittances from Tongans living overseas. Despite this, it enjoys a relatively healthy position in relation to average life expectancy (69 years), adult literacy (99 percent), formal schooling (7.1 years), high enrollment in primary and secondary schools (83 percent), and per capita gross domestic product (US$1,973 in 1996, US$1,868 in 1999). Its Human Development Index (HDI) ranking, relative to other Pacific

Island countries, has been very high. It was ranked second out of twelve Pacific developing-member countries (by the Asian Development Bank) in 1994, first in 1996, and fourth in 1999. Tonga's high rank in the Pacific reflects relatively strong economic growth linked to stagnant population growth, strong remittance flows, and sustained high levels of investment in social spending, especially education and health.[6]

With a Human Poverty Index (HPI) of 5.9, Tonga ranked first out of the twelve Pacific developing-member countries in 1999. This reflected a composite of people not expected to survive to age forty (8.4 percent), adults who were illiterate (1 percent), underweight children under age five (2 percent), and people without access to safe water (5 percent) or health services (nil). These sound indicators reflect consistently high levels of expenditure on education, especially primary education, and health, spread fairly evenly across all islands.[7]

Agriculture continues to be the sector of greatest significance, both in employment terms and as the main source of exports. Agricultural produce (now primarily squash and fish) accounts for over 90 percent of export earnings. Changes in the pattern of production have led to pressure on inhabitants of the outer islands to migrate to the main island, which is now the central export base. Weather and international price fluctuations have meant volatile earnings, contributing to the generally weak state of the kingdom's external account. Imports are consistently about five times the value of exports. This deficit has been partly covered in most years at the current account level by tourism earnings and remittances, and by the flows on the capital account. The generally weak state of the balance of payments has been reflected in the low level of import coverage by foreign reserves.

Tonga's extensive fisheries zone is a valuable resource, with fishing becoming an increasingly important source of export revenues.[8] Exports have been affected by weather conditions and the limited flights and expensive airfreight costs imposed on fresh fish exports to Japan. While Tonga attracts some tourists, travel to Tonga is predominantly for the purpose of visiting family.

▪ Polynesians

Tongans are Polynesians. They share similarities in language, culture, precontact societal structure, and physical features with Samoans; the Maoris of Aotearoa/New Zealand and the Cook Islands; the Polynesians of "French" Polynesia; Hawaiians, Niueans, Tuvaluans, Rotumans, and Lauans from Fiji; the Maohi of Rapanui (Easter Island); and the people of Wallis and Futuna.

Anthropologist Irving Goldman identified three different types of Polynesian society. The first, which he described as "traditional," included the Maori of New Zealand, and smaller-scale societies of the coral atolls and the smaller volcanic islands such as Tikopia, a Polynesian outlier in the Solomon Island archipelago. In such societies, seniority of descent provided *mana* (literally meaning "thunder," but including reputation and supernatural qualities, and the power to accomplish) and sanctity, defined rank, and allocated authority and power in an orderly fashion. A traditional society was essentially a religious system headed by a sacred chief and given stability by a religiously sanctioned gradation of worth. The second type, which Goldman described as "open," included Easter Island, the Marquesas in "French" Polynesia, and Samoa and Niue. In such societies, the importance of seniority was downplayed to allow political and military effectiveness to determine status and political control. Society was more strongly political and military than religious, and stability was maintained more directly by secular power. Status differences were not graded but tend to be more sharply defined. The third, which he described as "stratified," included Hawaii, Tahiti in "French" Polynesia, and Tonga. In such societies, clearly defined and hierarchically ordered social classes were highly developed. Because chiefs ruled thousands of people, genealogical connections could not be traced between all segments of society. "Because of the magnitude of their *mana,* the most powerful chiefs could not come into direct contact with commoners, and objects they touched were avoided. The chiefs formed a class unto themselves and married among themselves. The highest-ranking chiefs controlled all land, and their administrations were impersonal and authoritarian."[9]

History

Research indicates that the various Tongan islands were all settled more or less simultaneously during the period of about 900–850 B.C.E. The settlers were part of a population who are believed to have come out of Asia 4,000 years ago, and who, for the few hundred years before settlement in Tonga, had been exploring and occupying the islands of the Southwest Pacific. (Polynesians have been described as "the greatest ocean pathfinders the world has known.")[10] Evidence of settlement by this population has been found on the major islands of the Solomons, Vanuatu and New Caledonia, Fiji, and Samoa.[11]

The first Tu'i (King) Tonga, 'Aho'eitu, was said to be the son of Tangaloa, a god in Tongan (and Polynesian) mythology, and a woman of Tonga. He began his rule in 950 C.E. For many centuries the Tu'i Tonga dynasty ruled absolutely and unchallenged by the chiefs by means of the sacred *mana* of their line. They were *tapu* (sacred, prohibited), and any disrespectful action toward them invited the most severe penalties. During the twelfth and thirteen centuries, the Tu'i Tonga's domain extended over a number of neighboring countries, including Niue, Samoa, Tokelau, 'Uvea (Wallis) and Futuna, Rotuma (Polynesian outlier north of Fiji), and part of the Lau group of islands that make up southeastern Fiji.

Despite their supposedly unchallengeable status, several Tu'i Tonga were assassinated. Possibly in the fifteenth century, the twenty-fourth Tu'i Tonga relinquished his secular powers, designating his brother ruler of the kingdom, while he retained the privileges of the sacred *mana,* thus creating the Tu'i Ha'atakalaua, the second dynasty referred to earlier.[12]

After over seventy years of intermittent civil war in the late eighteenth and nineteenth centuries, a young chief of the ruling dynasty by the name of Taufa'ahau gradually defeated the recalcitrant chiefs and by 1852 put an end to the civil wars and reunited the kingdom. Taufa'ahau was at the forefront of contact with the Western powers moving into the region. At his baptism by Wesleyan (Methodist) missionaries in 1831, Taufa'ahau took the name Siaosi (George) from King George III of England, whose name had been venerated in Tonga since the visits of Captain James Cook in the 1770s. He later took the title Tupou, and was referred to by missionaries and his papalangi (European) contemporaries as King George Tupou. He was Tonga's first Christian monarch. He also introduced a series of legal codes and a constitution, emancipated landless serfs, and initiated land reforms. That is why he is referred to by historians as the "founder" of modern Tonga, though I prefer to refer to him as the "emancipator," because of the significance of the emancipation of the serfs, and the granting of land rights to all Tongans in 1862. His vigorous and skillful engagement with European powers, particularly Britain, contributed to Tonga not being directly colonized.

■ Codified Laws

The king introduced a series of legal codes, beginning with the Vava'u code of 1839 and ending with the constitution of Tonga of 1875. These legal codes progressively reduced the governing powers of the chiefs, and eventually made all people equal under the law; the king was also subject to the law. They introduced the role of judges, as distinct from chiefs, abolished serfs and the rights of chiefs over their people's property, and made land available to all men for a small rent, with the chief as landlord. Among other provisions, the final constitution established a range of rights and made the king a constitutional monarch by giving lawmaking power to a new class of chiefs, called nobles, and the elected representatives of the people.[13]

According to Ian Campbell, among the many political entities that make up the island states of the Pacific Ocean, Tonga is the only one that was not subject to direct colonial rule during the age of European hegemony. As with five other Polynesian Pacific Island groups (the Society Islands, now "French Polynesia," Hawaii, Fiji, Samoa, and the Cook Islands), Tonga grafted European institutions onto the traditional chiefly government to complement the imported religious and economic structures that were adopted during the nineteenth century. Political adaptation involved elevating chiefly autocracy into kingship, while at the same time limiting it by attaching to it representative institutions. In the process of foreign colonization in the other states, kingship did not survive; and when independence was restored to three of them, power was transferred to politicians elected for limited terms. In Tonga, however, kingship has survived, together with much of the ethos of the ancient chieftainship.[14]

The constitution of 1875 has remained virtually intact over the past 130 years, especially the declaration of rights. This was the constitution that was the focus of the political conflict in Tonga over the early years of this century. The current monarch, King Taufa'ahau Tupou IV, the nineteenth Tu'i Kanokupolu, is the great grandson of the founder of modern Tonga, King George Tupou I, who was the sixteenth Tu'i Kanokupolu.

■ Constitutional Amendments

On 3 June 2003 the attorney general and minister of justice submitted to the Legislative Assembly a draft bill to amend Tonga's constitution. This was the latest maneuver by the government in its blind determination to ban forever the newspaper *Taimi 'o Tonga*. The struggle over this offending newspaper itself has been one of the major political struggles in Tonga. The manner in which it was conducted gives an insight into Tongan political workings, and it seems likely that it also formed the immediate historical background against which His Majesty the King came to the remarkable decision to welcome greater popular representatives into the heart of government.

The bill emerged in the wake of two separate decisions on 26 May 2003 by the chief justice that two ordinances, banning the newspaper and invalidating its license to trade, passed by the king in Privy Council on 4 April and 16 May, were void. The chief justice further restrained other government actions on the matter. The original draft of the bill proposed to

- further delimit freedom of speech and expression and freedom of the media (clause 7);
- abolish the powers of the Supreme Court to judicially review all legislation passed by the Legislative Assembly and ordinances passed by His Majesty and the Privy Council and empower the assembly to declare what other matters shall be put beyond the reach of the courts (new clause 56A); and

- abolish the right to claim damages for any breach of the constitution and limit the remedy to declaratory relief (new clause 29A).

It was an amateurish piece of legal draughtsmanship and drew immediate criticism and admonishment from legal experts. According to Guy Powles, an expert on Tonga's constitution, "Removal of the judicial power to review law-making under the Constitution attacks the fundamental concepts of 'separation of powers' and 'checks and balances' which nations across the world have accepted as the essence of constitutional government. This constitutional amendment would render meaningless the notion of a Constitution that guarantees rights and freedoms. Laws or Ordinances could be passed and enforced against citizens, or by one citizen against another in breach of the Constitution, without any opportunity for the Courts to rule on the issue. The Constitution could be rendered unenforceable through the Courts."[15]

A media release from Tonga's Human Rights and Democracy Movement (HRDMT) on 13 June 2003 announcing the beginning of a public education campaign against the bill prompted a flurry of claims and counterclaims, and a suggestion that those responsible for the information reaching the media be charged with "contempt of parliament."[16]

A new draft of the bill was formally tabled in the Legislative Assembly in early July 2003, without the proposal to abolish the judicial review powers of the courts. Clause 7 of Tonga's constitution at the beginning of July 2003 read: "It shall be lawful for all people to speak, write and print their opinions and no law shall ever be enacted to restrict this liberty. There shall be freedom of speech and of the press for ever but nothing in this clause shall be held to outweigh the law of defamation, official secrets or the laws for the protection of the King and the Royal Family." This clause has remained virtually unchanged since 1875. The new draft of the bill proposed eight new conditionalities that could be used by government to delimit freedom of speech and media, and a new subclause seeking to strengthen the government's already considerable power to "regulate the operation of any media."

A further clause of the draft bill abolished the right to claim damages for any breach of the constitution and was clearly designed to provide some form of impunity "shield" for those instigating the raid on the country's constitution. In the original draft it was numbered "clause 29A." *But there was already a clause 29A*. This had been adopted in haste, at the behest of the king in January 1991, to make legal and constitutional the sale of passports of Tongan "nationals" to 426 mainly Asian buyers, including Imelda Marcos and her children. The government without a doubt must have regretted reminding the public of its earlier folly.

After the government's first two attempts to ban *Taimi 'o Tonga,* using the Customs and Excise Act and then the Prohibited Publications Act, were obstructed by the Supreme Court (which ruled them unconstitutional), the Privy Council went on an ordinance-making spree, for which it had legitimate authority. The ordinances passed by His Majesty in Privy Council on 4 April and 16 May 2003 were clearly attempts to stay one step ahead of the Supreme Court, so the chief justice's decisions, handed down on 26 May, were eagerly awaited.

■ The Government's Defense

The government's lines of defense in court, and the court's response, provided an outstanding opportunity to clarify fundamental aspects of the constitution, still largely as drafted in 1875. The first line of defense was that the Privy Council, containing as it does the king, is above the jurisdiction of the courts and immune from review (as is the queen in the British context, for example). However, Chief Justice Gordon Ward of the Supreme Court did not accept this, stating: "what is unusual about clause 30 (of Tonga's Constitution) when compared with the law in many other constitutional monarchies is that our King is clearly included in the Executive arm of Government. This feature distinguishes it from the position of the Queen in English law and from that of the Governor General as her representative in Australia."[17]

The government's second line of defense and the court's response clarified the role of the court in judicial review: "All acts of the Executive Government are subject to the scrutiny of the court in relation to the propriety of the action itself and the manner in which it was made. The fact any such regulation, rule or order may only be rescinded by the body which made it or by the Legislative Assembly does not prevent the court from considering whether it was a legitimate act of the Government in the first place." The chief justice added that the risk implicit in the government's contention is that a council order that is totally unlawful and that contravenes the rights of every citizen could remain in force without challenge in the Supreme Court until the next session of the Legislative Assembly—possibly many months away.

The third point clarified the notion of the monarch's "royal prerogative," distinguishing between "personal prerogatives," in which the court has no jurisdiction, and which include the power to pardon, the power to declare martial law, the power to consent to a royal marriage, the power to create a peer (nobleman), and "executive prerogatives" over which the court can exercise jurisdiction.

The chief justice stated, "I am satisfied that the intention of Tupou I (creator of Tonga's Constitution) was to codify and limit the King's personal prerogatives and so I cannot accept that the meaning of the second part of subsection 7(d) (of the Government Act) is to give the King the power to propose the creation of new personal prerogatives." In conclusion, the chief justice ruled void the ordinances to ban the newspaper.

Lifting of the Bans on *Taimi 'o Tonga*

This was not the end of the story, however. In spite of, or because of, Chief Justice Ward's very clear judgment lifting the bans on *Taimi 'o Tonga,* the government bureaucracy suddenly reverted into its normal go-slow gear, leading to a further order from the court to lift the ban forthwith. The government begrudgingly lifted the bans on 12 June 2003.

Undeterred, the government openly defied the chief justice's supplementary ruling of 26 May by submitting to the Legislative Assembly the Privy Council's ordinance to invalidate *Taimi 'o Tonga*'s license to trade.

Bills to Gag the Media

By the time the Legislative Assembly voted on this ordinance, on 29 July 2003, it had morphed into a "media operators" bill that proposed to limit foreign ownership of a newspaper operation in Tonga to 20 percent. Quite clearly, it was designed to lay the grounds to deny *Taimi 'o Tonga* an operating license in 2004 if its shareholding structure did not change by then. The government also tabled another bill for an "act to make provision for the regulating of newspapers." This bill proposed wide-ranging powers to the prime minister to grant, refuse, or revoke newspaper operating licenses, unilaterally set standards for print media, and unilaterally declare any newspaper published outside the kingdom a prohibited import. There is no questioning the need for setting standards for and regulation of the media in Tonga, but this bill proposed to give the prime minister absolute power and discretion.

What of the Constitutional Amendments?

Because of the unequal distribution of the thirty seats in the Legislative Assembly, it was doubtful that the amendment would be defeated in a ballot. Traditionally, the nobles' representatives have not voted against the government's wishes. But there were enough examples from their voting record in 2002 to suggest that they were not always beholden to government, which raised the hope among opponents of the amendment of a coup of sorts.

The constitutional-amendment bill had its first reading on 12 August 2003, and was adopted by a ballot of fifteen to eleven. Sensing a quick kill, the prime minister called for the second and third reading to be done immediately, but the legislative speaker sympathized with the opponents of the bill and granted a deferment until 7 October.

Public Actions

In the meantime, public actions of one kind or another were also under way. Members of the HRDMT, led by their seven people's representatives in the Legislative Assembly, started holding public meetings throughout Tonga in preparation for a major protest march on 6 October 2003. They also started gathering signatures for a petition to the king. Initially, they were not allowed paid airtime on public radio and television, but authorities changed their minds when church leaders protested and the government caught on and started hitting the airwaves itself, in addition to holding public meetings. The protest march in Nuku'alofa on 6 October, according to media reports, saw at least 8,000 marchers (mainly women), which was easily the largest protest march in Tonga's history. There were smaller protest marches in the administrative capitals of the outer islands of Vava'u, Ha'apai, and 'Eua.

Amendments Adopted

The second and third ballots on the amendments to the constitution took place on 16 October 2003 and were again adopted, this time by a vote of sixteen to eleven. The Legislative Assembly also passed a newspaper regulation act, and amended the country's civil legislation to ouster the application of English statutes from the country's jurisdiction, for good measure.

The general public was stunned. Members of HRDMT in the Assembly quickly regained their composure and drew up a petition to the king requesting that he not grant royal assent to the new legislation, but to no avail. His Majesty granted his assent on 21 November, and the amendments to the constitution and the two new media laws were enacted. This effectively meant that the *Taimi 'o Tonga* newspaper was banned again.

New Legal Challenge

Members of the HRDMT immediately started canvassing for public and financial support for a legal challenge to the constitutional amendments and the two new media laws, which were filed in March 2004. In October 2004, Chief Justice Robin Webster handed down his judgment on the legal challenge to the amendment to the constitution and the two new media laws, which had been lodged by a cross-section of media, church, and civil society representatives, and individuals.[18]

With regard to the constitutional amendments, the Supreme Court decided that some parts of them restricted or affected freedom of expression, but that other parts fell within the implied exceptions to freedom of expression because they were necessary in a democratic society in terms of a pressing social need and so were consistent with the constitution. Regarding the two new media laws, the chief justice found them inconsistent with the constitution, being severely restrictive of fundamental aspects of press freedom. He concluded that in general the newspaper regulation act could not stand because it was too widely expressed, too unclear in its limitations, and too intimidating, as a person could not be sure whether or not their writing would result in prosecution or even imprisonment. In each of the two media laws, the inconsistent provisions were so extensive and inextricably bound up with the other provisions that the latter could not survive independently. While regretting having to make such a finding, the chief justice considered it the clear duty of the court to uphold the constitution.

There was a huge collective sigh of relief from the public but no major jubilation, given the ministerial sackings that had occurred during the prior month.

■ Triple Ministerial Sackings

In August 2004 the government sacked the minister of police and the attorney general/minister of justice—the two cabinet ministers who were reportedly behind the raid on the country's constitution and civil legislation and the introduction of the new media laws. The government also sacked a third minister—of labor, commerce, and industries—for good measure. Although members of the Human Rights and Democracy Movement felt that their prayers had been answered, there was deep anger and sympathy for the three ministers because of the blatant disregard for justice and fair play in the way they were sacked. This was also the prevalent popular mood, especially among those who earned their livelihoods directly from the government, and even among members of the proestablishment "Kotoa Movement," who threatened to stage a massive protest march, though it never eventuated.

In his first public interview on the dismissals, the prime minister, His Royal Highness Prince 'Ulukalala Lavaka Ata, said that the three ministers had been sacked "Koe lelei fakalukufua 'a e fonua." This sounded very much like "in the public interest"—one of the eight new limitations placed on freedom of speech and the media that had been introduced through the amendment to clause 7 of the constitution. It is not clear whether the prime minister was aware of the irony that he was using a formulation supposedly inserted by former ministers of justice and of police to explain the dismissal of the same ministers from the cabinet. Nor is it clear whether he was aware of the extremely dangerous precedent he was setting for himself and the

Tongan government. In the future, he can use "in the public interest" again, and most likely will not hesitate to do so, to justify the unjustifiable.

▓ Proposal for Alternative Structure of Government

The HRDMT seized on the opportunity provided by the dismissals to revive its proposal for an alternative structure of government, first made public in 2002. The proposal suggested a new structure for Tonga's Legislative Assembly and underwent a number of very lively debates. In the final version, the membership size would remain at thirty, but the distribution was to change: nine seats reserved for nobles and six for women, with fifteen seats reserved for distribution geographically among the islands. (Significant changes were made during a movement workshop in debate of the proposal. The six women's seats remained from earlier versions, but if some of the current people's representatives had had their way, they would have removed these too. Luckily there were quite a few outspoken women at the workshop.)

The HRDMT also addressed a petition to the Legislative Assembly calling for a national referendum on whether the people should vote for all thirty members of the Assembly, and then whether the king should select his cabinet of twelve ministers from that limited field. The petition was voted out without discussion, although it was referred to a special committee of the Legislative Assembly.

▓ Weaknesses of the Human Rights and Democracy Movement

One of the major weaknesses of the HRDMT is the reluctance of the leadership to utilize new and innovative tactics and strategies in its public education and advocacy programs. For example, the strategy for the petition for the referendum should have been more inclusive of the nobles. The movement could have first approached each of the thirty-three nobles individually, and collectively, to seek their views and ultimately their support for the referendum. If the nobles were to be approached, and expressed dissatisfaction with the original wording of the petition, then it would need to be amended to take into account their concerns before being tabled in parliament. However, should the nobles be totally against the idea of a referendum, then it must be dropped altogether and the movement should develop new strategies.

New strategies could include proposing small changes to the present structure of government in a (for lack of a better term) "piecemeal" fashion. For example, the king could continue to appoint cabinet ministers from the whole of Tonga, but such appointments should be first endorsed by a committee made up of the nine people's and the nine noble's representatives in parliament. This would introduce an element of accountability,[19] similar to that in the US system, wherein the president's nominees for cabinet and the Supreme Court must be first confirmed, in public hearings, by a joint commission of the House of Representatives and the Senate. Such an innovation might be palatable to the nobles.

The nobles are important because they hold the balance of power in parliament. Historically they have voted with the government ministers, though with some exceptions in recent years. So the HRDMT's energies and resources must be focused on the nobles. Without their support in parliament, nothing will change. And as a number of the senior nobles have shown, they will support the movement's initiatives if it allows them room for maneuver. This is perfectly illustrated by His Royal Highness Prince Tu'ipelehake's initiative soon after the petition for a referendum was voted out. He initiated a "parliamentary motion" to establish a national committee to review the country's constitution, among other things. Although the motion was adopted only by the barest of margins, and is not binding on government, it signifies a small but major step forward.

The movement cannot afford to continue using the same old tactics of petitions and endless angry tirades against the ministers and nobles in parliament and the media that Akilisi Pohiva (founder of the HRDMT) has utilized successfully in the past and perfected over the years. Part of the reason for the reluctance to be more innovative is the tight control that the people's representatives (from parliament) have over the movement's executive committee, whose members will not support initiatives or tactics that may be interpreted by the voting public as kowtowing to the government or to the nobles, as it could hurt the latter's chances of reelection. This is a genuine fear, as numerous people's representatives have lost their seats because they were deemed, by the voting public, to have strayed too far from Akilisi Pohiva's modus operandi and style.

The other tactic that the movement might adopt is to get the people's representatives off the front pages of the newspapers and get them to boycott television, so that credit for the proposals for change can be "attributed" to the king and the nobles, because, as every Tongan child is taught very early in life, it is "from" them that all good things have flowed in the past. But keeping the people's representatives, and their rivals, off the front pages and off the air will take a miracle. There is also a real need for a movement that is independent of all sides and at the same time accessible to all sides, including government. The movement's vision, strategies, and tactics should not be beholden to the preferences and comfort zones of any one person or group.

■ Political Change

Political change in Tonga is possible and is definitely happening. For example, commoner and people's representative Feleti Sevele was appointed in 2004 by the government to chair the committee responsible for privatizing Fua'amotu Airport. This appointment marked the first time that a people's representative had ever been chosen to chair a government body. Heads of government departments are appointed for rather short, two-year fixed contracts, at the end of which they must reapply for their posts if they want to continue in office. This new methodology was unthinkable previously. Next could be the ministers. Acting ministers are now appointed from within the government departments (rather than from the nobles in the Legislative Assembly, as was the previous practice) and sit in parliament when the substantive minister is away. This change has made it possible for three women acting ministers (of finance, foreign affairs, and justice) to sit, talk, and vote in the current Legislative Assembly. The Office of Public Complaints, formally established in 2003, is another major alteration (though there are still doubts about its freedom to act). Peaceful protests, including the six-week public servants' strike in 2005 and the 2006 rallies and marches of Tongans in Tonga and also in New Zealand seeking political reform, have added momentum to the evolution of Tonga's political system.

These small changes have resulted in the decision to include people's representatives among cabinet ministers—consistent with the proposals put forth by the HRDMT and that culminated on 30 March 2006 with the appointment of Sevele as prime minister. Sevele had served as acting prime minister since the resignation of the former prime minister, Prince 'Ulukalala Lavaka Ata, on February 11. A longtime member of the prodemocracy movement, Sevele is the first commoner to be appointed as fully fledged prime minister of the kingdom. So great change, some planned, some unplanned, is definitely happening.

■ Weaknesses in the Existing Structure of Government

The first major structural weakness of the Tongan government is that identified in the US State Department's country report on Tonga for 2001: "The Government's human rights record was generally poor in several areas and the principal human rights abuse remained the severe restrictions on the right of citizens to change their government."[20] In other words, even though King Siaosi Tupou entrenched in the Tongan constitution of 1875 basic human rights and fundamental freedoms, such as freedom of speech, freedom of religion, the right to a fair trial, he did not include the right of the people to change their government or the structure of their government if they are unhappy with it.

The second major structural weakness is that neither the country's constitution nor the country's laws recognize women's rights as human rights. Women in Tonga are not given the same entitlement as men to resources such as land, citizenship, opportunities like educational scholarships in professions that are traditionally regarded as male domains, and opportunities for promotion at their workplaces or to positions of leadership. Approximately half of the country's population are women, but this is not reflected in the distribution of the country's resources and opportunities.

The third major structural weakness is that pointed out by the Supreme Court chief justice in 1998 in the *Wall Street Journal* case.[21] In his decision, the chief justice stated: "It is not shown to my satisfaction that the accused actually said that ('the King is a dictator') but if he did then, in their context those words can only mean, 'The King is an authoritarian ruler who ignores my repeated requests for accountability by Himself and his Ministers.' If he said this, it appears to me to be the truth. Taking account of evidence by the accused during the trial it appears to me not surprising that his attempts to obtain accountability in a system of government which does not provide for it are ignored."

The fourth major structural weakness is that the Tongan constitution of 1875, which survives today, is founded on the principles of unequal dignity, unequal value, unequal sanctity, and unequal human rights among the Tongan people. This is clearly illustrated by the country's defamation legislation. The punishment for criminal defamation of the king or members of the royal family is either a fine of US$400 or a prison sentence of up to two years. For criminal defamation of any of the thirty-three nobles or any of the thirty members of the Legislative Assembly, the punishment is a fine of US$200 or a prison sentence of up to one year. For criminal defamation of a commoner, the punishment is a fine of US$100 or a prison sentence of up to six months. For criminal defamation of the dead, the punishment is a fine of US$50 or a prison sentence of up to six months.

The fifth major structural weakness is the duplication of legislative and executive powers. For example, the constitution grants legislative powers to the Legislative Assembly, but the Government Act grants the same legislative powers to the king and the Privy Council. The preceding account of the array of mechanisms used to close the newspaper *Taimi 'o Tonga*—first bans imposed by the government, then ordinances imposed by the Privy Council—is an example of this duplication.[22]

In terms of duplication of executive powers, section 2 of the Government Act states, "The King in Council shall be the highest executive authority in the Kingdom." But the same section goes on to say, "and the Prime Minister shall be responsible for carrying out the Resolutions of the Privy Council." So in effect, the prime minister is an errand boy for the king and the Privy Council, but when he is in the Legislative Assembly he puts on the mantle of "leader" of government without express mandate.

The constitution does give the prime minister and cabinet ministers individual executive authority and responsibility, which in the final analysis can conflict with the authority of the king in Privy Council. But as illustrated by the sackings of the minister of education and the attorney general/minister of justice in 2002 relating to losses from Tongan trust funds, and the three ministerial sackings in 2004, when things go wrong, the ones who must fall on their swords never had any real executive authority.

Regarding the king's legislative powers, the Supreme Court's decisions in 2003 on the *Taimi 'o Tonga* bans were highly significant, for they clearly define the real and imagined legislative powers of the king and the degree of "absoluteness" of his rule.

■ Strengths of the Existing Structure of Government

The existing structure of the government of Tonga also has its strengths. First is the entrenchment of most of the basic human rights and fundamental freedoms in the country's constitution, from as long ago as 1875. Second is the emancipation law of 1862, which declared, "All chiefs and people are to all intents and purposes set at liberty from serfdom, and all vassalage, from the institution of the law; and it shall not be lawful for any chief or person, to seize or take by force, or beg authoritatively, in Tongan fashion anything from anyone." Third is the country's unique land tenure system, which gives every Tongan male (excluding females) a degree of autonomy not enjoyed in many other countries in the Pacific, nor in many other countries in the world for that matter. This system has its roots in the emancipation law of 1862, which also declared, "and the Chiefs shall allot portions of land to the people as they may need, which shall be their farm, and as long as the people pay their tribute, and their rent to the chief, it shall not be lawful for any chief to dispossess them, or any other person." Fourth is the general respect for rule of law. Except for the period 1885–1890, when those who refused to convert to the king's newly created Free Church of Tonga were openly persecuted, some of whom, including the king's own daughter, were sent into exile on the island of Koro in Fiji, and except for the banning of *Taimi 'o Tonga* in 2003, the government has in general respected the rule of law. Fifth is an independent and impartial judicial system. Sixth is a relatively vibrant media, recent events notwithstanding. Seventh is the political stability that the existing structure has underpinned for the past 130 years.

■ Role of the Military

Is there a role for the military in the political conflict in Tonga? The Tongan military (army, navy, marines) is well armed and well trained, undertaking frequent military exercises with US Marines stationed in Hawaii and French paratroopers stationed in Noumea, and regular training stints in New Zealand and Australia. Tonga has a platoon of forty-five soldiers currently serving in Iraq, and a contingent of police officers and some soldiers serving with the Regional Assistance Mission to the Solomon Islands (RAMSI). The usual scenario for a military training exercise involves the Tongan defense forces rescuing government leaders who have been taken hostage by a small but well-armed and organized group of rebels. The Tongan soldiers usually play the role of the "good guys."

So far, the military has played an unobtrusive role in national affairs. But recently, His Majesty appointed a former military commander minister of defense, and a former senior military officer (and former secretary of foreign affairs) as minister of foreign affairs. This may signal a bigger role for the military in national affairs, but then again it may simply be the government's response to the push from the US and Australian governments to join their "war on terror." It may also signal a bigger role in international peacekeeping for the Tongan military. In 2003, the Legislative Assembly amended the country's criminal-offense legislation to make "terrorism" a crime. The Human Rights and Democracy Movement's primary concern is that one of the definitions of "terrorism" in the law is almost identical to the definition of "sedition," and carries a much tougher penalty. When this point was raised in the Legislative Assembly, the response from the attorney general/minister of justice was that this was a matter for the courts.

However, any possible threat of internal military violence may be offset by a very strong Christian ethic of respect for human life and dignity in Tonga. A peaceful march led by democracy activist Akilisi Pohiva to the royal palace in the early 1990s (the biggest march at that time, though more recent marches have been larger) provides an example. The goal of the marchers was to present to the king a petition protesting abuse of authority and public resources by government ministers. As they marched, they sang a popular hymn of the Free Wesleyan Church of Tonga that includes the line, *Oku 'iai si'a tangi, 'I he fonua kotoa, kiha taha mafi ke tokoni* (There is a crying plea, from all over the land, for a truly strong but wise leader). Leading the march, Akilisi wept when he saw that the police and the soldiers who were escorting the marchers were themselves weeping as they joined in the singing.

◼ Conclusion

Tonga experienced a real *taupilo* in 2004. Out of it, however, His Majesty the King undertook a "road to Damascus" conversion, or at least turned in that direction, giving his subjects a direct role in governance of the kingdom. In taking this path, the king drew on some key models and traditions from Tonga's past, voluntarily devolving powers to others, while retaining the spiritual dimensions of Tongan kingship, and responding proactively to forces of change. Nobles and commoners (*kainanga e fonua,* or "eaters of the soil") are evolving a "road to Emmaus" type of dialogue. In this, the nobles, in response to and with the support of both the people's representatives in parliament and the populace, are working to negotiate ways forward for the monarchy and the kingdom. These ways forward involve both transformation of the monarchy and transplacement, as a combination of elite-led reform and popular pressure in a peaceful negotiation between the status quo and the forces of change. Despite the intensity of the process at times, Tongan community values have encouraged restraint.

Thus Tonga is managing this inherently tricky transition by drawing on its own values and institutions. Of course, these traditions and institutions have also taken shape in interaction with other forces and powers—the founding of "modern" Tonga is a story of the interaction of local and Western powers, not of autarchy. Not only the formal political institutions, and the social and political life that they have shaped, but also civil society and popular movements (and of course the media) draw from and contribute to institutions and movements throughout the region and internationally. The courts, and respect for the courts, are now integral to Tongan life and tradition, while simultaneously being part of an international (common law) tradition. But this interaction has taken shape in a way that has allowed genuine ownership of key institutions—sufficient at least to encourage the king to pay respect to a parallel Tongan tradition of devolution of powers. Whether or not these piecemeal changes will ever amount to thoroughgoing democratic changes and address or overcome the weaknesses in the existing structure of government remains to be seen. Nevertheless, Tonga may provide a thought-provoking indication of the potential for genuinely absorbing and making traditions and institutions one's own, while remaining distinctively oneself.

■ Editor's Note: The 2006 Riot

The report of the National Committee on Political Reform—a roadmap for political change and part of a community consultation process on democratization—was adopted in principle by the Legislative Assembly on 9 November 2006. The pace of political reform was increasing. However, on 16 November, a riot broke out in the capital of Tonga. It is believed that seven people died, probably in fires that were started by looters. Much of the town's business district was destroyed. There is debate about the factors behind the riot. However, efforts by prominent figures within the Human Rights and Democracy Movement to speed the pace of political reform by leading a protest march at delays in parliament at least sparked the action that degenerated into the riot. The riot and the deaths appear to have deeply shaken Tongans, and can be expected to change the political context and dynamic of the reform process. However, according to His Majesty King George Tupou V, they have not derailed the process of political reform in Tonga. While closing the annual parliamentary session, His Majesty said:

> The events of the last few days have shaken our constitutional founda-
> tions. But our cultural and constitutional roots are innately strong. And we
> have been prepared by more than a century of constitutional government
> to be able to face the political tasks that lie ahead.
>
> His Late Majesty was concerned that the Kingdom's political devel-
> opment was not keeping abreast with its economic development and the
> aspirations of his people. This led Him to set a precedent, momentous in
> Tonga, of appointments to Cabinet based on the recommendations of a
> Prime Minister elected by the people. This was the beginning of a new
> convention of the Sovereign voluntarily choosing to exercise his constitu-
> tional powers on advice of a Prime Minister from those elected to the
> House. . . .
>
> The Government subsequently tabled in Parliament the broad outline
> of the constitutional changes. . . . The Peoples' Representatives also sub-
> mitted their own proposals to the Assembly two weeks ago. All the pro-
> posals that are now in the public arena have the same ultimate aim—a
> more democratic form of parliament and government but appropriate for
> Tonga. The differences among these various proposals are not irreconcil-
> able, and can be resolved through dialogue.
>
> In 1875, the Constitution was a gift from King George Tupou I to the
> people of Tonga. Today, the Constitution is owned by all the people, and
> Tongan culture, Tongan traditions, Tongan strength, Tongan singing,
> Tongan voices, Tongan prayer and Tongan dignity must find new expres-
> sion and new strength.
>
> We would urge all Parliamentarians to continue discussion, and table
> their consensus at the next sitting of Parliament, including a timeframe for
> implementation.[23]

Notes

1. The highly respected Tongan monarch, His Majesty King Taufa'ahau Tupou IV, died on 10 September 2006. His eldest son, now King George Tupou V, ascended to the throne on 11 September 2006.

2. From the tenth century.

3. Tonga Broadcasting Commission, 2004.

4. "Divided and Ruled," *The Economist,* 24 July 1997, available at http://economist.com/surveys/displaystory.cfm?story_id=598593 (accessed 17 November 2005).

5. Emberson-Bain, *Country Briefing Paper,* p. 1.

6. Asian Development Bank, *Country Assistance Plan: Tonga;* Emberson-Bain, *Country Briefing Paper,* p. 1.

7. Asian Development Bank, *Country Assistance Plan: Tonga.*

8. Averaging under 2 million Tongan pa'naga (TOP) per annum in value in the five years to 1995, exports of fish averaged TOP4.5 million per annum in the period between 1996 and 2002, fluctuating from a low of TOP2.1 million in

1996–1997 to a high of TOP7.7 million in 1999–2000. Some revenue is also generated from fishing licenses from distant-water fishing nations such as the United States.

9. Irving Goldman, quoted in Kiste, "Pre-Colonial Times," p. 13.

10. Harry Luke, a former British governor in the Pacific region.

11. Campbell, *Island Kingdom,* pp. 1–4.

12. Ibid.

13. Ibid.

14. Ibid., p. xi.

15. Guy Powles, personal correspondence.

16. In 1996, 'Akilisi Pohiva, member of parliament and founder of the HRDMT; Kalafi Moala, publisher of *Taimi 'o Tonga;* and Filo 'Akau'ola, editor of *Taimi 'o Tonga* were charged with "contempt of parliament," tried by the Legislative Assembly, and sentenced to thirty days' imprisonment. They were released by order of the Supreme Court after twenty-one days' incarceration and were granted compensation for wrongful imprisonment in the latter part of 2003.

17. See *Lali Media Group Ltd v 'Utoikamanu,* Ruling [2003] TOSC 14; C 0124 2003 (17 March 2003), p. 9.

18. The challenge had been lodged by Alani Fisher Taione, a Tongan citizen resident in Auckland, New Zealand, who was charged under the newspaper regulation act with importing the banned *Taimi 'o Tonga* newspaper into Tonga; Kalafi Moala, chief executive officer of Lali Media Group Limited, owners of the banned *Taimi 'o Tonga* newspaper; Mateni Tapueluelu, editor of *Taimi 'o Tonga;* Po'oi Pohiva, publisher and deputy editor of *Kele'a,* who was initially not given a license to publish under the new newspaper act; Samiuela 'Akilisi Pohiva, people's representative in the Legislative Assembly; and 150 others, including other people's representatives, district and town officers, religious leaders, individuals, and organizations. For case notes, see *Taione v Kingdom of Tonga* [2004] TOSC 47, CV 374 2004 (15 October 2004).

19. In any case, the constitution allows the Legislative Assembly to impeach cabinet ministers for "maladministration, incompetence, destruction or embezzlement of Government property." This accountability mechanism, however, does not apply to the people's representatives in recognition (I am presuming here) of the fact they are elected under universal suffrage by the people.

20. US Department of State, *Country Reports on Human Rights Practices, 2001.*

21. In the case of *The King v SA. Pohiva,* see Michael J. Ybarra, "In Laid-Back Tonga, a Gadfly Commits Crime of Being Rude—The Monarchy Doesn't Like Akilisi Pohiva's Manners or His Reformist Attacks," *Wall Street Journal* (eastern edition), 23 August 1994, p. A1; Pacific Media Watch, "Tonga: Court Acquits Outspoken Publisher-MP," 9 March 1998, available at http://www.pmw.c2o.org/docs98/tonga1254.html (accessed 14 October 2005).

22. When the government imposed the first two bans in 2003, it first used the Customs and Excise Act and then the Prohibited Publications Act. When these bans were declared invalid by the Supreme Court, His Majesty, in Privy Council, created a new ordinance using section 7 of the Government Act. The Supreme Court also declared this ordinance invalid, then the government turned that same ordinance into the Media Operator's Act, which was declared void in October 2004.

23. L. Senituli, "Tongan Government Did Best to Facilitate Reform," *Pacific Islands Report,* 23 January 2007, available at http://archives.pireport.org/archive/2007/january/01-23-comm2.htm (accessed 3 February 2007).

14

Conclusion

M. Anne Brown

A CROSS MUCH of the Pacific Islands region, life in the villages, where most Pacific Islanders live, is relatively peaceful and orderly—without the presence of police. Talk of the problems the region faces can obscure the reality of its social cohesion and resilience. This cohesion is under great pressure, however, from the complex dynamics of far-reaching and rapid social, economic, and political change. As in postcolonial communities elsewhere, regional states and territories in the Pacific Islands face severe difficulties, as the chapters in this book have indicated: hardship and poverty, demographic pressures and unemployment, growing inequality, systemic leadership failures, mismanagement and corruption, intercommunal tension, serious erosion of law and order, environmental degradation, and HIV/AIDS.

These problems arise from a complex mix of causes. They are rarely, however, a consequence of the nature of Pacific Island life or social and cultural patterns per se (nor are they a result of introduced political traditions and international economic dynamics in themselves). Rather, problems are frequently the result of the interaction of indigenous factors with external forces—from the confusion between customary and state-based forms of legitimacy, authority, and justice, the tension between communally based and commercial economic life, and also from the sheer difficulty of being small, largely communally based economies operating within the demands of the postindustrial global economy. The problems with which regional states are grappling reflect the transitional nature of Pacific Islands political community—they are not failing states, but emerging states. Rather than faltering with state institutions as we know them, Pacific nations are engaged in a difficult but generative process of experimentation and adaptation as people and governments seek to build states that are grounded in and relevant to their own collective lives.

Perhaps the fundamental challenges facing Oceanic nations, then, concern how they can respond to and work with contemporary global dynamics and structures—liberal state institutions, the cash economy, and global markets—in ways that draw on, and do not destroy, the sources of resilience that sustain their societies.

Understanding the region as made up of emerging rather than failing states encourages a subtle but significant shift of perspective. Factors that come into greater prominence include the place of community in Pacific economic and political life, the interface between local and introduced traditions, the legitimacy (rather than simply the transfer) of state institutions and traditions, and the key role of citizenship in the development of strong political communities and strong states.

▪ Community and Citizenship

The centrality of community life in the Pacific Islands region has been referred to in a number of chapters in this volume. However, analysts from outside the region reflecting on the dilemmas confronting it often see the small-scale nature of Pacific Islands (particularly Melanesian) political organization, its social and cultural diversity, and the strong tendency to identify with clan ties, rather than with broader national or institutional affiliations, as leading problems for states and governance in the region. "Melanesian culture is warlike and tribal," Australian journalist Greg Sheridan asserts (overlooking the peaceful nature of most Melanesian life).[1] But smallness, diversity, and associated features of Pacific Islands societies also work as sources of strength.

The disconnection between society and state discussed in this volume can be seen as a struggle between opposing forces—as "a more fundamental conflict over which organisations . . . , the state or others, should make the rules."[2] While there is a gulf and often tension between the local and the national, and between society and state institutions in much of the Pacific Islands region, there is not necessarily an opposition. To cast the problem as one of a struggle between essentially "traditional" and "modern" processes is to abstract and fix these categories far too rigidly, while to pit local patterns of social life and value against liberal institutional models is to view events—and conceive of policy—in terms of an unwinnable and mutually diminishing conflict.

Development agencies have responded to development and security challenges in Oceania by mounting programs to strengthen government institutions (particularly justice, security, and financial institutions). This is important work, but the "state" is not reducible to central institutions; nor do central institutions work effectively or carry significant legitimacy if they fail to connect with the value structures or practical circumstances in which they are operating, as Abby McLeod has made clear in Chapter 4 regarding the limitations of police reform in Papua New Guinea (PNG). If the weaknesses of many state institutions are in significant part the result of their lack of grounding in society, then focusing on the interface between state and society is at least as important as focusing on the institutions alone.

Supporting a democratic state, then, lies in working not only with governments, although this is vital, but also with communities, and with the structures of authority and legitimacy that provide many of the working underpinnings of social order—what Marion Jacka in Chapter 2 has called state building from the "bottom up." Government at the local level is often involved in a very practical search for a marriage between introduced and local governance norms and mechanisms, between the (changing) values of custom and emerging civil society groupings, and between state institutions and the community. Equally, where states have little capacity to provide services, but where customary or local community authority remains significant, working with community-level governance in ways that complement rather than rival central government functions may be as valuable as supporting state institutions.

Customary political, social, and economic life is alive and evolving in the Pacific Islands; forms of the state are also undergoing change. Despite their lack of fit, they are already interwoven in practice, as a report on customary leadership in the Solomon Islands explains: "Traditional leadership and modern practices are not separate things, but influence each other, especially at the level of regional leadership," while "a good traditional leader is someone who is able to acquire new knowledge and skills of value to the community, while remaining knowledgeable in matters of custom and history."[3] Assisting the development of constructive relationships between communities and governments, and between customary and introduced political, social, and economic dynamics, is a way of drawing on the strengths of Pacific Island states to contribute to political and economic stability and vitality.

State building from the "bottom up" also involves supporting the growth of a more active grasp of citizenship. Political institutions are embedded in social relations; the quality of these institutions and of national political life is interdependent with the quality of citizenship. A key element of the weakness of state institutions and processes in much of the Pacific has been the lack of appropriate pressures for accountability, pressures that are significantly generated by citizens. However, citizenship, which develops very gradually, has arguably received much less support in the region than government institutions—perhaps because supporting citizenship seems a diffuse and elusive objective. Greater connection between government and communities, and the emergence of a broader understanding of national citizenship, is fundamental to a working democracy and to accountability at all levels.

As noted earlier, the strength of clan and community identifications in the Pacific region is sometimes seen as being in conflict with both national citizenship and the effective operation of parliaments and bureaucracy. There can be tension between competing obligations and between quite different constructions of community at the local and national levels. Except for the churches, broader forms of civil society (that can link local, national, and even international life) are still nascent in much of the region. This might suggest that building effective citizenship involves some form of rejection of local ties. However, endeavoring to build citizenship through undoing or ignoring the forms of sociality that already exist and through which people form their identities, is not likely to be productive. Citizenship, and a broader, more inclusive sense of community, could be sought through engagement with, rather than rejection of, community life at the local level. The evolving role of community governance could be explored as a context for the formation of citizenship. As Clive Moore notes in Chapter 9 in relation to the Solomon Islands, "First, the village is the key to understanding development in the Solomon Islands. Second, civil society (including the churches) is increasingly an important part of the nation, along side the formal government structure. Third, now is the time to radically rethink the role of . . . governments and their relationship with ordinary citizens." All three elements seem likely to be essential to supporting the state in Oceania.

Assistance for public education that fosters the community awareness and skills that underpin citizenship, that respects and engages actively with cultural norms, and that encourages cross-cultural and cross-ethnic respect in the many multicultural and multiethnic societies in the region, could also be a powerful tool in the region's movement toward governments well rooted in their own societies. This includes both basic education, such as literacy, as well as forms of civic education.

This dual emphasis of working with communities and with central government applies to enhancing economic growth as well as to supporting the emergence of state forms grounded in and able to sustain the lives and hopes of Pacific Islanders. Large economic projects are often centered around resource extraction or enclave developments. Community-based initiatives have the potential to expand the range of employment and income in rural areas, absorbing some of the expanding youth population. However, they could also be explicitly oriented to finding ways to both respect communal land tenure and encourage commercial initiative, and so serve as a bridge between customary and commercial economies: "Traditional leadership and leadership in the modern cash economy require different kinds of knowledge and skill, but may also be combined."[4] Local communities could be assisted to improve their ability to engage with, make sense of, and benefit from the pressures of economic, social, and political change they face, rather than being overwhelmed and undermined by those forces.

Recognizing the significance, endurance, and vitality of community and customary life in the Pacific Island region is not backward-looking, nostalgic, or romantic, as is sometimes claimed. On the contrary, it is a way of moving forward, by drawing on the resilience of Pacific societies in order to help work with the dilemmas and problems that are part of being an emerging state. The lens of conflict prevention brings into sharp relief the critical value of efforts on the part of those outside the region to take traditional or local forms of life and livelihood seriously. If preventing debilitating, embedded violence is a guiding value, then paying attention to the sources of social restraint and conflict management, of social cohesion, sustenance, and support, is a fundamental place to start.

The potential for destructive conflict in development trajectories also needs to be taken very seriously. Many of the cases of intercommunal violence discussed in this volume, for example, involve dispute over land, in particular tensions around traditional and commercial forms of land tenure. Significantly altering communal landownership arrangements, for example, can generate not only resource conflict, but also identity conflict (conflict over fundamental sources of meaning in life). Identity conflicts are notoriously difficult to resolve, and are unlikely to prove a path to growth. Customary land tenure arrangements are slowly evolving systems. Nevertheless, efforts to reconstruct Pacific Islands societies to fit external development and economic models in order to increase gross domestic product can be highly conflict-prone, and can override local constructions of accountability and appropriate behavior. Any such initiatives need to be assessed in terms of their capacity to fuel violent conflict and social fragmentation. Other paths to modest growth are available.

This is not to suggest that customary and community governance mechanisms have the "answer" to problems of governance in the region, that they are without serious problems of their own, or are capable of dealing with the complexity of contemporary international life. Customary systems did not evolve around or for states, but around lineage communities, and cannot be expected to deal with the particular needs of states, national economies, and international markets. Women and young people are consistently marginalized in customary forms around the region. Nor is there a homogeneous "indigenous system"; rather there exist a great variety of indigenous mechanisms and a range of approaches. The effort to bring together introduced state systems and various local approaches is not a search for a grand solution, but part of an ongoing exchange of experience from which somewhat new forms of political community will slowly take shape.

There are long-standing debates in the region around the marriage of indigenous and introduced governance norms. Some of these debates have focused on the search for constitutional solutions to the dilemmas posed by such a marriage. Experimentation and adjustment in state processes and governance is also ongoing in small, practical, and concrete terms "on the ground." This is a profoundly challenging task. As well as the marginalization of women and youth, involving customary leaders in formal governance "may lead to abuse of power or to diminished respect for leaders seen as bureaucratic appointees rather than as leaders recognized for their traditional knowledge, skill, and involvement with local communities."[5] Excessively formalizing customary authority, and so entrenching it as a form of conservatism rather than as a dynamic cultural exchange, is also a problem.

Experimentation can also be driven by political and social crises, although the challenge remains to avoid the severity of the crises of Bougainville, the Solomon Islands, Fiji, New Caledonia during the 1980s, or West Papua. In the Solomon Islands and PNG, there have been efforts, as Moore notes in Chapter 9, "to Melanesianize the system by devolving more government funds to the level of individual electorates, dispersed by individual politicians but through applications from community groups and with sufficient accounting and advisory procedures." Bougainville offers a striking example of ongoing conflict resolution through creative political solutions at the local, provincial, and national levels, including the negotiation of constitutional and political responses to the struggle over self-determination. As Anthony Regan notes concerning Bougainville in Chapter 5, "Out of the experience of conflict, new norms are emerging about the use of violence both by civil society and by the state." Deliberately slow political, social, and economic negotiation is also under way in New Caledonia in response to violent conflict in the 1980s (although some indigenous New Caledonians are concerned at what they consider to be continuing marginalization within national life).

▪ The Region and Beyond

While this volume has explored particular histories and circumstances, it has also indicated themes that have broader regional application. Despite the great diversity of the region, there is considerable cultural affinity and shared experience binding it, as well as patterns of common problems. Finding ways to deepen collaboration and build on each other's social, cultural, economic, and technical resources to mount regional responses to shared economic, political, and security challenges makes sense in Oceania.

The Pacific Islands region has an active network of intergovernmental agencies as well as civil society and faith-based linkages that build on cultural and historical affinities. The Pacific Islands Forum (PIF) is the premier political intergovernmental body, bringing together heads of governments and ministers from sixteen member states annually. Australia and New Zealand, the major powers in the broader region, are members of the PIF.

The Secretariat for the Pacific Community is one of the oldest regional institutions in the world (established in 1947) and provides technical, planning, and management assistance, and professional and scientific support to the region, including assistance with implementation of the UN's Millennium Development Goals. Other leading organizations include the Melanesian Spearhead Group (specific to Melanesia), the South Pacific Regional Environment Program, the South Pacific Applied Geoscience Commission, the South Pacific Tourism Organization, the Forum Fisheries Agency, and the University of the South Pacific, which has campuses across much of the region. The Pacific Islands Association of Nongovernment Organizations, the Pacific Concerns Resource Center, the Regional Rights Resource Team, the Pacific Conference of Churches, the Foundation of the Peoples of the South Pacific International, the Ecumenical Center for Research and Education, the Pacific Women's Network Against Violence Against Women, and the Pacific Islands News Association are some prominent examples of many active cross-regional nongovernmental organizations (NGOs).

While efforts to strengthen collaboration have been gathering pace, they face some thorny questions. The complexities of collaboration demand innovation, experimentation, and vision, but also patience, consultation, and long-term commitment to cooperative approaches. Closer economic cooperation faces complex questions of how to approach the subsistence economy and customary land tenure arrangements, discussed earlier in the volume. Efforts at the intergovernmental level to improve leadership and financial and political governance depend on agreement and backing from some of the governments that are themselves stymied by leadership and structural problems. Some of the more "technical" forms of cooperation (involving airlines, for example) touch sensitivities around sovereignty—a matter just as delicate in the Pacific as in other regions.

The emerging nature of states in the region also poses challenges for intergovernmental cooperation. Many forms of significant collaboration need to be grounded in Pacific societies to progress, yet governments are themselves not always so grounded. The Pacific Islands Forum, as the leading intergovernmental forum, has the task of reaching beyond this gulf to communicate and shape collaboration in ways that make sense both to Pacific communities and to governments. Pacific Islands societies at all levels value consultation and consensus. Regional cooperation in Oceania requires significant attention to collaborative initiatives at the level of communities and civil society as well as states.

Moreover, the PIF includes not only independent indigenous Pacific Islands states, but also New Zealand and Australia. There is an inevitable danger that economic collaboration, in particular, will move at the pace and conform too closely to the interests of its most powerful members, which, as developed economies and majority settler (rather than indigenous) states, naturally have interests and identifications that are profoundly different from those of their smaller neighbors. For example, there has been some debate about a free trade zone across the region, including possible currency harmonization, but this is a sensitive issue in the region, as the comparatively much stronger and bigger economies of Australia and New Zealand would dominate a free trade zone. The PIF faces the challenge of steering between this danger and its opposite: that suspicion of Australia and New Zealand among Pacific Islands governments will freeze moves toward potentially beneficial forms of collaboration and mutual support.

The Pacific Plan

At an intergovernmental level, the PIF has identified globalization, with its impact on Pacific Islands economies, and the international security environment, as challenges that the countries of the region could best face collaboratively. To stimulate and guide further collaboration, the Pacific Plan has been drawn up—a "living document" that sets out a ten-year working path to build on the region's interconnectedness. The plan is a measured approach to find ways for member countries to work together "for their joint and individual benefit," and there is interest in learning from the experiences of other regions.[6] Four foci have been identified: economic growth, sustainable development, good governance, and regional security.

The Pacific Plan seeks greater economic cooperation and common or more coordinated policies, services, and information systems across a broad scope of activities. There are concerns, however, that some of the more neoliberal economic measures discussed in the broader context of closer regional cooperation and in the lead-up to the plan would themselves intensify hardship and feed into conflict. Measures discussed include privatizing basic service delivery, for example, in areas where few have the ability to pay. The Australian Council for International Development, commenting on the draft plan, expressed concerns with economic and development models based on large-scale natural resource or land-based developments, "because of their historic relationship to conflict and corruption throughout the Pacific. . . . Exploration of the relative appropriateness of smaller-scale and more diverse economic opportunities should be a priority."[7]

The Pacific Plan also addresses regional security. Associated papers recognize "the link between social factors and security."[8] Weak economic growth, increasing inequality, lack of good governance, land issues, environmental degradation, the erosion of food security, disease, lack of access to basic social services, and a range of social tensions, including weakening traditional social support networks, growing squatter settlements, and increasing frustration and unemployment among young people, are identified as human security challenges in the region. The plan sketches a wide variety of ways to deepen understanding of and dialogue around security in the region.

The evolution of a regional approach to security is indicated by a number of joint declarations over the past decade and a half: the Honiara Declaration (1992), which points to cooperative law enforcement, intelligence gathering, training of security forces, and joint exercises as areas of possible security cooperation; the Aitutaki Declaration (1997), which seeks to strengthen regional security through conflict prevention measures, the encouragement of good social, economic, and environmental policies, and preventive diplomacy; the Biketawa Declaration (2000), which agrees on a range of practical political steps for responding to security crises; and the Nasonini Declaration (2002), which sets out the region's commitment to efforts to combat terrorism. There has also been some history of regional responses to national security crises: PNG supported the government of Vanuatu during a crisis shortly after independence; joint monitoring groups (staffed by New Zealand, Australia, Fiji, and Vanuatu, but led first by New Zealand and later by Australia) contributed significantly to the achievement of peace agreements on Bougainville; and the Regional Assistance Mission to the Solomon Islands (RAMSI) has been restoring order in the Solomon Islands. The subregional forum, the Melanesian Spearhead Group (PNG, the Solomon Islands, Vanuatu, and Fiji), was the structural context for PNG's support for Vanuatu in the 1980s, and has also lent some support to the Solomon Islands following political and security turmoil in early 2006.

Importantly, for the first time, RAMSI was deployed under the authority of a regional security agreement (the Biketawa Declaration), and with the explicit backing of the Pacific Islands Forum. Earlier regional responses to security crises were drawn from forum members; however, the PIF as a body was not involved in responding to the Bougainville or earlier crises. (There has also been some criticism of the PIF for its silence on West Papua.) The forum does not provide the leading mechanism for coordinated regional responses to crises. Intergovernmental regional security mechanisms are not yet highly developed, whether security is being addressed through the strategic or the developmental dimensions. Nevertheless, the organization is working toward common standards, policies, and values from which such mechanisms will increasingly emerge. It has also been monitoring sources and triggers of conflict across the region, and seeking greater integration of work on sustainable development and security in order to strengthen conflict prevention. The forum has been working to improve its shared policing of money laundering and the movement of small arms, and developing more common policing standards and training. These are all fundamental elements to creating a substantial framework of collaboration on difficult issues across the region.

Addressing governance, the Pacific Plan has given priority to supporting justice systems across the region, regionwide leadership codes and standards of accountability, and institutions (ombudsmen, attorneys general, auditing boards, and training schemes) to embed these principles. Civil society organizations have also been actively supporting regional links in this area, with human rights one focus of concern. Fiji is so far the only state with a formal human rights commission (the result of historical inter-communal tensions). However, a range of NGOs are active in the promotion of human rights, including economic and social rights, women's rights, active citizenship, reconciliation, and peacebuilding. Many of these NGOs draw on a combination of Christian and traditional values. Regional and national NGOs have participated in international human rights summits (such as the Vienna Conference on Human Rights) and are well-connected with international NGO and church networks. They hold regional confer-ences, workshops, and training programs. Across the region, there are also lively debates over the meaning of "human rights" in the Pacific context, with the position of women and the tension between individual rights and a collectivist culture being contentious issues.

Regionalism is growing in Oceania, with more active links among gov-ernments, civil society, and also customary community leaders, and seems likely to play an increasingly important role in development and security initiatives.

China and Taiwan

China and Taiwan are increasingly active in the region as donors and investors, but they are also in intense competition with each other for diplo-matic recognition. This competition has included very significant cash inducements to local politicians, provided most notably by Taiwan, a prac-tice that has proved destabilizing and corrosive to efforts to improve institu-tional and political integrity.[9] The duel between the two has reached deep into some states and regional agencies, with (for example) change in recog-nition sparking a change of government in Vanuatu in 2004, the suspicion of political campaigns being funded by Taiwan in Kiribati and the Solomon Islands, and the South Pacific Tourism Office the site of debilitating ongo-ing contest. The burning of Chinatown in the Solomon Islands in April 2006 (following the election of a candidate popularly believed to have bought his way into office using funds from Taiwan), though resulting from a complex mix of factors, is a warning of the additional volatility this struggle injects into the region.

Australia and RAMSI

Following decolonization, Australian foreign policy was guided by a combi-nation of significant bilateral aid and a careful effort at noninterference. The

Australian government was sensitive to charges of neocolonialism, and its policy was to provide aid—in the case of PNG, one of the largest bilateral aid programs in the world—but to support "local solutions."[10] The region has been close to the heart of Australia's aid program. However, New Zealand, which is home to a sizable Pacific Islands population, in addition to its own indigenous Maori, has been more intimately involved with Pacific life. Inevitably perhaps, given Australia's relative size, Australian actions often carried disproportionate effects in the region. In sweeping terms, Australia's footprint has outweighed its popular knowledge of and responsiveness toward the region. This has particularly been the case from since the early 1980s, following the end of the formal decolonization era.

Midway through 2003, however, key elements of Australian foreign policy toward the Pacific Islands region underwent a marked policy shift, toward a more hands-on engagement with the region and significantly greater expenditure. Triggered by conflict in the Solomon Islands and concerns about PNG, the Australian Agency for International Development (AusAID) stated, "Australia has sharpened its focus on the region . . . in the context of global security, increasing trans-boundary challenges and the understanding that a porous and undeveloped region is not in the interests of the Pacific or Australia."[11] The new orientation seeks to bring together development assistance, security assistance, and institutional reform in a "whole of government" approach to the region, and represents a notable effort to bring security and development to bear on each other.

The fundamental challenge of this approach, however, is to keep the forms of insecurity most experienced by *Pacific* states at the core of the Australian response, and then to build on regional strengths in combating these sources of insecurity. This is the most effective way to actually counter security problems and so to meet Australian and regional interests. The alternative is that security anxieties circulating in Australia overly dominate Australian responses. According to a major national daily newspaper, for example, "Terrorism and organised crime could flourish on Australia's doorstep, triggering an exodus of the displaced, if Pacific nations are allowed to collapse."[12] While organized crime, often originating outside the region, is increasingly a problem, security responses shaped according to concerns with terrorism and organized crime may not be best-suited to dealing with the region's underlying security problems.

The Australian government's policy shift was marked by a decision to deploy RAMSI in response to the deepening crisis in the Solomon Islands, in the Australian proposal to expand assistance to policing, law and justice, border management, economic management, and public sector management in Papua New Guinea (the Enhanced Cooperation Program), and by a more assertive position on questions of governance and corruption. The Australian government is prepared for RAMSI to be a long-term commitment, if it is desired by the Solomon Islands government; as such, it is a significant effort at sustained engagement that recognizes the long-term nature of postconflict state building.

The genuine difficulty facing RAMSI, however, is to establish engagement and partnership, while avoiding new, subtle forms of "colonization." There have been local criticisms that RAMSI is distant from the social and cultural realities of the population, which will work against partnership. Clive Moore comments in Chapter 9 that the "conflict resolution, human security, and development initiatives that have emerged so far are not sufficiently radical to redress the current instability of the Solomon Island central government." The central issues of reform, he argues, are the gulf between communities and government, and between indigenous systems of power and authority and modern liberal democratic governance structures. These questions are not the work of a regional assistance mission—fundamentally, responses must be nutted through by Solomon Islanders. They are, however, a challenge to partnership.

For Australia or other international interlocutors, it is critically important that acknowledging the need for local solutions in Oceania does not amount to a form of disengagement. While the shape of political community within the Solomon Islands, in this case, can only emerge from Solomon Islanders, the challenges they face are ones that in various ways are shared with others, and that deeply engage the broader region, including Australia and New Zealand. In greater and lesser ways, we have all been part of the historical emergence of these dilemmas concerning the nature of political community in Pacific Islands states; it makes sense that we support the process of generating creative solutions. Understanding and support over the long term in working with these fundamental and difficult questions of the emerging structure of political and economic community are the challenges of partnership. Partnership, however, involves mutuality and exchange—it is not primarily the delivery of a message from those with putative answers, to those seen to be defined by their problems. The evolution of the state in the Pacific may have new things to teach us all about the shapes of political community.

◼ Ways Forward

For those seeking to support constructive development and greater security in the region, guiding questions might be the following: How can the search for creative interaction between customary mechanisms and state forms of governance be supported? How can economic growth and employment levels for Pacific societies improve in ways that do not undermine but build on the frameworks sustaining community welfare?

To pursue development and security in the Pacific Island region as fundamentally linked and mutually supportive goals, it is important to recognize and work with the strengths of Pacific life. The high levels of social resilience that are largely grounded in Pacific Island community life constitute the foremost among these strengths. Partnership that recognizes the strengths as well as the weaknesses of the partners is a vital element of conflict prevention, as well as a strong and creative basis for working with security and development dilemmas in the region.

Pacific Islands states are better understood as emerging rather than failing states. Part of being an emerging state is that the links between the institutions of the state and the life and values of the community are still undeveloped and can work to undermine or distort each other. Many of the region's problems flow from this still-undeveloped relationship between state and society. Recognizing this has significant implications for efforts to enhance state building, governance, and justice, and encourages a somewhat different policy perspective than that provided by the framework of state failure. In particular, understanding the region as made up of emerging states, with a disconnection between state institutions and community values, encourages an emphasis on supporting a positive interface between communities and governments and on the development of citizenship.

Better-operating states, a growing sense of citizenship, improved economic well-being, and questions of land tenure are central to security and development in the Pacific. In working with these challenges, it is of fundamental importance to engage positively with communities as the basis for much of the social cohesion and resilience in the region. Engaging with communities is as important as working with governments and central institutions. The health of communities, which includes customary sociopolitical and economic life and their interaction with government, is central to states working well in the Pacific. The position of women could be taken as a major contributor to, and indicative of, the health of communities.

Economic well-being is not likely to be achieved by pushing through models of land tenure that are inimical to how most Pacific Islanders understand community, and that undermine food security. Customary land tenure is evolving: there is scope to search for imaginative solutions to the need for investment, and to explore the potential for smaller local enterprises to contribute to managing the tension between economic change and traditional values. Supporting local rural enterprise, compatible with community structures, is a significant way of contributing to community and economic health.

The region is still struggling with questions of self-determination, in both subtle and more conventional forms. Developments in West Papua warrant greater attention, while there is much value in international bodies exploring how best to assist the Indonesian government, the Indonesian army, and West Papuan groups in addressing the causes of serious violence in the territory.

When we are looking at questions of development and security in the Pacific Islands region, we are looking not only at the Pacific itself, but also at a network and history of relationships with the region. The context for understanding development and security is always a broader history of exchange, including, in this case, the complex exchanges that were part of coercive colonization. Phrases such as "basket cases" or "failed states," however, reflect and reinforce a sense of cleavage between "us" (as Westerners in this context) and "them" (as indigenous Pacific Islanders) and a lack of awareness of the extent to which our modern histories and contemporary realities are entwined. Those of us in Western developed states can sometimes approach the Pacific Islands region as if the task of development were to teach them how to do our institutions better. Developed states indeed have a depth of valuable experience in the operation of state institutions upon which Pacific Islands states do and could meaningfully draw. We all have things to learn from each other, however; how to live well with each other remains the fundamental challenge that we all share.

In addition, the nature of states and of state institutions is changing in complex ways in various regions. Developments in the Pacific Islands region are part of this process, and may offer valuable insights for other regions. Alan Patience, professor of politics at the University of Papua New Guinea, sums this up well: "If contemporary statist thinking is not approached more creatively—i.e., if modern state structures themselves are not radically interrogated in relation to the conditions and needs of PNG and its peoples—no form of sustainable state-making can occur in PNG (or for that matter, anywhere else in the South Pacific)."[13]

How would external actors approach the region if we really started to look at the Pacific as a place of innovative adaptation of international democratic and bureaucratic traditions—a place with clever people working on difficult problems (to borrow a comment by Anthony Regan)[14]—rather than as a place of failed or failing states?

▨ Notes

1. Greg Sheridan, "Melanesia Is a Huge Disaster," *The Australian,* 20 April 2006, p. 12.

2. Migdal, *Strong Societies and Weak States,* p. 37.

3. White, "Traditional Leaderships Report," p. 10.

4. Ibid., p. 10.

5. Ibid., p. 2.

6. Pacific Islands Forum Secretariat, *Pacific Plan for Strengthening Regional Cooperation and Integration* (9 December 2004), chap. 3, para 6.

7. Australian Council for International Development, *Comments on the Draft Pacific Plan, Submission to the Secretariat of the PIF* (Canberra, 2005), pp. 11–12.

8. Pacific Islands Forum Secretariat, *Regional Analysis Security Summary* (5 May 2005), p. 1, available at http://www.forumsec.org.fj (accessed 11 July 2006).

9. As of May 2006, Papua New Guinea, Fiji, Vanuatu, Samoa, Tonga, the Federated States of Micronesia, and the Cook Islands recognize the People's Republic of China, while the Solomon Islands, Tuvalu, Kiribati, Palau, Nauru, and the Marshall Islands recognize Taiwan.

10. This is a generalization. During the 1980s, which was also a turbulent time for parts of the Pacific, Australian policy was open to intervention upon the request of the relevant government. As Sinclair Dinnen has pointed out, Australia's more recent involvement in East Timor and elsewhere also contributed to the Australian government's willingness to intervene in the Solomon Islands on the request of the latter. Dinnen, "Lending a Fist?" p. 5.

11. Australian Agency for International Development, *Pacific Regional Aid Strategy, 2004–9* (Canberra, 2004), p. 11.

12. *Samantha Maiden,* "Support for Pacific States Not Indefinite: Costello," *The Australian,* 4 July 2006.

13. Patience, "The ECP and Australia's Middle Power Ambitions," p. 10.

14. Anthony Regan, verbal comments at the "Good News Workshop," Divine Word University, Madang, 24–26 November 2004.

Bibliography

Abrash, Abigail. *Development Aggression: Observations on Human Rights Conditions in the PT Freeport Indonesia Contract of Work Areas, with Recommendations.* Washington, D.C.: Robert F. Kennedy Memorial Center for Human Rights, 2002.

ACFOA (Australian Council for Overseas Aid). *Australia and the Pacific: Update on Current Issues and Trends.* Canberra, August 2002.

———. *Inquiry into Australia's Relationship with Papua New Guinea and Other Pacific Island Countries: Submission to the Senate Foreign Affairs, Defence, and Trade References Committee.* Canberra, July 2002.

Adams, Rebecca (ed.). *Gudpela Nius Bilong Pis: Peace on Bougainville—Truce Monitoring Group.* Wellington: Victoria University Press, 2001.

Aldrich, Robert. *France and the South Pacific Since 1940.* London: Macmillan, 1993.

Aleck, Jonathan. "Law and Sorcery in Papua New Guinea." PhD dissertation, Faculty of Law, Australian National University, Canberra, 1998.

Ali, A. *Plantation to Politics: Studies on Fiji Indians.* Suva: University of the South Pacific, 1980.

Allan, Colin H. "Customary Land Tenure in the British Solomon Islands Protectorate." Report of the Special Lands Commission. Honiara: Western Pacific High Commission, 1957.

Alpers, P., and C. Twyford. "Small Arms in the Pacific." Small Arms Survey Occasional Paper no. 8. Geneva: Graduate Institute of International Studies, 2003.

Anckar, D. "Westminster Democracy: A Comparison of Small Island States Varieties in the Pacific and the Caribbean." *Pacific Studies* 23(3–4), 2000, pp. 57–76.

Anderson, Tim. "A Grand Deceit: The World Bank's Claims of 'Good Governance' in Papua New Guinea." Report prepared for the Australian Conservation Foundation and the Center for Environmental Law and Community Rights. Papua New Guinea, 2003.

Angleviel, Frédéric (ed.). *Nouvelle-Calédonie: Terre de Recherches—Bibliographie Analytique des Thèses et Mémoires.* Noumea: Thèse-Pac, 2000.

Arréghini, Louis, and Philippe Waniez. *La Nouvelle-Calédonie au Tournant des Années 1990: Un Etat des Lieux.* Montpellier: Reclus, La Documentation Française, and Orstom, 1993.

Asian Development Bank. *Country Assistance Plan: Nauru, 1998–1999.* Manila, 2005.

———. *Country Assistance Plan: Tonga, 2001–2003.* Manila, December 2000. Available at http://www.adb.org/documents/caps/ton.pdf (accessed 24 May 2006).

———. *Country Strategy and Program Update, 2005–2006: Papua New Guinea.* Manila, 2006. Available at http://www.adb.org/documents/csps/png/2005/cspu-png-2005.pdf (accessed 1 February 2007).

———. *Economic Trends and Prospects in Asia, Nauru.* Manila, 2005.

———. *Priorities of the Poor in Papua New Guinea.* Manila, 2002.

———. *Responding to the Priorities of the Poor: A Pacific Strategy for the Asian Development Bank, 2005–2009.* Manila, 2004.

———. *Technical Assistance to Nauru for Strengthening the Ministry of Finance.* R345-00. Manila, December 2000.

ASPI (Australian Strategic Policy Institute). *Strengthening Our Neighbour: Australia and the Future of Papua New Guinea.* Canberra, 2004.

Audigier, François. "L'Affaire de la Grotte d'Ouvea et l'Élection Présidentielle de 1988." In Jean-Marc Regnault (ed.), *François Mitterrand et les Territoires Français du Pacifique, 1981–1988.* Paris: Les Indes Savantes, 2003, pp. 453–461.

AusAID (Australian Agency for International Development). "Australian Aid: Promoting Growth and Stability—A Whitepaper on the Australian Government's Overseas Aid Program." Canberra, 2006.

———. "The Contribution of Australian Aid to Papua New Guinea's Development, 1975–2000: Provisional Conclusions." Rapid Assessment, Evaluation, and Review Series no. 34. Canberra, June 2003.

———. "Framework: Australia's Aid Program to Papua New Guinea." Canberra, 2002. Available at http://www.ausaid.gov.au/publications/pdf/png_framework.pdf (accessed 1 February 2007).

———. "Framework for AusAID Assistance to Bouganville, 2004–2008." Canberra, 2004.

———. "Poverty Reduction Analysis." Background paper for PNG Law and Justice Sector Program. Canberra, 2004.

Bakeo, R. M. *The Crisis of Post-Independence Development in Vanuatu.* Suva: University of the South Pacific, 2000.

Baker, L. "Political Integrity in Papua New Guinea and the Search for Stability: Implications of the Organic Law on Integrity of Political Parties and Candidates 2001 for Political Stability in Papua New Guinea." *Pacific Economic Bulletin* update paper. Sydney: Australian National University and the Lowy Institute for International Policy, 21 May 2004.

Ballentine, Karen, and Jake Sherman. *The Political Economy of Armed Conflict: Beyond Greed and Grievance.* Boulder: Lynne Rienner, 2003.

Baloiloi, Misty. "Kumul 2020: A Twenty Year Development Plan for Papua New Guinea." Paper presented to the "State, Society, and Governance in Melanesia" seminar, Department of Political and Social Change, Australian National University, Canberra, 31 May 2001.

Banks, C. "Contextualising Sexual Violence: Rape and Carnal Knowledge in Papua New Guinea." In S. Dinnen and A. Ley (eds.), *Reflections on Violence in Melanesia.* Leichhardt, NSW: Federation Press, 2000, pp. 83–104.

———. "Deconstructing Violence in Papua New Guinea: The Primacy of Local Definitions." In C. Banks (ed.), *Developing Cultural Criminology: Theory and*

Practice in Papua New Guinea. Sydney: Institute of Criminology, 2000, pp. 79–128.

———. *Women in Transition: Social Control in Papua New Guinea.* Canberra: Australian Institute of Criminology, 1993.

Barbançon, Louis-José. *L'Archipel des Forçats: Histoire du Bagne en Nouvelle-Calédonie (1863–1931).* Paris: Presses Universitaires du Septentrion, 2003.

Bathgate, Murray A. *Fight for the Dollar: Economic and Social Change in Western Guadalcanal, Solomon Islands.* Wellington: Alexander Enterprise, 1993.

Bathgate, Murray A., Ian L. Frazer, and J. M. McKinnon. *Socio-Economic Change in Solomon Island Villages: Summary Team Report of the Victoria University of Wellington Socio-Economic Survey of the B.S.I.P.* Wellington: Department of Geography, Victoria University of Wellington, 1973.

Baxter, M. "Enclaves or Equity? The Rural Crisis and Development Choice in Papua New Guinea." *International Development* no. 54. Canberra: AusAID, 2001.

BCL (Bougainville Copper Limited). "The Economic Impact of Bougainville Copper." Supplement to *CRA Gazette* (Melbourne) 25(6), 12 October 1990.

Bedford, Richard, and Alexander Mamak. "Compensation for Development: The Bougainville Case." *Bougainville Special Publication* no. 2. Christchurch: University of Canterbury, Department of Geography, 1977.

Bello, Walden. "Globalization, Insecurity, and Overextension." In Annelies Heijmans, Nicola Simmonds, and Hans van de Veen (eds.), *Searching for Peace in the Asia-Pacific: An Overview of Conflict Prevention and Peacebuilding Activities.* Boulder: Lynne Rienner, 2004, pp. 67–84.

Bennett, Judith A. *Pacific Forest: A History of Resource Control and Contest in Solomon Islands, c. 1800–1997.* Cambridge: White Horse, 2000.

———. *Wealth of the Solomons: A History of a Pacific Archipelago, 1800–1978.* Honolulu: University of Hawaii Press, 1987.

Berdal, Mats, and David M. Malone (eds.). *Greed and Grievance: Economic Agendas in Civil Wars.* Boulder: Lynne Rienner, 2000.

Biles, D. (ed.). *Crime in Papua New Guinea.* Canberra: Australian Institute of Criminology, 1976.

Blair, Dennis, and David Phillips. "Peace and Progress in Papua." Report of an independent commission sponsored by the Council on Foreign Relations. New York: Council on Foreign Relations, 2003.

Blaser, Mario, Harvey A. Feit, and Glenn McRae. *In the Way of Development: Indigenous People, Life Projects, and Globalization.* London: Zed, 2004.

Blunt, P. "Cultural Relativism, 'Good' Governance, and Sustainable Human Development." *Public Administration and Development* 15(1), 1995, pp. 1–9.

Boege, Volker. *Conflict Potential and Violent Conflicts in the South Pacific: Options for a Civil Peace Service.* Hamburg: Universitat Hamburg–IPW, 2001.

Boege, Volker, and Lorraine Garasu. "Papua New Guinea: A Success Story of Postconflict Peacebuilding in Bougainville." In Annelies Heijman, Nicola Simmonds, and Hans van de Veen (eds.), *Searching for Peace in Asia Pacific: An Overview of Conflict Prevention and Peacebuilding Activities.* Boulder: Lynne Rienner, 2004, pp. 564–579.

Bolton, L. "Chief Willie Bongmatur Maldo and the Role of Chiefs in Vanuatu." *Journal of Pacific History* 33(2), 1998, pp. 179–195.

Bonay, Yohanes, and Jane McGrory. "West Papua: Building Peace Through an Understanding of Conflict." In Annnelies Heijman, Nicola Simmonds, and Hans van de Veen (eds.), *Searching for Peace in Asia Pacific: An Overview of*

Conflict Prevention and Peacebuilding Activities. Boulder: Lynne Rienner, 2004, pp. 452–453.

Bone, Robert C. *The Dynamics of the West New Guinea (Irian Barat) Problem.* New York: Cornell University Press, 1958.

Borrey, A. "Sexual Violence in Perspective: The Case of Papua New Guinea." In S. Dinnen and A. Ley (eds.), *Reflections on Violence in Melanesia.* Leichhardt, NSW: Federation Press, 2000, pp. 105–118.

Bougainville Constitutional Commission. "Brief of the 2nd Draft of the Bougainville Constitution." Buka, 4 April 2003.

————. "Report of the Bougainville Constitutional Commission: Report on the Third and Final Draft of the Bougainville Constitution." Buka, July, 2004.

Bourke, R. Michael, and Thomas Betitis. *Sustainability of Agriculture in Bougainville Province: Papua New Guinea.* Canberra: Land Management Group, Research School of Pacific and Asian Studies, Australian National University, 2003.

Boydell, S. *Land Tenure and Land Conflict in the South Pacific.* Suva: FAO, 2001.

Brown, S. *History of the Fiji Police.* Suva: Fiji Police Force, 1989.

Brundige, Elizabeth, Winter King, Priyneha Vahali, Stephen Vladeck, and Xiang Yuan. "Indonesian Human Rights Abuses in West Papua: Application of the Law of Genocide to the History of Indonesian Control." Paper prepared for the Indonesia Human Rights Network, Allard K. Lowenstein International Human Rights Clinic, Yale Law School, Yale University, 2003.

Budiardjo, Carmel, and Liem Soei Liong. *West Papua: The Obliteration of a People.* Surrey: Tapol, 1988.

Butt, Leslie, Gerdha Numbery, and Jake Morin. "Preventing AIDS in Papua: Revised Research Report." Jayapura: Universitas Cendrawasih, 2002. Available at http://www.papuaweb.org/dlib/tema/hiv-aids/butt-2002-prevent.pdf (accessed 12 March 2005).

Campbell, I. C. *Island Kingdom: Tonga Ancient & Modern.* Christchurch: Canterbury University Press, 1992.

Care, Jennifer Corrin. "Off the Peg or Made to Measure: Is the Westminster System of Government Appropriate to the Solomon Islands?" *Alternative Law Journal* 27(5), 2002, pp. 207–211, 244.

Carl, Andy, and Lorraine Garasu (eds.). "Weaving Consensus: The Papua New Guinea–Bougainville Peace Process." *Accord* (12). London: Conciliation Resources, 2002.

Carmody, Shane. "The South Pacific: Zone of Peace or Sea of Troubles." Presentation to the Australian Defence Studies Centre conference, Australian Defence Force Academy, Canberra, 17–18 August 2000.

Catholic Relief Services. *The Peacebuilding Toolkit: Learning from Good Practice: The Experience of Indonesian Peacebuilding.* Jakarta, 2003.

Chalmers, D., and Paliwala, A. *An Introduction to the Law in Papua New Guinea.* Sydney: Law Book Company, 1977.

Chand, Satish. "Papua New Guinea Economic Survey: Transforming Good Luck into Policies for Long-Term Growth." *Pacific Economic Bulletin* 19(1), 2004, pp. 1–19.

Chauvel, Richard. "Constructing Papuan Nationalism: History, Ethnicity, and Adaption." *Policy Study* (14). Washington, D.C.: East West Centre, 2005.

————. "Decolonising Without the Colonised: The Liberation of Irian Jaya." In Doleres Elizalde (ed.), *Las Relaciones Internacionales en el Pacifico: Colonizacion, Descolonizacion y Encuentro Cultural.* Madrid: Consejo Superiorde Investigacion Certificas, 1997, pp. 553–574.

————. "Essays on West Papua." Vol. 1. Working Paper no. 120. Victoria, Australia: Monash Asia Institute, Monash University, 2003.

————. "Essays on West Papua." Vol. 2. Working Paper no. 121. Victoria, Australia: Monash Asia Institute, Monash University, 2003.

Chauvel, Richard, and Ikar Nusa Bhakti. "The Papua Conflict: Jakarta's Perceptions and Policies." *Policy Study* (5). Washington, D.C.: East West Center, 2004.

Christnacht, Alain. "L'Œil de Matignon: Les Affaires Corses de Lionel Jospin." In *L'Épreuve des faits*. Paris: Le Seuil, 2003, pp. 9–100.

————. *La Nouvelle-Calédonie*. Paris: La Documentation Française, 2004.

Clements, Kevin. Foreword to Annelies Heijmans, Nicola Simmonds, and Hans van de Veen (eds.), *Searching for Peace in the Asia-Pacific: An Overview of Conflict Prevention and Peacebuilding Activities*. Boulder: Lynne Rienner, 2004, pp. ix–xii.

Clifford, W., L. Morauta, and B. Stuart. *Law and Order in Papua New Guinea*. Port Moresby: Institute of National Affairs and Institute of Applied Social and Economic Research, 1984.

Collier, Paul, and Anke Hoeffler. "On Economic Causes of War." *Oxford Economic Papers* 50(4), 1998, pp. 563–573.

Colombani, Jean-Marie. *Double Calédonie: D'Une Utopie à l'Autre*. Paris: Denoel 1999.

Commonwealth of Australia. *A Pacific Engaged: Australia's Relations with Papua New Guinea and the Island States of the South-West Pacific*. Canberra: Foreign Affairs, Defence, and Trade References Committee, August 2003.

"Conflict in Bougainville: Part 3—Successes of the Bougainville Revolutionary Army: An Interview with Sam Kauona Sirivi." *NZine*, 30 June 2000. Available at http://www.nzine.co.nz/features/bville3.html (accessed 12 June 2005).

Connell, John. "Compensation and Conflict: The Bougainville Copper Mine, Papua New Guinea." In John Connell and Richard Howitt (eds.), *Mining and Indigenous Peoples in Australasia*. Sydney: Sydney University Press, 1991, pp. 55–75.

————. "The Panguna Mine Impact." In P. Polomka, *Bougainville: Perspectives on a Crisis*. Canberra: Strategic and Defence Studies Centre, Australian National University, 1990.

————. "Taim Bilong Mani: The Evolution of Agriculture in a Solomon Island Society." Australian Development Studies Monograph no. 12. Canberra: Australian National University, 1978.

Coppet, Daniel de. "'Land Owns People': In Honour of the Late Allki Nono'ohimae Eerehau." In R. H Barnes, Daniel de Coppet, and R. J. Parkin (eds.), *Contexts and Levels: Anthropological Essays on Hierarchy*. Occasional Paper no. 4. Oxford: JASO, 1985, pp. 78–90.

Corris, Peter. *Passage, Port, and Plantation: A History of the Solomon Islands Labour Migration, 1870–1914*. Melbourne: Melbourne University Press, 1973.

Counts, D. "All Men Do It: Wife Beating in Kaliai, Papua New Guinea." In D. Counts, J. Brown, and J. Campbell (eds.), *To Have and to Hit: Cultural Perspectives on Wife Beating*. Urbana: University of Illinois Press, 1999, pp. 73–86.

Cox, E. "Appropriate Development: Twenty-five Years of Changing Non-Government Efforts and Organizations." *Development Bulletin* (50), October 1999, pp. 6–10.

Crocombe, Ron. "Enhancing Pacific Security." Report prepared for the Pacific Islands Forum Regional Security Committee meeting, July 2000.

Crocombe, Ron, and Christine Geise. "Nauru: The Politics of Phosphate." In Ron

Crocombe (ed.), *The Politics of Micronesia.* Suva: Institute for Pacific Studies, 1989, pp. 29–54.

Crossland, K. J. "The Ombudsman Role: Vanuatu's Experiment." State, Society, and Governance in Melanesia Discussion Paper no. 00/5. Canberra: Research School of Pacific and Asian Studies, Australian National University, 2000.

Curtin, Tim, Hartmut Holznecht, and Peter Larmour. "Land Registration in Papua New Guinea: Competing Perspectives." State, Society, and Governance in Melanesia Discussion Paper no. 1. Canberra: Research School of Pacific and Asian Studies, Australian National University, 2003.

Davenport, William, and Gulbun Coker. "The Moro Movement of Guadalcanal, British Solomon Islands Protectorate." *Journal of the Polynesian Society* 76(2), 1967, pp. 123–175.

Davies, Matthew. "Indonesian Security Responses to Resurgent Papuan Separatism: An Open Source Intelligence Case Study." Working Paper no. 361. Canberra: Strategic and Defence Studies Centre, Australian National University, 2001.

Denoon, Donald. *Getting Under the Skin: The Bougainville Copper Agreement and the Creation of the Panguna Mine.* Melbourne: Melbourne University Press, 2000.

——— (eds.). *Rabuka: No Other Way.* Moorebank: Doubleday, 1988.

Denoon, Donald, et al. (eds.). *The Cambridge History of the Pacific Islanders.* Cambridge: Cambridge University Press, 1997.

Development Studies Network. "Discussion: Development—Papua New Guinean Perspectives." *Development Bulletin* (50), October 1999, pp. 4–5.

Dinnen, Sinclair. "Building Bridges: Law and Justice Reform in Papua New Guinea." State, Society, and Governance in Melanesia Discussion Paper no. 2. Canberra: Research School of Pacific Studies, Australian National University, 2002.

——— (ed.). *A Kind of Mending: Restorative Justice in the Pacific Islands.* Canberra: Pandanus, 2003.

———. *Law and Order in a Weak State: Crime and Politics in Papua New Guinea.* Honolulu: University of Hawaii Press, 2001.

———. "Lending a Fist? Australia's New Interventionism in the Southwest Pacific." State, Society, and Governance in Melanesia Discussion Paper no. 5. Canberra: Australian National University, 2004.

———. "Praise the Lord and Pass the Ammunition: Criminal Group Surrender in Papua New Guinea." *Oceania* 66(2), 1995, pp. 103–118.

———. "Restorative Justice in Papua New Guinea." *International Journal of the Sociology of Law* (25), 1997, pp. 245–262.

———. "The Trouble with Melanesia." In Ivan Molloy (ed.), *The Eye of the Cyclone: Issues in Pacific Security.* Sippy Downs: University of the Sunshine Coast/PIPSA, 2004, pp. 70–72.

———. "Violence, Security, and the 1992 Election." In Y. Saffu (ed.), *The 1992 PNG Election: Change and Continuity in Electoral Politics.* Canberra: Department of Political and Social Change, Research School of Pacific and Asian Studies, Australian National University, 1996, pp. 77–104.

Dobell, Graeme. "The South Pacific: Policy Taboos, Popular Amnesia, and Political Failure." In Ivan Molloy (ed.), *The Eye of the Cyclone: Issues in Pacific Security.* Sippy Downs: University of the Sunshine Coast/PIPSA, 2004, pp. 244–246.

Docker, E. W. *The Blackbirders: The Recruiting of South Seas Labour to Queensland, 1867–1907.* Sydney: Angus and Robertson, 1970.

Donald, J., and A. Rattansi (ed.). *"Race," Culture, and Difference.* London: Sage, 1992.

Doorn, R. J. *A Blueprint for a New Nation: The Structure of the Nagriamel Federation.* Hicksville, N.Y.: Exposition, 1979.

Douglas, Bronwen. "Almost Constantly at War? An Ethnographic Perspective on Fighting in New Caledonia." *Journal of Pacific History* 25(1), 1990, pp. 22–46.

Downs, I. *The Australian Trusteeship Papua New Guinea, 1945–1975.* Canberra: AGPS, 1980.

Durutalo, S. *The Paramountcy of Fijian Interests and Politicization of Ethnicity.* Suva: Forum, 1986.

Ellis, Albert. *Ocean Island and Nauru: Their Story.* Sydney: Angus and Robertson, 1936.

Elmslie, Jim. *Irian Jaya Under the Gun: Indonesian Economic Development Versus West Papuan Nationalism.* Belair, South Australia: Crawford, 2002.

Elsham. *Laskar Jihad dan Satgas Merah Putih Meningkatan Aktivitas Latihannya.* Unpublished report. Jayapura, 2002.

Emberson-Bain, 'Atu 'o Hakautapu. *Country Briefing Paper: Women in Tonga.* Asian Development Bank, 1998. Available at http://www.adb.org/documents/books/country_briefing_papers/women_in_tonga/women_ton.pdf (accessed 6 June 2006).

Erickson, T. H. *Ethnicity and Nationalism: An Anthropological Perspective.* London: Pluto, 1993.

Faberon, Jean-Yves (ed.). *L'Avenir Statutaire de la Nouvelle-Calédonie.* Paris: La Documentation Française, 1997.

———. "La Nouvelle Calédonie et la Révision Constitutionelle de Mars 2003 sur l'Organisation Décentralisée de la République." *Revue Juridique, Politique et Économique de Nouvelle Calédonie* (1), January 2003, p. 3.

Faberon, Jean-Yves, and Jean-Raymond Postic (eds.). *L'Accord de Nouméa: La Loi Organique et Autres Documents Juridiques et Politiques de la Nouvelle-Calédonie.* Noumea: Ile de Lumières, 2004.

Fairbairn, T., and D. Worrell. *South Pacific and Caribbean Island Economies: A Comparative Study.* Adelaide: Foundation for Development Cooperation, 1996.

Filer, Colin. "The Bougainville Rebellion, the Mining Industry, and the Process of Social Disintegration in Papua New Guinea." In Ronald J. May and Matthew Spriggs (eds.), *The Bougainville Crisis.* Bathurst: Crawford, 1990, pp. 112–140.

Firth, Stewart. "The Impact of Globalisation on the Pacific Islands." Briefing Paper for the Second Southeast Asia and Pacific Subregional Tripartite Forum on Decent Work, International Labour Office, Melbourne, 5–8 April 2005.

Fraenkel, Jon. "Clash of Dynasties and Rise of Demagogues: Fiji's Tauri Vakaukauwa of May 2000." *Journal of Pacific History* 35(3), 2000, pp. 295–308.

———. *The Manipulation of Custom: From Uprising to Intervention in the Solomon Islands.* Wellington: Victoria University Press, 2004.

France, P. *Charter of the Land.* Melbourne: Oxford University Press, 1969.

Fraser, Helen. *Your Flag's Blocking Our Sun.* Sydney: ABC, 1990.

Frazer, Ian. "To'ambaita Report: A Study of Socio-Economic Change in North-West Malaita." Wellington: Department of Geography, Victoria University, 1973.

Friedlaender, Jonathan. "Why Do the People of Bougainville Look Unique? Some Conclusions from Biological Anthropology and Genetics." In Anthony J. Regan and Helga M. Griffin (eds.), *Bougainville Before the Conflict*. Canberra: Pandanus, 2005, pp. 57–70.

Fry, Greg. "Framing the Islands: Knowledge and Power in Changing Australian Images of 'The South Pacific.'" *Contemporary Pacific* 9(2), 1997, pp. 305–344.

Garap, Sarah. "Gender in PNG: Program Context and Points of Entry." Gender analysis paper for draft Project Design Document (PDD). Port Moresby: Government of Papua New Guinea, Law and Justice Sector Program, 2004.

———. "Struggles of Women and Girls: Simbu Province, Papua New Guinea." in S. Dinnen and A. Ley (eds.), *Reflections on Violence in Melanesia*. Leichhardt, NSW: Federation Press, 2000, pp. 159–171.

Ghai, Yash, and Y. K. Pao. *News Archives,* June 28, 2000. Background analysis. Available at http://www.lookinglassdesign.com/fijicoupmay2000/june2000/628-bghongkong-pc.html (last revision 25 June 2000).

Ghai, Yash, and Anthony Regan. "Bougainville and the Dialectics of Ethnicity, Autonomy, and Separation." In Yash Ghai (ed.), *Autonomy and Ethnicity: Negotiating Competing Claims in Multi-Ethnic States*. Cambridge: Cambridge University Press, 2000, pp. 242–265.

Giay, Benny. "Against Indonesia: West Papuan Strategies of Resistance Against Indonesian Political and Cultural Aggression in the 1980s." In Benedict R. Anderson (ed.), *Violence and the State in Suharto's Indonesia*. New York: Cornell Southeast Asia Program, 2001, pp. 129–138.

———. "Hai: Motif Pengharapan 'Jaman Bahagia' di Balik Protes Orang Amungme di Timika, Irian Jaya dan Isu HAM." *Deiyai* (1), 1995, pp. 5–8.

———. *Menuju Papua Baru: Beberapa Pokok Pikiran Sekitar Emansipasi Orang Papua*. Jakarta: Deiyai/Elsham Papua, 2000.

———. "Towards a New Papua." *Inside Indonesia* (57), July–September 2001, pp. 8–9.

———. "Zakheus Pakage and His Communities: Indigenous Religious Discourse, Socio-Political Resistance, and Ethnohistory of the Me of Irian Jaya." Amsterdam: Department of Cultural Anthropology/Sociology of Development, Vrije University, 1995.

Gibson, John, and Scott Rozelle. *Results of the Household Survey Component of the 1996 Poverty Assessment for Papua New Guinea*. Washington, D.C.: World Bank, 1998.

Goddard, M. "The Rascal Road: Crime, Prestige, and Development in Papua New Guinea." *Contemporary Pacific* 7(1), 1995, pp. 55–80.

Golden, Brigham. "Letter to the Editor." *Van Zorge Report,* 30 November 2000, pp. 33–34.

———. "Political Millenarianism and the Economy of Conflict: Reflections on Papua by an Activist Anthropologist." Asia Society, Asian Social Issues Program, 2003. Available at http://www.asiasource.org/asip/papua_golden.cfm#golden (accessed 10 July 2005).

Gordon, R., and M. Meggitt. *Law and Order in the New Guinea Highlands*. Hanover: University Press of New England, 1985.

Government of Australia. "New Memorandum of Understanding Signed with Nauru." Media release, minister for foreign affairs. Canberra, 5 March 2004.

———. *Solomon Islands: Rebuilding an Island Economy*. Canberra: Department of Foreign Affairs and Trade, Economic Analytical Unit, 2004.

Government of Fiji. *20 Year Plan*. Suva, 2001.

———. *Constitution of 1965*.

————. *Constitution of 1970.*

————. *Constitution of 1990.*

————. *Constitution of the Republic of Fiji, 1997.*

Government of New Zealand. *NZAID Annual Review, 2002/03.* Wellington: NZAID, 2003.

————. *NZAID Annual Review, 2003/04.* Wellington: NZAID, 2004.

Government of Papua New Guinea. *Final Report of the Constitutional Planning Committee.* Port Moresby, 1974.

————. *Medium Term Development Strategy, 2005–2010.* Port Moresby, 2005.

————. "Report of the Committee to Review Policy and Administration on Crime, Law, and Order" (Morgan Report). Port Moresby: Department of Provincial Affairs, 1983.

Government of Papua New Guinea and United Nations. *Millennium Development Goals: Progress Report for Papua New Guinea, 2004.* Port Moresby, July 2004.

Government of the Solomon Islands. "Draft Federal Constitution of Solomon Islands, 2004." Honiara: Provincial Institutional Strengthening and Development Unit, Department of Provincial Government and Constituency Development, October 2004.

————. *Human Development Report 2002: Building a Nation.* Vol. 1. Brisbane: Government of the Solomon Islands and the UNDP.

————. *National Economic Recovery, Reform, and Development Plan, 2003–2006: Strategic and Action Framework.* Honiara: Department of National Reform and Planning, 2003.

————. *Provincial Development Profiles, 2001.* Honiara: Rural Development Division, Ministry of Provincial Government and Rural Development, 2001.

————. *Report on the 1999 Population and Housing Census: Analysis.* Honiara: Statistics Office, 2002.

Griffin, James. *Bougainville: A Challenge for the Churches.* North Sydney: Catholic Commission for Justice and Peace, 1995.

————. "Napidakoe Navitu." In R. J. May (ed.), *Micronationalist Movements in Papua New Guinea,* Political and Social Change Monograph no. 1. Canberra: Australian National University, 1982, pp. 113–138.

Hanson, L., B. Allen, R. Bourke, and T. McCarthy. *Papua New Guinea Rural Development Handbook.* Canberra: Land Management Group, Department of Human Geography, RSPAS, Australian National University, 2001.

Harris, B. *The Rise of Rascalism: Action and Reaction in the Evolution of Rascal Gangs.* Port Moresby: Institute of Applied Social and Economic Research, 1988.

Hassall, G., and C. Saunders. *Asia Pacific Constitutional Systems.* Melbourne: Cambridge University Press, 2002.

Hau'ofa, E. *A New Oceania: Rediscovering Our Sea of Islands.* Suva: University of the South Pacific, 1993.

Hegarty, David. "Through and Beyond the Arc of Instability." In Ivan Molloy (ed.), *The Eye of the Cyclone: Issues in Pacific Security.* Sippy Downs: University of the Sunshine Coast/PIPSA, 2004, pp. 50–54.

Heijmans, Annelies, Nicola Simmonds, and Hans van de Veen (eds.). *Searching for Peace in the Asia-Pacific: An Overview of Conflict Prevention and Peacebuilding Activities.* Boulder: Lynne Rienner, 2004.

Howard, M. "State Power and Political Change in Fiji." *Journal of Contemporary Asia* 21(1), 1991, pp. 78–106.

Howard, Richard, Rodd McGibbon, and Johnathon Simon. *Resistance, Recovery, Re-empowerment: Adat Institutions in Contemporary Papua.* Washington, D.C.: US Agency for International Development, Civil Society Support and Strengthening Program, 2002.

Howley, Pat. *Breaking Spears and Mending Hearts: Peacemakers and Restorative Justice in Bougainville.* Annandale, NSW: Federation Press, 2002.

Hughes, Anthony V. "Tenure Conversion in the Solomons (1965–1969)." *South Pacific Bulletin* 20(1), 1970, pp. 41–47.

Hughes, Helen. "Aid Has Failed the Pacific." *Issue Analysis* (33). St. Leonards: Centre for Independent Studies, 2003.

———. "Can Papua New Guinea Come Back from the Brink?" *Issue Analysis* (49). St. Leonards: Centre for Independent Studies, 13 July 2004.

———. "From Rags to Riches: What Are Nauru's Options and How Can Australia Help?" *Issue Analysis* (50). St. Leonards: Centre for Independent Studies, 18 August 2004.

———. "Helping the Islands to Help Themselves." *Quadrant,* July–August 2003, pp. 47–49.

———. "The Pacific Is Viable." *Issue Analysis* (53). St. Leonards: Centre for Independent Studies, 2 December 2004.

———. "The Political Economy of Nauru." *Economic Record* (40), 1964, pp. 508–534.

Hughes, Helen, and Steve Gosarevski. "Does Size Matter? Tuvalu and Nauru Compared." *Policy* 20(2), 2004, pp. 16–20.

International Crisis Group. *Dividing Papua: How Not To Do It.* Jakarta, 9 April 2003.

———. "Indonesia: Ending Repression in Irian Jaya." *Asia Report* (23). Jakarta, 20 September 2001.

———. "Indonesia: Resources and Conflict in Papua." *Asia Report* (39). Jakarta, 13 September 2002.

Ipo, John. "Land and Economy." In Hugh Laracy (ed.), *Ples Blong Iumi: Solomon Islands—The Past Four Thousand Years.* Suva: Institute of Pacific Studies, University of the South Pacific, 1989, pp. 121–136.

Ivoro, J. "Conflict Resolution in a Multi-Cultural Urban Setting in Papua New Guinea." In S. Dinnen, A. Jowitt, and T. Newton Cain (eds.), *A Kind of Mending: Restorative Justice in the Pacific Islands.* Canberra: Pandanus, 2003.

Jacka, M. "Australian Aid: Investing in Growth, Stability and Prosperity." Paper for master's in international social development, UNSW, November 2003.

———. "Papua New Guinea: Promoting Papua New Guinean Solutions to Development." Report prepared for Australian Council for International Development, Canberra, 2006.

Jenkins, R. *Re-thinking Ethnicity: Arguments and Explorations.* London: Sage, 1997.

Kaman, J. "Peace Studies as a Process of Peace Building: An Alternative Approach to Violence in Papua New Guinea, 25 Years and Beyond." In D. Kavanamur, C. Yala, and Q. Clements (eds.), *Building a Nation in Papua New Guinea: Views of the Post-Independence Generation.* Canberra: Pandanus, 2003.

Kamma, Freerk. *Koreri: Messianic Movements in the Biak-Numfor Culture Area.* The Hague: Koninklijk Institute, 1972.

Kaputin, J. "The Law: A Colonial Fraud?" *New Guinea* 10(1), 1975, pp. 4–15.

Kavanamur, D. "The Politics of Structural Adjustment in Papua New Guinea." In P. Larmour (ed.), *Governance and Reform in the South Pacific.* Canberra:

National Centre for Development Studies, Australian National University, 1998, pp. 99–120.

Kavanamur, D., C. Yala, and Q. Clements (eds.). *Building a Nation in Papua New Guinea: Views of the Post-Independence Generation.* Canberra: Pandanus, 2003.

Keesing, Roger M. "Creating the Past: Culture and Identity in the Contemporary Pacific." *Contemporary Pacific* 1(2–3), 1989, pp. 19–39.

———. "A Tin with the Meat Taken Out: A Bleak Anthropological View of Unsustainable Development in the Pacific." In Ton Otto (ed.), *Pacific Islands Trajectories: Five Personal Views.* Canberra: Department of Anthropology, Research School of Pacific Studies, Australian National University, and Centre for Pacific Studies, University of Nijmegen, Netherlands, 1993, pp. 29–55.

Kele-Kele, Kalkot Matas. "The Emergence of Political Parties." In Chris Plant (ed.), *New Hebrides: The Road to Independence.* Suva: IPS and USP, 1977, pp. 17–34.

Kennedy, Danny, and Abigail Abrash. "Repressive Mining in West Papua." In Geoff Evans, James Goodman, and Nina Lansbury (eds.), *Moving Mountains: Communities Confront Mining and Globalisation.* Sydney: Otford and the Mineral Policy Institute, NSW, 2001, pp. 83–98.

King, Peter. *West Papua and Indonesia Since Suharto: Independence, Autonomy, or Chaos?* Sydney: UNSW, 2004.

Kirksey, S. Eben. "From Cannibal to Terrorist: State Violence, Indigenous Resistance, and Representation in West Papua." Master's thesis in economic and social history, University of Oxford, 2002. Available at http://www.papuaweb.org/dlib/s123/kirksey2/_mph.doc (accessed 12 March 2006).

Kiste, Robert C. "Pre-Colonial Times." In K. R. Howe, Robert C. Kiste, and Brij V. Lal (eds.), *Tides of History: The Pacific Islands in the Twentieth Century.* St. Leonards: Allen and Unwin, 1994, pp. 3–28.

Kituai, A. "My Gun, My Brother: The World of the Papua New Guinea Colonial Police, 1920–1960." Pacific Islands Monograph no. 15. Honolulu: University of Hawaii Press, 1988.

Kjar, Renée. "The Invisible Aristocrat: Benny Giay in Papuan History." Bachelor of arts honorary thesis, Canberra, Faculty of Asian Studies, Australian National University, 2002.

Knauft, B. *Good Company and Violence: Sorcery and Social Action in a Lowland New Guinea Society.* Berkeley: University of California Press, 1985.

Kolig, E. "*Kastom,* Cargo, and the Construction of Utopia on Santo, Vanuatu: The Nagriamel Movement." *Journal de la Societe des Oceanistes* 85(2), 1987, pp. 181–199.

Kothari, U., and M. Minogue (eds.). *Development Theory and Practice: Critical Perspectives.* Hampshire: Palgrave, 2002.

Lal, B. "Chiefs and Thieves and Other People Besides: The Making of George Speight's Coup." *Journal of Pacific History* 35(3), 2000, pp. 281–293.

Laracy, Hugh (ed.). *Pacific Protest: The Maasina Rule Movement, Solomon Islands, 1944–1952.* Suva: Institute of Pacific Studies, University of the South Pacific, 1983.

Larmour, P. "Conditionality, Coercion, and Other Forms of Power: International Financial Institutions in the Pacific." *Public Administration and Development* (22), 2002, pp. 249–260.

———— (ed.). *Governance and Reform in the South Pacific.* Canberra: National Centre for Development Studies, Australian National University, 1998.

————. "Land Policy and Decolonisation in Melanesia: A Comparative Study of Land Policymaking and Implementation Before and After Independence in Papua New Guinea, Solomon Islands, and Vanuatu." PhD dissertation, Department of History and Politics, Macquarie University, Sydney, 1988.

Law and Justice Sector Working Group. *The National Law and Justice Policy and Plan of Action: Toward Restorative Justice.* Port Moresby: Government of Papua New Guinea, 1999.

Lawrence, P. "The State Versus Stateless Society in Papua and New Guinea." In B. J. Brown (ed.), *Fashion of Law in New Guinea: Being an Account of the Past, Present, and Developing System of Laws in Papua and New Guinea.* Sydney: Butterworths, 1969, pp. 15–37.

Lawson, S. *The Failure of Democratic Politics in Fiji.* Oxford: Clarendon, 1991.

Legorjus, Philippe. *La Morale et l'Action.* Paris: Fixot, 1990.

Lepani, C. "Perspective: Strengthening PNG's State and Australia's Role." In H. White and E. Wainwright (eds.), *Strengthening Our Neighbour: Australia and the Future of Papua New Guinea.* Canberra: Australian Strategic Policy Institute, 2004.

Lindstrom, L. *Achieving Wisdom: Knowledge and Politics on Tanna.* Berkeley: University of California Press, 1981.

Lini, W. *Beyond Pandemonium: From the New Hebrides to Vanuatu.* Suva: University of the South Pacific, 1980.

Lowry, Robert. *The Armed Forces of Indonesia.* St. Leonards: Allen and Unwin, 1996.

MacClancy, J. V. "*Vanuatu* and *Kastom*: A Study of Cultural Symbols in the Inception of a National State in the South Pacific." PhD dissertation, Department of Anthropology, Oxford University, 1983.

Maclellan, Nic. *Australia and the Pacific: Update on Current Issues and Trends.* Canberra: Australian Council for Overseas Aid, August 2002.

————. "Conflict and Reconciliation in New Caledonia: Building the Mwâ Kâ." State, Society, and Governance in Melanesia Discussion Paper no. 2005/1. Canberra: Australian National University, 2005.

————. "Creating Peace in the Pacific: Conflict Resolution, Reconciliation and Restorative Justice." In Annelies Heijmans, Nicola Simmonds, and Hans van de Veen (eds.), *Searching for Peace in Asia Pacific: An Overview of Conflict Prevention and Peacebuilding Activities.* Boulder: Lynne Rienner, 2004, pp. 526–542.

————. "Fiji, the War in Iraq, and the Privatisation of Pacific Island Security." Austral Policy Forum no. 06-11A. Melbourne: Nautilus Research Centre.

————. "Self-Determination or Territorial Integrity?" *Inside Indonesia* (67), July–September, 2001.

MacLeod, Jason. "Gagged." *Arena Magazine* (68), December 2003–January 2004, pp. 30–34.

MacWilliam, Scott. "Post-War Reconstruction in Bougainville: Plantations, Smallholders, and Indigenous Capital." In Anthony J. Regan and Helga M. Griffin (eds.), *Bougainville Before the Conflict.* Canberra: Pandanus, 2005, pp. 224–238.

Maino, C. "Serious Economic Crime: The Threat to Us All." Paper presented to the Twelfth International Symposium on Economic Crime, Cambridge, Jesus College, 11–17 September 1994.

Mamak, Alexander, and Richard Bedford. "Bougainvillean Nationalism: Aspects of Unity and Discord." Bougainville Special Publication no. 1. Christchurch: Department of Geography, University of Canterbury, 1974.

Martinez, Jean-Claude (ed.). *La Nouvelle-Calédonie: La Stratégie, le Droit et la République*. Paris: Pedone, 1985.

May, Ronald J. "From Promise to Crisis: A Political Economy of Papua New Guinea." In P. Larmour (ed.), *Governance and Reform in the South Pacific*. Canberra: National Centre for Development Studies, Australian National University, 1998, pp. 54–73.

May, Ronald J., and Matthew Spriggs (eds.). *The Bougainville Crisis*. Bathurst: Crawford, 1990.

McCulloch, Lesley. "Trifungsi: The Role of the Indonesian Military in Business." Paper presented at the international conference "Soldiers in Business: Military as an Economic Actor," Jakarta, 17–19 October 2000.

McDonald, Hamish, Desmond Ball, James Dunn, Gerry van Klinken, David Bourchier, Douglas Kammen, and Richard Tanter. "Masters of Terror: Indonesia's Military and Violence in East Timor in 1999." Canberra Paper on Strategy and Defence no. 145. Canberra: Strategic and Defence Studies Centre, Australia National University, 2002.

McGee, R. "Participating in Development." In U. Kothari and M. Minogue (eds.), *Development Theory and Practice: Critical Perspectives*. Hampshire: Palgrave, 2002, pp. 92–116.

McGibbon, Rodd. "Plural Society in Peril: Migration, Economic Change, and the Papua Conflict." *Policy Study* (13). Washington, D.C.: East West Center, 2005.

———. "Secessionist Challenges in Aceh and Papua: Is Special Autonomy the Solution?" *Policy Study* (10). Washington, D.C.: East West Center, 2004.

Meava, J. "Wide Bay Conservation Project." *Echoes from the Fores: Papua New Guinea Eco-Forestry Forum,* 17 July 2002. Available at http://www.eco-forestry.org.pg/echoes/echoes%2014.pdf (accessed 30 May 2006).

Migdal, J. S. *Strong Societies and Weak States: State-Society Relations and State Capacities in the Third World*. Princeton: Princeton University Press, 1988.

Mitchell, Donald. "Frozen Assets in Nagovisi." *Oceania* (53), September 1982, pp. 56–66.

Molisa, Grace, Nikenike Vurobaravu, and Howard Van Trease. "Vanuatu: Overcoming Pandemonium." In Ron Crocombe and Ahmed Ali (eds.), *Politics in Melanesia*. Suva: IPS and USP, 1982, pp. 82–115.

Moore, Clive. "Australia's Motivation and Timing for the 2003 Intervention in the Solomon Islands Crisis." *Royal Historical Society of Queensland Journal* 19(4), 2005, pp. 732–748.

———. *Happy Isles in Crisis: The Historical Causes for a Failing State in Solomon Islands, 1998–2004*. Canberra: Asia Pacific Press, 2004.

Morgan, M. *Integrating Reform: Legislative Needs Assessment, Republic of Vanuatu*. Suva: United Nations Development Programme, 2001. Available at http://www.undp.org.fj/gold/docs/vanuatul.pdf (accessed 10 August 2005).

———. "Political Fragmentation and the Policy Environment in Vanuatu, 1980–2004." *Pacific Economic Bulletin* 19(3), 2004, pp. 40–48.

Muria, J. "The Role of the Courts and Legal Profession in Constitutional and Political Disputes in the Pacific Islands Nations." *Journal of South Pacific Law* 6(2), 2002.

Muwali, A. "South Pacific: Macroeconomic Crisis and Structural Reforms in Papua

New Guinea." Economics Division Working Paper no. 97/1. Canberra: National Centre for Development Studies, Australian National University, 1997.

Nage, James. "Immigrant Settlements in Honiara, Solomon Islands." In Leonard Mason and Pat Hereniko (eds.), *In Search of a Home*. Suva: Institute of Pacific Studies, University of the South Pacific, 1987, pp. 93–102.

Naidu, V. "State and Class in the South Pacific." Unpublished PhD thesis, University of Sussex, 1989.

———. *Violence of Indenture*. Suva: Pacific Institute of Applied Studies, 2004.

Naitoro, John Houainamo. "Solomon Islands Conflict: Demands for Historical Rectification and Restorative Justice." Update on the Solomon Islands. Canberra: Asia Pacific School of Economics and Management, Australian National University, 2002.

Nandan, S. *Requiem for a Rainbow*. Canberra: Pacific Indian Publications, 2001.

Narayan, J. *The Political Economy of Fiji*. Suva: South Pacific Review, 1985.

Narokobi, B. *Lo Bilong Yumi yet: Law and Custom in Melanesia*. Goroka: Melanesian Institute for Pastoral and Socio-Economic Service, and University of the South Pacific, 1989.

———. *The Melanesian Way*. Suva: Institute of Pacific Studies, 1983.

Nash, Jill, and Eugene Ogan. "The Red and the Black: Bougainville Perceptions of Other Papua New Guineans." *Pacific Studies* 13(2), 1990, pp. 1–17.

Nelson, Hank. "Bougainville in World War II." In Anthony J. Regan and Helga M. Griffin (eds.), *Bougainville Before the Conflict*. Canberra: Pandanus, 2005, pp. 168–198.

Newton Cain T., and A. Jowittt. "National Integrity Systems: Country Study Report, Vanuatu." Blackburn: Transparency International Australia, 2004.

Niditauae, T. *Pastors in Politics: The Question of Political Involvement and Church Leadership in Vanuatu*. Suva: Pacific Theological College, 1985.

Norton, R. *Race and Politics in Fiji*. St. Lucia: University of Queensland Press, 1994.

OECD (Organization for Economic Cooperation and Development). *Development Co-operation Reports, 1971–2000*. Paris.

Ogan, Eugene. "Copra Came Before Copper: The Nasioi of Bougainville and Plantation Colonialism, 1902–1964." *Pacific Studies* 19(1), 1996, pp. 31–51.

———. "The Cultural Background to the Bougainville Crisis." *Journal de la Societe des Oceanistes* (92–93), 1992, pp. 61–67.

Okole, Henry T. "Enhancing Nation Building Through the Provincial Government System in Papua New Guinea: Overtures Toward Federalism." In David Kavanamur, Charles Yala, and Quinton Clements (eds.), *Building a Nation in Papua New Guinea: Views of the Post-Independence Generation*. Canberra: Pandanus, 2003, pp. 51–67.

———. "Insights from the DWU Symposium." *The National*, 1 April 2004.

———. "Institutional Decay in a Melanesian Parliamentary Democracy: Papua New Guinea." *Development Bulletin* (60), December 2002, pp. 37–40.

Oliver, Douglas. *Black Islanders: A Personal Perspective of Bougainville 1937–1991*. Melbourne: Hyland, 1991.

Osborne, Robin. *Indonesia's Secret War: The Guerilla Struggle in Irian Jaya*. Sydney: Allen and Unwin, 1985.

Otter, Mark. "Is the 'Solomon Islands Paradox' an Australian Responsibility?" School of History, Philosophy, Religion, and Classics Seminar paper. Brisbane: University of Queensland, 1 May 2003.

Oxfam Community Aid Abroad. *Mining Ombudsman Annual Report, 2003.* Melbourne.

———. *"The Raim Story": East New Britain Sosel Eksen Komiti.* Melbourne, n.d.

———. "Submission to the Senate Foreign Affairs, Defence, and Trade References Committee Inquiry into Australia's Relations with Papua New Guinea and the Island States of the South-West Pacific." Melbourne, 2002.

Papua New Guinea–Australia Development Cooperation Program. *Law and Justice Sector Review.* Canberra: AusAID, 2001.

Patience, Allan. "The ECP and Australia's Middle Power Ambitions." State, Society, and Governance in Melanesia Discussion Paper no. 2005/4. Canberra: Australian National University, 2005.

———. "Failed and Vulnerable States." Unpublished inaugural lecture at the University of Papua New Guinea, Port Moresby, 30 April 2004.

Peebles, D. *Pacific Regional Order.* Canberra: Australian National University, 2005.

Perlez, Jane, and Raymond Bonner. "Below a Mountain of Wealth, a River of Waste." *New York Times,* 27 December 2005.

Permanent Mission of the Republic of Indonesia to the United Nations. *Questioning the Unquestionable: An Overview of the Restoration of Papua into the Republic of Indonesia.* New York, 2003.

Pitts, M. *Crime, Corruption, and Capacity in Papua New Guinea.* Canberra: Asia Pacific Press, Australian National University, 2002.

Plenel, Edwy, and Alain Rollat. *Mourir à Ouvea.* Paris: Editions La Découverte/Le Monde, 1988.

Pollard, Alice Aruhe'eta. *Givers of Wisdom, Labourers Without Gain: Essays on Women in the Solomon Islands.* Suva: Institute of Pacific Studies and Solomon Islands Center, University of the South Pacific, 2000.

Pollock, Nancy. "The Mining of Nauru and Its Aftermath: Political Implications of Rehabilitation." In Don Rubinstein (ed.), *Pacific History.* Guam: University of Guam, 1992, pp. 281–292.

———. "Nauru: Decolonising, Recolonising—But Never a Colony." In Donald Dcnoon (ed.), *Emerging from Empire? Decolonisation in the Pacific.* Canberra: Australian National University, 1997, pp. 102–106.

———. *Nauru Bibliography.* Wellington: Department of Anthropology, Victoria University, 1992.

———. "Nauru's Post-Independence Struggles." In Brij Lal and Hank Nelson (eds.), *Lines Across the Sea.* Brisbane: Pacific History Association, 1995, pp. 49–56.

Polomka, P. (ed.). *Bougainville: Perspectives on a Crisis.* Canberra. Strategic and Defence Studies Centre, Research School of Pacific Studies, Australian National University, 1990.

Prasad, S. "Industrial Relations in Vanuatu: Constraints and Potential." In S. Prasad and K. Hince (eds.), *Industrial Relations in the South Pacific.* Suva: School of Social and Economic Developments, University of the South Pacific, 2001, pp. 131–150.

Premdas, Ralph. "Constitutional Challenges: The Rise of Fijian Nationalism." *Pacific Perspective* 9(2), 1980, pp. 30–44.

Price, Charles, with Elizabeth Baker. "Origins of Pacific Island Labourers in Queensland, 1863–1904: A Research Note." *Journal of Pacific History* 11(1–2), 1976, pp. 106–121.

PSRMU (Public Sector Reform Management Unit). "A Review of the Law and Justice Sector Agencies in Papua New Guinea: Opportunities to Improve Efficiency, Effectiveness, Coordination and Accountability." Unpublished draft report. Port Moresby: Government of Papua New Guinea, Department of Prime Minister and National Executive Council, 2002.

Ranck, S., and S. Toft (eds.). *Domestic Violence in Urban Papua New Guinea.* Port Moresby: Papua New Guinea Law Reform Commission, 1986.

Ratuva, S. "Addressing Inequality? Post-Coup Affirmative Action Policies in Fiji." In H. Akram-Lodhi (ed.), *Confronting Fiji Futures.* Canberra: Asia-Pacific Press, 2001, pp. 226–248.

———. "Anatomising the Vanua Complex: Communal Land Conflict in Fiji." Paper presented to South Pacific Land Tenure and Conflict Symposium, Suva, University of the South Pacific, 2002.

———. "Ethnic Politics, Communalism, and Affirmative Action in Fiji: A Critical and Comparative Study." Unpublished PhD thesis, Institute of Development Studies, University of Sussex, 1999.

———. "The Paradox of Multi-Culturalism: Managing Differences in Fiji's Syncretic State." Paper presented to International Conference on Plurality and Differences, University of New Caledonia, organized by the government of France, 2002.

———. *Participation for Peace: A Study of Inter-Cultural and Inter-Religious Perception in Fiji.* Suva: Ecumenical Center for Research, Education, and Advocacy, 2002.

———. "State Induced Affirmative Action, Economic Development, and Ethnic Politics: A Comparative Study of Fiji and Malaysia." Sociology Working Paper no. 1/2001. Suva: University of the South Pacific, 2001.

———. "Storm in Paradise: The 1987 Coups in Fiji." Research report, pt. 1. Uppsala, Sweden: Life and Peace Institute, 2003.

Ravuvu, A. *The Façade of Democracy.* Suva: Reader Publishing, 1991.

Regan, Anthony J. "Bougainville: Beyond Survival." *Cultural Survival Quarterly* 26(3), 2002, pp. 20–24.

———. "The Bougainville Conflict: Political and Economic Agendas." In Karen Ballentine and Jake Sherman (eds.), *The Political Economy of Armed Conflict: Beyond Greed and Grievance.* Boulder: Lynne Rienner, 2003, pp. 133–166.

———. "The Bougainville Political Settlement and the Prospects for Sustainable Peace." *Pacific Economic Bulletin* 17(1), 2002, pp. 114–129.

———. "Causes and Course of the Bougainville Conflict." *Journal of Pacific History* 33(3), 1998, pp. 269–285.

———. "Clever People Solving Difficult Problems: Perspectives on Weakness of the State and Nation in Papua New Guinea." *Development Studies Bulletin* (67), April 2005, pp. 6–12.

———. "Identities Among Bougainvilleans." In Anthony J. Regan and Helga M. Griffin (eds.), *Bougainville Before the Conflict.* Canberra: Pandanus, 2005, pp. 418–446.

———. "Why a Neutral Peace Monitoring Force? The Bougainville Conflict and the Peace Process." In Monica Wehner and Donald Denoon (eds.), *Without a Gun: Australia's Experience of Monitoring Peace in Bougainville, 1997–2001.* Canberra: Pandanus, 2001, pp. 1–18.

Regan, Anthony J., and Helga M. Griffin (eds.). *Bougainville Before the Conflict.* Canberra: Pandanus, 2005.

Regan, Patrick M., and Daniel Norton. "Greed, Grievance, and Mobilization in Civil Wars." *Journal of Conflict Resolution* 49(3), 2005, pp. 319–336.

Regnault, Jean-Marc (ed.). *François Mitterrand et les Territoires Français du Pacifique (1981–1988).* Paris: Les Indes Savantes, 2003.

Reid, Anthony. "*Merdeka:* The Concept of Freedom in Indonesia." In David Kelly and Anthony Reid (eds.), *Asian Freedoms: The Idea of Freedom in East and Southeast Asia.* Cambridge: Cambridge University Press, 1998, pp. 141–160.

Reilly, Benjamin, and Kennedy Graham. "Conflict Through Asia and the Pacific: Causes and Trends." In Annelies Heijmans, Nicola Simmonds, and Hans van de Veen (eds.), *Searching for Peace in the Asia Pacific: An Overview of Conflict Prevention and Peacebuilding Activities.* Boulder: Lynne Rienner, 2004, pp. 9–22.

Rimoldi, Max, and Eleanor Rimoldi. *Hahalis and the Labour of Love: A Social Movement on Buka Island.* Oxford: Berg, 1992.

Roberts, S. *Order and Dispute: An Introduction to Legal Anthropology.* Harmondsworth: Penguin, 1979.

Rodman, William L. "The Law of the State and the State of the Law in Vanuatu." In V. S. Lockwood, T. G. Harding, and B. J. Wallace (eds.), *Contemporary Pacific Societies: Studies in Development and Change.* Englewood Cliffs, N.J.: Prentice Hall, 1993, p. 56.

RPNGC (Royal Papua New Guinea Constabulary). "Draft Report." Unpublished document. Port Moresby: Administrative Review Committee, 2004.

———. "Report on Community Perceptions of the Police in Papua New Guinea." Unpublished project document. Port Moresby: Development Project, Phase III, 2004.

Rumbiak, John. "From the Ashes of Empire." *Inside Indonesia* (67), July–September 2001.

———. "Human Rights in Papua: Some Remarks." In Sigfried Zollner, *Autonomy for Papua: Opportunity or Illusion,* papers presented at the conference "Autonomy for Papua: Opportunity or Illusion?" Berlin: Friedrich Ebert Foundation, West Papua Network, and Watch Indonesia! 4–5 June 2003.

———. "A Struggle for Dignity, Justice, and Peace." In Ben Bohane, Liz Thompson, Jim Elmslie (eds.), *West Papua: Follow the Morning Star.* Melbourne: Prowling Tiger, 2003, pp. vi–viii.

Rutherford, Danilyn. "Waiting for the End in Biak: Violence, Order, and a Flag Raising." In Benedict R. Anderson (ed.), *Violence and the State in Suharto's Indonesia.* New York: Cornell Southeast Asia Program, 2001, pp. 189–212.

Ruthven, David. "Land Legislation from the Protectorate to Independence." In Peter Larmour (ed.), *Land in Solomon Islands.* Suva: Institute of Pacific Studies, University of the South Pacific, 1979, pp. 239–248.

Saltford, John. *The United Nations and the Indonesian Takeover of West Papua, 1962–1969: The Anatomy of Betrayal.* London: Routledge Curzon, 2003.

———. "United Nations Involvement with the Act of Self-Determination in West Irian (Indonesia West New Guinea), 1968 to 1969." 2001. Available at http://www.fpcn-global.org/united-nations/wp-68-69.html (accessed 23 April 2001).

Sanday, J. "The Military in Fiji: A Historical Development and Future Role." Working Paper no. 201. Canberra: Strategic and Defence Studies Centre, Australian National University, 1989.

Sanguinetti, Alexandre, et al. *Enquête sur Ouvea.* Paris: EDI, 1989.

Saussol, Alain. *L'Héritage: Essai sur le Problème Foncier Mélanésien en Nouvelle-Calédonie.* Paris: Musée de l'Homme, 1979.

Scaglion, R. "Spare the Rod and Spoil the Woman? Family Violence in Abelam Society." In D. Counts, J. Brown, and J. Campbell (eds.), *To Have and to Hit:*

Cultural Perspectives on Wife Beating. Urbana: University of Illinois Press, 1999, pp. 137–154.

Schoeffel, Penelope. "The Pacific Islands: Past, Present and Future." Unpublished paper presented at the Brisbane Dialogue Conference, Foundation for Pacific Development Cooperation, November 2000.

Sekretariat Keadilan Perdamaian–Keuskupan Jayapura [Office for Justice and Peace–Catholic Diocese of Jayapura, West Papua]. "Recent Developments in Papua: Special Autonomy—Its Process and Contents." *Socio-Political Notes* (5). Jayapura: December 2001.

Senituli, Lopeti. "Indigenous Peoples in the Pacific Context." Unpublished paper for the United Nations Development Programme, Suva, July 1999.

Shears, R. *The Coconut War: The Crisis on Espiritu Santo.* Sydney: Cassell Australia, 1980.

Shlomowitz, Ralph, and Richard Bedford. "The Internal Labor Trade in the New Hebrides and Solomon Islands, c. 1900–1941." *Journal de la Société des Océanistes* (86), 1988, pp. 61–85.

Slatter, Claire. "To Djubelly." In 'Atu Emberson-Bain (ed.), *Sustainable Development or Malignant Growth? Perspectives of Pacific Island Women.* Suva: Marama, 1994.

Sokomanu, A. G. "A Presidential Crisis." In H. van Trease (ed.), *Melanesian Politics: Stael Blong Vanuatu.* Christchurch: Macmillan Brown Centre for Pacific Studies, 1996.

Spate, O. *Fijian People: Economic Problems and Prospects.* Suva: Government Press, 1959.

Spencer, Michael, Alan Ward, and John Connell (eds.). *New Caledonia: Essays on Nationalism and Dependency.* St. Lucia: Queensland University Press, 1988.

Spriggs, Mathew. "Bougainville's Early History: An Archaeological Perspective." In Anthony J. Regan and Helga M. Griffin (eds.), *Bougainville Before the Conflict.* Canberra: Pandanus, 2005, pp. 1–19.

Spriggs, Matthew, and Donald Denoon (eds.). *The Bougainville Crisis: 1991 Update.* Canberra: Australian National University in association with Crawford, 1992.

Standish, B. "Elections in Simbu: Towards Gunpoint Democracy?" In Y. Saffu (ed.), *The 1992 PNG Election: Change and Continuity in Electoral Politics.* Canberra: Department of Political and Social Change, Research School of Pacific and Asian Studies, Australian National University, 1996, pp. 277–322.

———. "Papua New Guinea Politics: Attempting to Engineer the Future." *Development Bulletin* (60), December 2002, pp. 28–32.

Stavenhagen, R. *Ethnic Conflict and the Nation State.* London: Macmillan, 1996.

Stella R. "PNG in the New Millennium: Some Troubled Homecomings." In D. Kavanamur, C. Yala, and Q. Clements (eds.), *Building a Nation in Papua New Guinea: Views of the Post-Independence Generation.* Canberra: Pandanus, 2003, pp. 11–24.

Strathern, M. "Legality or Legitimacy: Hageners' Perception of the Judiciary." Unpublished paper, 1971.

———. "Report on Questionnaire Relating to Sexual Offences as Defined in the Criminal Code." Boroko, Port Moresby: New Guinea Research Unit, 1975.

Sumule, Agus. "Social and Economic Changes in Papua Since the Law on Special Autonomy Came into Effect." In Sigfried Zollner, *Autonomy for Papua:*

Opportunity or Illusion, papers presented at the conference "Autonomy for Papua: Opportunity or Illusion?" Berlin: Friedrich Ebert Foundation, West Papua Network, and Watch Indonesia! 4–5 June 2003.

———. "Swimming Against the Current: The Drafting of the Special Autonomy Bill for the Province of Papua and Its Passage Through the National Parliament of Indonesia." *Journal of Pacific History* 38(3), 2003, pp. 353–369.

Sutherland, W. "Globalization, Nationalism, and the National Agenda." Draft occasional paper, 1999.

———. "State and Capitalist Development." Unpublished PhD thesis, University of Canterbury, 1985.

Sutherland, W., and R. Robertson. *Government by the Gun: Unfinished Business of May 2000.* Annandale: Pluto, 2001.

Tanis, James. "Nagovisi Villages as a Window on Bougainville in 1988." In Anthony J. Regan and Helga M. Griffin (eds.), *Bougainville Before the Conflict.* Canberra: Pandanus, 2005, pp. 447–472.

Tapol (Indonesia's human rights campaign). "West Papua: Secret Operation Launched to Undermine and Destroy All Pro-Independence Activities." News release, 12 October 2001. Available at http://www.gn.apc.org/tapol (accessed 15 October 2001).

Tebay, Neles. *West Papua: The Struggle for Peace and Justice.* London: Catholic Institute for International Relations, 2005.

Telapak and EIA (Environmental Investigation Agency). "The Last Frontier: Illegal Logging in Papua and China's Massive Timber Theft." Bogor, Indonesia, 2005. Available at http://www.telapak.org/publikasi/download/the_last_frontier_en.pdf (accessed 11 April 2005).

Tepahae, P. "Chiefly Power in Southern Vanuatu." State, Society, and Governance in Melanesia Discussion Paper no. 97/9. Canberra: Research School of Pacific and Asian Studies, Australian National University, 1997.

Thompson, Liz. *Breaking Bows and Arrows* (video). Firelight and Tiger Eye, 2001.

Thompson, Roger. "Edge of Empire: Australian Colonisation of Nauru 1919–1939." In Don Rubinstein (ed.), *Pacific History.* Guam: University of Guam, 1992, pp. 273–280.

Timmer, Jaap. "Living with Intricate Futures: Order and Confusion in Imyan Worlds, Irian Jaya, Indonesia." PhD dissertation, Centre for Pacific and Asian Studies, University of Nijmegen, Netherlands, 2000.

———. "The Return of the Kingdom: Agama and the Millennium Amongst the Imyan of Irian Jaya, Indonesia." *Ethnohistory* 47(1), Winter 2000, pp. 26–65.

Tjibaou, Jean Marie. *Cibau Cibau: Kamo pa Kavaac.* Noumea: ADCK, 1998.

———. *La Présence Kanak.* Paris: Editions Odile Jacob, 1996.

Toata, Teuea. "Keeping the Nauru Economy Afloat." *Pacific Economic Bulletin* 19(2), 2004, pp. 123–128.

Toft, S. (ed.). *Domestic Violence in Papua New Guinea.* Port Moresby: Papua New Guinea Law Reform Commission, 1985.

Toft, S., and S. Bonnell. *Marriage and Domestic Violence in Rural Papua New Guinea.* Port Moresby: Papua New Guinea Law Reform Commission, 1985.

Togolo, Melchior. "Torau Response to Change." In Anthony J. Regan and Helga M. Griffin (eds.), *Bougainville Before the Conflict.* Canberra: Pandanus, 2005, pp. 274–289.

Tonkinson, R. "Vanuatu Values: A Changing Symbiosis." *Pacific Studies* (2), Spring 1982, pp. 44–63.

"Towards an Amungme History: The Pre-Freeport Era." *Papua Web.* Available at http://www.papuaweb.org/dlib/tema/amungme/muller/amungme-pre-freeport. rtf (accessed 21 July 2005).

Transparency International. *The 2004 Corruption Perceptions Index.* Available at http://www.transparency.org/policy_research/surveys_indices/cpi/2004.

Trumbell, Robert. "Smallest and Richest." In Robert Trumbell (ed.), *Tin Roofs and Palm Trees: A Report on the New South Seas.* Canberra: Australian National University, 1977, pp. 215–233.

Tryon, Darrell. "The Languages of Bougainville." In Anthony J. Regan and Helga M. Griffin (eds.), *Bougainville Before the Conflict.* Canberra: Pandanus, 2005, pp. 31–46.

2003/04 Review Team. "Towards Sustainable Timber Production: A Review of Existing Logging Projects—Draft Observations and Recommendations Report." Prepared for the government of Papua New Guinea, May 2004.

UNCTAD (United Nations Conference on Trade and Development). "UNCTAD Calls for End to Development Pessimism: Domestic Productive Capacities Could Make International Trade Work for Poverty Reduction." Press release, 27 May 2004. Available at http://www.unctad.org/templates/webflyer.asp?docid= 4813&intitemid=2068&lang=1.

UNDP (United Nations Development Programme). *Human Development Indicators: Basic Indicators for Other UN Member Countries.* New York.

———. *Human Development Indicators for Papua New Guinea, 2003.* New York. Available at http://hdr.undp.org/statistics/data/countries.cfm?c=png (accessed 5 July 2006).

———. *Human Development Report, 2003: Human Development Indicators— Nauru.* New York.

———. *Human Development Report, 2003: Millennium Development Goals—A Compact Among Nations to End Human Poverty.* New York.

———. *Human Development Report, 2004.* New York.

———. *Multi-Country Programme Outline for the Pacific Countries, 2003–2007.* Report no. DP/MPO/PIC/1. New York, 2002.

———. *National Human Development Report, 2004: The Economics of Democracy: Financing Human Development in Indonesia.* BAPPENAS and UNDP. Available at http://www.undp.or.id/pubs/ihdr2004/ihdr2004_full.pdf (accessed 17 July 2005).

———. *National Strategic Plan on HIV/AIDS in Papua New Guinea: Gender Audit Report.* Port Moresby, 2005.

———. *Pacific Human Development Report 1999: Creating Opportunities.* Suva, 1999.

———. *Sustainable Human Development in Vanuatu: Moving on Together.* Suva: UNDP and the government of Vanuatu, 1996.

UNICEF (United Nations Children's Fund). *Children and HIV/AIDS in Papua New Guinea.* Port Moresby, 2005.

United Nations. *Papua New Guinea Common Country Assessment, 2001.* Port Moresby: United Nations Country Team.

US Department of State. *Country Reports on Human Rights Practices, 2001: Tonga.* Washington, D.C.: Bureau of Democracy, Human Rights, and Labor. Available at http://www.terrorismcentral.com/library/government/us/statedepartment/ democracyhumanrights/2001/eastasiapacific/tonga.html (accessed 18 March 2006).

———. *Vanuatu Human Rights Practices, 1994.* Washington, D.C.

van den Broek, Theo. "Restoring Human Dignity." Paper presented to the meeting

"Passionists Proclaim the Word of the Cross: Formation for Solidarity in the Service of Justice," Passionists of Asia-Pacific, Madang, Papua New Guinea, 28 September–2 October 2003.

van den Broek, Theo, and J. Budi Hernawan. *Memoria Passionis di Papua: Kondisi Hak Asasi Manusia dan Gerakan Aspirasi Merdeka—Gambaran 1999*. Jakarta: SKP and LSPP, 2001.

van den Broek, Theo, J. Budi Hernawan, Frederika Korain, and Adolf Kambayong. *Memoria Passionis di Papua: Kondisi Sosial-Politik dan Hak Asasi Manusia 2001*. Jakarta: SKP and LSPP, 2003.

Van Fossen, A. "Financial Frauds and Pseudo-States in the Pacific Islands." *Crime, Law, and Social Change* 37(4), 2002, pp. 357–378.

———. "Money Laundering, Global Financial Instability, and Tax Havens in the Pacific Islands." *Contemporary Pacific* 15(2), 2003, pp. 237–275.

Van Trease, Howard. "The History of Land and Property Rights in Vanuatu." Thesis. Waikato: Waikato University Press, 1983.

——— (ed.). *Melanesian Politics: Stael Blong Vanuatu*. Christchurch: Macmillan Brown Centre for Pacific Studies, 1996.

———. *The Politics of Land in Vanuatu*. Suva: Institute of Pacific Studies, University of the South Pacific, 1987.

Vernon, Don. "The Panguna Mine." In Anthony J. Regan and Helga M. Griffin (eds.), *Bougainville Before the Conflict*. Canberra: Pandanus, 2005, pp. 258–273.

Viviani, Nancy. *Nauru: Phosphate and Political Progress*. Canberra: Australian National University, 1970.

"Waigani Seminar." In A. Sawyerr (ed.), *Economic Development and Trade in PNG: Proceedings of the Fourteenth Waigani Seminar*. Port Moresby: University of Papua New Guinea, 1981.

Wainwright, Elsina. "How Is RAMSI Faring? Progress, Challenges, and Lessons Learned." *Strategic Insights* (14). Canberra: Australian Strategic Policy Institute, April 2005.

———. *Our Failing Neighbour: Australia and the Future of Solomon Islands*. Canberra: Australian Strategic Policy Institute, 2003.

———. "Responding to State Failure: The Case of the Solomon Islands." *Australian Journal of International Affairs* 57(3), 2003, pp. 485–498.

Warner, B., and A. Yauieb. "The Papua New Guinea Economy." *Pacific Economic Bulletin* 20(1), 2005, pp. 1–13.

Weeranmantry, Christopher. *Nauru: Environmental Damage Under International Trusteeship*. Melbourne: Oxford University Press, 1992.

Wehner, Monica, and Donald Denoon (eds.). *Without a Gun: Australia's Experience of Monitoring Peace in Bougainville, 1997–2001*. Canberra: Pandanus, 2001.

Weightman, Barry, and Hilda Lini (eds.). *Vanuatu: Twenti Wan Tingting Long Team Blong Independens*. Suva: IPS and USP, 1980.

Weill, Henri. *"Opération Victor": GIGN et Services Secrets dans le Pacifique*. Paris: Balma, 1990.

Wesley-Smith, Terrence. "Development and Crisis in Bougainville: A Bibliographic Essay." *Contemporary Pacific* 4(2), 1992, pp. 408–432.

Wesley-Smith, Terrence, and Eugene Ogan. "Copper, Class, and Crisis: Changing Relations of Production in Bougainville." *Contemporary Pacific* 4(2), 1992, pp. 245–269.

White, Geoff. "Traditional Leaderships Report." UNDP-SIG Isabel Province Development Project, October 2004.

Wickler, Stephen, and Matthew Spriggs. "Pleistocene Human Occupation of the Solomon Islands." *Antiquity* (62), 1988, pp. 703–706.

Williams, Maslyn, and Barrie Macdonald. *The Phosphateers.* Melbourne: Melbourne University Press, 1985.

Windybank, Susan, and Mike Manning. "Papua New Guinea on the Brink." *Issue Analysis* (30). Sydney: Institute for Independent Studies, 12 March 2003.

Wing, John, with Peter King. *Genocide in West Papua? The Role of the Indonesian State Apparatus and a Current Needs Assessment of the Papuan People.* Sydney: West Papua Project, Centre for Peace and Conflict Studies, University of Sydney: Elsham, 2005.

World Bank. *Enhancing the Role of Government in Pacific Island Economies.* Washington, D.C., 1998.

———. "Papua New Guinea: World Bank Approves the Release of the Second Tranche under the Governance Promotion Adjustment Loan." News release no. 2002/170/S, 21 December 2002.

———. *World Development Indicators, 2001.* Washington, D.C., 2001. Available at http://www.eldis.org/static/doc8744.htm (accessed 1 February 2007).

World Bank and IMF (International Monetary Fund). *Review of the Poverty Reduction Strategy Paper Approach.* 15 March 2002. Available at http://www.imf.org/external/np/prspgen/review/2002/031502a.pdf (accessed 18 November 2005).

World Bank and National Research Institute. *Papua New Guinea Environment Monitor, 2002.* Boroko, Papua New Guinea.

Zimmer-Tamakoshi, L. "Wild Pigs and Dog Men: Rape and Domestic Violence as 'Women's Issues' in Papua New Guinea." In C. Brettell and C. Sargent (eds.), *Gender in Cross-Cultural Perspective.* Upper Saddle River, N.J.: Prentice-Hall, 1997, pp. 538–553.

The Contributors

M. Anne Brown is a research fellow at the Australian Centre for Peace and Conflict Studies at the University of Queensland and formerly served in the Australian Department of Foreign Affairs and Trade. She works on applied as well as research projects on conflict prevention and peacebuilding in the Pacific Island region, Southeast Asia, and Australia. Her work focuses primarily on questions of political community across difference.

Paul de Deckker is professor of political anthropology at the University of New Caledonia, where he was elected vice chancellor in 2000. He has taught at the universities of Auckland, Paris, Brussels, and Bordeaux.

Graham Hassall is professor of governance at the University of the South Pacific. He has previously taught in Australia, Papua New Guinea, and Switzerland. He has published widely on governance and the Pacific Islands.

Marion Jacka works in the Department for Community Development in Port Moresby, Papua New Guinea, as an Australian volunteer assisting with policy development and community learning. She has previously worked as a trade union official, and as a researcher for the Australian Council for International Development.

Nic Maclellan has worked in journalism, research, and community development in the Pacific Islands. He has written and broadcast on development, human rights, and the environment in the South Pacific for a range of media, including Radio Australia, *Islands Business,* and *Pacific Magazine.* He is coauthor of *La France dans le Pacifique: De Bougainville à Moruroa, After Moruroa: France in the South Pacific,* and *Kirisimasi.*

Jason MacLeod is researching the nonviolent struggle in West Papua at the Australian Centre for Peace and Conflict Studies at the University of Queensland. He has a background in community development, advocacy, conflict transformation, training, and popular education. He has worked on issues related to West Papua, East Timor, and Indonesia since the early 1990s.

Abby McLeod is an ARC postdoctoral fellow at Australian National University. She is an anthropologist whose primary research interests are women and the law in Melanesia, and the cultural impediments to police reform in developing countries.

Clive Moore is a historian at the University of Queensland, teaching in the areas of Australia and the Pacific, colonial and race relations history, and the history of gender. His research interests include the histories of Australia, Queensland, the Pacific Islands, New Guinea, Papua New Guinea, the Solomon Islands, and Melanesia, on which he has published widely. He has had a long engagement with the Solomon Islands and Papua New Guinea, and was awarded the Cross of the Solomon Islands for services to that country in 2006.

Max Quanchi teaches Pacific Island history at the Queensland University of Technology. His research interests include Australia's historical and contemporary relationship with the Pacific Islands, imaging and representation in colonial-era photography, and the history of cross-cultural encounters. He is an executive member of the Pacific History Association, and has taught in Australia and the Pacific Islands. From 1995 to 2001 he cocoordinated a regional professional development program for history teachers in the Pacific Islands. He has authored or coauthored *Pacific People and Change, Culture Contact in the Pacific, Messy Entanglements, Jacaranda Atlas of the Pacific Islands,* and *The Historical Dictionary of Discovery and Exploration of the Pacific Islands.*

Steve Ratuva is a political sociologist and a fellow in governance at the University of the South Pacific. He has worked at the Research School of Pacific and Asia Studies, Australian National University, and the University of New South Wales, and as a researcher and resourcer for institutions including the Pacific Island Development Program in Hawaii, the Life and Peace Institute in Sweden, and the International Working Group for Indigenous Affairs in Denmark.

Anthony Regan is a constitutional lawyer and a fellow in the State, Society, and Governance in Melanesia Program of the Research School of

Pacific and Asian Studies at Australian National University. His main field of research concerns the law and politics of constitutions, with particular reference to conflict and conflict resolution. Regan has lived and worked for over seventeen years in Papua New Guinea and Uganda, including more than two years in Bougainville assisting in the development of the autonomous region's constitution. He has been directly involved in peace processes and postconflict constitution-making processes in Uganda, Bougainville, East Timor, the Solomon Islands, Nagaland, and Sri Lanka.

Lopeti Senituli is press secretary and political adviser to the prime minister of Tonga, Feleti Vaka'uta Sevele (the first commoner and first elected people's representative to be appointed prime minister). This position follows a long career as a public advocate working on issues of human rights abuse, corruption, environmental degradation, fair trade, and indigenous rights in Tonga and across the Pacific. He is also a lay preacher with the Free Wesleyan Church, and a former teacher, public servant, and board member of the Tongan Rugby Union.

Orovu Sepoe teaches political science at the University of Papua New Guinea. The position of women in PNG has been a major scholarly and practical focus for her. She has also served in capacities supporting political and electoral integrity and legislative review, and is a council member of the Divine Word University, where she is active in gender and development programs.

Index

About the Book

REFLECTING A GROWING awareness of the need to integrate security and development agendas in the field of conflict management, the authors of this original volume focus on the case of the Pacific Islands. In the process, they also reveal the sociopolitical diversity, cultural richness, and social resilience of a little-known region. Their work not only offers insight into the societies discussed, but also speaks to the realities of political community and state-building efforts throughout the developing world.

M. Anne Brown is research fellow at the Australian Centre for Peace and Conflict Studies at the University of Queensland. She is author of *Human Rights and the Borders of Suffering: The Promotion of Human Rights in International Politics.*